LAST SECOND
IN DALLAS

LAST SECOND
IN DALLAS

Josiah Thompson

University Press of Kansas

Published by the University
Press of Kansas (Lawrence,
Kansas 66045), which was
organized by the Kansas
Board of Regents and is
operated and funded by
Emporia State University,
Fort Hays State University,
Kansas State University,
Pittsburg State University,
the University of Kansas, and
Wichita State University.

Library of Congress Cataloging-in-Publication Data

Names: Thompson, Josiah, author.
Title: Last second in Dallas / Josiah Thompson.
Description: Lawrence : University Press of Kansas,
2020. | Includes index.
Identifiers: LCCN 2020016290
     ISBN 9780700630080 (cloth)
Subjects: LCSH: Kennedy, John F. (John Fitzgerald),
     1917–1963—Assassination.
Classification: LCC E842.9 .T485 2020 | DDC
     973.922—dc23
LC record available at https://lccn.loc.gov/2020016290.

British Library Cataloguing-in-Publication Data is
available.

Printed in the United States of America

10 9 8 7 6 5 4 3

The paper used in this publication is acid free and meets
the minimum requirements of the American National
Standard for Permanence of Paper for Printed Library
Materials Z39.48–1992.

This book is for Nancy.

History unfolds as always in the midst of distraction, misunderstanding, and partially obscured sight lines.

—Geoffrey O'Brien

CONTENTS

This is a book about the forensic evidence of the assassination of President John F. Kennedy, who was murdered by rifle fire while riding in an open limousine in a motorcade in Dallas, Texas, on November 22, 1963. You will find no conspiracy theories here, only the cold facts of a terrible crime and the logical conclusions that an intelligent and seasoned investigator has drawn from them.

"Forensic" is an old word. It derives from the name of the Roman Forum, the place of assembly in ancient Rome where judicial and other public business was conducted. It refers then to legal evidence—evidence collected to establish the facts of a crime in a court of law. No such court was ever convened to assess the facts of President Kennedy's assassination because the alleged killer, a young ne'er-do-well and ex-Marine named Lee Harvey Oswald, was himself shot dead in plain view two days later in a crowded basement hallway at the headquarters of the Dallas police. Since Oswald's death prevented him from confronting his accusers, a fundamental constitutional right, he could not be tried.

In lieu of a trial, Kennedy's successor, President Lyndon B. Johnson, appointed a special commission headed by the chief justice of the US Supreme Court, Earl Warren, to conduct an extended inquiry. The Warren Commission labored for eleven months, produced twenty-six volumes of testimony and evidence, and concluded that Oswald was Kennedy's sole shooter and acted alone.

Americans were initially relieved by the commission's conclusions. But despite those twenty-six volumes, doubts began to accrue. Many more than twenty-six volumes of journalistic, historical, professional, and amateur investigation, speculation, and theorizing followed in the wake of the assassination itself and of the commission report. The author of this book, Josiah Thompson, himself published one of those volumes, *Six Seconds in Dallas*, which drew on his work as a consultant on the case for LIFE magazine. Since its publication in 1967, it has become one of the few highly respected books on the Kennedy assassination.

The killing of a national leader flows outward in every direction from its transfixion of time and space like the shock wave from a nuclear explosion, shattering complacency and permanently marking lives. Like many other people, I have second-order connections to the Kennedy assassination—three, in fact, two of which are relevant here: Josiah Thompson is an old friend from university days, and I helped Nobel laureate physicist Luis W. Alvarez, who figures importantly in Thompson's story, write his memoirs. It was Alvarez's forensic work that originally convinced me that Thompson was wrong in *Six Seconds in Dallas*, that the Warren Commission was right, and that there was no second shooter. And it is Thompson's careful reexamination of the forensic evidence in this book that has changed my mind. I never would have imagined doing so, but for what it's worth, I now think the weight of that evidence supports Thompson's conclusions.

Along the way through Thompson's meticulous reinvestigation, you will meet a fascinating human being. Thompson was a professor of philosophy before he abandoned a securely tenured academic career to become a private investigator. Before that, for his doctoral dissertation, he learned Danish well enough to read, study, and write a biography of the nineteenth-century Danish philosopher Søren Kierkegaard, the grandfather of the modern philosophical movement known as existentialism. Existentialism is about understanding the meaning and mystery of our existence without anchoring it in unsupported certitudes. That seems to me what Thompson has spent his life pursuing: giving up certitude, as it were, and casting off into a sea of risk. Very few investigators—or let's call him a historian, since the case went cold long ago—are prepared to revise a central conclusion of their previous major work, as Thompson does here. I salute him for it. To borrow his own metaphor, he has taken a jigsaw puzzle that he thought he had solved before, pulled it apart, found some missing pieces, and put it together again to create a startling new picture.

No truth of the past can ever be established with complete certainty. I learned that lesson during my sophomore year in college in a seminar on writing history. The history professor, Lewis B. Curtis, gave us references to evidence on the beheading of the seventeenth-century English king Charles I. A week later, we all reported back with great confidence about what we had found. Then Professor Curtis swung his axe. None of us had proven that Charles I had been beheaded. I had found a parliamentary order dispensing money for black paint to paint the platform on which the tyrant king would lose his head. Paint isn't proof, said Professor Curtis, nor is an official order for regicide, nor anything else we had discovered. Any of these cherished bits of evidence could be mistaken, misconstrued, or downright fraudulent. Certitude about the past is not available to us. Unattainable as it is, we must make do with something less. We can only marshal evidence, weigh it, assess it, and make reasonable judgments about its authority.

That is what Josiah Thompson does here. Based on what he has found, although we'll never know for certain, I believe he's right.

PREFACE

We know that it happened in one way rather than another. But what was that way?

The president of the United States is shot down at high noon in the public square of a major American city. Hundreds of witnesses are looking on, many taking photos. Almost fifty law enforcement officers are present. And now, almost fifty-five years after the event, we still do not know what happened.

In itself, this fact is extraordinary. In the usual history of a murder case, what happened is the first thing known and remains the one thing known most certainly. Any murder case produces numerous questions that are only partially answered or not answered at all. But the core of the case—the narrative of what happened—is almost never subject to controversy. It is that framework of agreed-upon fact that supports all the other questions. Therefore, to find that what happened in Dealey Plaza is still controversial more than half a century later is in itself noteworthy.

This book has a twofold purpose. On the one hand, it is a personal narrative of my experiences over the past five decades of trying to figure out what happened. At the same time, it is a kind of detective story that ends up disclosing what I found.

Let's start with an analogy. Have you ever pulled out an old jigsaw puzzle and tried to assemble it only to find that some of the pieces belong to another puzzle? You pick a particular piece and try again and again to make it fit. You move various pieces around, but they refuse to come together. Frustrated, you put the offending pieces off to the side. If no original pieces were thrown away, and if you guessed right about which pieces do not belong in the puzzle, who knows? You might just end up solving the puzzle.

Something like this happened in the Kennedy assassination. The evidence package was never clearly defined since even at the beginning, no one knew clearly what it was. Back in the summer of 1966, I visited the National Archives every few weeks, and on each visit the archivist would produce new

documents that had just been declassified. This pattern of sequential and partial release of evidence has continued over the decades. From the very outset the evidence in the case has been a moving target, never settling into a
single agreed-upon form. Even worse, for some time after the House Select
Committee on Assassinations released its report in early 1979, the evidence
was contradictory. Over time, some real facts were mistakenly discarded, and
nonfacts worked their way into the mix. No matter how hard anyone tried,
the evidence simply would not come together. It had become like that puzzle
with the extra pieces.

There was a simple reason for this. The case never went to trial because the
accused killer of the president was murdered two days later in Dallas Police
Headquarters on national television. With the alleged assassin dead, there
was no judicial process to identify evidence and to establish the basic facts of
the event. In any ordinary murder case, the looming reality of a trial casts its
shadow over everything that happens in the case investigation. Witnesses are
interviewed on tape by law enforcement, and every piece of physical evidence
is described and safeguarded, its provenance documented. Original tapes of
911 calls and police radio logs are kept locked in an evidence locker. In this
case, the loosened restrictions meant that dispatchers were free to distribute
copies of radio logs to their friends. Only recently has it become clear that
critical copies of radio logs earlier thought to be originals were in fact second-
and third-generation copies contaminated by later dubbings. For decades,
that contamination made it seem as if an audio record of the shooting was
not valid, even though the sequence and timing of the shots in that record
matched the sequence and timing of the shots' impact in the Zapruder film.

For comparison, think of the O. J. Simpson trial in 1995, broadcast live to a
rapt national radio audience, where, in a completely transparent procedure,
exhibits and transcripts were presented in open court, providing a perma-
nent record of evidence and testimony. In contrast, the Kennedy case was
placed in the hands of the Warren Commission, whose proceedings were
sometimes secretive and often opaque, attended by intermittent press reports
discussing matters that later became evidence or failed to become evidence.
Ten months after the killing, the commission issued a report that was universally applauded as delivering the last word on what happened. For a time,
the commission's conclusion that Oswald had acted alone was accepted as
settled history.

That lasted until the commission published its twenty-six volumes of *Hearings and Exhibits*, laying out the supposed evidence for its conclusions. Very

quickly, these volumes disclosed the opposite of what the commission hoped for. Instead of quieting any discussion of whether Oswald had acted alone, it ignited precisely that discussion. Continuing the analogy of the jigsaw puzzle, it became apparent that many pieces of evidence would not fit the commission's picture. Some pieces had been shaved a bit and then forced into the puzzle where a good fit was otherwise impossible. Other pieces had simply been buried and not disclosed by the commission in its report or in its supporting volumes. This hothouse mixture of fact, conflicting evidence, and confusion proved to be fertile ground for crackpot conspiracy theorists, who in turn transformed the JFK assassination into fodder for supermarket tabloids.

But as conspiracy theories flourished and Kennedy assassination research came to be portrayed as the province of wackos and wing nuts, a small community of serious students quietly grew. People in this group were able to separate conspiracy hype from the underlying evidence. Before long I found myself counted among them. In 1966 and 1967, I worked for LIFE magazine on its assassination investigations. What I learned through my own research and that investigation was published in *Six Seconds in Dallas* in November 1967.

In the years that followed I continued my interest in the case, although tempered now by the demands of making a living and raising a family. In retrospect, the satisfaction I experienced in investigating the assassination must have played some role in my later decision to abandon my life as a college professor and become a private investigator. Thirty-five years spent actually investigating criminal cases sharpened my eye and improved my judgment when I returned to the Kennedy case in 2011.

For decades, polls indicated that less than half the population thought Lee Harvey Oswald had acted alone. But over time, as various conspiracy theories turned out to be groundless, the public's exhaustion with the endless arguments and unproven claims took its toll. In addition, the periodic appearance of ill-informed press and television reports helped move the pendulum of belief back toward the "respectable" position of the Warren Report.

Were it this simple—if the case came down to a battle of words between woolly-headed "conspiracy theorists" and "respectable" analysts—I would not have written this book. The Kennedy killing is not such a cartoon battle but is a murder case like thousands of others that are investigated every year and either solved or not solved on the basis of the available evidence. There is no mystery here. The work involves patient effort in exposing what is hidden. In most cases, this consists of putting together witness testimony and photographic and audio records plus whatever physical evidence is available.

In the Kennedy case, we have these different varieties in abundance. Over the decades, the core evidence in the case has expanded and contracted as a result of continued scrutiny and new forensic discoveries—sometimes in only minor ways and sometimes in ways that are truly tectonic.

Because I was involved with this case from the beginning, I recognized in 2011 that the first decade of the new century had produced evidentiary change at a rate not seen since the 1960s. New scientific work removed certain facts long considered axiomatic, breaking what had been an impasse with conflicting schemes of evidence resulting in endless rehearsals of old arguments.

By 2011, however, the evidence appeared to have shifted in a fundamental way that pointed towards a new and compelling narrative. It seemed almost as if the earlier fifty years had been necessary to permit the conflicting evidence to ripen and, in that ripening, to eject the "facts" that did not belong there. Just as important, this new narrative is the product of rigorous, disciplined science that combines what has been known for fifty-plus years with new breakthroughs. The result is a virtually seamless account of the last second of the shooting—the instant when everything important happens—when audio and visual evidence combines with witness testimony to produce a textured narrative of great power that has no loose ends.

Before beginning to read, however, the reader should be warned. This book is about the final second of John Kennedy's life. What happened in that final instant is shown in all-too-graphic detail by the Zapruder film and the autopsy photos. It is profoundly unsettling for both author and reader to examine a man's death in such graphic detail. Yet we must. For it is in that last second of the shooting that a central reality of the event is to be found. We must immerse ourselves in these details if we are to reach that reality, unsettling and uncomfortable as it may be.

As we burrow deep into these details, we should remember that true inquiry is not some free-floating logical exercise carried out by disembodied spirits. Inquiry is something we as humans do, and for that reason, it is filled with all the absurdity and comedy of our lives. This book is therefore not just a history of the ebb and flow of our knowledge of the Kennedy assassination. It is also a story of my own all-too-human pursuit, failure, and final success in searching out a hidden truth. It tells the story of what happened in the last second of the shooting and how, with many missteps and halting moves along the way, I found it out.

Since almost every fact in this case has been challenged by someone with some sort of argument, and given the importance of addressing these arguments, the notes discuss these issues and provide additional information of interest to the academic and assassination research communities.

The two technical appendices comprise scientific papers by Dr. James Barger and his colleague Richard Mullen, providing links to publicly available materials and the related information needed to replicate their studies.

Regarding the images, a conscientious effort has been made to obtain the best photographs available. With respect to the Zapruder film, the frames reproduced here may well be the highest-quality versions ever published.

Due to the historic importance of many photographs and film images in these pages, none have been subjected to any alteration via Photoshop or similar applications. The only exception is Plate 3a in the color photo gallery, where the yellow tint of an original Ektachrome copy of Zapruder frame 313 has been color balanced and a close-up portion then shadow enhanced to reveal relevant detail. Frame images both before and after modification are shown.

ACKNOWLEDGMENTS

f I were to try to acknowledge all the people who helped me bring this book to fruition, this section would become a chapter in itself. Instead, I will limit myself to acknowledging those whose contributions were of singular importance.

That list must begin with writer John Grissim, who began as my editor and who ended up as both editor and collaborator. When John and I first met in the early 1980s, we quickly learned we had both served in the US Navy, John as communications officer on a fleet oiler operating near Yankee Station during the early stages of the Vietnam War. John had cut his journalist's teeth writing for *Rolling Stone* in the sixties and early seventies while publishing several books with New York publishers. He lived just a few miles down the coast in Stinson Beach, and his journalism background made him an obvious hire to do PI work. We did a couple of cases together and John handled well several tough and uncooperative witnesses.

In 1988, with the publication of *Gumshoe*, I had learned that, for the most part, New York editors no longer edited books but largely just made deals. So by the fall of 2012, I knew I would need to hire my own editor for *Last Second in Dallas*. By then I knew a lot about John. In addition to authoring eight books, he had edited a magazine, had founded, and later sold, a respected quarterly journal about ocean events, had written a column for a local newspaper, and self-published two books. A few years previously he and his wife, Susan, had moved from the Bay Area up to Washington State, but with telephone and internet available this was no obstacle. I reached out to him, we worked out a deal, and before year's end he was my editor.

By the summer of 2013, *Last Second in Dallas* was finished in its first form. But when John and I recognized that confirmation for what we had written so far lay in the long-discredited acoustic evidence, we put aside our author and editor hats and became investigators. At one point, in 2017 when we were struggling with the Ramsey Panel's central argument, I remember saying to John, "Will you see what you can make of it? It just makes my head hurt." John devoted a couple of weeks to the task and came up with a counter argument of great simplicity. When our small group of expert readers vouched for John's discovery, *Last Second in Dallas* became not just my book, but our book, as he had become a true collaborator. His hand is found on virtually every page.

As to our expert readers, from 2015 through 2018 John and I worked closely with a smaller subset—a six member email discussion group solely devoted to the acoustics evidence, in particular the Ramsey Panel report. Joining us were James Barger, PhD, emeritus Chief Scientist of Raytheon BBN laboratory; Don Thomas, PhD, author of *Hear No Evil* (2010), the powerful, meticulous examination of the forensic evidence of the assassination, including the Ramsey Panel's arguments; and Michael O'Dell, a California mathematician widely respected by the assassination research community for his thorough research on the sound recordings.

The four years we worked together were crucial and hugely productive. We called ourselves the Gents, this being our shorthand group email salutation. It was through this discussion that John and I (liberal arts guys) learned how real science is done and how to talk about it. Don Thomas's thoughtful critiques and insights were especially helpful, while Michael O'Dell's work with algorithms provided corrected audio tracks of unprecedented accuracy and detail. Together their contributions helped Jim Barger, aided by his colleague Richard Mullen, perform a breakthrough quantitative analysis of the crosstalk in the assassination's audio recordings.

Jim Barger's singular achievement not only restored the validity and importance of the acoustic evidence that he and his BBN team developed for the HSCA in 1978; he was also notable for his grace in handling dumb questions from non-scientists like John and me. I am truly grateful for the memorable experience of working with these remarkable "Gents."

Many members of the "assassination buffs" community have helped my investigation over the decades. Several who materially assisted in my research for this book deserve special mention.

Physicist Paul Hoch and I became friends in the late sixties when, as recounted in chapter 9, he was working under Professor Luis Alvarez at the Lawrence Radiation Lab in Berkeley. An early member of the buffs, in September 2012, Paul allowed me to make prints from his negatives of Alvarez's melon-firing tests, as well as photocopies of his notes and ancillary documents. He also gave me permission to publish the material.

A year later, Paul put in my hands an even more important trove of documents—367 pages of the Ramsey Panel's internal papers. These offered a completely new and defining account of the Panel's proceedings. None had ever before been made public. Paul's willingness to turn over this material to me demonstrates his commitment not only to the buff community but also to the rules and rigor of serious scholarship. I am enormously grateful for his contribution.

Then there is Chris Scally. For decades from his home in Ireland, Chris has carried out the hard work of scholarship in tracking the provenance of both the Zapruder film original and the original Dictabelt and Audograph recordings of the shooting. When Chris learned what we were doing, he wrote a twelve-page, single-spaced study: "The History of the DPD Channel 2 Audograph Discs: A Report for Josiah Thompson (May 21, 2016)." We relied upon it, along with an earlier monograph by Chris, in drafting our chapters on the acoustics evidence. Chris Scally's work stands as a remarkable model of what painstaking, honest research in the Kennedy case can produce.

Patrick McCarthy, Doug Desalles, MD, and Gary Aguilar, MD have been my friends and counselors over the last decade. Early on in my research for *Last Second in Dallas*, Patrick was a great help when I was trying to figure out how best to analyze the three time streams of the acoustic evidence. For years Doug and Gary have advised me on the medical evidence in the case. Gary and I have traveled to various conferences where his presentations, together with his published research, confirm his reputation as the premier expert on the medical evidence in the case.

Arthur Snyder of the Stanford Linear Accelerator Laboratory (SLAC) has generously assisted our researches by giving his opinion of particular theories and the equations, notably the technical arguments underlying the blur illusion. Thanks also go to Peter Goldberger, a student of mine and friend from the 1970s, whose sharp legal mind pointed up evidentiary problems in 2015.

Aside from the contributions of the buffs, I extend my appreciation to Rex Bradford of the Mary Ferrell Foundation website (maryferrell.org) for proofreading an earlier version of the manuscript and helping us determine the proper URLs for various documents on the Mary Ferrell site.

Thanks to David Wimp and Keith Fitzgerald for their contributions that helped break the impasse that has long stymied the case. Steve Barber, who first reported hearing the crosstalk that broke the Ramsey Panel's own impasse, was very helpful and supportive, providing me helpful documents and photos to help tell his story. For contributions that made him an honorary buff, grateful thanks to John Grissim's brother Tony Grissim of Leica Geosystems who helped develop the use of its 3-D laser scanner for crime scene reconstruction, for his technical advice on creating excellent explanatory diagrams. For insights on witness memory recall, thanks also to psychiatrist Robert Baron,

MD. For his meticulous reading of the manuscript, thanks go to Matt Douthit for the additional facts he conveyed with respect to the medical evidence.

For very different reasons I am grateful to Geoffrey O'Brien for his uncannily relevant epigraph quote which came from his review of Darryl Pinckney's *Black Deutschland* in *The New York Review of Books*, March 24, 2016.

As the notes make clear, The Sixth Floor Museum at Dealey Plaza will become the repository for numerous documents from my files that are referenced in *Last Second in Dallas* when no copies are known to exist anywhere else. Curator Stephen Fagin, Executive Director Nikola Langford, and Director of Collections and Interpretations Megan Bryant have all extended to me numerous kindnesses and help as we prepared the book for production. Thank you all so very, very much.

One person who deserves special recognition is Laurie Tanguay of Lobo Designs (Sequim, Washington) to whom we turned in early 2013 when the decision was made to fully integrate the photos, figures and tables—in short, the evidence—with the text for ease of comprehension and impact. Laurie's extensive background in book design and her technical expertise enabled her to create a gorgeous bound manuscript, not once, but four times, until the book was finally ready in 2019 to submit to publishers. Working with her has been a privilege and a joy, and I am deeply grateful to her for her essential contributions.

Many helped in the effort to get this book published—Dan Alcorn, Nicholson Baker, Erroll Morris, and Jeffrey Toobin, as well as Phyllis Theroux and Michael Fischbach. Literary agent Molly Friedrich read an early draft and generously shared essential insights and recommendations. Premier investigative journalist Mark Dowie, cofounder and former editor of *Mother Jones* magazine, provided remarkable counsel drawn from his knowledge of academic publishing. Sincere thanks to you all.

But it is to Richard Rhodes and Michael Briggs that I ascribe my great good luck in finding my way to the University Press of Kansas (UPK). Dick and I have known each other since we were both undergraduates in New Haven sixty years ago. Rustling around in Luis Alvarez's autobiography, I noticed that Dick had been hired as a kind of "book doctor" to beat the book into shape. Subsequently, he had moved to a coastal community south of San Francisco. I contacted him and we had a convivial lunch together down there. I gave Dick the latest manuscript of *Last Second in Dallas*, not knowing then that he was conversant with the Kennedy assassination, having written a whole chapter about Lee Harvey Oswald in an earlier book where he accepted the Warren Commission story of both Oswald and the shooting. I was elated two weeks later when he let me know that I had "turned him around" on the case. He offered to try to get the book published and within a few weeks I was in touch with Michael Briggs, the recently retired editor in chief of UPK. Mike had published earlier books on the assassination and knew the field. Like one of the editors of old, not only did he devour the book but for weeks peppered me with questions that tested the validity of various points. Having satisfied himself that the arguments in the book were valid, he enthusiastically recommended it not only to the present editor in chief, Joyce Harrison, but also to the director of the press, Conrad Roberts. Mike has been a loyal and interested friend of both the book and me ever since.

Working with the crew in Lawrence reminds me of the early days of *Six Seconds in Dallas*. Bernard Geis Associates (BGA) was a tiny but powerful publisher with offices on 55th Street and Lexington in New York. Over the months of book production, the small staff spent long hours ironing out all the difficulties of production which were immense in a book filled with photos, diagrams, and odd scientific equations. *Last Second in Dallas* proved itself to be a worthy sibling to *Six Seconds in Dallas* by being even more of a bear to produce. Under Bethany Mowry's careful editorial eye, everyone at UPK pitched in to produce a volume that would make the very best use of each diagram and photo and would be free of even the smallest typo. Karl Janssen designed a superb cover. Kelly Chrisman Jacques kept everything flowing together into a seamless whole and caught errors that John and I missed. Michael Kehoe kept our publicity options open. Connie Oehring carried out a masterful job of copyediting much better than I ever received at Doubleday, Knopf, or Little Brown. Andrea Laws became our heroine as she pushed ahead day after day obtaining permissions, where frustration and difficulty proved to be part of her daily routine. It is a magnificent crew that produced this book and they have my undying gratitude.

Finally, my family. Nancy claims to be massively bored by the Kennedy assassination but she continued to make herself available to give judgment on any particular paragraph or chapter—no small achievement after fifty-four years. My son, Ev, read the whole manuscript and suggested the title we used as well as using his PI information databases to find people. My grandson, David Fuchs, produced a singularly useful database of all the photo materials in our files. Another grandson, Andrew Fuchs, took the author's photo and offered excellent design advice about the cover. To all of them, I am truly grateful.

RAIL YARD
SWITCHING TOWER →

ZAPRUDER
PEDESTAL

TRIPLE UNDERPASS

GRASSY KNOLL

ELM ST.

MAIN ST.

TEXAS
SCHOOL BOOK
DEPOSITORY
BUILDING

DAL-TEX
BUILDING

RECORDS
BUILDING

CRIMINAL
COURTS
BUILDING

HOUSTON ST.

PART I

BEGINNINGS—THE 1960s

On that August day in Dallas in 1966, it was only 8:30 in the morning and already getting hot. I was sitting in Dealey Plaza on the concrete steps, looking out over Elm Street. The part of Dealey Plaza where the shooting happened is small. That's what you don't get from the pictures. Just ten feet to the right is the concrete pedestal on which Abraham Zapruder stood filming with his 8-mm movie camera, barely seventy feet from John Kennedy when the shot hit him in the head, spewing gore over the motorcycle outriders and throwing his body backward like a rag doll. Maybe that's why Zapruder stumbled away from the pedestal, crying like a baby. I sat there taking in the scene, trying to imagine the confusion, the screams, people hitting the ground and then getting up and looking around. The shots came from so close in. Everyone standing along Elm Street felt they were inside whatever was going on. It was over in a matter of seconds—and now I was trying to put it back together, millisecond by millisecond.

A middle-aged couple with a girl of about six were making their way up the steps to my right. They were talking about what happened. When they got to the top of the steps, the girl with blond pigtails reached down and picked up a twig. She held it up for her mother to see and then put it in her pocket. I'd been told this is the way it's always been—tourists visiting Dealey Plaza, picking up a leaf or twig or blade of grass, something, anything, from where "it" happened. For after Dallas came Vietnam and Memphis and Los Angeles and Kent State, the Pentagon Papers, Cambodia, and Watergate. After Dallas, it seemed, nothing would ever be the same. On this killing ground, the young king had been murdered and here something like a mystery had begun to take form. For the how and the why of the murder remained hidden, connected—if only by our subconscious—with all that has happened since.

Three years earlier, on Friday, November 22, I had been walking up York Street in New Haven, Connecticut. It was 1:45 in the afternoon, and Nancy and I had just had lunch together at a lunch counter on Chapel Street across the street from her job at the Yale Art Gallery. We had spent the last year in

Copenhagen, where I had written my dissertation on the Danish philosopher Søren Kierkegaard. Now we were living in a $65-a-month apartment a few blocks away on Dwight Street while Nancy worked as an assistant curator and I made a little money as a teaching assistant in the philosophy department. We had married five years earlier in December 1958, within weeks of my return from a six-month deployment to the Mediterranean. Our first months together were spent living on a decrepit cabin cruiser moored near the naval base on St. Thomas (US Virgin Islands) while I went through four months of advanced underwater training run by my unit, Underwater Demolition Team (UDT) 21. Service in a UDT brought with it extra pay—demolition pay and hazardous-duty pay—which Nancy and I quickly blew on a year in Europe at Oxford and in Vienna. Then back to New Haven for graduate school. We were happy.

As I passed the preppy clothing stores of Fenn-Feinstein and J. Press at the Broadway corner, I was thinking of the dinner party we were going to the next night. It was at Alex Mourelatos's place out on Whitney Avenue, and his parties were always fun. Suddenly, a woman ran out of Cutler's record store yelling, "Kennedy's been shot!" My first reaction was "That can't possibly be. She must be mistaken."

After lunch, Nancy had gone to the library of the art and architecture building across York Street from the art gallery. When the news broke, people in the library got up from their research and streamed out of the building. Everyone needed to talk with someone else about what had happened. Nobody wanted to be alone. The feeling, she said, was "uncontainable."

In the hours that followed, the nation came to a standstill, and every radio and television set was broadcasting the news. Reports said shots had been fired from the sixth floor of the Texas School Book Depository as the president's motorcade passed. By late afternoon, the Dallas police announced that they had an assassin in custody, a Marxist sympathizer–nutcase named Lee Harvey Oswald. Just prior to his capture, Oswald had shot and killed Dallas patrolman J. D. Tippit. As hour followed hour, the sense of the enormity of what had just happened grew. I felt strangely numb. I think we all were.

The dinner party the next night at Alex Mourelatos's place was anything but "fun." The mood was somber, the conversation muted, the dinner guests oddly disconnected. It felt as if the normal social bonds had been weakened. Along with deep sadness went an unspoken recognition that the ground under our feet had shifted, that something had happened of which the consequences were unknown. As we were getting our coats, Alex made a remark that stuck with me. "Oswald," he said, "will never live to stand trial." Driving home, I thought of what Alex had said. When we pulled up on Dwight Street in front of our tiny apartment next to the Celantano Funeral Home, I turned to Nancy and said, "That's just Alex. Europeans see conspiracies everywhere."

The next morning, a Sunday, we decided to drive to Washington, DC. We had been glued to our twelve-inch Sony black-and-white TV for two days and wanted to get away from the shadows on the screen. We wanted to share in what was happening in a richer way, a more direct, more personal way. We wanted to actually walk past the casket in the Capitol Rotunda and on Monday stand on Constitution Avenue in the cold sunlight as the funeral cortege passed.

Yet even as we drove south to the Capitol, bizarre events continued to unfold. Millions were watching on national TV as authorities walked a handcuffed Oswald from the basement of the Dallas Police Department (DPD) headquarters to a car that would transfer him to the nearby county jail. Suddenly, a man stepped from the crowd and fired a revolver point-blank into Oswald's midsection, killing him. The shooter was Jack Ruby, operator of a Dallas strip club with supposed underworld ties.

From the very beginning, there had been a strangeness to November 22. The date has often been described as a kind of tectonic shift, like the one that occurred on December 7, 1941. Just as December 7 marked the end of the uneasy peace between world wars, so November 22 marked the end of the prosperity and stability of the 1950s. And just as December 7 ushered in World War II and the enormous changes it brought about, so November 22 ushered in a similar era of war and change.

But November 22 was different.

There was a reason for December 7. The Japanese Greater East Asia Co-Prosperity Sphere was running into constrictions. The United States was blocking Japanese expansion. Thus, the attack on Pearl Harbor was in some way expected, even inevitable. There was an explanation for it. There was a why.

Not so November 22.

It erupted out of nowhere, a bullet blowing up our young president's head at high noon in a public square with hundreds looking on. As the days passed—when you'd expect a why to begin taking shape—it made even less sense. That was what Nancy and I talked about with strangers that chilly Sunday night in the long line stretching into the Capitol.

The next Wednesday, LIFE magazine came in the mailbox. LIFE had purchased the film taken by Abraham Zapruder that captured the shooting from beginning to end. I sat in our Dwight Street apartment, poring over the black-and-white frames from the film that LIFE had published. It was clear that the Texas School Book Depository was directly behind President Kennedy when he was hit. "That's strange," I said to myself, pulling the New York Times off the coffee table. There it was—an article reporting a Dallas surgeon had made a tracheotomy incision in the front of Kennedy's throat right through a small bullet hole. But Kennedy could not have been shot in the front of the throat from a building directly behind him. It made no sense.

What I did next made even less sense.[1]

With the New York Times clutched in one hand and LIFE magazine in the other, I set out to walk to Church Street, where the FBI had an office. I almost turned back a couple of times. Finally, I found myself talking with an agent and explaining the conflict between these two arcane sources of information. He listened politely, took my name, and thanked me for my comments. After I left, he and the other agents probably had a good laugh over the weirdness of Yale graduate students.

In the months that followed, the Kennedy assassination faded to the back pages of newspapers. In September 1964, the Warren Commission issued its findings, the outcome of a vast multiagency investigation, resulting in an 888-page report accompanied by twenty-six bound volumes of supporting documentation. The commission concluded that there had been three shots, all fired by Lee Harvey Oswald from a sixth-floor corner window of the depository building. They said one shot had missed, but they could not determine which one. Another had struck President Kennedy in the back, emerged from his throat, and struck Governor John Connally behind his right shoulder. This bullet then smashed through the right side of Connally's chest, splintering his fifth rib and continuing on to shatter his right wrist bone at its widest point before lodging in his left thigh. The report described this bullet as the one found on the hospital stretcher used to carry Connally. The third bullet hit President Kennedy in the back of his head and blew out a large hole on the right side, killing him instantly.

The networks and all print media covered the commission's report with adulation. Like almost everyone, I thought it was all over.

I'd gotten my PhD that summer, and our daughter, Lis, was born in July. Yale hired me in the Philosophy Department, and Nancy quit her job at the Yale Art Gallery. As I went about doing the things a new faculty member was expected to do, every now and then the Kennedy assassination would touch the back of my mind. I found the commission's twenty-six volumes in the Yale Library and from time to time would wander into the stacks and pick up a volume. There was no index, and it seemed a jumble of disconnected documents and testimony.

But in early 1965 analyses and critiques of the report began to appear in print. One of the critics was Vincent Salandria whose articles analyzing the evidence appeared in obscure periodicals such as *Liberation* and *The Minority of One*. Other than the fact that he was a lawyer for the Philadelphia School Board, Salandria's credentials indicated no special expertise. But when I casually consulted the twenty-six volumes to verify what he was saying, his criticisms all checked out. The more I read, the more interested I became.

Reading left-wing periodicals critical of government pronouncements might have been reasonably normal behavior for Yale graduate students in the early 1960s. But it wasn't normal for me. Given my background, it was very far from normal.

I came from a comfortable but not wealthy family in a small town on the Ohio River named East Liverpool. It probably had its best days toward the close of the nineteenth century. Because of clay deposits along its riverbanks, the town early on became home to the pottery industry, and Thompsons had been part of that industry for over a hundred years. My father was sales manager of a local pottery and a Republican. The Thompsons had always been Republicans, and not just Republicans but Republicans of a very conservative stripe—"Taft Republicans." When World War I broke out, my father and his brother both enlisted. On November 10, 1918, my father was a first lieutenant and artillery observer just north of Verdun. He was wounded by shrapnel from a German shell just hours before the Armistice.

I went to public elementary school and two years of high school in East Liverpool. Since my father had gone to Andover and Yale forty years earlier, so did I. In the mid-1950s, Yale was essentially apolitical, and so was I. My friends and I talked a lot about literature and philosophy. We read Hemingway and Fitzgerald and the usual poets. Since the draft was in force when we entered college, almost all of us joined Reserve Officers' Training Corps units. With the end of the Korean War and the decline of McCarthyism, the political world seemed frozen by the stalemate between the major powers. The economy was doing just fine, so we were not worried about finding a good job out of college.

It wasn't Yale that moved my political center of gravity. It was what happened next.

In June 1957, I graduated and received a commission in the US Navy. I volunteered for UDT training to become a navy "frogman," a designation later changed to Sea, Air, and Land Team (SEAL). A year later, I had completed training and been assigned to UDT 21. Immediately, I was put in charge of a twenty-two-man UDT detachment deployed to the Mediterranean. I was there when the crisis in Lebanon broke out in July, triggered by a military coup in Iraq that overthrew the pro-Western king. Fearing the spread of "international Communism," President Eisenhower ordered the landing of a large US Marine Corps force at Beirut to bolster pro-Western Lebanon against any threat from Syria. At the same time, the British dropped paratroops into Jordan.

As our ship approached the Lebanese coast, it seemed as if we were in a war movie from the 1940s. Live ammunition was broken out and loaded into the 3"/50 antiaircraft guns as two jets from a British carrier swooped low overhead. The captain of the ship opened his safe and passed out top-secret operational orders that had precious little to do with the situation we would encounter.

The tactical situation required an additional landing north of Beirut to cut the coast road and prevent Syrian armor from coming down that road and attacking our beachhead. My unit was assigned the job of carrying out the combat reconnaissance of two beaches along the coast road north of the city. Arriving under cover of predawn darkness the next morning, we found the target beach empty. I took a position along a nearby railroad embankment, along with a radioman. Shortly after dawn, two carrier-based AD-6 Skyraiders began flying figure-eight patterns overhead. Two destroyers, each with six five-inch guns, were stationed less than a mile offshore. Both were on my radio net. Supposedly, each would deliver ordnance on any coordinates I gave them.

As it turned out, no hostile forces showed up anywhere near the planned landing site. The beach reconnaissance went forward with no opposition from the Lebanese, and the subsequent landing went off flawlessly. Later histories indicated that the entire Lebanon operation was based upon faulty intelligence. All US forces were withdrawn within a couple of months. As for our small detachment, we took it all in stride. The whole thing was just another JANFU—Joint Army-Navy Fuckup.

When I went back to Yale in 1960 for graduate studies, I remembered all this. I remembered that, as a twenty-three-year-old with little experience or knowledge of his surroundings, I had been given a devastating amount of firepower with the accompanying potential for making awful mistakes. I remembered too that all the grandiose justifications for our invasion bore little resemblance to what had actually taken place. All the noble phrases about defending the free world from communism seemed a bit silly when our forces ended up leaving two months later. I had seen the power of our military unleashed against a small country that couldn't fight back, and it wasn't pretty.

Something like this was in my head in early 1963 when I started dropping by the library of the US Embassy in Copenhagen and browsing its stacks. I found there a book by Fred Cook on the Alger Hiss case. Cook offered a powerful counterargument to the claim that Hiss had betrayed his country. Using the tools of historical scholarship, Cook was able to expose fissures in the received wisdom about the case. This was a use of scholarship that no one had ever told me about. Scholarship did not have to be about things found only on dusty shelves in the library. It could be applied to present controversies and used to expose contemporary untruths. Almost thirty years later, scholarship yielded new revelations that showed Hiss to be guilty after all.

After getting my PhD and being hired by the Yale Philosophy Department at its lowest rank, I was given what was called an "experimental ethics course" to teach. I never learned what that meant, but I took it to mean "movies." So I showed a lot of movies with moral dilemmas. Late in the winter, Yale sociologist Staughton Lynd put together a document called A Declaration of Conscience against the War in Vietnam and appeared at a Yale rally promoting it. I went to the rally and later assigned the document as the focus for a paper in the "experimental" course.[2] The son of a rich alumnus was in the class, and his father complained to Yale's president. I met with President Kingman Brewster in his office and ended up drafting a defense for using the document.

In June 1965, our years at Yale came to an end. My dissertation had been picked up for publication, and I had landed a really good job as assistant professor at Haverford, a well-regarded Quaker liberal arts college in Philadelphia. Shortly after I joined the Haverford faculty that fall, Nancy and I began attending peace marches and protests.

It was at this juncture that an extraordinary coincidence occurred that set the path for everything that followed.

When in January 1966 the local sheriff of Delaware County said he would arrest any "peaceniks" who came into his jurisdiction, another professor and I drove over and started handing out American Friends Service pamphlets about Vietnam.[3] The police arrested us for "littering," and we spent a couple of hours in cells before an American Civil Liberties Union (ACLU) attorney arrived. He did a masterful job of bluffing. We were brought out of our cells into the squad room, where various police officers were gathered. Entering the squad room, the attorney spoke to us in a loud voice: "We've been in touch with Attorney General Katzenbach, and when the FBI agents arrive . . . [looking at his watch] I want you to tell them that not only have your civil rights been violated but you are suing for false arrest . . . [*pointing at the various officers*] Officer So-and-So, Sergeant So-and-So, Lieutenant So-and-So and Captain So-and-So."

We were released in less than two minutes. Outside, the ACLU attorney introduced himself. He was Vincent Salandria.

Meeting Vince Salandria proved significant. At that time, I knew practically nothing about the Kennedy assassination. With great generosity, he brought me into the fold of people who were opening up the case. These were not professional historians or public affairs wonks. They were ordinary people who, for reasons as various as their backgrounds, had smelled something wrong with the official story and were going after it. There were Mary Ferrell, Penn Jones, Sylvia Meagher, Paul Hoch, Cyril Wecht, Maggie Fields, Harold Weisberg, Shirley Martin, Ray Marcus, Lillian Castellano, David Lifton, and many more.[4] Several housewives, a lawyer for the school board, the editor of a small paper, a graduate student, a young professor, and a World Health Organization (WHO) official. We were little people—people who had only a few things in common: curiosity, an unwillingness to be intimidated by public attitudes, more than a little tenacity, and—best of all—a willingness to laugh at ourselves. None of us had any money or hoped to make any money out of this. We were doing it for its own sake. In Calvin Trillin's words from the piece he wrote about us in the *New Yorker*, we were "assassination buffs."[5]

I met several over the phone when visiting Vince at his home. Information was passed around as soon as it was discovered. Over the winter months, I began to educate myself. By the time summer rolled around, Vince thought I knew enough to make a trip to the National Archives worthwhile.

When classes let out in May 1966, Vince and I started making trips to Washington. We would work there in the giant reading room of the archives, now and then asking the curator, Marion Johnson, to bring us files from the Warren Commission section. Additional commission documents were becoming available nearly every month, so every trip brought new discoveries.

For me, the real shocker was the moment in a screening room of the archives when I saw the Zapruder film for the first time. I literally gasped aloud as I watched the president's head explode and snap backward as if his right temple had been struck by a baseball bat. Everything indicated that the shot that had hit him had come from in front of the limousine, not from behind. What also struck me was the realization that the Zapruder film had never been shown to the public—for example, on network television—and if it were, that viewers would intuitively draw the same conclusion.

We studied 35-mm slides made from the film and spent long hours in the reading room going over documents and ordering photocopies. Vince pointed out to me something that Ray Marcus, one of our fellow assassination researchers, had spotted. Governor Connally was turning to the right in his seat when suddenly his right shoulder collapsed. Since he was shot just under his right armpit, this collapse could signal the impact of the bullet that hit him. But Connally at this point was facing Zapruder. If one were deeply skeptical that this bullet had first penetrated Kennedy—and we were—this meant the bullet that hit him could not have come from the depository but rather came from somewhere across the street. There was a building there, and we knew from extensive commission testimony by Connally's thoracic surgeon that the downward angle of the bullet that had gone through Connally was 27 degrees.

I wondered what that trajectory would line up with. Nowhere in the archives could we find an answer. Nobody had ever asked the question.

Vince was a careful guide and mentor. Over time, we decided to write a joint article on our findings for a national magazine such as the *Atlantic Monthly* or *Harper's*. I had free time in the summer to write, while Vince had his day job as a school board attorney. But after a few weeks, we started to disagree about evidence. Vince was committed to the hole in Kennedy's throat being a bullet entry hole, while I doubted it. Regrettably—but perhaps understandably—our collaboration broke down.

I continued on alone. By late August 1966, I had a sixty-page draft and, by great good fortune, a recommendation from John Silber, chairman of the University of Texas Philosophy Department, to his friend Willie Morris, editor of *Harper's* magazine. Early one morning in September, I drove up to New York for my appointment with Morris, only to learn that his schedule had changed and he could not see me until after 5:00 that day. With seven hours to kill, I called Don Preston, a Vermont neighbor of another Haverford professor who had expressed interest in what I was finding out in the Kennedy case. Don was also the executive editor of Bernard Geis Associates (BGA), a small but powerful publisher. He invited me to come by, and after about an hour's conversation, he excused himself and came back with an invitation for lunch with Bernard Geis. At the end of lunch, Geis asked Preston to write up a contract for me. "You're going to write a book for us, Thompson," he said. The advance was $500, but they would pay for expenses.

What had started out with Salandria as a kind of earnest hobby had now morphed into something quite different. My life had been just fine, thank you, without the Kennedy assassination. Nancy and I had spent two years together in Europe without children. Now we had two kids under two years of age.

Nancy was blond and beautiful and twenty-nine, and I was thirty-one. We were happy living on a picture-perfect campus where I had a tenure-track job and a rosy future. As long as the Kennedy assassination was a kind of weird hobby, that was one thing. But this was different. A New York publisher had given me an advance to actually write a book about it. Where could I possibly find time to do it while teaching full time? Would that rosy future survive diving into a historical argument that remained extremely controversial? In 1966, pursuing questions about the Kennedy assassination was not as bad as believing in flying saucers, but around certain academic dinner tables, it was on its way there.

The more I thought about it, the clearer it became that I couldn't help myself. I had all these thoughts in my head. It was as if the Warren Commission had played a vicious trick on the rest of us. They had put out a report that was universally acclaimed and then published twenty-six volumes of evidence to support it. If anyone ventured into that morass of evidence, they would quickly recognize that it pointed away from the commission's conclusions. It was as if the commission had declared that it had solved a giant jigsaw puzzle, failed at the job, and then laid out the hundreds of thousands of pieces that would have to be put together to really solve it. The challenge was addictive. The questions never ceased bubbling up. Falling asleep, driving to the supermarket, walking up the hill to my office on the campus—one question would lead to another and that one to another. The more I read, the more questions I had.

Nancy and I had never had any real money, and it had never mattered. As a new assistant professor at Haverford, I was getting $7,500 a year. Lis had been born in July 1964 and Ev in February 1966, so we were spending everything I made. To make any real progress investigating the Kennedy assassination, I needed money, and now Geis had promised to provide it. For the first time, I had some backing and could start trying to answer the questions that kept popping up in my head. First and foremost, it meant that I could finally go to Dallas and see Dealey Plaza with my own eyes. In addition, the timing was right—my book on Kierkegaard had been revised and was at the press. I hadn't thought about it or Søren Kierkegaard for months. As soon as I got back from New York, I started planning the trip.

I knew what I wanted to do in Dallas. Foremost in my mind was that backward snap of Kennedy's head under impact. I wanted to explore the area to the right front of the limousine to see what was there, to assess whether a shooter could have fired from there. As for the Connally problem, I knew I'd need a special tool. The day before my departure, I found an engineering supply house in the phone book and drove out to North Philadelphia. I told the guy at the counter that I didn't want a transit or anything complicated, just something that would let me measure an elevation from one point to some other point. He said, "I think I've got just what you need. It'll cost you $67.50. Can you handle that?" I said I could, and he disappeared into the aisles behind him. He returned a moment later with a little box. "This is called an Abney level," he said. Then he showed me how it worked. There was a bubble that aligned between two marks and a dial marked in degrees with a small telescope that swiveled. "You set the bubble and align the crosshairs in the scope on your point. That's about it."

I paid him and headed back to Haverford.

The following evening, I landed at Love Field and took a cab to downtown Dallas. I had the cabbie let me off at Dealey Plaza. It was too late to see anything, but I found a hotel at the northeast corner of the plaza. It was pretty much a fleabag, but I didn't care. I wouldn't be there long.

In those years, the Dallas police were thought by many to have been involved in the assassination. Hence, when a loud banging on my door woke me up at 2:00 a.m., my first thought was "The Dallas police! They must have followed me from the airport!" It never crossed my mind that I was too innocuous to have attracted attention from anyone. I went to the door and slowly opened it. A drunk was stumbling down the corridor. Apparently, he'd been trying to get into the wrong room.

The next morning, a Sunday, was beautiful. I dropped the Abney level in my pocket and set off across the plaza. I'd brought some photocopies of photos and a map of Elm Street giving Kennedy's location during the shooting. That was how I came to be sitting on the steps near Zapruder's pedestal for a long time, taking in the scene, trying to imagine what it had been like.

After a while, I stood and walked down the sidewalk to look over at Zapruder's pedestal. Clearly, he had chosen the perfect spot from which to photograph the assassination. To my left (and Zapruder's right) were the steps that led down to the Elm Street sidewalk. One witness, Emmett Hudson, had been standing on that little cement landing during the shooting. And directly across the street was where another witness, Mary Moorman, had taken her famous photograph of Kennedy as the shots hit him. Behind Hudson and those trees was the five-foot-tall wooden stockade fence that separated the parking lot and railroad yards from Dealey Plaza. I walked up the cement stairs and ambled over behind the fence. About five feet away from the fence along its length were railroad ties, placed to keep cars from banging into the fence. Just in front of the fence was where witness S. M. "Skinny" Holland and his rail-yard coworkers had spotted smoke during the shooting. And right where I was standing—maybe eight or ten feet up from the corner of the fence—was where Holland and the others had found fresh footprints, cigarette butts, and new mud on a fence strut.

I looked over the stockade fence in the direction of Elm Street to where the president's limousine had been when the shots were fired. I tried to imagine a shooter firing from my position, likely steadying a rifle barrel atop the fence while bracing one foot on the fence strut, the other in the mud. I didn't have to try. It was all right there in front of me—the target's slow left-to-right movement coming toward the shooter, the short distance, the concealment of the overhanging bushes, the support of the fence—almost every component made this a textbook example of a sniper's ideal spot.

I turned around and looked back at the railroad yard. Dominating everything was the railroad tower from which signals operator Lee Bowers had observed the shooting and the two men behind the fence. On this Sunday, there were only a few cars parked here. I walked between them and the fence until I came to the railroad overpass. I walked out onto the middle of the overpass and looked up Elm Street. Here was where Holland and the other railroad men had watched the assassination, Kennedy's limousine heading toward them and then disappearing underneath. What a perfect place to watch from. They could see everything and not be in the line of fire.

Looking up Elm Street, I could see the Texas School Book Depository building with the Hertz sign on its roof. Right on the corner was the sixth-floor window from which at least some shots had come. Across Houston Street from the depository was the Dal-Tex Building, where Zapruder had his office. Like the depository, it was an older redbrick building, while across Elm Street and kitty-corner to the depository was the Records Building—modern-looking and light-colored. Once again, it struck me: How close everything was!

For a moment, as I stood there, a wave of doubt hit me. How could I have been so misguided as to think that a young professor with a paltry $500 advance, zero connections, no credibility, no track record, and not a lot of time could possibly mount any challenge to the findings of the US government with its vast resources—findings that, moreover, had been embraced by the media, the pundits, the establishment, and various powers that be as settled historical fact?

Then I thought about the Abney level in my pocket, about the 27 degrees Connally's surgeon had calculated, and how I had been reading about the assassination for months and had found no mention that anyone—not the Dallas police, not the FBI, not the Warren Commission—had ever asked the question: What would that 27-degree bullet trajectory line up with if you looked back along it?

"Maybe that was the problem all along," I thought. "Maybe the sheer momentum of the narrative let loose just hours after the shooting so dominated everything that it ended up determining the outcome. Was this momentum so forceful that it literally pushed aside all doubts and reservations?"

I remembered how in November 1963, we had all hoped there was no conspiracy, how we had all hoped that the president's death was a stroke of blind misfortune, like Air Force One being struck by lightning. Combined with the nation's need for closure and reassurance, had this initial narrative gained such power that no one had ever asked the right questions?

I climbed up on Zapruder's pedestal and watched a few cars move down Elm Street. There wasn't much traffic, and the cars were going much faster than the eight to eleven miles per hour of Kennedy's limousine. I got out my charts and figured out where Connally had been when his shoulder collapsed between Zapruder frames 237 and 238 and he directly faced Zapruder. Imagining Connally facing me at that location, I could determine roughly the direction from which the shot that hit him had come.

I looked beyond him across the plaza and saw the modern face of the Dallas County Records Building on Houston Street. Moving down to the sidewalk, I took a few practice shots with the Abney level. I waited until the light at Elm and Houston changed and then darted out into the center lane. Within a few feet of where Connally had been that November day, I set my feet and took a reading with the Abney level precisely to the roof of the records building. Damn! I couldn't believe it. Feeling a small jolt of adrenaline, I went back to the sidewalk and over the next several minutes carefully repeated the process three more times.

Each time the result was the same: 27 degrees.

CHAPTER 2 *LIFE* MAGAGINE

While I was making my first reconnaissance of Dealey Plaza and worrying about how I would ever gain access to interview key witnesses, let alone complete a book, publisher Berney Geis, unbeknownst to us, was exploring a possibility that soon would catapult me into the heart of a high-pressure, deadline-driven investigation of the Warren Commission Report by LIFE magazine. How this happened is a reflection on the culture of publishing at that time.

Back in 1966, that world was quite small and almost exclusively centered in New York City, where it seemed everyone knew everyone else. Berney Geis was no exception, having earlier that year published *Valley of the Dolls*, a steamy roman à clef penned by actress-turned-author Jacqueline Susann. It chronicled the Hollywood/Broadway careers of three women and their rise to fame and eventual self-destruction ("dolls" was a slang term for downers). The novel was an instant blockbuster (eventually selling an astonishing thirty million copies) and made many people rich, including Berney, who, with a touch of whimsy, remodeled his office by installing a fire pole to allow easy access to the company's offices on the floor below.

One of Berney's personal friends was Loudon Wainwright Jr., a prominent writer and columnist for LIFE whose well-regarded weekly column, "The View from Here," had made him a household name among the magazine's huge audience (LIFE's circulation was thirteen million). Parenthetically, LIFE had recently run a puff-piece profile of Jacqueline Susann. Believing that Wainwright might be sympathetic to what we were doing, Berney called him. Wainwright was not only interested, he said that LIFE was considering a reinvestigation of the events of November 22. He suggested that he, together with a couple of LIFE editors, meet with Berney and me at Berney's office—preferably sooner rather than later.

Apparently what had sparked LIFE's interest was the publication that summer of two books critical of the Warren Commission, both credible and well reviewed. *Rush to Judgment*, written by attorney Mark Lane, took issue with the conclusions of the commission, arguing that there had been a conspiracy to assassinate Kennedy, and that Lee Harvey Oswald had likely been set up as the fall guy. The second book, *Inquest*, authored by Edward Jay Epstein, grew out of a thesis he had written while a graduate student in government at Cornell University. Epstein's principal focus was the internal workings of the Warren Commission during its probe. The combined message of the two books was that there were clearly problems in the Warren Commission account that simply could not be wished away.

Thus, one morning in mid-October, as I drove up from Philadelphia to Manhattan for the meeting at Berney's office, I found myself once again amazed at how quickly events were happening and how unexpectedly—and easily—I was being given access to resources that could literally supercharge what I was trying to do. Yet, as I gazed out on the leaves turning yellow and red alongside the New Jersey Turnpike, I was of two minds.

On the one hand, it did not seem strange at all that I should be meeting with LIFE editors about the Kennedy assassination. I was writing a book about it. They wanted to hear what I had to say. They had the Zapruder film, and I wanted to see it—in fact could hardly wait to see it. That was the only thing that mattered.

On the other hand, none of this seemed real to me. It appeared to be happening on a stage distant from my real life of preparing the next day's classes and shopping with Nancy at Penn Fruit. I was about to get a glimpse inside the Time-Life universe, the home of two weeklies that together were arguably the most influential magazines in America. This was the heyday of the national magazine, and cover stories in TIME and LIFE often set the national agenda. In the case of TIME (circulation 3.3 million), it conveyed and defended a Republican perspective on the Vietnam War. LIFE was more focused on photojournalism than news, but both periodicals were extremely powerful institutions. Who was I to be playing on this stage?

The meeting in Berney's office started about 11:00 a.m. Wainwright brought along two associate editors, Ed Kern and Dick Billings.[1] Kern had recently written the major part of a series on the Roman Empire. Billings was LIFE's chief of investigative reporting. The atmosphere was amiable but businesslike.

Had I stopped to think about it, I would have recognized that this was an audition for me. But I didn't treat it that way. I began by asking Kern and Billings what they knew concerning various issues. From the answers they gave, it was clear that they were just starting out. I asked about the so-called missing frames of the film that had recently become an issue. Billings explained that the controversy was a waste of time. Yes, the original film had broken and had been spliced with a few frames left out. But the frames were there in the first-day copy that LIFE also owned. It was an example, he said, of how silly things can get out of hand.

I described the kind of investigation I wanted to carry out. I had a list of ten or fifteen witnesses in Dallas and across the country whom I wanted to interview. There were some items of evidence in the National Archives that I wanted to examine and photograph. And there were some measurements I wanted to carry out on frames from the Zapruder film.

The meeting went swimmingly. By its close, it had become clear that this was a winning situation for everyone. I wanted to be able to study the Zapruder film to begin answering a number of questions about the event. LIFE could also get me access to witnesses and to important pieces of evidence. From the LIFE editors' point of view, they needed immediate guidance into the center of the growing controversy. While the magazine owned the critical evidence in the case, it would be of no value unless they learned quickly what to do with it. That was where I came in. With several months' time, an editor could be brought up to speed on the assassination controversy. But LIFE did not have several months. They needed to start their investigation right away with the goal of publishing their findings in late November, less than six weeks away.

After the meeting, our group adjourned to Laurent, an upscale restaurant across the street, while Wainwright headed back to the Time-Life Building for another meeting. Over lunch, we continued discussing the kind of investigation I had in mind. Kern and Billings, while not yet conversant with the assassination, were very bright men with good judgment about how investigations turned out in the real world. Berney tried to get them to commit LIFE to helping me with the editorial heavy lifting and even endorsing or condensing the book. They insisted that they weren't authorized to make any such decisions. In the midafternoon, Kern, Billings, and I hopped into a cab and made our way across town to the Time-Life Building at Rockefeller Center.

Getting out of the cab at the corner of Fiftieth and Sixth Avenue, I looked up at the forty-eight stories of green glass windows jutting into the mid-October sky. There was a sculpture in the plaza and in the lobby large wall murals and the entrance to an elegant Latin American–themed restaurant, La Fonda del Sol. "Funny world you've got yourself into, Thompson," I said to myself. Since we were going to LIFE's editorial offices, we had to go through some security formalities before being admitted to the correct bank of elevators.

We went to Billings's office on the twenty-ninth floor, and there I was introduced to fellow assassination researcher Ray Marcus. He was a nice-looking guy of about forty with a high forehead and curly hair combed straight back. He ran a business in Los Angeles making vinyl plastic items for the household. I had never met Marcus before or even talked to him on the telephone. I had seen on Salandria's shelf a spiral-bound copy of a monograph Marcus had written on commission exhibit (CE) 399, the bullet that the commission had determined had wounded both Kennedy and Connally. In addition, he had made some important finds on the Zapruder film. During our meeting and lunch, Marcus had been in Billings's office studying frames from the Zapruder film. Was he going to be hired too? Would we be working together?

Soon we were all sitting in a conference room with a projector and a screen. Billings began talking about the case and the Zapruder film. I could barely disguise my anticipation. Finally, after a few minutes, the lights were dimmed and the projector started up. For the life of me, I can't recall whether we watched an 8-mm or 16-mm copy of the film, but whichever, it was flat-out gorgeous! The images were sharp, the colors vivid, the outlines firm. Compared with the muddy copy Vince and I had seen at the archives, this was infinitely better—still shocking, still breathtaking.

They ran the film twice, after which Billings produced about 150 35-mm transparencies of individual frames that he had brought from his office and that Marcus had been studying. I took a quick look at the frames around 313 and several others in the 230s. They were glorious! There was no question about the awful damage to Kennedy's head and the point in time when Connally had been hit.

Marcus was ushered out, and I spent an hour or so describing in more detail what I had in mind for an investigation. I pointed out that the National Archives copies of the film were so muddy that measurements of the president's head after impact would have been eaten up by measurement error. Given the clarity of what I had just seen, I now knew that those measurements could be made with real accuracy. I never did find out what Marcus's role in all this was to be. His name was never mentioned again by Kern or Billings.

As soon as I left the building, I went to a pay phone and called Don Preston at Berney's office. "Look, I don't know where this is going, Don," I said. "The Zapruder film is glorious. You can see all the details. Connally was hit later, just as he and his wife have always insisted. You can see the impact of the bullet on him. The single-bullet theory is dead. It's all there on the film. Obviously, Oswald didn't act alone. LIFE is going to break this all within the month!"[2] At this point I had all but forgotten the book. What I had seen changed everything. LIFE was going to explode this case, and it was going to do it with the film to which the Warren Commission had paid only lip service.

LIFE was shooting for an article in late November to coincide with the third anniversary of the assassination. Doubtless fueling the magazine's need to move quickly was a report that the New York Times had assembled a team of investigative reporters to conduct its own examination. It was obvious that everything I wanted to do could not be done in a month. Kern and Billings had their own ideas as to what they wanted to focus on first. I was also concerned as to how I could work out commuting to Dallas in the framework of the classes I was teaching. It could be done, I figured, because my classes were grouped together during the week. This would make a four- or even five-day trip to Dallas possible if I included the weekend. In addition to Dallas, there would be trips to the archives and a couple of interviews to do in Washington. It would be tight but doable.

LIFE had given up its Dallas bureau earlier in the 1960s. We worked out of a small, cramped temporary office in the city's downtown section that was nicknamed the "Sub-rosa Bureau" by the two LIFE staffers who worked there, Holland McCombs and Patsy Swank.

With his closely cropped white hair and lanky build, Holland McCombs reminded me of actor Lee Marvin. I never did understand what McCombs did for LIFE, but apparently it was important. Important, yes, but also mysterious—things that not everyone was privy to.

Patsy Swank was one interesting woman.[3] An attractive woman in her mid-forties with light brown, shoulder-length hair, she possessed a sharp intelligence and a wonderful West Texas laugh. She had been a stringer for LIFE since 1961 and did most of the real work: contacting witnesses, running down films and photos, sweet-talking us into places we couldn't otherwise have gotten into. Her husband, Arch Swank, was an architect of real distinction in Dallas. The couple had four young children. We had dinner one night at their home in an upper-middle-class neighborhood. It had an interesting design with a lot of dark oak paneling.

During the first few days, I learned the inside story of how LIFE had landed the Zapruder film. It was through Patsy.

When the assassination happened, Patsy stayed by her phone, and soon calls came in from her news contacts. Early on, she heard about Abraham Zapruder and his film. When the LIFE Los Angeles bureau chief, Dick Stolley, flew into Dallas that Friday afternoon to take charge of the LIFE reporting, Patsy immediately told him about Zapruder. Together, they began calling Zapruder's home every fifteen minutes. Zapruder was busy getting the film processed at the Kodak plant, then having copies made, then finding Secret

Service Agent Forrest Sorrels, and finally dropping off two copies of the film at the Dallas Secret Service office.

Around 11:00 p.m., Stolley and Patsy finally reached Zapruder. He and Stolley agreed to meet early the next morning. At that meeting, Stolley persuaded Zapruder to sell the film to LIFE and walked out of Zapruder's office with the original in his briefcase, thus assuring LIFE a dramatic scoop. That Saturday morning, LIFE agreed to pay Zapruder $50,000 ($376,200 in inflation-adjusted dollars) for just the print rights to the film. The following Monday, Stolley went back and signed a replacement contract to purchase the ownership and all rights to the film and took away with him the single copy Zapruder had retained. In return, LIFE paid Zapruder $150,000 ($1,128,000 in inflation-adjusted dollars).[4]

Patsy had connections, and she was prepared to use them to get us where we wanted to go. I was ready to point out just where that was.

Three years out from the killing, the initial investigations had left clear signs of where the problems lay. Both the twenty-six volumes of follow-up to the Warren Report and the thousands of documents becoming available month after month in the National Archives identified specific areas where investigation might turn up answers to outstanding questions. There were two such areas that especially interested me.

First, given the hazy outlines suggesting that a shot had been fired from the right front of Kennedy's limousine, I wanted to interview witnesses whose positions in Dealey Plaza made what they had to say relevant to this question.

Second was Parkland Hospital, where Kennedy had been taken immediately after the shooting. The descriptions of the president's wounds provided by various doctors there were at odds with the official autopsy report. I decided to pursue this line of inquiry first, to interview the individual doctors involved one-on-one, plus any other hospital staff who might have useful information.

Parkland had closed its doors to journalists many months or years before, but somehow Patsy got us in. Besides having the full backing of LIFE, it might have been that she knew the administrator of the hospital, C. J. Price, through her husband. As we drove over to the hospital, I explained to her that I wanted to pursue just one event, the finding of the so-called magic bullet, CE 399. Here, some background is in order.

In the short time that the presidential party was at Parkland Hospital, a bullet—"projectile" in forensic terminology—was found on a gurney in the hall of the Emergency Department. The 6.5-mm projectile was later matched to the rifle found on the sixth floor of the depository. The problem was the condition of the bullet. It would be wrong to say that the bullet was "pristine."

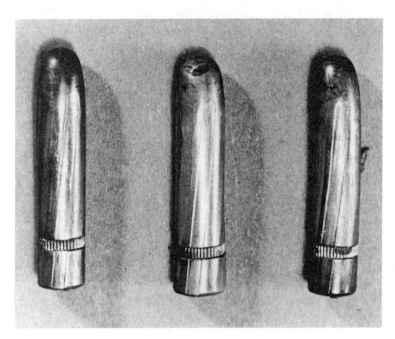

Photo 2-1. CE 399 is the bullet in the middle. The bullets on each side were fired into long tubes of cotton waste for firearms ID purposes.

It was not. It was slightly damaged—squeezed a bit—along its rear third. It looked just like the bullets that Federal Bureau of Investigation (FBI) agents had test-fired from the rifle into long tubes of cotton waste. Both CE 399 and these test bullets were somewhat deformed.

But CE 399 had not been fired into a tube of cotton waste. According to the Warren Commission, this bullet had entered Kennedy's back, exited his neck without striking bone, and then passed through Governor Connally, piercing his right shoulder and shattering five inches off a rib before punching out an exit hole the size of a fifty-cent piece in the front of his chest. The bullet continued on to penetrate his left wrist, breaking the wrist bone at its thickest point, and then finally embedded itself in Connally's left thigh. On this particular finding, Cyril Wecht, MD, a leading forensic pathologist and past president of the American Academy of Forensic Scientists, had not minced words when I had talked to him. He told me that for a projectile to have done all this and to remain in only slightly damaged condition was "utterly impossible."[5]

The bullet was found by a hospital engineer, Darrell Tomlinson, on a gurney shoved against the wall near the men's room in the Emergency Department. It

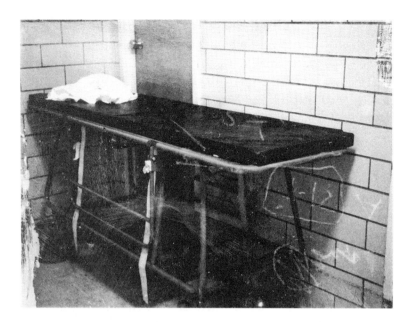

Photo 2-2. Polaroid photos taken at Parkland Hospital with help from Tomlinson and Wright show bullet nestled against gurney pad.

was lying alongside the gurney's black vinyl pad, between the pad and metal edge. Tomlinson took the bullet to Parkland's security director, O. P. Wright, and described how he had found it. Wright examined the bullet and then went to find a federal officer to take custody of it. He got a refusal from one FBI agent but ultimately passed it on to Secret Service Agent Richard Johnsen. Agent Johnsen wrote a note saying that on the gurney with the bullet were "rubber gloves, a stethoscope and other doctor's paraphernalia." Johnsen carried the bullet back to Washington in his pocket and personally gave it— and the note—to Chief James Rowley of the Secret Service. Later that night, the bullet made its way to the FBI Laboratory. Testing was easy since the bullet was in such good shape. It had been fired from the rifle found on the sixth floor of the book depository.

When Patsy and I arrived at Parkland, we were told that no tape recorders were allowed. We had no LIFE photographer with us, but I had managed to bring along a clumsy Polaroid camera. One of the first people I interviewed was Rosa Majors, a nurse's aide. She had been on duty when a two-and-a-half-year-old child named Ronnie Fuller had been brought into the Emergency Department at the same time as Kennedy and Connally. Fuller had fallen and cut his cheek, and it was bleeding badly. Given the equipment left on various gurneys, it looked as if the gurney on which the bullet had been discovered had been used in the care of Ronnie Fuller. What Rosa Majors told me about where Fuller's gurney was last seen and what was on it confirmed that the bullet had been found on Ronnie Fuller's gurney—a gurney in no way connected to the care of either President Kennedy or Governor Connally.

Then there was the bullet itself. I had come to Parkland carrying several bullet photos. One showed two undamaged .38-caliber projectiles; another showed the firearms identification projectiles fired from the 6.5-mm Carcano into long tubes of cotton waste; and finally, an eight-by-ten-inch black-and-white print of CE 399 showed the bullet reportedly found on the gurney.

Showing hospital engineer Darrell Tomlinson bullet photos was largely a waste of time. He was not familiar with bullets and had no eye for recognizing them. Security Director O. P. Wright was another matter entirely. Wright had spent thirty years with the Dallas police and had ended as deputy chief. As I sat in his cramped little office, he looked at me with that old cop's look. I could see it in his eyes: "What's a thirty-year-old college professor doing hanging around with LIFE magazine? Couldn't they have gotten a professional? Some homicide detective who's retired and could use the money? Is he trying to invent some dizzy conspiracy theory?"

We started talking about November 22, and he told me the same things I had already read in the report he had written. Earlier, when Wright had accompanied me as I had reenacted with Tomlinson his finding of the bullet, he had supplied a .30-caliber projectile that he had in his desk. I was turning it in my hand as we talked. I asked him what the gurney bullet looked like, and he said it had a pointed tip "like the one you got there in your hand." I looked at the .30-caliber bullet in my hand. We talked some more, and then I drew

Photo 2-3. CE 399.

three bullet shapes on a white legal pad: one pointed like the .30 caliber, another long with a rounded tip like CE 399, and yet another rounded and squat like a .38 caliber.

He picked the shape with the pointed tip—the one most like the .30 caliber in my hand—as most similar to the gurney bullet. We talked some more about what had happened that day, and then I pulled the photos out of my gray Danish book bag. I showed him first the squat .38-caliber projectile. He just shook his head. Then I tried the firearms identification rounds, CE 572.

"Look," Wright said impatiently, "I told you it had a pointed tip. Just like that bullet you have there." Finally, I

Photo 2-4. .30-caliber projectile from O. P. Wright photographed in hotel room.

pulled out the photo of CE 399, the bullet Tomlinson was supposed to have found on the gurney and given to him and which he in turn had given to Secret Service Agent Johnsen. "That's just like the last two. Same answer."

We talked a while longer and then made our way out into the vestibule, where Patsy was waiting. With her looking on, I showed Wright the photo of CE 399, and he rejected it again as the bullet he had handled on November 22. An hour or so later, when we were getting ready to leave, Wright approached me and asked, "Say, that single-bullet photo you kept showing me . . . was that the one that was supposed to have been found here?"

"Yes," I answered.

He looked right at me, his face expressionless, and said, "Uh . . . huh." Then he turned and went back to his office.

Wright let me keep the .30-caliber projectile. That night, back in my room at the Sheraton, I photographed it using a room key for scale.

Although Patsy and I often worked together in Dallas, we always recognized that the investigation was being run out of New York by Billings and Kern. Both had the title "associate editor." For his part, Dick Billings looked the part of head of investigative reporting. If he had ever played football, he would have been a tight end. He was about six feet tall with an athletic build, straightforward and articulate, yet you had the impression he knew all the angles. He was the kind of guy who, in another life, would have been a federal prosecutor or an agent. If Billings was tuned to action, Ed Kern was tuned to language. Smaller than Billings, he was a feature writer. He looked like he wrote for the *New Yorker*. He was somewhat of an introvert, and during the interviews we did together, it was always apparent how smart he was.

It was never clear just what role I was supposed to play in this investigation. My contract stated only that I would "act as a consultant to LIFE in an examination of the Warren Report and the assassination of President Kennedy." I would be paid a one-time fee of $1,500 and $200 per month plus expenses. Nobody really knew what I was supposed to be doing, and that was just fine with me.

At the outset, the plan was for me to point out targets whom others would interview. Once we started, however, it became clear that this approach wouldn't work. The others hadn't read enough to know how a witness fit into the case and hence what to ask them. If Kern or Billings or Patsy or McCombs interviewed any witnesses by themselves, I never heard of it.

What Patsy and I did understand was that there was a level of the LIFE investigation beyond our participation or understanding. I never knew what McCombs was supposed to be doing, and it was apparent that I was not supposed to know. During my whole time with LIFE, I never met the editor, George Hunt. In the early part of the investigation, we were pointing toward an article in November that would highlight a new interview with Governor Connally, but when that time came, I was kept far away. Looking back, I suspect that LIFE did not want me anywhere near the governor, as I might blurt out something that would make a mess of things.

Because I was on such a long leash, I could do pretty much whatever I wanted to do in Dallas. From the outset, I had no interest in the conspiracy theories making the rounds. People could argue these things forever, yet I doubted that any of them could be proven. But what had happened in Dealey Plaza was something else entirely. The assassination had happened one way rather than another. That much was clear. The threshold question was equally clear: Was President Kennedy fired upon from any location other than the sixth-floor corner window of the book depository? If all the basic facts of the assassination could be explained by shots from the sixth-floor window, then Occam's razor would cut against conspiracy as an explanation, and the theorists would be in for a rough ride. On the other hand, if the threshold question could be affirmatively answered based upon a meticulous, impartial examination of the evidence, then the whole question of whether or not there had been a conspiracy would be settled as historical fact.

This threshold question decided for me how I wanted to bend the LIFE investigation. And bend it I did.

I never told Patsy my thinking on all this, nor my reasons for picking the witnesses to interview. If the truth be told, I don't think Patsy ever believed anything but what the Warren Report said. She saw me as a young college professor who had somehow gotten himself wrapped into the LIFE package. We were just people working on a story, the gist of which was that the critics of the Warren Commission were on to something. I had simply refined that something into a focus on the threshold question. That this made sense from LIFE's point of view is very likely why I never got any grief from Kern or Billings. They knew I was bending the investigation in a particular direction and, I think, approved of it. Oddly, we never talked about it.

I had picked out for interviews a particular class of witnesses based on their locations on November 22. I had already made up a chart showing the location of witnesses in Dealey Plaza along with Zapruder frame numbers showing the location of the limousine as it moved down Elm Street. The crowd thinned dramatically along Elm Street toward the Triple Underpass. Only a scattered few were standing near the place where Zapruder frame 313 showed Kennedy being struck in the head by a bullet. I was interested in those witnesses who were close enough to that impact to have seen something important. It was a short list—something our small investigation team could handle.

There was another reason for picking these witnesses to interview. Since first seeing the Zapruder film in the archives, I had never quite gotten over the image of that impact, of seeing President Kennedy slammed backward and to the left in his seat. In LIFE's copy, it was even more vivid and compelling. It looked exactly as if he had been hit in the right temple with a baseball bat. There is no question about it being the very climax of the Zapruder film, the instant when President Kennedy is struck down. Everything else in the film is either prologue or postscript. Strangely, it is not mentioned even once in the 888-page Warren Report or in the tens of thousands of pages making up the twenty-six volumes of *Hearings and Exhibits*. It is as if the sequence didn't exist—as if it never happened.

To me it was understandable why the Warren Commission had ignored this sequence. It didn't fit its official narrative—that all the shots had been fired from directly behind the president. How could a bullet from the rear have slammed him left and backward toward the very rifle that shot him? Lacking an answer, the commission appeared to have decided not to even ask the question. For me, this behavior flashed a clear, if unintended, message: Here was blood in the water. Here was the place to focus our investigation.

I was aware of a lot of other evidence that pointed to the impact at frame 313 having come from a shot fired from the right front, from the already infamous "grassy knoll." This witness testimony largely came from the same people who were already on my list—people who were close to the president when he was shot in the head.

Given that these witnesses were so few in number, this meant that I could talk to them myself and judge their credibility. This was important since I had seen how witness reports had begun shifting after November 22. It is a well-established phenomenon that many witnesses begin tailoring their recollections to received opinion as to how an event happened. Within an hour or so of the shooting, a primary narrative gained traction: Oswald, the lone assassin, fired all the shots from the sixth-floor corner window of the depository. In the months that followed, government sources, and then the Warren Commission itself, endorsed this account. It should come as no surprise that over time, many witnesses tailored their recollections to match this official story. This meant that the earliest report by a witness was the most important because it was the most trustworthy. Here, Patsy Swank was an enormous asset. Because of her connections with local reporters and TV stations, she and I could run down the first recorded interviews with many of these witnesses and sometimes even audio or video tapes that had never been broadcast.

Before going to Dallas, I had started collecting material for witness folders. I organized the folders with the first and most important report or tape going first in the folder. Even in those cases where a witness was unavailable through death or a decision on their part, I made up a file folder containing all the transcripts, FBI reports, and videotape interviews of the witness. Patsy quickly learned which witnesses were unavailable (for example, Dallas police officers) when she started making calls. Ordinary people such as S. M. Holland or Bill and Gayle Newman gave her no trouble when she called to set up interviews. I never heard of anyone asking Patsy for money to do an interview.

First on the list were Bill and Gayle Newman. When Kennedy was shot in the head, they were standing at the north curb of Elm Street, only ten to twelve feet from the president. Then there was Emmett Hudson, who was standing between the stockade fence on the knoll and the limousine. Lee Bowers was running the railroad tower behind the knoll and saw two men behind the stockade fence at the time of the shooting.

S. M. Holland had probably the best view of any of the witnesses. He was standing on the railroad overpass overlooking Elm Street and therefore was able to watch the whole tableau developing in front of him. Marilyn Sitzman and Abraham Zapruder stood on a concrete pedestal as Zapruder filmed the shooting. James Altgens was an Associated Press (AP) photographer on the south curb of Elm Street, only twenty or so feet from Kennedy when he was hit in the head.

Then there was a gaggle of Dallas policemen. The four motorcycle officers were riding just off the right and left rear of the limousine and hence were only feet from Kennedy when he was hit in the head. Joe Marshall Smith was a patrolman who ran to the knoll area with his gun drawn only seconds after the shooting. There were a few others, but their law enforcement interviews did not indicate that they had much of interest to report. This was a good enough list to start with.

CHAPTER 3   WITNESSES
The Bystanders

Bill and Gayle Newman

Photos from Dealey Plaza show Bill and Gayle Newman with their two boys standing on the north curb of Elm Street.[1] The limousine sweeps down the street and passes within ten or twelve feet of them. When Kennedy is hit in the head, the Newmans are closer to him than any other civilian witnesses. Immediately, they throw themselves on the ground to protect their children. Within half an hour of the shooting, they are whisked to a TV studio to tell their story on the air. No other witnesses were this close to what happened or were interviewed so quickly. This was why I put the Newmans at the top of our priority list of witnesses to interview.

The afternoon I drove out to the Newmans' home in the middle-class Dallas suburb of Oak Cliff, this was pretty much everything I knew about the Newmans except for one outstanding fact—the Warren Commission had never called them to testify or to be deposed in Dallas. They had executed affidavits on November 22, and two FBI agents had interviewed them two days later. Why hadn't the Warren Commission been more interested in these exceptional witnesses?

Various interviews over the years have filled in many details about who the Newmans are and what they observed.[2] On the day of the assassination, Bill was twenty-one and Gayle was twenty-two. Both had been born in Dallas and raised in Oak Cliff. For much of Bill's late childhood he had lived on North Beckley Street, only three or four blocks from Oswald's rooming house on the same street. Bill was starting a career as an electrician and earlier that week had taken the state electrician's exam. Gayle was a stay-at-home mom, her days filled with taking care of their two sons, Billy, four, and Clayton, two.

Neither was interested in politics. They were just regular people, in Bill's words, "living day to day, making a living, going to a movie, going to church."[3] The president coming to town was not an everyday event, so they decided to drive to Love Field to see him. They thought it would be good for the boys.

Photo 3-1. Newmans on the ground with their boys moments after the shooting.

They were going to bring their 8-mm movie camera but inadvertently left it at home on top of a bureau.

At Love Field, the Newmans were unable to get anywhere near the president and Mrs. Kennedy. Consequently, they drove to downtown Dallas, parked a few blocks east of Houston Street, walked down to Dealey Plaza, and picked a spot along the curb away from other people. They waited there for about fifteen minutes until the president's limousine made its turn onto Elm Street.

After the shooting they were dazed and scared and remained lying on the ground for several minutes. Eventually, they were picked up by two TV station staffers and driven to the nearby studio of WFAA-TV, where a cooking show was in progress. The show was interrupted, and the Newman family was soon on live television being interviewed by newsman Jay Watson. Bill recalled, "We were on the air within half an hour of the shooting."

At WFAA, Patsy Swank and I had viewed a clip of the Newmans' interview with Watson. The Newmans and their children were seated at a news desk while Watson hovered over them with a microphone. Watson told Bill Newman, "Tell me what you saw and what you felt. What happened to you?"

NEWMAN: We were . . . We had just come from Love Field after seeing the president and the first lady. And we were just in front of the Triple Underpass on Elm Street at the edge of the curb . . . getting ready to wave at the president. . . .

WATSON: You were down. you were down under the viaduct, so to speak, weren't you?

NEWMAN: Well, we were halfway between . . .

WATSON: On the grass.

NEWMAN: . . . the Triple Underpass. We were at the curb the instant it happened. But the president's car was some 50 feet in front of us, coming towards us, when we heard the first shot. And the president . . . I don't know who was hit first, but the president jumped up in his seat, and I thought it scared him. I thought it was a firecracker because he looked . . . you know . . . fear, and then as the car got directly in front of us, well, a gunshot apparently from behind us hit the president in the side [*demonstrating with his finger to his right temple*] . . . side of the temple.

WATSON: Do you think the first gunshot came from behind you, too?

NEWMAN: I think it came from the same location . . . apparently back up on the . . . the mall. I don't know what you call it. . . .

WATSON: Do you think a shot came from up on top of the viaduct toward the president; is that correct?

NEWMAN: Yes, sir, not, no, not on the viaduct itself but up on top of the hill . . . of the mound of ground, there's a garden.

WATSON: How far away would you say that is from where the president was? A couple, 300 yards, something like that?

NEWMAN: Well, I have no idea. I didn't see the . . . where the gunshot come from. We were looking directly at the president when he was hit, and he was

Photo 3-3. Newmans on the ground after the shooting.

Photo 3-4. Minutes later, people stream onto the grassy knoll.

more or less directly in front of us, and we didn't realize what happened until we seen the side of his head. When the bullet hit him in the head.

WATSON: Did you see the blood coming from the president's head?

NEWMAN: Yes, sir, we seen. I seen, I don't know if my wife did, but I seen that.[4]

The children were restless. After interviewing Gayle, Jay Watson let her get up and walk around with Clayton. Two plainclothes detectives from the sheriff's office arrived at WFAA during the Newmans' interview. They asked the Newmans to come with them to the sheriff's office, where they each signed affidavits.

From Bill's affidavit:

> By this time he was directly in front of us and I was looking directly at him when he was hit in the side of the head. Then he fell back and Governor Connally was holding his middle section. Then we fell down on the grass as it seemed we were in the direct line of fire. . . . Then the car sped away and everybody in that area had run up on top of that little mound. I thought the shot had come from the garden directly behind me, that was on an elevation from where I was as I was right on the curb. I do not recall looking towards the Texas School Book Depository. I looked back in the vicinity of the garden.[5]

From Gayle's affidavit:

> Just about the time President Kennedy was right in front of us, I heard another shot ring out and the President put his hands up to his head. I saw blood all over the side of his head. About this time, Mrs. Kennedy grabbed the President and he kind of lay over to the side kind of in her arms. Then my husband, Billy, said, "It is a shot!" We grabbed our two children and my husband lay on one child and I lay on the other one on the grass.[6]

When the Newmans finally got home that night, they were shaken and scared by what they had seen. Because they were prime witnesses, they feared that someone might want to harm them. That night and the next they took the boys in their bedroom, and Bill loaded a 20-gauge shotgun and kept it near the bed.[7] On Sunday when they returned from church, two FBI agents were waiting for them. While they were being interviewed, a news report flashed that Oswald had been shot in the basement of the Dallas Police Headquarters.

The FBI interview reports[8] reprise the Newmans' earlier interviews on television and their affidavits from the sheriff's office. What is oddly absent from the agents' reports is any indication from the Newmans of where they thought the shot that hit President Kennedy in the head came from. Both Newmans made clear in their earlier interviews that they threw themselves on their children because they thought they were "in the line of fire," that the shots were coming from behind them, from the "mall" or "little garden" on the knoll. Paraphrasing Gayle Newman, the agents' reports said, "After the shots were fired, she and her husband each grabbed a child and lay down on the grass fearing that they might be hit by gunfire." Paraphrasing Bill Newman, they said, "Newman first thought the President and Governor were playing some kind of a game and suddenly realized they had been shot and that he was perhaps in the line of fire because officers started running toward the arcade directly back of him and his wife. He grabbed one child and his wife the other. They both lay down on the grass until after the procession passed."

These early reports were confusing. Where did Bill and Gayle think the shot that hit Kennedy in the head came from? I wanted to nail down what Bill Newman meant by the term "mall." And precisely where was the "little garden"?

I pulled up in front of their modest home on Clarendon Drive and went in. Bill, Gayle, and I sat down in their living room. After some pleasantries, I turned on the tape recorder, and we began to talk.

What became clear right away was the fact that they had hit the ground after the head shot because they were genuinely afraid of being hit themselves. "We were in a bad situation from the standpoint of getting shot," said Bill. "I thought the shots were coming from right off the tops of our heads."[9] Bill went on to describe the moment when the president was hit in the head. He drew a diagram that put the impact near the right ear. "The way he was hit, it looked like he had just been hit with a baseball pitch," said Bill, throwing his head back and to the left. "Just like a block of wood fell over his head . . . When he was hit, I was looking right at him, and of course immediately I knew he was shot, because it went white, like that, and then blood, gook just started bulging out." Bill Newman, of course, had not seen the Zapruder film, but I had—many times. What he was describing was exactly what the film shows.

Our interview continued.

THOMPSON: Now, could I ask you a little more about this? Try to get your immediate response? I take it, it was your immediate response—in your affidavit of the 22nd—that the shots were somehow right back of you: that's what I'm trying to get at.

BILL NEWMAN: That's right. Well, of course the president's being shot in the side of the head by the third shot—I thought the shot was fired from directly above and behind where we were standing. And that's what scared us because I thought we were right in the direct path of gunfire. And—

THOMPSON [interrupting]: By "the president's head" you mean the actual appearance of the impact on the side of his head here and the way his head flipped back over this—

BILL NEWMAN [*interrupting*]: Right, right. My thoughts were that the shot entered there, and apparently the thoughts of the Warren Commission was that the shot came out that side.

THOMPSON: But it's your feeling that the shots were coming from over your . . . right behind you, just based on (1) the sound of the shots, (2) the impact on the president's head, and (3) the movement of the president's head after this impact. Would that be a—?

BILL NEWMAN [*interrupting*]: Right. Well, I think everybody thought the shots were from where I'm saying, behind us, because everybody went in that direction. Must have.

THOMPSON: Do you have . . . this is probably pushing your own recollections too far, but I'll try it anyhow. When you say in back of you, do you have any feeling . . . [*getting up and standing in front of Newman*] say, if I stand here, and I say "in back of me," do you have any feeling if it was "back of me" in this direction? Or "back of me" in this direction? Did it appear to you to be in back of you towards the Texas School Book Depository or towards the general area of the stockade fence and the railroad? Do you have any recollection at all?

BILL NEWMAN: Well, this is going to sound peculiar too, but I was thinking more just the opposite of the building. Actually, the thought never entered my mind that the shots was coming from the building.

THOMPSON: Is that right? Is that right?

BILL NEWMAN: But of course I talked to people, and they say, at that height, it echoes.

THOMPSON: But to take . . . It's your first impression that the shots were coming a little bit from the right front of the vehicle?

BILL NEWMAN: The thought never entered my mind that it was coming from the building.

THOMPSON: Well, look, we have to be careful at this point. A lot of people have said a lot of things. The Warren Commission has come out with their judgment. Don't let what anyone has said contaminate what you heard and felt, and if you—I think it's very important—it's people like you who are going to make our investigation, people who won't budge, you know. So it's your judgment. So it's your judgment . . . I'm not pushing this, I hope. Is it your general recollection that the shots came from behind you, certainly, back of you, right back of you, so much that you were afraid of being hit?

BILL NEWMAN: That's right.

THOMPSON: And now, tell me as to the direction.

BILL NEWMAN: As far as saying one way or the other, I don't know. But I would lean to thinking it came from the opposite direction.

THOMPSON: From the general area of the stockade fence?

BILL NEWMAN: Right.

Bill Newman went on to say that his first thought was that someone had thrown out firecrackers. With respect to the shots, he had heard two close together. He recalled them as a "boom-boom" and estimated they were perhaps a second apart. There was a pause that Newman estimated to be about ten seconds, and then Kennedy was hit in the head with a third shot. Newman went on to say that there could have been a fourth shot, but he could not be sure. To close the interview, I asked Newman if there was anything he thought we ought to pursue.

THOMPSON: Is there anything that you'd like to tell me that you think is significant? Any lead that we ought to pursue? Let's say that if you had the time and money at your disposal, that you'd pursue trying to figure this thing out?

BILL NEWMAN: No, except exactly where the bullet went in and where the bullet went out. That's what would be of great interest to me.

THOMPSON: Well, that's what we're pursuing, and you'll be glad to know that we're showing the Zapruder film tomorrow to Dr. Kemp Clark, the neurosurgeon who worked on the president's head. I take it that the reason you said that's important is that . . . well, the fact is that it appeared to you that the president was hit in the side of the head. [Part of the tape is unintelligible here for what appears to be at least several sentences.] What's your evidence? How would you characterize it?

BILL NEWMAN: Well, just on the hole was made of course. I actually saw a hole, a void. I don't even see there, but it just looked like his ear disintegrated, just blowed his ear off, just was suddenly real white and right behind that it was red with blood and stuff gushing out, and of course by that time the president had fallen over.

THOMPSON: Over to his left?

BILL NEWMAN: Over to his left side. Just went stiff.

I started the Hertz rental car and pulled away from the curb thinking of that last exchange with Newman. If he were in my place, he had said, he would pursue what happened when Kennedy was hit in the head. "My thoughts were that the shot entered there," he had said, "and apparently the thoughts of the Warren Commission was that the shot came out that side." He was troubled because the official version did not match what he believed he had seen.

Another of Bill's points, however, didn't stand up when I thought about it. He had said that "everybody thought the shots were from where I'm say-ing, behind us, because everybody went in that direction. Must have." Bill was right that perhaps more than one hundred people had run into the knoll area in front of the rail yards shortly after the shooting. We have photographs showing that this happened, but it proves very little. Crowds are influenced by odd things. If one person started to run in that direction, others would fol-low, and still others would follow them. So the undisputed fact that many ran toward the knoll and not the Texas School Book Depository means very little.

In addition, Bill's remark that people had suggested that "at that height . . . echoes" might make a shot from the depository seem as if it had come from the knoll is just plain wrong. The knoll is covered with trees and grass and a wooden fence, all sound-absorbing materials. The facade of the depository and the buildings along Houston Street would reflect sound. Just the reverse of what Bill had been told is true. A shot from the knoll might well produce echoes making people think it had come from the northeast end of Elm Street but not the other way around.

Marilyn Sitzman

The offices of Jennifer Juniors, Abraham Zapruder's clothing firm, were located in the Dal-Tex Building, just across Houston Street from the depos-itory. I wanted to talk to Zapruder. Not about what he had seen of the assas-sination—that was recorded frame by frame in his film. It was what he had heard that interested me. Like Bill Newman, who had told me there might have been a shot after he saw the president's head explode, Zapruder had said much the same thing when interviewed by Jay Watson on WFAA-TV. This was perhaps an hour after the Newmans were interviewed by Watson. Zapruder told Watson,

> And I got on top there, there was another girl from my office, she was right
> behind me. And as I was shooting, as the president was coming down from
> Houston Street making his turn, it was about a halfway down there, I heard a
> shot, and he slumped to the side, like this [demonstrating]. Then I heard another
> shot or two, I couldn't say it was one or two, and I saw his head practically open
> up, all blood and everything, and I kept on shooting.[10]

I wanted to ask Zapruder what he meant when he said, "I heard another shot or two, I couldn't say [whether] it was one or two."

I never found out whether Zapruder's absence that day was deliberate or

Photo 3-5. Abraham
Zapruder with Jay Watson
at WFAA-TV.

accidental. It was clear to both Patsy and me that his office staff had run out of
patience with the Kennedy assassination. Zapruder may have made a bundle
out of selling the film, but his office staff had gotten only headaches. They were
tired of it and wished the celebrity of their boss would slip away. I got the same
impression from Marilyn Sitzman, the "girl from the office . . . right behind me"
on the concrete pedestal. She too had been bothered by the press but had never
given a statement to either the Dallas authorities or the FBI. In her early twenties when the assassination happened, she was the receptionist for the office.
On November 22 she was wearing what appears to be a tan wool dress. Photos
show her towering over Zapruder as he tracks the limousine with his camera.

Before I turned on the tape recorder we chatted for a few moments about
nothing in particular. She seemed easy to talk to, a friendly young woman,
even somewhat garrulous. Perhaps it was a mistake, but I decided then to get
into what I wanted to talk to her about. I could go back over the point later
with the recorder on if necessary. The first thing to do was to see whether it
was true.

I had received a report that she had mentioned a very important detail in
a phone call. The report came from Jones Harris, whom I had talked to from
time to time on the telephone but never met face-to-face. Jones was the son of
actress Ruth Gordon and Broadway director Jed Harris. He traveled in upper-
class circles and lived on the Upper East Side of Manhattan. Jones was not
really part of the assassination underground at the time. According to Jones,
Sitzman had told him in a telephone interview that the shot that hit Kennedy
came from her right and was close in. She said her right ear was ringing from
the sound of the shot long after the sound of the shots had died away.

I asked her about it. She recalled the phone conversation with Jones Harris
but denied that she had ever told "Mr. Harris any such thing." She pointed

out that there was a similarity in the sound of the early shots and the shot that hit President Kennedy in the head. They all came from the left, she said, and there was no great difference in their loudness. She said she was surprised that Jones Harris had told me such a thing.

I turned on the tape recorder and asked her to describe what she had experienced on November 22.

> SITZMAN: Well, he stood up there, and he asked me to come up and stand behind him, 'cause when he takes the pictures looking through the telescopic lens, he might get dizzy, and he wanted me to stand behind him, so in case he got dizzy I could hold on to him. So I got up behind him, and we saw the motorcade turn the corner at Main onto Houston. He hadn't started taking the pictures there then, and we watched them as they came down Houston.
> ... There was nothing unusual until the first sound, which I thought was a firecracker, mainly because of the reaction of President Kennedy. He put his hands up to guard his face and leaned to the left, and the motorcade, you know, proceeded down the hill. And the next thing that I remembered correct ... clearly was the shot that hit him directly in front of us, or almost directly in front of us, that hit him on the side of his face.
>
> THOMPSON: Where on the side of the head did that shot appear to hit?
>
> SITZMAN: I would say it'd be above the ear and to the front.
>
> THOMPSON: In other words, if one drew a line vertically upward from the tip of the ear, it would be forward of that line?
>
> SITZMAN: Yeah.
>
> THOMPSON: It would then mean the left ... back of the temple, but on the side of the head, back of the temple?
>
> SITZMAN: Between the eye and the ear.
>
> THOMPSON: Between the eye and the ear.
>
> SITZMAN: And we could see his brains come out, you know, his head opening. It must have been a terrible shot because it exploded his head, more or less.[11]

I asked if she had noticed any movement of Kennedy's head and body when the shot hit him "on the side of his face." She said she had not and went on to stress that the loudest thing she heard that day was the siren. She mentioned a young black couple who had been eating their lunch and drinking Cokes while sitting on a bench only feet from Zapruder and Sitzman. When the shooting started, they "had thrown down their Coke bottles . . . and just started running towards the back." According to Sitzman, "the pop bottles crashing was much louder than the shots."

I was very disappointed as Patsy and I made our way out of Zapruder's offices and the Dal-Tex Building into the brightly lit Dealey Plaza. Zapruder had conveniently absented himself, and Marilyn Sitzman had told me nothing of importance. A black couple had been having lunch on a bench near the pedestal on which she and Zapruder had stood. This was hardly world-shaking news. According to Sitzman, both the siren that went off after JFK was shot in the head and the sound of Coke bottles breaking near her were louder than the shots she heard. This seemed strange. Even stranger was the fact that she had noticed no movement of Kennedy's head and body when the shot hit him in the head. The Zapruder film shows almost exactly what Sitzman must have seen. The climax of the film shows not just the shot she saw hit him "on the side of his face" but the simultaneous left and backward snap of his head and body. How could she have missed it? I had done too few interviews then to recognize that this often happens in criminal cases. Most interviews don't produce anything new or startling. Real breakthrough interviews are the exception and not the rule.

Emmett Hudson

On November 22, Mary Moorman and her friend Jean Hill had come to Dealey Plaza not just to see President Kennedy and take his picture. Both had friends in the Dallas police who were riding motorcycles in the motorcade. Mary had brought her Polaroid camera, and they stationed themselves in the grass center of Dealey Plaza across from the pergola and the pedestal from which Zapruder took his film. In many well-known photos of the assassination, Moorman in a blue coat and Hill in a red coat can be seen standing next to the south curb of Elm Street as the limousine passes. Just one-ninth of a second after the president was struck in the head, Moorman snapped a photo that has become one of the iconic images of that day. In addition to showing the relative positions of Zapruder and Sitzman on the concrete pedestal and Bill Newman by the curb, her photo shows three men standing on the concrete landing leading down to the street. Of these three men, Emmett Hudson is in the middle wearing a cap. He appears to have on a khaki-colored shirt and pants with a dark colored jacket.

On the afternoon of November 22, Hudson went to the Dallas County sheriff's office and executed a sworn affidavit. In that affidavit, he said he was fifty-six (he was actually fifty-eight) and had been employed by the Dallas Parks Department for the past six years. His job was groundskeeper for Dealey Plaza and the fountain in front of Union Station. This is Hudson's description of what he heard and saw:

Photo 3-6. Muchmore frame: Emmett Hudson (*center*) and two others on the steps.

Photo 3-7. Muchmore frame enlarged: Hudson in center.

This day I was sitting on the front steps of the sloping area and about halfway down the steps. There was another man sitting there with me. He was sitting on my left and we were both facing the street with our backs to the railroad yards and the brick building. At the same time, the President's car was directly in front of us, I heard a shot and I saw the President fall over in the seat. . . . This man said "Lay down!" and we did. I definitely heard 3 shots. The shots that I heard definitely came from behind and above me. When I laid down on the ground, I laid on my right side and my view was still toward the street where the President's car had passed. I did look around but I did not see anything unusual, either anyone running and I did not see any firearms at all. This shot sounded to me like a high-powered rifle.[12]

Hudson's statement was witnessed by Forrest Sorrels, the Secret Service agent in charge of the Dallas office. This may account for why Hudson was interviewed by two FBI agents three days later.

The agents referred to a newspaper copy of the Moorman photo, which had been published in the Sunday *Dallas Times Herald*. According to their report, Hudson looked at the photo and said, "That is me in the light-colored clothing and that is where I was standing at the time the President was shot." The report went on to say,

> Hudson said the shots sounded as if they were fired over his head and from some position to the left of where he was standing. In other words, the shots sounded as if they were fired by someone at a position which was behind him, which was above him, and which was to his left. He again called attention to the photograph referred to above, and particularly to the corner of the Texas School Book Depository building appearing in such photograph and said the shots sounded as if they were coming from that building (Texas School Book Depository building).[13]

The Texas School Book Depository building appears nowhere in the photograph, although the corner of the concrete pergola does. The depository was not behind Hudson but instead facing him many hundreds of feet up Elm Street.

Efforts to identify the two men standing with Hudson on the concrete landing have been unsuccessful. As time passed, it was apparent that Hudson's testimony was manipulated by his government questioners. On the afternoon of the shooting, Hudson said simply in his affidavit that the shots "came from behind and above me." Three days later two FBI agents mistakenly transformed the pergola into the Texas School Book Depository and elicited Hudson's agreement that "the shots sounded as if they were coming from that building." Nine and one-half months later, on July 22, 1964, Hudson was deposed by Wesley Liebeler of the commission staff.[14] Hudson told Liebeler that he saw the president hit in the head with what he called "the second

Photo 3-8. Moorman photograph with shot trajectory.

shot." According to Hudson, this shot hit the president "a little bit behind the ear and a little bit above the ear" on Kennedy's right side. Hudson and his companions threw themselves to the ground, and he heard a third shot "coming from above and kind of behind." Liebeler transformed "from above and kind of behind" Hudson into "behind the motorcade" by asking Hudson, "You heard it come from sort of behind the motorcade and then above?" Hudson agreed, and Liebeler later tried but failed to nail down the depository as the source of the shots. At the end of the deposition, he asked a somewhat confused Hudson how much time separated the first shot from the second shot. He said, "Probably two minutes" and then added, "It might not have been that long."

It is difficult to know what to make of Hudson's various reports. In reporting its findings in 1978, the HSCA used Hudson as an example of how a witness's testimony can be bent by the questioning of law enforcement and government attorneys.[15] Films show that Hudson and his companions dropped to the ground after the president was struck in the head. Hudson described this but also surprisingly stated that this next-to-last shot was almost immediately followed by a final shot:

Photo 3-9. Minutes after the shooting, Hudson (*in white ellipses*) remains sitting on the steps' landing where he threw himself.

MR. LIEBELER: After you saw him hit in the head, did you hear another shot?
MR. HUDSON: Yes, sir. (7H560)

Hudson went on to say that after seeing the president hit in the head by the next-to-last shot, he and the others threw themselves to the ground. "I just laid down over on the ground and when that third shot rung out," says Hudson, "I was close to the ground" (7H560). In what proved to be a normal-length interview, Hudson reiterated three times that a final shot followed the one that hit President Kennedy in the head. When Liebeler pressed him on whether it was the second—or next-to-last—shot that exploded the president's head, Hudson replied, "Yes; I do believe that—I know it was" (7H560).

Time pressures made it impossible to interview Hudson in November 1966. Hence, we are left with the somewhat puzzling evidence from his various law enforcement interviews.

James Altgens

On the other side of the street from Marilyn Sitzman, Abraham Zapruder, Bill Newman, and Emmett Hudson was Associated Press photographer James Altgens. Because of his position, he was an equally important witness to the shot that struck the president in the head. I don't remember precisely why he

Photo 3-10. AP photographer James Altgens's photo of the motorcade snapped at Zapruder frame 255.

was unavailable for interview when Patsy Swank tried to reach him. Perhaps he was away on assignment.

With his Nikkorex F 35-mm camera and 105-mm lens, Altgens had already gotten shots of the presidential limousine on Main Street and again on Houston Street. Then he had run across the plaza to the south curb of Elm Street to take one of the most famous photos of the assassination. Taken simultaneously with Zapruder frame 255, it shows the limousine from the front with its motorcycle outriders. President Kennedy has already been hit, and his elbows are upraised.

Altgens wanted to get one more shot, he told the Warren Commission, so

Photo 3-11. Frame 342: James Altgens with camera raised.

Photo 3-12. Frame 347.

he prefocused his camera on 15 feet and let the limousine approach. "I had refocused to 15 feet," said Altgens, "because I wanted a good close-up of the President and Mrs. Kennedy and that's why I know it would be right at 15 feet because I had pre-focused in that area, and I had my camera almost to my eye when it happened, and that's as far as I got with my camera."[16]

Since Altgens appears in the Zapruder film from frame 339 through frame 353, we can see exactly where he was when he raised the camera to his face to take another photo of the president. As the limousine glides by Altgens, we can see that he has his "camera almost at eye level" and is approximately 15 feet from the president and Mrs. Kennedy.

What did he see? He told the Warren Commission the following:

There was not another shot fired after the President was struck in the head. That was the last shot—that much I will say with a great degree of certainty. . . . What made me almost certain that the shot came from behind was because at the time I was looking at the President, just as he was struck, it caused him to move a bit forward. He seemed as if at the right time—well, he was in a position—sort of immobile. He wasn't upright. He was at an angle but when it hit him, it seemed to have just lodged—it seemed as if he were hung up on a seat button or something like that. It knocked him just enough forward that he came right on down. There was flesh particles that flew out of the side of his head in my direction from where I was standing, so much so that it indicated to me that the shot came from out the left side of his head. Also, the fact that his head was covered with blood, the hairline included on the left side—all the way down, with no blood on his forehead or face—suggested to me, too, that the shot came from the opposite side, meaning in the direction of this Depository Building, but at no time did I know for certain where the shot came from.

Strangely, Altgens made no mention of the left and backward snap of the president's head that is so shocking in the Zapruder film. In addition, he saw impact debris flying toward him—that is, forward from the impact on the president's head. He believed the head shot had come from the direction of the depository. This makes him the perfect witness to rebut claims that the president was hit in the head from the right front. He was used to rebut these claims when he appeared on a CBS Reports program on June 26, 1967. He described there what he had experienced:

> And as they got in close to me, and I was prepared to make the picture, I had my camera almost at eye level; that's when the President was shot in the head. And I do know the President was still in an upright position, tilted, favoring Mrs. Kennedy. And at the time that he was struck by this blow to the head, it was so obvious that it came from behind. It had to come from behind because it caused him to bolt forward, dislodging him from this depression in the seat cushion, and already favoring Mrs. Kennedy, he automatically fell in that direction.[17]

In June 1967 I watched this program and wondered what Altgens's report meant. He was an experienced press photographer and had no reason to change or embellish his story. Yet his report ran directly counter to what we see in the Zapruder film and the reports of the motorcyclists riding to the left rear of the limousine. The film shows that Kennedy was struck a strong blow by the shot that drove him backward. The motorcyclists were hit with large amounts of impact debris, and they were behind the limousine on its left-hand side. Altgens, however, reported seeing almost exactly the opposite. I had no idea how to understand this conflict. It would be thirty-six years before this would be explained to me and I would come to understand how what Altgens saw matched both the film and what other witnesses reported. Likewise, for an understanding of why Emmett Hudson surprisingly recalled a final shot after President Kennedy's head exploded or why Abraham Zapruder said on television within minutes of the shooting, "I heard a shot, and he slumped to the side, like this [demonstrating]. Then I heard another shot or two, I couldn't say it was one or two, and I saw his head practically open up, all blood and everything, and I kept on shooting."

The Police Officers

O utside the president's limousine, only the motorcycle police outriders were closer than the Newmans to the president when he was hit in the head. President Kennedy was sitting in the right rear corner of the limousine. In the early Zapruder frames, his right elbow extends over the right side of the car as he waves to the crowd. Riding just off the limousine's right rear fender were Officers James Chaney and Douglas Jackson. On the other side, Officers Bobby Hargis and B. J. Martin were riding just off the limousine's left rear fender. On the next page, the famous Altgens photograph shows Hargis, Martin, and Chaney during the shooting. Jackson is just out of frame to the left.

Several of these officers had been deposed by the Warren Commission, but their testimony left ambiguities that I wanted to resolve. In addition, I wanted to interview Officer Joe Marshall Smith who had been directing traffic at the corner of Houston and Elm Streets and who had run into the knoll area within seconds of the shooting. He too had been deposed by the Warren Commission, but his testimony raised more questions than it answered.

The DPD would not permit interviews by anyone—period. By November 1966, the department had repeatedly been maligned in the national press, while various conspiracy theorists had charged it with complicity in the event. In short, the Dallas police had had it with the national press corps, and LIFE was no exception. After being turned down officially, any attempt to contact these officers at their homes would invite only refusals and bad publicity for LIFE. The door was solidly locked.

This meant that we would have to rely upon the available interviews and sworn testimony.

In 1966 I put together what I could find of the available material. Since then, several of the officers have granted interviews that permit us to know in better detail what they observed on November 22.

Photo 4-1. Altgens photograph taken at frame 255. Note Officer Chaney looking to his left at President Kennedy and Officers Hargis and Martin riding well to the left rear of the limousine. Officer Doug Jackson is out of frame to the left of Officer Chaney.

Officer Douglas C. Jackson

Douglas Jackson was riding the outboard motorcycle trailing the limousine's right rear fender. Riding inboard of Jackson was Officer James Chaney. As far as can be discovered, Jackson never filled out a report on the events of that day or gave an interview about it. He avoided the press, the Warren Commission, and numerous others who were digging into the events of November 22. That included us. Fortunately, Jackson picked a solitary and quiet solution to his brush with history. He went home that Friday night and jotted down in his child's school notebook what he could recall of the day. The account, which became available years later, is affecting in its simplicity and directness.

Jackson began by describing how November 22 "started out cold and raining, a dark day."[1] Back in 1961, he had escorted President Kennedy when he had come to Dallas to visit the ailing Speaker of the House Sam Rayburn. He had hoped to get the chance again. The original plan was to have two officers riding in single file on each side of the limousine to keep anyone from getting too near the car. Jackson wrote that President Kennedy did not want this arrangement, and so the two officers were told to ride side by side at the rear bumper of the car. It was still raining just before 9:00 when "we rode our motorcycles out of the garage that morning. By ten," he remarked, "it was beginning to clear off."

Uneventfully, the motorcade rolled along from Love Field into the downtown. The crowd got thicker as it started down Main Street. Jackson recalled, "Several times my right handle bar and right hand hit people in the stomach because they weren't watching me but looking at the President." A young man with a camera darted towards the car, and "one of the Secret Service men caught him just in front of my motor and bodily threw him between me and Chaney into the crowd." Finally, the motorcade reached Dealey Plaza:

> Then we turned west onto Elm Street. Drove only a short way traveling very slowly. About that time I heard what I thought was a car backfire and I looked around and then to the President's car in time for the next explosion and saw Mr. Connally jerk back to his right and it seemed that he look [sic] right at me. I could see a shocked expression on his face and I thought "Someone is shooting at them." I began stopping my motor and looking straight ahead first at the railroad overpass and saw only one policeman standing on the track directly over the street. I looked back toward Mr. Kennedy and saw him hit in the head. He appeared to have been hit just above the right ear. The top of his head flew off away from me. Mrs. Kennedy pulled him toward her. Mrs. Connally pulled Mr. Connally down and she slid down into the seat. I knew that the shooting was coming from my right rear and I looked back that way but I never did look up. Looking back to the front again I saw the Secret Service Agent lying down across the car over Mr. and Mrs. Kennedy. The presidential limousine was beginning to pick up speed.

Jackson and Chaney sped off to Parkland Hospital with the limousine. When they got there, Jackson stepped off his motorcycle and over to the limousine:

> An Agent opened the car door and started to get Mrs. Kennedy out but Mrs. Kennedy said no. It's no need, she said, and raised up from over Mr. Kennedy. I could see the top of his head was gone, his left eye was bulged out of socket. The agent said "Oh no!" and started crying, pulled his coat off and placed it over Mr. Kennedy's head. I saw someone rolling a stretcher up and I said "Let's get Mr. Johnson out then." Thinking that Mr. Connally was Mr. [Vice President Lyndon] Johnson, I reached in the car and got ahold of him under his arms. Some other officers got ahold of Mr. Connally and we laid him on the stretcher and he was taken inside. I looked back to Mr. Kennedy as Mrs. Kennedy said, "Alright but I'm going with him."
>
> I reached in and got ahold of him at his shoulders and helped lay him on a

stretcher. I stepped back and some agents started pushing Mr. Kennedy into the hospital. Mrs. Kennedy walked beside the stretcher.

A woman with a small boy walked up and asked Jackson if it was true about the president being shot. "How bad is he hurt?" she asked. Jackson replied, "I don't know, Mam [sic] . . . and if I did I couldn't tell you." Then Jackson lit a cigarette:

> This was the first chance I had to relax a little bit and I lit a cigarette. I noticed I had blood on my hands, looked and I had blood on my left sleeve, down the left side of my riding breeches and on the outside of my left boot. I suppose I got this on me as I helped get Mr. Kennedy out of the car.

Although Jackson had blood on his hands, left sleeve, pants, and boot, he said this came from reaching into the blood-soaked backseat of the limousine to help get the president onto a stretcher. He made no mention of being hit by any blood or brain debris from the impact on Kennedy's head and reported that "the top of his head flew off away from me."

In the early 1970s, he was interviewed for a book on the shooting.[2] When asked if he had been "hit by any spray," Jackson replied, "No. I guess his brains and hair or what-have-you that came off the top of his head went towards Hargis and B. J. Martin on the left side of the car. And uh, the force of the bullet caused it to go that way. I didn't get anything on me until I got to Parkland Hospital."

Officer James Chaney

Jackson went home and stayed home that night. James Chaney, who had been riding inboard alongside Jackson, did not. He was found by news reporters that night at police headquarters and was interviewed. During the interview, Chaney was wearing his motorcycle helmet from that morning.

> ABC NEWSMAN BILL LORD: I understand that you were riding next to the president's car when the assassination took place.
> CHANEY: I was riding on the right rear fender.
> LORD: What happened?
> CHANEY: Well, we had proceeded west on Elm Street at approximately fifteen to twenty miles an hour. When we heard the first shot, I thought it was a motorcycle backfiring. And I looked back over to my left. And also President

Kennedy looked back over his left shoulder. Then, when the second shot came, I looked back just in time to see the President struck in the face by the second bullet. He slumped forward into Mrs. Kennedy's lap. And uh, apparently . . . [unintelligible] . . . I went ahead of the President's car to inform Chief Curry that the president had been hit. And he instructed us over there to take him to Parkland Hospital and he had Parkland Hospital stand by. I rolled up ahead . . . to notify the officers who were leading the escort that we had been hit. We were going to have to move him out.

LORD: You did not see the person who fired the shot?

CHANEY: No, it was back over my right shoulder.

LORD: What preventive measures had been taken to preclude such an incident?

CHANEY: I don't know. . . .

LORD: Thank you.[3]

The Chaney interview ends, and newsman Bill Lord is seen back at a desk in the ABC studio. Lord speaks into the camera: "This patrolman was so close to the president that following the three shots, his uniform was splattered with blood."

It is difficult to know what to make of Lord's statement. What we see of Chaney gives no indication of any blood spatter. The Lord interview with Chaney lasted less than ninety seconds. Additional videotaped interviews were done with Chaney at Dallas police headquarters that night, probably within minutes of the Lord interview. As in the Lord interview, Chaney is standing in a corridor wearing his motorcycle helmet. In the taped WBAP-TV interview Chaney answers questions from a battery of reporters for four minutes and forty-one seconds. A KRLD-TV tape overlaps with the WBAP tape but contains four minutes and sixteen seconds of additional questions from numerous reporters. Nowhere in this additional eight minutes of interviews does Chaney or any of the reporters indicate that he was "splattered with blood."[4]

Chaney was subsequently interviewed a couple of times by the FBI, but in no interview or official report is there any mention of him being "splattered with blood." Chaney was interviewed by the FBI on November 28, 1963, but was asked only about his chance contact with Jack Ruby in Dealey Plaza on November 23, 1963.[5] He was interviewed again by the FBI on September 8, 1975, yet once again he made no mention of being blood-spattered.[6] This is especially interesting due to the circumstances that led to this 1975 interview.

A few days before Chaney's interview, a Dallas FBI agent was standing on a corner in downtown Dallas talking with Lieutenant Jack Revill of the Dallas police.[7] According to the agent's report, Revill told him that former Dallas

Photo 4-2. Officer James Chaney at Parkland hospital only moments after the shooting. Note absence of any blood or brain tissue on him.

police chief Jesse Curry had told him he still believed that two men had been involved in the Kennedy assassination. "Why?" asked the agent. Revill replied that Curry had said it was because one of the motorcycle officers had said "he had ridden through a spray of blood at the time the shots were fired." Revill added that only a few moments before meeting Dallas FBI Agent Brown, he had been talking with Officer James Chaney. Chaney had told Revill "that he had never been interviewed by anyone following the assassination."

The report on the Revill conversation worked its way up to FBI headquarters, and soon a request came down to interview both Chaney and Jackson. Both were interviewed within ten days with no surprises. They related the same stories told earlier in Jackson's school notebook and Chaney's TV interviews. Since the FBI's interest in both was kindled by Curry's remark concerning a motorcycle officer being hit with "a spray of blood," it is curious that neither was asked if they had been hit with any blood spray. Since Jackson said he had gotten his bloodstains from climbing into the back of the limousine, it would appear that he had received none from the bullet hits. And Chaney?

Had he had bloodstains on his uniform or helmet when Bill Lord and others interviewed him Friday night? Like his partner, Jackson, had he climbed into the limousine and gotten bloodstains on his uniform that way? We just don't know.

Officer Bobby W. Hargis

Like Chaney, Officer Bobby Hargis, who was the inboard rider immediately to the rear of the limousine's left-rear fender, submitted no report on his experiences on November 22. The first account of Hargis's experiences came from an interview on November 23 by a reporter for the *New York Sunday News* whose story was published the next day in the newspaper. Hargis said that when he heard the first explosion, he "knew it was a shot." He thought "Governor Connally had been hit when I saw him turn toward the President with a real surprised look." Then there was the impact on the president's head:

> As the President straightened back up, Mrs. Kennedy turned toward him and that was when he got hit in the side of his head, spinning it around. I was splattered with blood. Then I felt something hit me. It could have been concrete or something, but I thought at first I might have been hit. Then I saw the limousine stop, and I parked my motorcycle at the side of the road, got off and drew my gun.[8]

Photographs show Hargis doing exactly as he described. He got off his motorcycle by the south curb of Elm Street, turned toward the knoll area, and then crossed the street toward it.

Unlike either Jackson or Chaney, Hargis was deposed under oath by the Warren Commission the following April. He recalled only two shots and was asked about that by Commission Counsel Samuel Stern. He said that two was all he could remember, but "everything was moving so fast at the time that there could have been 30 or more shots that I probably never would have noticed them." He was asked next about being splattered with blood. He replied,

> Yes; when President Kennedy straightened back up in the car the bullet hit him in the head, the one that killed him and it seemed like his head exploded, and I was splattered with blood and brain, and kind of bloody water. It wasn't really blood. And at that time the Presidential car slowed down. I heard somebody say, "Get going." That is when the Presidential limousine shot off, and I stopped and

got off my motorcycle and ran to the right hand side of the street behind the light pole.[9]

Before continuing his narrative, Hargis was asked about his impression of the source of the shots. He replied,

> Well, at the time, it sounded like the shots were right next to me. There wasn't any way I could tell where they were coming from but at the time there was something in my head that said that they probably could have been coming from the railroad overpass, because I thought since I had got splattered with blood—I was just a little back and left of—just a little back and left of Mrs. Kennedy, but I didn't know. I had a feeling that it might have been from the Texas School Book Depository, and these two places was the primary place that could have been shot from.

Hargis was asked whether he "ran up the incline on your side of the street" and replied,

> Yes, sir; I ran to the light post, and I ran up to this kind of a little wall, brick wall up there to see if I could get a better look on the bridge, and, of course, I was looking around that place by that time. I knew it couldn't have come from the county courthouse because that place was swarming with deputy sheriffs over there.

He was asked if he had ever gone behind "the picket fence" and replied that he didn't remember any picket fence. Finally, he went back to his motorcycle:

> Then I got back on my motorcycle, which was still running, and rode underneath the first underpass to look on the opposite side in order to see if I could see anyone running away from the scene, and since I didn't see anyone coming from that direction I rode under the second underpass which is the Stemmons Expressway and went up around to see if I could see anyone coming from across Stemmons and back that way, and I couldn't see anything that was of a suspicious nature, so I came back to the Texas School Book Depository.

During a much later interview, Hargis recalled that he was walking from the depository to the Dallas County Sheriff's Department when another officer saw something on his lip: "And old Bud Brewer says, 'Bob, you got something on your lip.' And he did like that (flick at it) and it was a piece of Kennedy's brain and a piece of skull bone."[10]

Photo 4-3. Officer Hargis turns toward the knoll.

Officer B. J. Martin

Riding outboard of Officer Bobby Hargis to the left rear of the limousine, Officer B. J. Martin was only a couple feet from the south curb of Elm Street when President Kennedy was hit in the head. Martin gave no interviews to the press but, like Hargis, was deposed by the Warren Commission in April 1964.

Commission Counsel Joe Ball carefully took Martin through his experience of the shooting.[11] Martin pointed out that the limousine was going only four or five miles per hour when it made its turn onto Elm Street, and he was not aware of it picking up appreciable speed until after the shooting. When he heard the first shot, he thought the limousine was moving "between 5 and 10 miles per hour." He estimated his motorcycle was "5-foot to the left and approximately 6- to 8-foot to the rear" of the president's limousine at the time of the shooting. Hargis, he pointed out, was "3- or 4-foot closer than I was." He heard a shot and could see that the president was leaning forward. He could see the left side of the president's face and noticed that "he had no expression on his face." He heard two more shots but noted, "You couldn't tell just where they were coming from." There was a breeze blowing that day out of the southwest that would have been blowing somewhat left to right as they headed down Elm Street. "It seemed," said Martin, "like we were going to turn into the wind as we turned off of Houston onto Elm."

When he got to Parkland Hospital, he noticed bloodstains on his helmet:

> During the process of working traffic there, I noticed that there were blood stains on the windshield of my motor and then I pulled off my helmet and I noticed there were blood stains on the left side of my helmet. It was just to the left—of what would be the center of my forehead—approximately halfway, about a quarter of the helmet had spots of blood on it. . . . There was other matter that looked like pieces of flesh. . . . There was blood and matter on my left shoulder of my uniform . . . and just below the level of the shoulder. . . . There was blood and other matter on my windshield and also on the motor. . . . They weren't large splotches, they were small—it was not very noticeable unless you looked at it. . . . It was just in the front [of his front fender]—right on the front just above the cowling on the motorcycle.

Officer Joe Marshall Smith

Officer Joe Marshall Smith was directing traffic at the corner of Elm and Houston Street at the time of the shooting. Back in 1966, it was not about the shooting that I wanted to talk with him. It was what he experienced after the shooting that made him a priority witness. Once again, however, the Dallas police would not permit an interview.

In the weeks after the assassination, the Dallas police officers who were at the scene were eagerly sought out by the press. Ronnie Dugger, editor of the *Texas Observer*, a respected liberal newspaper out of Austin, somehow found Smith. I had met Dugger during a visit to Austin and admired his in-your-face but cerebral style of journalism. Somehow, Dugger had run into Joe Marshall Smith in that first week of December and published Smith's recollection that he had "caught the smell" of gunpowder behind the stockade fence on the knoll.[12] Smith had said, "I could tell it was in the air." This report prompted the US attorney for Dallas to send a communication to the FBI mistakenly claiming that Smith had "definitely distinguished the aroma of gunpowder near the underpass."[13]

Smith's report must have leaked before Dugger was able to publish it because on December 9 two FBI agents interviewed Smith. Their report stated,

> The shots echoed so loudly he had no idea at the time where they had been fired from. He stated he did smell what he thought was gunpowder but stated this

smell was in the parking lot by the TSBD Building and not by the underpass. He advised he never at any time went to the underpass and could not advise what was the smell of gunpowder in the underpass. He stated he did not see the President when he was shot. After the shots were fired, there was a great deal of confusion, and he left his post for a few minutes to go in the area where the President had been shot but did not go in the TSBD Building.[14]

Six months later, when Smith was deposed by the Warren Commission, he was never asked about smelling gunpowder. Instead, an odd encounter came to light:

OFFICER SMITH: And this woman came up to me and she was just in hysterics. She told me, "They are shooting the President from the bushes." So I immediately proceeded up here. . . . I was checking all the bushes and I checked all the cars in the parking lot.

LIEBELER: There is a parking lot in behind this grassy area back from Elm Street toward the railroad tracks, and you went down to the parking lot and looked around?

SMITH: Yes, sir; I checked all the cars. I looked into all the cars and checked around the bushes. Of course, I wasn't alone. There was some deputy sheriff with me, and I believe one Secret Service man when I got there. I got to make this statement, too. I felt awfully silly, but after the shot and this woman, I pulled my pistol from my holster, and I thought, this is silly, I don't know who I am looking for, and I put it back. Just as I did, he showed me that he was a Secret Service agent.

LIEBELER: Did you accost this man?

SMITH: Well, he saw me coming with my pistol and right away he showed me who he was.

LIEBELER: Do you remember who it was?

SMITH: No, sir; I don't—because then we started checking the cars. In fact, I was checking the bushes, and I went through the cars, and I started over here in this particular section.

LIEBELER: Down toward the railroad tracks where they go over the triple underpass?

SMITH: Yes.[15]

I was dying to interview Smith. The questions were obvious: Where exactly did you encounter the Secret Service agent? What was he wearing? What did he look like? Are you sure he was a Secret Service agent?

Two of these questions were answered by author Anthony Summers when he interviewed Smith extensively in 1978.[16] Why did Smith believe he had been shown Secret Service credentials and not some other federal identification? Smith said, "The man, this character, produces credentials from his hip pocket which showed him to be Secret Service. I have seen those credentials before, and they satisfied me and the deputy sheriff. So I immediately accepted that and let him go and continued our search around the cars." What did the man look like? Smith said, "He looked like an auto mechanic. He had on a sports shirt and sports pants. But he had dirty fingernails, it looked like, and hands that looked like an auto mechanic's hands. And afterwards it didn't ring true for the Secret Service."

The Railroad Men

Lee E. Bowers Jr.

When I asked Patsy Swank to get in touch with Lee Bowers, she said, "It was in the paper. He died in an auto wreck a couple of months ago."

The accident had happened the week after I first visited Dallas. Bowers had been driving alone on State Route 57 south of Midlothian, Texas. His car had struck a bridge abutment.

Since we could not interview him, we had to reconstruct what Bowers had seen on November 22 based on what he said to investigators and what others recalled.

On that Friday morning, it took Lee Bowers about forty-five minutes to drive to work.[1] It was raining when he turned into the parking lot by the rail yards just west of the Texas School Book Depository. By 10:00 or 10:30, the rain had stopped, and it was becoming a beautiful day with temperatures in the mid-60s. Bowers had made this trip every weekday for the previous ten years. He was a switchman for the Union Terminal Railroad and worked the "first trick" from 7:00 a.m. until 3:00 p.m.

Bowers was thirty-eight on November 22, 1963. He was married, and one of his bosses described him as "all business. [He] didn't talk very much . . . [and] was somewhat of an introvert."[2] A coworker described him as "a very kind man . . . the nicest person I knew down there. Everybody liked him. He was friendly and he didn't tell any exaggerated stories. . . . You could bet on the truth when he said something." When asked if Bowers was intelligent, the coworker replied he was "more so than some of the other railroad men."

Bowers was seventeen when he joined the navy in 1942. He stayed in until 1946 and then attended Hardin-Simmons University, a small college in Abilene, Texas, for two years before going on to Southern Methodist University for two more years, majoring in religion. A coworker said he "didn't know for sure if he [Bowers] was very religious, but I never heard him curse or use bad language." For the previous fifteen years, Bowers had worked for the

Photo 5-1. Lee Bowers in 1966.

L. E. BOWERS, JR.

Union Terminal Railroad, moving from lower- to higher-ranking jobs until, by November 1963, he was in charge of the day shift in the switching tower just north of Dealey Plaza. A coworker said "he seemed to like to work the tower." Like many men who worked for the railroad and got off at 3:00 p.m., he also ran a small business as a builder.

From his perch in the switching tower fourteen feet above the maze of tracks, he could look south toward Dealey Plaza. He could not see the plaza itself from his perch. It was hidden by a concrete pergola, trees, and a wooden stockade fence that ran east to west along the brow of what has come to be called "the grassy knoll." On Bowers's side of the fence was a parking lot that was open to the public. On the morning of the president's visit to Dallas, the lot was filled with cars, with one row parked abutting the fence and three to five feet out. In railroad lingo, Bowers worked in what was called an "interlocking tower." As the senior switchman, he ran the switches and signals controlling the maze of tracks that ran in several directions below the tower. Contemporary photos show that nine tracks crossed the Triple Underpass southwest of Bowers's tower. Other tracks came in from the east. By moving heavy steel levers in his tower, Lee Bowers controlled which trains went where. Contemporary photos show that Bowers wore glasses. The nature of his job, however, required that he have good corrected vision to control the movement of train traffic in the yards below him.

Bowers described how, immediately after the shooting, the rail yards were very quickly sealed off by law enforcement. He was ordered to make sure no trains moved, and he did so. He had to stay put in his tower after his shift

Photo 5-2. Photo taken by author in 1966 shows Bowers's view from the switching tower toward the pergola, stockade fence, and Dealey Plaza. Two men were seen in the area shown in inset within the white rectangle.

ended at 3:00 p.m. because the cordon was so tight that his relief switchman couldn't get in. In his tower, Bowers talked "to a DPD sergeant; then . . . to a lieutenant, then . . . to an inspector." Finally, the relief got in, and Bowers was taken by squad car to Dallas police headquarters and to the office of Captain Will Fritz. When Oswald was brought to Fritz's office, Bowers was moved to a small cubicle just outside the office.

What had Bowers told the series of police officers that made him such an important witness? An affidavit executed by Bowers that afternoon tells us:

I work at North Tower Union Terminal Co. RI-8-4698 7 a.m. to 3 p.m. Monday thru Friday. The tower where I work is West and a little north of the Texas Book Depository Building. I was on duty today and about 11:55 a.m. I saw a dirty 1959 Oldsmobile Station Wagon come down the street toward my building. This street dead ends in the railroad yard. This car had out-of-state license plates with white background and black numbers, no letters. It also had a Goldwater for "64" sticker in the rear window. This car just drove around slowly and left the area. It was occupied by a middle-aged white man with partly grey hair. At about 12:15 p.m. another car came into the area with a white man about 25 to 35 years old driving. This car was a 1957 Ford, Black, 2 door with Texas license. This man appeared to have a mike or telephone in the car. Just a few minutes after this car left at 12:20 p.m. another car pulled in. This car was a 1961 Chevrolet, Impala, 4 door, am not sure that this was a 4 door, color white and dirty up to the windows. This car also had a Goldwater for "64" sticker. This car was driven by a white male about 25 to 35 years old with long blond hair. He stayed in the area longer than the others. This car also had the XXX [*strikeout*] same type license plates as the 1959 Oldsmobile. He left this area about 12:25 p.m. About 8 or 10 minutes after he left, I heard at least 3 shots very close together. Just after the shots the area became crowded with people coming from Elm Street and the slope just north of Elm.[3]

Bowers's report of the three cars circling the parking lot was sufficiently important to get him interviewed by FBI Special Agents Barrett and Almon later the same day. Their report covers the same facts laid out in Bowers's affidavit. Just what these three cars were doing has never been explained. They may simply have been looking for a parking place. Alternatively, at least the second car may have been law enforcement since the driver "appeared to have a mike or telephone in the car." Whether Bowers told either the Dallas police or the FBI about seeing two men milling about the stockade fence is not known. He may have mentioned it, and they disregarded it as too insignificant to put in their reports, or he may not have mentioned it because he didn't think it was worth mentioning.

Bowers's report about the two men first surfaced in the transcript of his sworn testimony before Warren Commission Counsel Joe Ball on April 2, 1964.[4] Ball asked him whether he had seen anyone standing between his tower and where "Elm Street goes down under the underpass." Bowers replied that he had seen two men, "one man, middle-aged, or slightly older, fairly heavy set, in a white shirt, fairly dark trousers. Another younger man, about mid-twenties, in either a plaid shirt or plaid coat or jacket." They were standing within "10 or 15 feet of each other" and "were facing and looking up towards Main and Houston."

At the time of the shooting, Bowers could see only the man in the white shirt; "the darker dressed man was too hard to distinguish from the trees." Bowers was asked whether he saw any activity in this area after hearing the first of three shots. "At the time of the shooting," he said, "there seemed to be some commotion." He was asked by Ball what he meant by "commotion" and replied, "I just am unable to describe rather than it was something out of the ordinary, a sort of milling around, but something occurred in that particular spot which was out of the ordinary, which attracted my eye for some reason, which I could not identify it."

The questions of the two men and the "commotion" came up later when Bowers was interviewed by attorney Mark Lane (author of *Rush to Judgment*) and producer Emile de Antonio two years later for a film they were making.[5] Like Counsel Ball, Lane began with an open-ended question to Bowers:

QUESTION: Mr. Bowers, did you see any pedestrians at any time between your tower and Elm Street that day?

ANSWER: Directly in line, there of course is—uh—there leading toward the Triple Underpass there is a curved decorative wall, I guess you'd call it. It's not a solid wall but it is a part of the park. And to the west of that there were at the time of the shooting in my vision only two men. These two men were standing back from the street somewhat at the top of the incline and were very near two trees which were in the area. And one of them, from time to time as he walked back and forth, disappeared between a wooden fence which also is slightly to the west of that. These two men to the best of my knowledge were standing there at the time of the shooting. One of them, as I recall, was a middle-aged man, fairly heavy-set without a coat and a white shirt. He remained in sight practically all of the time. The other individual was slighter build and had either a plaid jacket or a plaid shirt on and he, in walking back and forth, was in and out of sight, so that I could not state for sure whether he was standing there at the time of the shots or not. But he was in the immediate area. Other than these two and the people who were over on the top of the underpass who were, for the most part, were railroad employees or were employees of a Fort Worth welding firm who were working on the railroad, there were no strangers out on this area. Now, down below there could have been, but this part was not visible to me.

QUESTION: Did you recognize these two men who were standing around or near the wooden fence on the occasion as men who were employed by the Union Terminal or any other agency in the area?

ANSWER: No. These two men, to the best of my recollection, I had never seen before nor since. I did not recognize them. They didn't strike any chord or any sense of recognition with me at all.

QUESTION: After the shots were fired, Mr. Bowers, what did you see?

ANSWER: Immediately after the shots were fired, there was, of course, mass confusion, to put it mildly. But the area was immediately sealed off by, I would say, at least fifty police within three to five minutes.

Bowers went on to give a more detailed description of the "commotion" he had mentioned to Ball:

At the time of the shooting in the vicinity of where the two men I've described were, there was a flash of light or an—as far as I'm concerned—something I could not identify. But there was something which occurred which caught my eye in this immediate area on the embankment. Now what this was I could not state at that time and, at this time, I could not identify it other than there was some unusual occurrence, a flash of light or smoke or something which caused me to feel like something out of the ordinary had occurred there.

A few months after the Lane interview, Bowers was killed in a single-car accident. Conspiracy theorists have claimed ever since that he was murdered because of what he saw on November 22. These claims cannot be taken seriously inasmuch as Bowers had already testified to the Warren Commission and given the filmed interview to Mark Lane. Dave Perry, a very smart ex–insurance adjustor and executive, looked into the crash and reported that Bowers may have fallen asleep or lost concentration due to the allergy medicine he was taking.[6]

Also not to be taken seriously are reports from people who knew Bowers that he claimed to have seen one of the men he described put a rifle in the trunk of a car. These reports surfaced in the 1990s when various TV producers were in search of a story. The same cannot be said of the reports of two individuals who, like Bowers, worked for the Union Terminal Railroad.

Both suggest that Bowers saw more than he revealed when questioned by Joe Ball and Mark Lane.

The first is Olan DeGaugh. As yardmaster, he was several levels above Bowers in the railroad company hierarchy. In an oral history interview in 2002, he described Bowers as "a good person, a good worker, a good man . . . . He was one of my best friends." When asked if he had talked to Bowers about the Kennedy assassination, he replied, "Several times. I don't know how many times. Not a real long conversation." When asked if Bowers ever varied his story about what happened that day, DeGaugh said, "I don't think he ever changed it."

And what did Bowers tell DeGaugh about the assassination?

DeGaugh said, "Well, the day Kennedy was assassinated, he [Bowers] was looking out the window and there was a car parked next to the board fence out here barely where the street ends and he saw someone holding the trunk of a car put something in it and drive off. And it had been assumed that it had been Oswald. It may have been Oswald." DeGaugh said the car "was a coupe of some kind . . . an old car."[7]

The second is Barney Mozley, the switchman who relieved Bowers by taking the "second trick" in the tower that Friday afternoon.[8] Also in 2002,

Mozley gave an oral history interview. After explaining his difficulty in getting through police lines to relieve Bowers, Mozley pointed out that from the tower, "you can't see the assassination. I mean, when there was actually shooting. You could hear it, but you couldn't see it. That was the way it was." He did talk to Bowers about the assassination within days of November 22.

QUESTION: Did he ever talk to you about the assassination at all ever?

ANSWER: Yeah, he did, but he didn't want it to be repeated. And I never did say anything about him, but I can say something about him now. He was a . . . yeah, he would do that and tell you, "Now, don't go around talking about it because," he said, "It's dangerous." But he never said dangerous from whom.

QUESTION: How long after the assassination did he tell you that?

ANSWER: Oh, it was just a few days.

Mozley went on to describe how a lock had to be put on the switching tower door to keep curious people—journalists and others—from coming into the tower and bothering the operator. Mozley was asked if Bowers was ever interviewed in his tower by such people and replied,

No, no one did. He was. Why he was first questioned and put under questions for so long was because he said that he saw somebody coming around the wooded area on the day he was shot, the President was assassinated, with a . . . a trench coat, you know, on with [sic] it looked like something was under it, like a . . . like a rifle or something. And that's. . . . And he said that, too, you know. He said that, and that's what he shouldn't have done (chuckling). He should have played, "Don't know much about it, didn't see it," and he'd probably be better off. And it's . . . even today, I look back and people will ask me, did I think it was a . . . a conspiracy. And I said, "Yes, it definitely was" (chuckling).

Bowers is important as a witness not because of what Mozley and DeGaugh later reported he told them. The facts they recounted seem garbled at best. Is it significant that Bowers told Mozley within days of November 22 that Bowers had "dangerous" information? Perhaps and perhaps not. Bowers was a mild-mannered, hardworking person who may have been simply expressing fear about being in the crosshairs of a national event with the media and law enforcement looking on. Bowers is an important, if frustrating, witness, not because of what he failed to tell Ball and Lane but because of what he did tell them. He is important because his observation of the two men behind the fence amplifies the experience that day of a much more important witness.

S. M. "Skinny" Holland

What Lee Bowers could not see from his perch in the switching tower, his boss, S. M. "Skinny" Holland, could see. Standing on the railroad overpass under which Elm Street passed and which Bowers could only partially see, Holland had a kind of cockpit view of the assassination.

As signals and track supervisor for the Union Terminal Railroad, Skinny Holland was Lee Bowers's and Barney Mozley's immediate supervisor. Born in 1906, Holland had worked for various railroads for over forty years, twenty-five for the Union Terminal. He was lanky, and his face had a leathery quality, the product of too many summers in the West Texas sun and too many cigarettes.

Holland's interviews with government investigators show that he did not suffer fools gladly. He had signed an affidavit at the sheriff's office on November 22 and two days later had been interviewed by the FBI. In March 1964, he was interviewed by Samuel Stern, a young lawyer for the Warren Commission. The sheriff's affidavit and the FBI interview report make clear that Holland heard four—and possibly five—shots.[9]

Given that what Holland had to say clashed dramatically with the government's scenario of what happened, it comes as no surprise that Samuel Stern struggled to reduce Holland's four or five shots to three.

"The FBI report that I have," Stern told Holland during his deposition, "said that you heard either three or four shots fired together, and I gather the impression of the agent was that you were uncertain whether it was three or four."[10] Holland paid no attention to the ploy and calmly denied telling the agents what Stern said he had told them. Instead, he referred Stern to his earlier signed affidavit that makes clear he heard four shots. Holland then reminded Stern, "I have also told those two, four, six Federal men that have been out there that I definitely saw the puff of smoke and heard the report from under those trees."

Holland was an independent—one might even say stubborn—man, certainly an odd choice for a government gadfly.[11] He was a personal friend of Dallas County Sheriff Bill Decker, who had authorized Holland to carry a pistol for sixteen years as a special deputy. He was a longtime solid citizen of nearby Irving, Texas, who had contributed to civic clubs and had coached Little League Baseball for years. One of his three adopted children was a police officer. For all of these reasons, I wanted to talk with Holland directly. Was he a credible witness, or was he some cranky old codger who wanted to get his name in the paper and stick it to the authorities at the same time?

Photo 5-3. S. M. "Skinny" Holland.

Thus, late on a chilly Wednesday afternoon in November 1966, Ed Kern and I visited Holland at his home in Irving. It was a modest middle-class dwelling with furnishings from the 1940s and 1950s. We sat in the living room. At first Holland was taciturn and all business. We showed him identification, and he said he had checked on us with his friend, Sheriff Bill Decker. We were the people we claimed to be. (Sometime earlier that year Mark Lane had used the name "Blake" in interviewing Holland.) When he asked what angle LIFE magazine was going to take, we answered that we had only just begun our investigation and simply wanted to find out what happened.

"That sounds nice," he shot back. "That's what government investigators told me, but it hasn't turned out that way."

It took a while, but finally Holland began to loosen up and tell us his story. He spoke it almost without stopping, telling us what he had told others time after time:

> Well, on the morning of the assassination, it'd been raining that morning, and I had some welders up on the overpass doing some welding, and, oh, about 11 o'clock I walked up to check on the welders, and there was a couple of police up on the triple underpass . . . overpass. And they asked me if I would come back and identify the people that worked for the Union Terminal or the railroad that was . . . had authority or was supposed to be up on the triple underpass. And I told 'em I would after lunch.
>
> In the meantime, I had my welders move off the overpass, and they drove off before lunch and went down to the south end of the station to do some welding down there. About thirty or forty minutes after I ate my lunch, I went back on up there and talked to the two policemen. Well, we stood around there and talked for thirty or forty minutes. And I went on identifying each one that was coming

Photo 5-4. Holland on the overpass pointing toward the fence. Note Bowers's switching tower in the background.

up, where they worked, who they were. One or two that worked for a different railroad, that I knew worked for the railroad, but I didn't know 'em personally, I'd tell them, well, I know that they work for the railroad, but I don't know the people personally. And you could go over and check their credentials.

About the time for the parade, well, I walked right up on the [overpass] . . . leaned against the banister of the triple overpass, looking up the street for the motorcade. Everything was perfectly normal. People was happy when they turned off from down Houston Street and then turned off on Elm Street. People were waving, hollering, and smiling, and they didn't much more than turn onto Elm Street when I heard a loud report. And President Kennedy leaned over like that and put his hand up. And Governor Connally was sitting on the right in the jump seat, and he started to turn to his right. Anyway, he was sitting so close to the door that he turned back to his left, similar to that, and that's the position that he was in when the second shot was fired, and he just crumpled down.

And in a matter of just another two or three seconds, there was another report; it wasn't nearly as loud. It came from behind the picket fence, up on top of the grassy knoll, and about the same instance, there was a louder report that came from up the street, and they were so close together you could say, well, you could say they were just [snaps his fingers together twice, one immediately after another

Photo 5-5. Holland on the overpass during the assassination as Mrs. Kennedy crawls to the back of the vehicle.

to indicate the closeness of the sounds of the shots]. But one of them wasn't nearly as loud as the fourth report, and it knocked President Kennedy completely over; just almost turned a flip.

And Mrs. Kennedy climbed out of the car, not to help a Secret Service man in, because he was still in the car when she came up on the back of the car. He jumped out of the car and came up and pushed her back in the car, and they stopped momentarily, almost right underneath me. All that took place in a period of four, five, or six seconds. Then we all . . . four of us broke around this fence where we saw the smoke [and the] shot. [There was a] steam line. One of the boys stumbled. When he jumped over, he jumped over against Mr. Simmons. And he stumbled and fell. He almost caused Mr. Simmons to fall. And Mr. Simmons and Mr. Dodd were within four or five foot of me and were trying to thread our way through the cars.

And I got over to the spot where I saw the smoke come from and heard the shot. I was looking for empty shells or some indication that there was a rifleman or someone was over there. Well, you know it'd been raining that morning and behind the station wagon from one end of the bumper to the other. It was about two feet from this picket fence—backed up about two feet from this picket fence. You could've counted the foot marks—footprints from one end of that bumper to the other, I expect you could've counted four or five hundred footprints down there. And on the bumper, oh about twelve or eighteen inches apart, it looks like someone had been standing up there. Either that, or just cleaning the mud off their feet, because there was two big muddy spots, real mud on the bumper. I looked under the car, in the cars, all around.[12]

Since we had a tape running, I didn't have to take any notes and just listened to Holland's story as it rolled out of his mouth in a West Texas twang. I was familiar enough with the documents to know that Holland hadn't varied from the account he had first given on November 22. I also knew that Simmons had corroborated Holland's account of seeing the smoke near the fence in an FBI interview and that several other witnesses from the overpass had also seen the smoke.[13] Even more important, two Dallas police officers reported encountering "railroad men" on the knoll and being told within minutes of the shooting "that the smoke from the bullets came from the vicinity of a stockade fence."[14]

The smoke Holland and others saw near the stockade fence at the same time that they heard the next-to-last shot is perhaps the most controversial element in Holland's account. It was not the smoke that focused their attention on this area. Rather, the sound of the shot drew their attention there, and then they saw the smoke. Holland described how the sound of the next-to-last shot was different and how it drew his attention to the left, to the area of the stockade fence and the trees. "There was definitely a sound direction where it was coming. . . . That's what brought my attention to my left. [And the president] was knocked over. Then, it was just like you'd hit somebody with your fist and knock him down. . . . That was the third and fourth shot. I looked right across there, which was just a glance over from where he was hit, and there was a puff of smoke."

We asked Holland what the puff of smoke looked like, and he gave us this description:

Right under these trees, right at that exact spot, about ten or fifteen feet from this corner, the corner of the fence here, back this way right under this clump of trees, right under this tree . . . That's where it was, just like somebody had clump [sic] a firecracker out and leave a little puff of smoke there; it was just laying there. It was white smoke. It wasn't black smoke or like a black powder. It was like a puff of a cigarette. . . . The smoke was about nine foot from the ground up to the tree, but it would be just about in line with, or maybe just a little bit higher than that fence, but by the time it got out underneath the tree, well, it would be about eight or nine feet.[15]

Photo 5-6. Holland retraces his steps on November 22.

Photo 5-7. Holland's view from the overpass: Holland and others see smoke in the circled area.

Photo 5-8. Area behind the stockade fence in the summer of 1967.

Holland was simply making the point that the ground fell away on the south side of the fence and that the smoke was fence-top high but nine feet above the embankment when they saw it under the trees.

"Could the smoke have come from a cigarette?" Kern asked. "Maybe a spectator behind the fence blows a puff of smoke that hangs in the air?"

"He couldn't have blown the smoke that far," Holland answered. "'Cause the tree is about ten or fifteen feet from that fence."

I asked if the smoke might have come from one of the police motorcycles nearby. Holland replied that was impossible since the nearest motorcycle was at least seventy-five feet from where he saw the white smoke. He added, "I saw the smoke before any motorcycle left the street."[16]

Finally, Kern raised the point that "many critics have said, in defense of the Warren Commission criticizing your testimony, that rifles no longer sent out puffs of white smoke. They used to when our ancestors hunted with flintlocks."

Holland interrupted Kern to tell him that flintlocks gave off quantities of black smoke, not white smoke. Then he went on,

The powder still fires. Now I know this much about hunting and guns: the smoke is not near like it was years ago. When you shoot you see a black puff of smoke

Photo 5-9. Holland standing behind the stockade fence.

. . . just like a steam engine. They have it refined now. But you fire a gun, any gun, from a light underneath this shade you'll see a puff of smoke that'll linger there. It'll be, just like I say, dim, like a cigarette or maybe firecracker smoke, but mister, if it's powder, it's going to smoke. The powder we're using now is pale, like a puff of cigarette smoke. Smokeless powder will still smoke.[17]

It was the sound of the next-to-last shot that led Holland, Dodd, and Simmons to focus on the eastern end of the stockade fence, eight to ten feet west of the fence's corner. They saw Kennedy bowled over and at the same time noticed the puff of smoke aligned with the top of the fence.

They immediately reacted. They ran to that spot, climbing over bumpers and hoods in what Holland called "a sea of cars" to get there. The area near the stockade fence "isn't a parking lot," Holland commented. "It was just railroad property that was vacant, and people just drove in there and stopped their cars in every position you could think of . . . helter-skelter." Holland pointed out that the railroad had placed railroad ties along the stockade fence to prevent cars from backing into it. This created a space of two to three feet between the rear bumper of a car and the fence.

"There was nothing growing in there," said Holland, "just dirt between the ties and the fence." It had rained lightly earlier that morning, and the intervening space had turned to mud. In the mud were "several hundred" footprints that overlapped. It was clear someone had been there earlier that morning, pacing back and forth.[18]

I asked Holland if they were men's or women's footprints, and he replied that they were men's. "That was the mystery to me," said Holland, "that they didn't extend further from one end of the bumper to the other. It looked like a lion pacing a cage." Kern asked if Holland had stooped down to examine them. Holland replied,

> I didn't stoop. I squatted down there to see if I could see an empty shell. I didn't get on the footprints. I got on the edge of them. I squatted down and looked under the station wagon, looked under the black car, and I looked under the car next to it, and I looked around the mud behind this car and underneath the station wagon bumpers for empty shells of some sort, something we could tie in.[19]

To clarify things, I asked Holland to work on a diagram with us. While drawing, Holland remarked that he had also noticed "three, four, or five cigarette butts. They was trampled under, just like you would trample grass, but there were four or five cigarette butts." Holland noticed "two large spots of mud" on the station-wagon bumper:

> HOLLAND: On this bumper [*the station wagon's bumper*]. On the . . . it would be on the right side of the bumper.
> THOMPSON: On the east side, given the diagram.
> HOLLAND: On the east side, going on this diagram. Actually, he had a . . . what is it? . . . a bumper guard. There was one mud spot on this side of the bumper guard and a mud spot on that bumper guard, about twelve or fourteen inches apart. . . . It was mud like you'd clean your shoes off on a sharp instrument or something—about twelve or fourteen inches apart. Exactly like someone was standing up there looking over the fence. That was the position of the mud on the bumpers.[20]

The two railroad men who ran with Holland to the fence, Richard Dodd and James Simmons, corroborated virtually every detail of Holland's account.[21] James Simmons even added a detail. He pointed out to the Warren Commission that not only were there footprints in the mud between the cars and the fence, but "on the fence there was a wooden brace or rail and there were muddy footprints on it."

Holland, Dodd, and Simmons were likely not the only people to see the muddy footprints behind the fence. A minute or two after the three arrived there, and while Holland was squatting down looking under the cars for

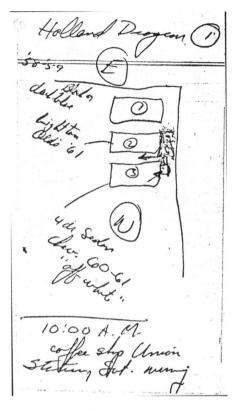

Photo 5-10. Holland's diagram of cars and footprints behind the stockade fence.

cartridge cases, a group of men who looked "like law enforcement" came up and were "milling all around there." "They were dressed up," said Holland. "One or two that came up to where I was, like they was looking over my shoulder."[22]

One of these men, may have been Sheriff's Deputy Seymour Weitzman. He was watching the motorcade from near the corner of Main and Houston. After the shooting he ran across the plaza and up into the grassy knoll area. He burned his hands climbing over a steam pipe to get into the area behind the fence. In his Warren Commission deposition, he was asked if he noticed anything "in the railroad yards." He said he was there with "other officers, Secret Service as well" and that "we noticed numerous kinds of footprints that did not make sense because they were going different directions."[23]

It was now pitch dark outside, and I had run out of questions. There was one thing I wanted to do, but it would require Holland visiting Dealey Plaza with us. We made an appointment to meet him at a coffee shop in Union Station at 10:00 Saturday morning.

Driving back to Dallas and the Sheraton Hotel, neither Ed nor I said anything for a long time. Finally I broke the silence. "Pretty detailed, eh?" He agreed, adding that it wasn't just Holland's story.

"What's so impressive is the fact that other people were there," he continued. "And their stories corroborate everything Holland said. What's more, those footprints are about as real as anything else in this case. Now, give me a nice clean explanation as to why someone interested in seeing the motorcade would huddle behind the fence instead of joining everyone else out there on the bank in front of the fence? That question also applies to the two guys

Photo 5-11. Holland behind the stockade fence, as seen from Moorman's position.

Photo 5-12. Inset showing Holland standing behind the stockade fence.

Bowers saw standing behind the fence where Holland and the others found the footprints. Why would someone who came down there to see the parade stay behind the fence?"

I thought for a moment and then said very slowly, "I don't know."

We lapsed back into silence.

Saturday morning, Holland was waiting for us when we got to the coffee shop in Union Station. He was dressed almost formally: hat, gloves, brown overcoat, dark suit with a white shirt and dark tie. I remembered one of AP photographer James Altgens's photos showing Holland on the overpass, dressed nearly the same. This was the uniform Holland wore to work, and I gathered he took what he was doing this Saturday to be work. Funny, we weren't paying him a dime.

We set off north along the tracks from Union Station. It was less than a quarter mile to the overpass with the parking lot and Bowers's tower beyond. I wanted to check out something with Holland.

I had with me an eight-by-ten-inch copy of the Moorman photo that showed Zapruder, Sitzman, Bill Newman, and Emmett Hudson all standing on the north side of Elm Street.[24] It has become one of the most published photos of that day. Through photogrammetry we can determine that it was taken one-ninth of a second after the president was struck in the head. Moorman's placement is crucial. Although the limousine is in the foreground, the "grassy knoll" with its stockade fence is visible in the background. I had always thought this photo might offer a way to confirm or disprove the idea that a shot was fired from the fence. Since it was taken almost simultaneously with the shot to the president's head, the gunman who fired the shot should be visible in the photo. If he was not, the absence would cast considerable doubt on the whole theory.

I had found in that photo what I called "an anomalous shape" along the fence line. By "anomalous" I meant I couldn't think of any reason for it to be there. With respect to another shape along the fence, I had been able to determine that it was a fixed feature of the site, a railroad signal tower in the background. But this anomalous shape was something else. It was temporary, only there at the instant the photo was taken. In scale, it was the right size to be the upper portion of a human head. I wanted Holland's help in trying to figure out what it was.

We stopped on the overpass to take in Holland's view on November 22. Then he led us north towards Bowers's tower to where he and the others had climbed over the steam line. We made our way across the railroad property to where cars were parked behind the stockade fence. When we got to the area

Photo 5-13. Moorman photograph.

Photo 5-14. Moorman photograph inset showing an anomalous shape on the fence.

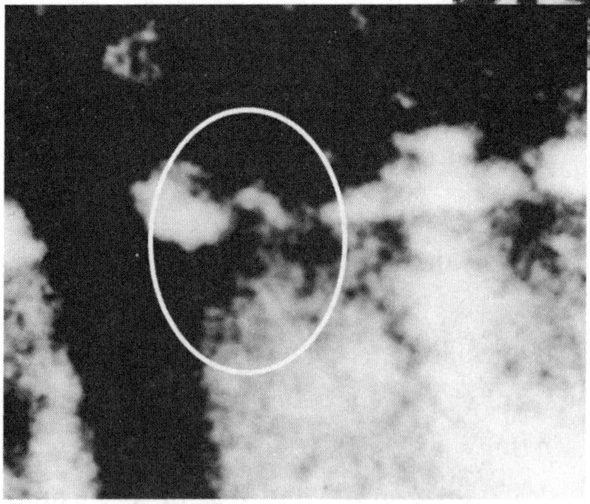

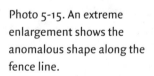

Photo 5-15. An extreme enlargement shows the anomalous shape along the fence line.

where Holland had found footprints and cigarette butts just west of the fence corner, I asked Holland if he remembered telling us of the two places where mud had been left on the rear bumper of the station wagon. He said he did. He said they were about a foot and a half apart on either side of the passenger-side mud guard. I told him, "I want you to stand right behind the fence at that point and look down towards me and Elm Street."

I then walked around the fence and across Elm Street to Moorman's position. It was easy to locate since a couple of lines of sight were apparent in her photo. From her position, I took a photo of the knoll showing Holland's position behind the fence.

Back then it took several days to get film developed, but I knew immediately what I had seen through the camera's viewfinder. Holland's position in that photo would match up exactly with the anomalous shape, as indeed it did when I later compared the two photos (see Photos 5-11 and 5-13). Where Holland and his coworkers found footprints on the bumper of the car and in the mud is precisely the same point along the fence where the anomalous shape appears. When I returned to Holland and Kern, Holland looked at me crookedly.

"What do you think?" he asked.

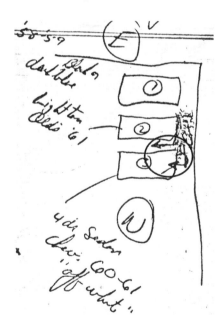

Figure 5-16. Holland's diagram of cars and footprints behind the stockade fence. The lower arrow inside the black ellipse points to the car trunk.

"Damn, Skinny," I said, "I gotta believe you now. But there's just one thing I don't quite get. How did this guy get away?"

"Remember when we talked back at the house?" he replied. "How I told you that these cars were all parked in a jumble so that the last car in would have to move to let other cars out?"

We nodded.

"That means that no car was getting out of there fast. . . ."

"And then the cops threw a cordon around the whole area," I said. "So how did the shooter get away?"

"You got that drawing we made while we were talking about all this at the house?"

I produced the drawing. Holland went on, pointing at the drawing.

Now, from the end of this bumper to the end of this bumper, in this two-foot space, there would be three or four hundred footprints, if a man could've counted 'em, because they was just like a lion pacing a cage, from this end of the bumper to this end of the bumper; there's only two sets of footprints that was left there that I could find. They could of course have gone to this car and climbed in and pulled the lid down. . . . Just to the west of the station wagon there was two sets of footprints that left that . . . the east end of this bumper where I squatted down to look under the cars and to look for evidence of any empty shells, and I noticed the two footprints leaving; now, they could've stepped out between the second and third cars on the gravel, or they could've got in the trunk compartment of this and pulled the lid down.[25]

I asked Holland if he knew whether the police had searched the trunks of cars as they left. He said he didn't know. "There's one other possibility," I said. "The shooter could have put the rifle in the trunk, flipped it shut, and behaved like all the bystanders who rushed in. Then, after a few minutes milling around with the others, he could have just casually walked away."

In the days that followed, Patsy Swank and I made inquiries of knowledgeable authorities in Dallas. No trunks had been searched. We knew the cordon surrounding the railroad yard and the parking area would have prevented anyone from entering or leaving for several hours. This was why Lee Bowers's relief could not reach him at the usual time. Then, word came that Oswald was in custody, and the investigation focused on the Texas School Book Depository. The cordon was lifted, and the police left the scene. Cars were permitted to come and go as they pleased.

CHAPTER 6 "A MATTER OF REASONABLE DOUBT"

U nbeknownst to me when I first met Ed Kern and Dick Billings in New York, LIFE had more immediate plans for cashing in on the assassination controversy. The editors had listened to my plan for an investigation aimed at answering "the threshold question," and they liked the fact that the witnesses relevant to this question were limited. But senior management was always interested in selling magazines. There was one issue in the assassination controversy that was ready-made for LIFE coverage.

One of the flash points in the gathering controversy was the Warren Commission's acceptance of the so-called single-bullet theory—the view that both Kennedy and Connally were struck by the same bullet. Given the constraints in timing based on how rapidly the sixth floor rifle could be fired and what the Zapruder film showed, this theory was the only way the crime could be packaged as the work of a single shooter. Edward Epstein's book *Inquest* had already revealed that the commission had split down the middle on whether to accept this controversial theory advanced by one of its lawyers. None of the witnesses in Dealey Plaza saw it this way, and none of the assassination films showed it happening this way. More importantly, Governor Connally and his wife had maintained, both publicly and in testimony, that the theory was wrong, both insisting the governor had been hit by a separate shot after the one that struck the president in the back. Whether or not the single-bullet theory was the Achilles heel of the Warren Commission, it was a vulnerable point in the commission's claims, and it lent itself to coverage by LIFE, especially since the magazine owned the Zapruder film.

About ten days after our meeting in New York, Kern called and said he and Billings were focusing on the single-bullet theory.[1] They wanted to talk with Connally's doctors to get more information on his wounds. Kern asked which of the doctors might give them the most information relevant to the single-bullet theory. I said I thought Dr. Robert Shaw was the obvious choice since he had worked on Governor Connally's chest wound. Unfortunately, he was out of the country working on the SS *Hope*, a hospital ship providing services to Third World countries. My next choice was Dr. Charles Gregory, who had worked on Connally's fractured wrist. I knew Dr. Gregory was a close associate of Dr. Shaw and that both had publicly stated in Washington that they doubted the single-bullet theory.

A couple of days later, Kern called back to report that he and Billings had interviewed Governor Connally over the weekend. I was amazed. LIFE moves fast. "Like you suggested, we're going down to see Dr. Gregory on Wednesday. Want to come along?"

Could there be any doubt? Kern gave me Dr. Gregory's Dallas office address, and we agreed to meet there at 5:00 p.m. two days later. This was the first interview we would be doing together, and Dr. Gregory was an important witness.

I was already in Dr. Gregory's office and talking with him when they arrived. I had made photocopies of his deposition, and Kern and Billings had brought with them the four-by-five-inch Ektachrome transparencies from the Zapruder film. I did most of the questioning, and Kern and Billings showed the transparencies on a light table.

After the transparencies were laid out, I asked Dr. Gregory to look closely at what happens between frames 237 and 238, three-quarters of a second after the president has clearly been hit. We moved the other transparencies aside and looked closely at 237 through 240.

In this series of frames Governor Connally is turning in his seat to the right. This means that the angle between his right shoulder and the car door gets smaller over time. Then, quite suddenly, it reverses direction and gets larger. What brings about this change in angle is the collapse of Connally's right shoulder. But that is not all. In frames 238, 239, and 240, Connally's cheeks puff out and his hair is disordered.

I pointed this out to Dr. Gregory and asked his opinion about what caused it. He explained that the epiglottis is like a trapdoor at the top of the windpipe. A shot through the chest such as Connally received would shock the chest wall and force air upward through the epiglottis. Since it couldn't all escape from his mouth immediately, it would puff out his cheeks. The three effects we were seeing, Gregory said, were the effects of a bullet driving through the chest. I asked him what was the maximum time before frame 238 when the bullet could have hit Connally. He thought for a moment and then replied, "A quarter of a second. Maybe 234 at the earliest." This was generally in line with his testimony before the commission, where he said that "in frames marked

234, 235 and 236, Governor Connally was in a position such that a single missile . . . could have passed through his chest."[2] Obviously, this was much too late for Connally to have been hit by the same bullet that hit Kennedy. I glanced at Kern and saw a hint of a smile developing around his lips.

But there was more.

We mentioned to Dr. Gregory that we had looked forward to talking with Dr. Shaw but that he was unavailable. Dr. Gregory said he and Shaw had talked about the wounding of Connally, and both believed that Connally and Kennedy had been hit by separate shots. Why? Because of the character of Connally's back wound, Gregory explained. It was small and elliptical in shape. But most importantly, it had very clean edges. No fibers had been carried into Connally's back wound, while his wrist wound was fouled with numerous fibers from his wool suit. Dr. Gregory pointed out that he'd been a field surgeon during the Korean War and later had made a study of gunshot injuries, examining more than five hundred gunshot wounds. It was his opinion, supported by Dr. Shaw, that the small, clean and elliptical wound in Connally's back had come from a projectile that had hit nothing else first. He added that it was a pity that Dr. Shaw was not present, as Shaw would have echoed everything he said.

Billings scooped up the Ektachrome transparencies. We thanked Dr. Gregory and left. In the drive back to the Sheraton, I was elated. "Really great interview," I said. "If you guys are going after the single-bullet theory, you couldn't ask for anything better."

Patsy Swank was waiting for us when we got back to the hotel. In addition, Hank Suydam had flown in from Miami, where he was bureau chief. Billings and Suydam had previously worked together in the Washington office. When it was time to go out for dinner, Suydam said he wasn't hungry and elected to stay behind. Patsy, Ed, Dick, and I trooped out to the nearby Cattlemen's restaurant. The waitresses wore short shorts and carried replica six-guns. I had prime rib.

It was just after nine o'clock when we returned. I was interested in the Ektachrome transparencies made from the original by the LIFE photo lab. They were sitting on a table by an easy chair. I picked them up and began to count them. Why count them? I don't know why. Something kicked off in my brain— possibly from my time in the navy—that said, "If you're going to take custody of something, make sure you know what you have!" I counted up to the 230s and then stopped short. Four frames from the 230s were missing. We had had them that afternoon. I laid down 230 and started counting: 231, 232, 233. . . . I can't now recall exactly which ones were missing, but there were four in all, and they were in serial order. I pointed this out to the others. They looked puzzled. "There's no way I'm taking these out of this room tonight," I said. I handed them to Billings and went to bed.

The next morning, Kern and Billings were off to New York. Patsy Swank had gone directly home from the restaurant and therefore didn't know about the missing Zapruder transparencies. Within the next week, I learned from Kern that he had lured Suydam out of his room while Billings had searched it, with no result. The whole thing made little sense since the LIFE photo lab could replace the four missing frames. I had no clue what was going on. I took it to be a symptom of some kind of power struggle within LIFE (see color photo gallery, Plates 9 and 10).

During the next week, our article began to take shape in New York. It was going to showcase Governor Connally's examination of the four-by-five-inch transparencies and his conclusion that he was not hit by the same bullet that hit Kennedy. The title was "Did Oswald Act Alone? A Matter of Reasonable Doubt." On the cover would be Zapruder frame 230 to illustrate the point that Kennedy was hit and Connally wasn't. I went up to New York that week and the next. At one point I was given the first twelve pages of the article for fact-checking. I made suggestions about evidentiary matters that were sometimes followed and sometimes not. I thought it better not to ask either Kern or Billings about the frames that had gone missing in Dallas.

The more I thought about it, the more it seemed to me that something ought to be done. I had seen in the National Archives what had been officially preserved of the Zapruder film: a muddy print of the film and some equally muddy slides. I had also seen what LIFE had. I had no clue what was going on in the LIFE executive suite concerning this film, but the disappearance of four frames while in Hank Suydam's custody was just bizarre. Furthermore, I needed copies of the film to work on in Philadelphia. I wanted to make very precise measurements of the movement of Kennedy's head and the change in Connally's shoulder angle.

The discussions between Geis, Preston, Kern, and Billings had left open to what extent we would get permission to publish selected frames. What we had heard suggested that this would not be a huge problem and would be decided later on, when the book was done and we knew what we needed. But right now it seemed like a really good idea for good copies of the critical frames to reside somewhere else than in the offices of LIFE magazine. Would Kern and/or Billings give me permission to make copies? Probably not. It was magazine policy to hold these copies closely. Kern and Billings really didn't have the authority to do anything with the transparencies except show them to witnesses and let me study them. If copies of critical frames were to exist outside the Time-Life Building, I would have to bring that about on my own.

In Dallas I'd been carrying around in my briefcase a cassette tape recorder and a Polaroid instant camera. To copy the LIFE transparencies I would need some additional equipment—a bellows, a cable release, and a couple of extension tubes—for the 35-mm Nikon camera I already owned. A Haverford senior, David Butterworth, was a photographer and agreed to help. Together we went to a photo store and bought the equipment. Out of materials from the Haverford biology lab, we constructed a copying stand to hold the camera. We experimented by shooting a few shots of transparencies over a light table until I got the feel of it.

By the week of November 14, I was ready. On Friday I drove up to New York after a morning class, arriving at the Time-Life Building in the late afternoon. Walking up to the security desk, I was pleased that I'd put a couple of gift-wrapped housewarming gifts on top of the camera and the film. The guard cleared me by a call to Kern's office, and I went to Kern's office on the thirtieth floor. We chatted for a while before visiting Billings's office on the twenty-ninth floor. Once again I avoided any questions about Suydam and the missing transparencies.

Finally I took a shot. "Look, gang, I've been working for you for three weeks, and I haven't yet had a chance to study those transparencies you've been carrying around. How about I take the lot of them to Philadelphia this weekend?" Kern looked at Billings who, as chief of investigative reporting, was his senior.

"No," Billings said. "I don't think that's a very good idea."

"Okay," I said. "So how am I going to do this?"

Kern said, "Why don't you take them up to my office? You can use my office tonight to work on them."

Billings picked up from his desk a stack of four-by-five-inch transparencies wrapped with a rubber band, about 150 in all, in numerical sequence, each encased in a transparent plastic sleeve, and handed the stack to me.

I smiled and said, "Can't be too careful. Let's see what's here."

I counted them out, and one was missing. I can't remember what the frame number was, but I pointed this out to both Kern and Billings.

When Kern and I returned to his office, I went to the light table while he went to his desk. He hung around for perhaps another half hour and then said, "When you get done with those things, put them in that cabinet over there and lock the door when you go out. Just turn the button, and the door will lock when you go out."

I said, "Okay." Kern left.

I started examining the transparencies with a jeweler's loupe that was sitting on the light table. I looked at them sequentially and took notes. It was fascinating work, and I was fully engrossed. After a couple of hours, I broke out the camera. I had a dozen or so rolls of film, more than half of it Plus X black-and-white film for prints and the remainder for Ektachrome slides. I set up the copying stand with its base adjacent to the light table and placed two books along its base to hold it steady. There was a problem with the overhead lights reflecting off the light table, so I draped my overcoat over it. Then I loaded a roll of Ektachrome into the camera and placed it in the copying stand with the shutter release cable installed. I fiddled with both the focus and the exposure setting until I was satisfied. Then I started to shoot. The shutter release cable meant I didn't have to touch the camera to fire the shutter. Each time I had to make sure the focus was right because there was some small variation in how far above the glass a transparency would lie. I started shooting around 8:30 p.m. After about an hour, a cleaning woman came in. I said, "The wastebasket is over there." She picked up the wastebasket and dumped it in her cart. Then she put it back and closed the door.

About 11:15 p.m. I heard the door open and looked back over my shoulder from the light table. It was Kern. I was startled, having thought he'd gone home for the day.

He said, "Photographing, eh?" If he was surprised, he didn't show it.

"Yeah," I replied casually. "I want some copies to take down to Philadelphia. I got some measurements to make." Whether or not my no-big-deal nonchalance successfully masked my acute awareness that I had just been caught red-handed copying a priceless artifact belonging to the all-powerful Time-Life empire, I will never know. Kern simply nodded, then asked a few questions about Kennedy's head movement, which we had discussed earlier.

A moment later he went over to his desk and said, "Look . . . I left some record albums here." He picked up a package of what appeared to be 33⅓ LPs and started out the door. He turned toward me and said, "Hey, Tink, be careful of those photos. Right?"

"Okay," I answered. He closed the door and left.

I got back to work and finished the copying job about three-quarters of an hour later. I put all the frames in serial order and wound the rubber band around them. In doing so, I noticed that the frame I could not find in Billings's office was there. I wrote a note to Kern:

By the way, Ed, I found the frame we couldn't find in Dick's office. It's in the bunch now with the rest. What did you mean by "careful"? Do you mind if I show these frames to Salandria in Philadelphia? Tink[3]

I left the note on his desk and put the transparencies in the cabinet. Then I turned the door button to lock it and pulled the door shut behind me. I signed out of the building with the security guard at around midnight. Then I had the long drive on the Jersey Turnpike back to Philadelphia. I was dead tired by the time I got back to our little apartment on College Lane. Nancy and our children were asleep.

Late the next morning, I called Kern at his home.

"Ed, I want to be absolutely certain that I know what you mean when you said 'be careful' because I don't want to get your tail caught in the door. I left a note in your office asking whether I could show these to Vince Salandria."

There was a pause, and Ed said slowly, "As far as I'm concerned, I didn't come back last night."

"Okay. I understand. And you're right; it doesn't make any sense to show these to anybody. I won't show them to anyone." Then I went further than I'd ever gone before. "Look, I want you to know why I wanted those copies in the first place. Yes, I need them to do some measurements down here. That's all true. But after what happened in Dallas, I don't know what's going on with LIFE. I wanted to make damn sure there are copies of that film in a bank vault somewhere."

"Well, I really don't care why—and that's that," he said, his tone slightly dismissive. "Let's just forget it."

As far as I knew, it was forgotten. Neither Kern nor Billings ever mentioned it to me again. A year would pass before I would know the full story. A few weeks later, LIFE signed a contract with me.

To make sure there would be no surprises for Kern, I kept close tabs on the copies. David Butterworth and I tried to develop a few frames of the Plus X and ended up spoiling a couple frames. It turned out not to be important since they were duplicates. After that I took all the rolls of Plus X to Ted Hetzel, a professor of engineering at Haverford and an avid photographer. I explained to Ted that I had an agreement with my LIFE editors that the copies could not go out of my hands. He had his own equipment and photo lab and personally developed all the black-and-white film. The Ektachrome color shots were another matter. They could not be developed privately but had to be processed by Kodak. With some anxiety, I sent them off for processing and was happy when they created no waves and came back with fine resolution and color. I kept the original negatives and most of the transparencies in a safety deposit box and never let copies out of my hands. As I understood it, this was part of my understanding with Kern; I would protect him by protecting the copies.

When the LIFE issue came out, I was disappointed. Much of the material we had discovered had not made it into the article, and what had was watered down. Earlier I had talked to former Yale classmate and author Bud Trillin about it because he had once worked for TIME as a reporter. Bud told me that when he went to work for TIME, he had to sign something that said he was just a "researcher." He explained, "If you put something in the top of the meat grinder, something much different comes out the bottom." He was right. Although a series of Zapruder frames in the 230s was part of our article, no mention was made of the dramatic changes in Connally at 238 that we had discussed with Dr. Gregory. Even worse was a serious mistake near the end of the article that I had not been able to fact-check. It said that the downward bullet track through Governor Connally (27 degrees) exactly matched the inferred back-to-front downward track through Kennedy. This was not only false, it was the reverse of what was actually the case. The two tracks didn't match up at all, and the track through Kennedy was actually at a slight upward angle.

I complained about this to Kern and even wrote a letter correcting the mistake. Kern took me down to the "Letters to the Editor" desk and told the editor, "Thompson is working for us as a consultant on this. Try to put it in." The letter never got in, and I got an unsigned form letter back from LIFE thanking me for my interest in the case.

I returned to Dallas regularly, working on the assumption that LIFE intended to run more articles challenging the Warren Commission's findings. In January, I spent two and a half days in Washington at the archives photographing evidence with LIFE photographer Arthur Schatz. One evening Kern and I interviewed autopsy surgeon Dr. J. Thornton Boswell in his suburban Maryland home not far from Bethesda.

When not in Dallas or Washington, I went up to New York about every ten days. Kern and I would huddle in his office, discussing various issues and developments. Occasionally I would encounter Billings during these visits, which would last from midafternoon to early evening. One Monday in early February, I found Kern at his desk looking over manuscripts from Time-Life Books.

"What's going on?" I asked.

"They took me off the case this morning," he replied. "I suppose toward the end of this month it will all wrap up."

Later that day, I walked down to Billings's office and asked him if what Kern had said was true. He confirmed that the investigation was wrapping up. They would pay me for all of February, and I would continue to send them information picked up in the assassination underground. That evening I walked out of the Time-Life Building for the last time.

When I got back to Haverford, I pulled my LIFE contract out of a drawer. I just wanted to be sure. Yes, it was all there as I remembered: "The material you supply will become the property of LIFE, but it will be released to you for the purpose of publishing a hard cover book on or after July 1, 1967 or after LIFE has published the last article of its series, whichever comes first."[4]

In the midst of my work for LIFE, I had essentially forgotten the book. In some sense, I suppose I thought LIFE would do the job and I would never have to write it. Now that was over. I was on my own. For whatever reasons, LIFE did not want to pursue this investigation—but I could. After July 1, I could use everything we had turned up—the witness interviews, the films and photos, and the work in the archives.

Now I had to figure out how to do that.

CHAPTER 7 PUZZLING THE PIECES

Over the last few months, events had happened at a furious pace, and I had simply rolled with them, not paying much attention to where it was all going or what it all meant. Now that my LIFE assignment was over, I had a chance to step back and take in the landscape.

In hindsight, LIFE's commitment to investigating the assassination was much thinner than I had thought. The magazine was not risking much by emphasizing what Governor Connally was saying—and had been saying for over three years—certainly nothing that would get the "conspiracy theory" brickbat thrown its way. Moreover, the magazine could exploit its ownership of the Zapruder film one more time by using it to illustrate the governor's point of view. Like the New York Times before it, LIFE had fielded an investigative team and then closed it down before it produced anything significant.

What did strike me as odd was that investigations by two major publications with enormous resources had been so short-lived. However, when I thought about it, I saw a likely explanation. I had discovered early on that the staff writers at LIFE didn't know enough about the evidence to do the kind of searching interviews we wanted, and it seemed reasonable that the New York Times was in the same predicament. Neither publication was about to invest enough money and time to enable one of its own people to reach that level of understanding. As a result, journalists working on the case were hamstrung by its complexity and their lack of the time needed to properly research it. In contrast, time was what we amateurs had in abundance, and it was why LIFE had hired me.

As for the books already published about the assassination, it struck me that virtually all had focused, in one way or another, on picking apart the Warren Commission's conclusions. None had looked at the core evidence in the case and tried to pull all the pieces together into a single coherent whole. We had heard enough about how wrong the Warren Commission's reconstruction was, but what was right?

Looking ahead to writing my own book, I asked myself what I was really trying to do. From the outset, I had never been a conspiracy theorist. In fact, I had taken great pains to stay far away from what seemed to me a febrile breeding ground for endless speculation. To my mind, there remained a bright line between conspiracy theories—with their endless permutations—and the basic question of whether there had been a conspiracy at all. Here, it seemed to me, everything boiled down to what happened in Dealey Plaza and a single question: Was there more than one shooter? If the answer from Dealey Plaza was yes, and if the presence of a second shooter was confirmed by the shooting itself, then the debate ended. But the debate also ended if the answer was no.

From the very beginning, the government had been claiming that the shooting was an unhinged act by a single individual firing three shots from a $12 Italian army rifle. It was—according to this scenario—an amateur assassination. But most amateur assassinations do not succeed since single individuals acting alone cannot bring enough force to the point of attack. The Kennedy assassination was efficiently carried out and devastatingly effective. These are the hallmarks of a professional hit. If a conspiracy was involved, it would never have been permitted to go forward with only one individual shooting from an upper floor of a nearby building. Such a plan would have been rejected as too risky, too vulnerable to failure. Therefore, it all came down to the threshold question: Was there more than one shooter? If the answer was yes, then that fact would show itself in the details of the shooting. Finding those details—if they existed—would be the task of my book. And if they did not exist, that too would make the book worthwhile. In either case, the book would not stray beyond what happened in Dealey Plaza on November 22.

Hardly had I clarified the task before me in the winter of 1967 than I became aware of the immense problems facing me and my publisher. The first problem was time: we had precious little of it. Berney Geis had already told me he wanted a publication date of November 22, 1967, which was only ten months away. How could we possibly put this book together in so short a time?

The second problem was evidence. Much of what we had was fragmentary, and a good deal of that was in motion, with more material being declassified and released almost monthly. This meant that what we took to be evidence one day might not be evidence the next.

The third problem was me, the amateur researcher with the aforementioned abundance of time. My day job as a professor would take up a lot of time during the next ten months. Thank God for the summer vacation, which would free me up to work full-time on the book. But could I do it? I had written a dissertation that would be published in the fall, but that did not mean I knew how to write a book.

I turned to the materials—to the pieces of the puzzle—that our LIFE team had gathered. First were the witness interviews I had done alone or with Ed Kern. Some were quite long. The transcript of the Holland interview ran to seventy-one pages. The clarity and simplicity of Holland's memories were impressive, as was the fact that he hadn't just observed events but had acted in concert with others in response to what they had all observed.

I poked around in my desk for the bullet that O. P. Wright had given me at Parkland Hospital. There it was, a copper jacket with a pointed tip. Certainly what Wright had told me was new and important. What we had learned about the gurney on which the bullet was discovered led inevitably to the conclusion that it had not been used in the care of either Kennedy or Connally. Likely what Patsy Swank and I had turned up at Parkland Hospital would make a chapter in itself.

There was the interview that Ed and I had done with Dr. J. Thornton Boswell, one of the autopsy doctors at Bethesda Naval Hospital. His was the first interview given to the press by any of the autopsy doctors, and it raised more questions than it answered. In response to some questions, he was direct and candid. In answering others, he seemed equivocal, even evasive. He told us that all three of the doctors had stuck their pinkie into Kennedy's back wound and found no exit. He also said a second autopsy face sheet with his notes on it had apparently been lost. These were odd details, but they helped illustrate what an appalling mess the official autopsy had been.

Then there was the gorilla in the room: the Zapruder film.

In the archives I had seen the Warren Commission's poor copy of this film and the 35-mm slides of individual frames. Compared to the original film in LIFE's possession and the four-by-five-inch transparencies made from it, they were awful. Yet I now had in hand very good Ektachrome and Plus-X copies of all the relevant frames, many in close-up. I was no forensic expert, but I could see that more information could be extracted from the film that could prove or disprove claims made about what happened. In short, I was in a position to carry out studies that the government might have done but never had. Specifically, I wanted to take precise measurements that would provide confirmation of what appeared to be changes that took place between individual frames in two sequences from the film.

The first study was the run of frames that showed Governor Connally turning to his right and then being hit by a bullet. The previous summer, when Vince Salandria and I had made our trip to the archives, Vince had told me that Ray Marcus had discovered between frames 237 and 238 of the Zapruder film—one-eighteenth of a second—dramatic changes in Governor Connally that could not be seen when the film was run at speed. Our informal inspection confirmed this finding. It surely looked to us as if this was the instant when a bullet crashed into Connally's back, less than half a second after Kennedy emerged from behind the sign with his elbows splayed upward, clearly hit. If this was the instant of impact, Connally's back faced the Records Building, not the depository, and my Abney level had told me that a 27-degree elevation from his position carried a straight line to its roof.

According to the autopsy, Kennedy received only a superficial back wound—the one all three doctors had probed with their pinkies, finding no exit or projectile—while Connally took a bullet that blew five inches out of a rib and caused a hole the size of a silver dollar in his chest. If they were hit by the same bullet, why did Kennedy react first and Connally only much later?

In Dallas, we had shown the frames to the governor's surgeon, Dr. Charles Gregory, who had explained that we were seeing the momentum transfer effects of a bullet: the change in the angle of Connally's shoulder, the puffing of his cheeks, and the way his hair was disordered. The analysis was straightforward. All I needed were blow-ups from the film and a protractor to measure the angle between Connally's shoulder and the top of the limousine door.

The second study—measuring the movement of Kennedy's head just before and after the impact on his head at frame 313—was much more complicated.[1] Here, I was fortunate to have the help of the Haverford Physics Department. Physics professor Bill Davidon had been arrested with me when I had first met Vince Salandria in January 1966. He was interested in the project, and one of his best students, Bill Hoffman, was recruited to help work on it.

Vince and I had studied this impact at the archives using the 35-mm slides and copy of the Zapruder film. It was gruesome. With elbows splayed upward, Kennedy seems to lean toward his wife. Gradually, his elbows sink, and he tilts forward. Then, suddenly and violently, Kennedy's head explodes above the right temple, and his body is slammed backward and to the left, his head leading the movement, seeming to pull the rest of his body with it. He hits the upright seat back and bounces forward. Mrs. Kennedy looks down into the tangle of blood and brain. Clearly, a large portion of Kennedy's head has been blown away. With her arm around his shoulder, he disappears forward out of sight in the limousine.

The oddest part of this sequence is invisible when the film is run at speed. At speed, it looks as if someone has hit Kennedy with a baseball bat high above the right temple, driving his head backward and to the left. But using the 35-mm slides and comparing the impact slide with the one just before it, we could see that Kennedy's head jumps forward in that one-eighteenth of a second. It must have been a couple of inches. This made no sense, but the movement was undeniable and could be measured. What could cause it? It was beginning to look as if Kennedy was hit by a virtually simultaneous volley of bullets, first from the rear and then from the right front.

Obtaining precise measurements would be no easy job because the limousine was moving during this sequence, and its angle to Zapruder's camera was changing slightly during the sequence. Some of the frames were unusable due to blurring, and calculating the transformation of distances on two-dimensional photographs to actual distances in space was far beyond me. Still, it could be done.

In sum, it appeared that we had come up with something genuinely new and extremely important in terms of evidence. The more I thought about it, the more convinced I was that what appeared to be a double impact on the president's head would end up being the centerpiece of the book. Moreover, these two movements fit into an already familiar dual pattern. So much evidence in the case seemed to come in patterns of two, each piece pointing in a different direction.[2]

For starters, there was the duality of witness reports concerning the origin of the shots. I had cataloged where the witnesses thought the shots came from. Of the sixty-four witnesses whose opinions had been recorded, twenty-five thought shots came from the general direction of the Texas School Book Depository, while thirty-three thought shots came from the knoll area. On the one hand, witnesses saw someone shooting from the sixth floor corner window of the depository; cartridge cases were found near that window, and the rifle was found on the same floor. On the other hand, witnesses such as Holland and the others heard a shot fired from behind the stockade fence on the knoll, saw smoke there, and later discovered muddy footprints and cigarette butts at that location.

Most striking were the observed effects of Kennedy being shot in the head. There was the obvious catapulting of his body backward and to the left, clear evidence of the shot coming from the right front. Accompanying this impact was a spray of blood and brain matter together with skull fragments cast over the motorcyclists riding to the left rear of the limousine. A bullet fired from the right front would have struck the president above the right temple—a tangential hit—and driven his head to the left and back while throwing impact debris in the same direction. All this happened at the most dramatic moment in the Zapruder film, when the president's head explodes, yet the Warren Commission made no mention of it in its 888-page report or in the twenty-six volumes of hearings and exhibits. Ignoring this elementary core evidence, the Warren Commission instead emphasized a second spray of blood and brain tissue that flew forward as far as the hood ornament. The commission noted that blood spots were found on both the interior (back) surface of the windshield and the exterior (front) surface. The windshield itself was cracked on its interior surface by a fragment that left a lead smear. A second fragment dented the rear surface of a chrome strip above the windshield. In addition, two fragments later identified as having been fired from Oswald's rifle were found in the front seat area. Only a double impact could account for this dispersion of impact debris—of blood, brain matter, and skull and bullet fragments—in two quite different directions. Because it had no way of explaining the backward and leftward movement and the trajectories of the impact debris, the Warren Commission did the easiest thing. It just never mentioned these details.

A similar duality is reflected in the medical evidence. On the one hand, the Bethesda Hospital autopsy surgeons found a small entry hole low in the back of Kennedy's head with a massive defect in the skull running seventeen centimeters forward from this point, while reports from Parkland Hospital painted a somewhat different picture. Doctor after doctor reported seeing a significant exit wound—in medical parlance an "avulsive" (meaning "ripped-open") wound—in the right rear of the president's head.

While the double-impact scenario would be the logical center of my recon-struction, I knew that any successful reconstruction had to explain all the evi-dence in the case, not just part of it. For example, there was that troubling small hole in the center of President Kennedy's throat. Disagreement over what had caused that hole had ended the collaboration between Vince Salan-dria and me. Vince was persuaded that the hole was due to a shot from the front. I didn't buy it. The spinal column was only a few inches behind that hole. Any bullet entering there must have shattered the spinal column before blowing a hole out the back of Kennedy's neck.

The Warren Commission explained the hole as the exit of the bullet that hit Kennedy in the back.[3] This did not make much sense since the back wound was lower than the throat wound, and the supposed bullet track hit no bone. In this theory, a bullet fired from the depository window six stories above Ken-nedy would have had to take an upward trajectory through his body, not a downward one. Any bullet exiting through that hole would have continued on to hit Connally. Connally and his wife had told LIFE they were sure this had not happened, and I had to agree with them.

If both the Warren Commission and Vince Salandria were wrong about

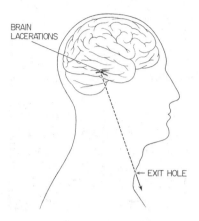

BRAIN
LACERATIONS

← EXIT HOLE

Figure 7-1. The possible path of a
bone or bullet fragment from the
head impact out the throat.

what had caused this little hole, what
had caused it? I found a third possibility.

First, the hole in the throat was
extremely small. The surgeon who cut
through it to perform a tracheotomy
said the next day that it was only three
to five millimeters across. This is about
three-quarters of the diameter of an
ordinary pencil. Most important, the
hole was bracketed above and below
by vertical damage to the president's
throat. The autopsy doctors located
a couple of lacerations deep in the
president's brain near the bottom of
the brain pan. Then there was what
appeared to be an up-and-down track of bruising, laceration, and blood-filled
tissue both above and below the tiny hole in the throat. Although it was not
a slam dunk, one had to take seriously the notion that Dr. Perry's small entry
hole was actually the exit point of a piece of bone or metal driven downward
by the explosion of the president's head. Both *Newsweek* and the *Journal of the
American Medical Association* contained stories in December 1963 and January
1964 claiming that this had happened.[4]

I was getting somewhere clearing up the loose pieces of the puzzle. There
was, however, one enormous obstacle. While most people heard three shots,
the accumulating evidence indicated that four shots were fired, the final two
almost simultaneously. With two of the four shots fired virtually simultaneously, four shots would likely be heard as three. Yet according to the four-shot
reconstruction I was putting together, only two of the shots came from the sixth
floor corner window of the depository (the remaining two were from the grassy
knoll and the roof of the Dallas County Records Building). Yet not two but three
expended cartridge cases were found in the depository. How could that be?

The first thing that popped into my head was something the Warren Commission's major witness had said.[5] His name was Howard Brennan, and he
was sitting on the wall just across Elm Street from the depository. Before the
shooting, he noticed a man at the sixth floor window in the southeast corner.
There was a noise that Brennan took to be a "backfire." He had no recollection of hearing another shot but looked up to the sixth floor window and saw
the man taking very "deliberate aim" with a rifle that was pointed down Elm
Street. What caught my attention was the fact that Brennan talked about only

two shots. He heard one that he took to be a backfire and looked up to see a gunman in the window taking his time to make his last shot.

Brennan also told the FBI the next day that he saw "two Negro men on the next lower floor, immediately below the window where the man was observed with the rifle." These men appear in a famous Tom Dillard photo of the front of the depository only seconds after the shooting.[6] They were working in the depository and were less than ten feet from the open sixth floor sniper's window. On the afternoon of the shooting, one of them—Bonnie Ray Williams—signed an affidavit saying, "I heard 2 shots. It sounded like they came from just above us."[7] Later, it turned out that there was plaster in Williams's hair, the result of the sonic concussions coming from just ten feet above him.[8] One of Williams's companions that day even heard the expended cartridge cases hitting the floor above them.[9]

All this had been in my head back in December when LIFE photographer Arthur Schatz and I had visited the National Archives to photograph the evidence. Arthur came equipped with special lighting equipment, and the archives staff permitted us to arrange the evidence in whatever way we wanted. We put on gloves, and I held Oswald's rifle in my hands. It had an odd-looking sling, and I asked the archives technician about it. He knew nothing. It felt strange—even a bit eerie—to hold that rifle, but I was interested in something else. I worked its action and was surprised to learn how stiff it was, much stiffer than the duplicate Carcano I'd purchased earlier that had been made by the same gun factory as Oswald's only four months earlier than his. Arthur used his special lighting to take a dramatic photo of CE 399—the so-called magic bullet—and used a macrolens to take a wonderfully detailed photo of CE 842, the tiny lead fragments removed from Governor Connally's wrist.

Things got really interesting when we photographed the three cartridge cases found near the corner window of the sixth floor of the depository and the live round found in the rifle.[10] I noticed something never mentioned in all the expert testimony or shown in any of the Warren Commission photographs. If you laid out the three cartridges alongside the live round, you could see a dent on the shoulders of two of the cases where they abutted the chamber of the rifle. The live round showed a similar but much less prominent mark. In contrast, the third cartridge case, designated CE 543, had no dent on its shoulder but a sharp dent in its lip. In its present form, this cartridge would not accept a projectile.

Back on the Haverford campus, I asked the obvious question: Might the case have been dented after being fired from the sixth floor corner window? Photos of the sniper's nest show a painted brick wall, so I figured a brick wall

Photo 7-2. This Dillard photo taken seconds after the shooting shows Bonnie Ray Williams (*left*) and James Jarman (*right*) only ten feet below the sniper's window.

would have been the hardest surface the case could have struck after ejection. With a pair of pliers, I pulled the projectiles out of fifteen rounds and poured out the powder. Then I set up a chair and started throwing the cases against a brick wall in the Hall Building. I threw them hard at the wall but could not get one to dent. Lacking powder or projectile, the case itself was not heavy enough to dent. What was going on here?

I turned to the documents containing the testimony of firearms examiners about these cartridge cases. One of the examiners, Joseph Nicol, expressed the opinion that the one with the dented tip (CE 543) had likely been given a "dry-run" by being inserted into the breech by hand, then rammed forward by the bolt, to be ejected as the bolt is pulled back.[11] He pointed out that all three of the cartridge cases had firing pin and bolt marks showing they had been in Oswald's rifle when the trigger was pulled. However, with respect to the cartridge case with the dented lip, the trigger could have been pulled on it when it lacked powder or a projectile.

Nicol found three marks on this cartridge case that were not found on the

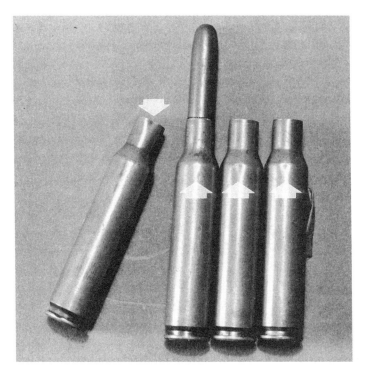

Photo 7-3. Three of the four cartridge cases bear chambering marks characteristic of Oswald's rifle. The fourth not only lacks identical chambering marks and has a dented lip, but its unique markings indicate that it was dry-fired in a second rifle, not Oswald's.

Photo 7-4. CE 543: This dented cartridge case found on the sixth floor of the Texas School Book Depository could not, in this condition, have held a projectile on November 22, 1963.

other two.[12] He believed two of the marks were from the extractor (the metal clamp that grabs the case and pulls it backward when the bolt is operated) and the third from the ejector (another part of the mechanism that throws the cartridge case out of the breech). But these marks apparently didn't come from the extractor and ejector on Oswald's rifle since they were absent from the other two cases and the live round. If I understood him correctly, Nicol seemed to be saying that these marks did not come from Oswald's rifle. Was there a second Mannlicher-Carcano rifle involved in this case that we had never heard of?

I looked in vain for any mention by Nicol of the shoulder dents on the two cases and the live round. These had been so obvious to Arthur Schatz and me; why weren't they obvious to Nicol?

What else could I find? I found a letter from FBI Director J. Edgar Hoover to the commission, written two months after Nicol testified.[13] Hoover reported that the other two cartridge cases had marks showing that each one had been in the chamber of Oswald's rifle when it was fired. According to Hoover, there was no mark like this on CE 543, only the magazine follower mark and the three strange marks mentioned by Nicol.

But the magazine follower mark could not have been caused on November 22 because that mark is caused by a lever under spring tension at the bottom of the magazine that presses against only the last round in the clip. Since the live round found in the rifle was the bottom round in the clip on November 22, it had its own follower mark. Even more important, Hoover's letter mentioned that the three marks described by Nicol were absent not only from the other cartridge cases and the live round but also from the many cartridge cases produced in test firings of Oswald's rifle. That clinched it: the cartridge case with the dented lip also had marks from a second Carcano, not Oswald's.

CE 543 was looking stranger and stranger. When "dry-fired" in Oswald's rifle, it picked up firing pin and magazine follower marks. During that dry-firing with no projectile, its lip apparently struck some irregularity in the mechanism and became dented so that it could no longer accept a projectile. Joseph Nicol himself noted that "the weight of the empty shell would be different, of course, from one which had a projectile in it, so that its dynamics might be different."[14] That could explain why, like the others, it had no dent in its shoulder and instead had a sharp dent in its lip. Did this mean that only two shots had been fired from the sniper's nest and not three?

Finally, there were things I'd discovered at LIFE that were just weird. For example, there was the figure we called "the Umbrella Man." Ed Kern and I found him while studying photos of the motorcade and the shooting. It had rained in the early-morning hours of November 22 but cleared by about ten o'clock. By the time of the president's arrival, it had become a beautiful day with bright sun and temperatures in the high 60s. In the crowd scenes we looked at—Love Field, downtown Dallas streets, Main and Houston Streets— no one had an open umbrella. Yet when we looked at shots of Dealey Plaza, there he was: "the Umbrella Man." Dressed in a conservative dark suit, a thin white man holding an open black umbrella was standing by the Stemmons Freeway sign. And when the limousine got to this position, that was when shots began to rain down on it. The only open umbrella in all of Dallas that Friday at 12:30 p.m. seemed to be held open at the very point where shots were first fired. "This couldn't be a coincidence," I said to myself. "Or could it?"

When the dust settled from all these forays into puzzling the pieces, I was pleased but not surprised that vexing pieces of the puzzle were not fixed in stone. The forward and backward movement of the president's head under impact seemed to be something we could measure. It was a quantifiable fact. Given the Warren Commission's ostentatious ignoring of the massive left and backward snap together with the spray of impact debris over the motorcyclists riding to the left rear, the existence of the double movement itself would be news to most readers. To be sure, other pieces of the puzzle were not grounded in demonstrable fact and hence were somewhat speculative. It certainly bothered me that I had no really good reason for why an extra cartridge case would have been dropped near the sixth floor window. But the availability of alternative explanations to the Warren Commission conclusions was itself reassuring.

Finally, the reconstruction was complete: the first shot came from the depository's sixth floor window, the second from the roof of the Dallas County Records Building, the third from the sixth floor window of the depository, and the fourth and final one from the knoll. Four shots from three locations in just under six seconds. Those facts suggested a title for the book: *Six Seconds in Dallas.*

CHAPTER 8 *SIX SECONDS IN DALLAS*

To a casual visitor in the late winter of 1967, Haverford College would have seemed to be a place of bucolic beauty and tranquility. The faculty lived mostly on campus in apartments or houses provided at a low rent by the college. The wider community was the Main Line of Philadelphia, where Haverford was squeezed between Bryn Mawr and Ardmore on the string of wealthy suburbs constituting what had once been the main line of the Pennsylvania Railroad. Nancy and I and our two young children lived in a six-room apartment with a porch overlooking Merion Field and the Duck Pond. When it got cold in the wintertime, faculty and their children would skate on the frozen pond that otherwise was a sanctuary for ducks and Canada geese. Faculty kids used the hill beyond for sledding, and I sometimes watched them as I walked up the hill to class.

Haverford was expanding a bit, so a new class of young faculty had come in with us the year before. Most of us had young families, and we'd often arrange dinner parties similar to the graduate student dinners we all had known earlier at various universities. When I looked around at the collection of hundred-year-old trees and buildings dating back to the 1840s or at the portraits of distinguished Quaker professors inside those buildings, I sometimes felt as if I had stumbled onto the set of a movie about a small liberal arts college.

In those days, Haverford was a good place, a safe place, a happy place. Yet also in those days, the world beyond the campus was neither good nor safe nor happy. It was swiftly becoming a darker and more dangerous place. We heard about it each night on the evening news when Walter Cronkite reported on the latest ratcheting up of the meat grinder in Vietnam. My old unit, UDT 21, had provided cadres for the formation of SEAL Team 2 in 1962. Now both SEAL teams and UDTs were being deployed to Vietnam in increasing numbers. My friends from a decade earlier were probably now becoming casualties.

In July US Army General William Westmoreland had asked for 200,000 additional reinforcements to supplement the 475,000 troops already in Vietnam. In August China shot down two US fighter-bombers that had accidentally strayed across the border after raids in North Vietnam. In September and October, US Marine Corps forces were besieged just south of the Demilitarized Zone, and the United States responded with B-52 strikes. In 1966, the United States suffered 5,000 dead and 30,000 wounded. In 1967, these figures nearly doubled to 9,378 dead and 56,013 wounded. In October LIFE magazine renounced its earlier support of President Johnson's war policies. That same month a national poll showed that 46 percent of Americans believed US military involvement in Vietnam was a "mistake."

At Haverford, opposition to the war had to do largely with how old you were. The older faculty tended to just look on and observe what was happening. The students were involved initially because they might be drafted as soon as they left. The younger faculty were in between but generally sided with the students. Together with younger colleagues from Bryn Mawr and Swarthmore, we wrote letters to various local newspapers, joined peace marches, and spoke at rallies. There was very little risk in doing any of this. No one would get fired for speaking at an antiwar rally. When a local newspaper gave me the nickname "Hanoi Hannah's Helper," it was a source of mirth, not embarrassment. The term "credibility gap" was often used in those days to signify a growing distrust of government pronouncements. Surely the Kennedy assassination was a flagrant example of this, and equally surely, what I was doing would increase that gap. In some roundabout way, then, increasing the credibility gap would help the antiwar movement. But that wasn't why I was doing it. I was just trying to figure the damn thing out.

Did the faculty know what I was doing? A few did. The people I asked for help did. But I had asked them not to talk about it, and they probably didn't. At the dinner tables of older conservative faculty, what I was doing would have been seen as not unlike studying flying saucers. Since my degree was in philosophy, not history, my "research" would be seen as similar to digging up dirt for a supermarket tabloid. But the Quakers are nothing if not tolerant. Had Nancy told other women at the Faculty Women's Club what I was doing, someone would have replied with a smile, "Well, isn't that nice." Nancy would have received the same response had she said her husband had spent the previous summer in the attic trying to construct a model of the Cutty Sark out of toothpicks for insertion into a wine bottle.

As the winter turned to spring and the first buds began to form on the sycamores along College Lane, I was left alone. I started writing chapter drafts of the book that now bore the working title Six Seconds in Dallas. I wrote in longhand in a spiral notebook. Late at night I would type the drafts, revising them as I went. By choice during this time, I distanced myself from the assassination buffs community, with the exception of Sylvia Meagher, a brilliant and thoughtful researcher who coincidentally was writing her own book on the subject, *Accessories after the Fact*. We were in frequent touch, sharing documents and ideas and discussing many points over the phone.

Every week or so, I'd drive up to New York for meetings at BGA, headquartered on the top two floors of a four-story office building on Fifty-Sixth Street just west of Lexington. Berney's office was on the top floor, as was the office of Don Preston, his executive editor. The year before, Berney had cut a six-foot-diameter hole in the top floor and installed a brass firehouse pole. We would all experiment with sliding down it to the floor below.

Letty Pogrebin handled publicity. She was an attractive young mother only a couple of years older than I. Often the three of us would huddle in Don's or Berney's office, talking about the latest thing that had come up. Now and then Berney's wife, Darlene, would join us. We were a small group but an energetic one. There was always much joking around, but there was also intense interest in the latest findings I had turned up or had heard about through the network of assassination buffs. This was a different kind of book than anything BGA had ever published. As month followed month and the chapter drafts became stronger, our little group worked harder and set our sights higher. Might the mountain of assembled evidence change public attitudes about this event? Could the book prompt a new investigation? Sometimes it seemed silly to even think that. At other times, it didn't. What I didn't foresee was the roller coaster awaiting all of us.

I don't believe I ever saw any other editors at BGA during those visits I made to New York. Don Preston was a wonderful editor but was too busy to take on the editing of *Six Seconds*. Berney relied on freelance editors, and that summer he quickly turned to *Esquire* magazine for help. John Berendt had edited an issue of *Esquire* devoted to various assassination theories and ideas. Not only was he familiar with much of the material, but he had his own sources within the assassination network. He was hired to edit what I was pumping out with my portable Underwood. For a two- or three-week period in August, I came up and stayed at a hotel while John and I beat the book into its final form.

By the middle of June, a central problem had become acute.[1] Back in April, I had written to Dick Pollard, director of photography for LIFE, for permission to use twenty-five frames from the Zapruder film. I told him the frames filled important "holes" in my book, and I hoped we could "work out some arrangement" for their use. The fall before, I had talked to Kern and Billings about this. Their reply was vague but positive in terms of being able to work something out. Pollard was anything but positive. He said he could not grant such permission because if he did, he would have to grant permission to a "myriad" of other magazines seeking the same.

We kicked the problem upstairs to Douglas Hamilton, our copyright attorney from Columbia Law School. He got in touch with LIFE's editorial counsel, John Dowd. For a few days, it seemed as if this lawyer-to-lawyer contact might deliver the permission we wanted. Finally Dowd told Hamilton that Time Inc. viewed the Zapruder film as "an invaluable asset of the corporation." Berney and I decided to make a last-ditch effort to gain permission. We agreed to turn over all my royalties and all Berney's profit from the book in exchange for permission to use the frames we wanted. Later I heard that this offer went all the way to the Time Inc. board of directors, where it was turned down along with a parallel request for TV use from CBS News.

When we got the final refusal, there was no dramatic meeting in New York with Doug Hamilton. We all just kept working. Doug directed us to cut the number of frames we were going to publish to a bare minimum, crop those frames as much as we could, and finally have an artist make copies or artist's renderings of these frames. He said if we did this, we would probably be sued by Time Inc., but we would probably win the action. I wasn't all that happy with the "artist's renderings," but I knew nothing about the law and figured it was useless to press for anything else.

That summer was one of nonstop activity. Everybody on Fifty-Sixth Street was pitching in and taking care of the many details a book like this required. Arthur Hawkins was hired to do the artist's renderings of the Zapruder frames and also to design the book. I had eight-by-ten-inch black-and-white copies of the chosen frames printed, and then we cropped those down as far as we could. I hired a medical illustrator in Philadelphia to take care of the medical illustrations. As for the demanding task of creating the book's index, by good fortune, Sylvia Meagher, who was skilled at building indices, agreed to do the job. Don Preston recruited a graphic artist to prepare graphs and diagrams. Extremely heavy, high-quality paper was chosen to show the photos to advantage. The typography was complicated by one of the appendices including mathematical equations with arcane characters. In short, the book was a bear to produce, and there was no question of missing the publication date of November 16.

In late September, Don Preston called me with big news. The *Saturday Evening Post* had purchased condensation rights to *Six Seconds*. They were going to publish it in November along with a cover and two editorials backing its conclusions. This didn't mean a lot to me at the time, but then it began to sink in. We were getting breaks no one could have foreseen. A few more breaks like this, and we might change the whole public perception of the case. A new investigation? Not likely, but just maybe.

Very soon Don Preston and I visited the *Post*. Jim Atwater was senior articles editor and responsible for the condensation. He welcomed us to the magazine and showed us around. He was very gun-shy about the Zapruder frames. Don had brought along copies of some of the most important artist's renderings, but Atwater was not about to publish them. He set up a scheme whereby an artist would sit with me and one of the renderings and then go into another room to draw what he had seen. The results were pitiful, more like stick figures than the accurate renderings we had brought along. However, the *Post* art department had put together a stunning cover. Don made arrangements for us to use it as our book jacket and then gave orders to jettison something like twenty-five thousand book jackets that had already been printed.

Atwater made it clear to us that the Curtis family, who published the *Post*, was not at all pleased with his decision to buy *Six Seconds* and run it with a cover and two editorials. The head of the family lived on an estate on the Main Line and had seen the local newspaper articles calling me "Hanoi Hannah's Helper." He wanted to know why Atwater was publishing this book by "that commie professor." I knew Atwater was also a Yalie, so I made some remark about commies and Yale. Atwater just asked me to be a good boy and stay out of trouble until that issue of the *Post* appeared. I agreed.

The day before Saturday, October 21, I had been in New York working on the final details with Jim Atwater. I was heading back to Philadelphia at dusk on the New Jersey Turnpike, the latest galleys from the *Post* in my briefcase, when I passed army truck after army truck heading south to the Pentagon. I thought about those trucks as I entered Pennsylvania, and I thought about them when I fell asleep that night. When I woke up early the next morning, Nancy was still asleep. I wrote a note to her, walked up to the college, and boarded one of the buses chartered to take students and faculty to the march on the Pentagon. It would be difficult to explain why I did this since I couldn't really explain it to myself. I slept on the way down, and it was a beautiful day as thirty thousand of us marched to the Pentagon across one of the Potomac bridges. There, troops began herding people away from the building as officers with handheld loudspeakers ordered the crowd to disperse, warning that anyone who did not move would be arrested. I didn't, and I was. More than 650 of us were arrested. I ended up in a police van for four hours with Noam Chomsky. I don't remember if I introduced myself to him, only that I hoped he might begin talking about linguistic theory, but he seemed to be interested only in politics.

We were housed that night in a giant dormitory at some correctional facility in Lorton, Virginia. I had the *Post* galleys in an inside pocket and got a bit of work done that night. I had trouble sleeping and remember looking over after 1:00 a.m. to see Norman Mailer making his way to the toilets. I noticed that he walked on the balls of his feet like a fighter. He couldn't have known anyone was watching, so it must have come naturally to him. The next morning, we were all released after pleading no contest to some minor misdemeanor. I made my way to Union Station and took the train back to Philadelphia. I don't think Jim Atwater or anyone outside my family ever knew of that arrest.[2]

About a week later, I got an urgent call from Don Preston. He wanted me to immediately fax him my contracts with various Dallas residents for the use of their photos in *Six Seconds*. He explained that Time Inc. had a legal team at the offices of the *Saturday Evening Post*. They were threatening to go into federal court in the Southern District of New York to obtain an order restraining the *Post* from publishing the *Six Seconds* condensation. The grounds would be twofold: first, that the *Post* had violated LIFE's copyright on the Zapruder film and second, that LIFE had exclusive contracts with the individuals involved for the publication of their photos. I told Don that my contracts also specified exclusivity, and I would send them right up.

It all turned out to be more bark than bite. The crude black-and-white drawings made by an artist after looking at a Zapruder frame could not possibly infringe the copyright. And the contracts? It turned out that both contracts were exclusive, and my contracts had been signed earlier than LIFE's. LIFE might want to sue the individuals involved, but there was no possible action against us or the *Saturday Evening Post*. No federal judge would issue a prior restraint injunction against the *Saturday Evening Post* on such a flimsy basis.

We had synchronized the publication date for *Six Seconds* with the appearance on the newsstands of the *Saturday Evening Post* that contained its condensation. The big date was November 16. Either that day or the day before, all hell broke loose. Time Inc. brought suit against me as author, BGA as publisher, and Random House as distributor. Immediately Random House caved and said it would not distribute the book. Also immediately Berney rented trucks and sent them to the Random House warehouse to pick up the fifty thousand or so copies of the book waiting there to be distributed. In addition, he had his attorneys tell Random House it would be facing a breach-of-contract lawsuit that it could not win. Within hours Random House caved back in our direction and agreed to distribute the book. So much for the First Amendment spine of large book publishers.

In its complaint, Time Inc. claimed that the Zapruder film had been "stolen surreptitiously" by me at the instigation of Berney Geis. Later discovery in the case showed that I had legal permission to have copies because my possession of them had been made known to the editor of LIFE before he signed a contract with me. But the legal action by Time Inc. was costly to both BGA and me. Together we financed the defense of all three defendants in the case. All my royalties went to the lawyers, as did all Berney's profits on the book and more. LIFE's lawsuit dried up paperback offers for the book that were running in six figures. It also meant that we were inhibited in what we could say in advertisements. Berney was a real prince about everything. He backed the book with a big advertising and publicity budget. My contract with him made me liable for all legal expenses. Very quickly by letter, he limited my liability to the author's earnings on the book. During Haverford's spring vacation, he sent Nancy and me to Barbados for a vacation at his expense.

Letty Pogrebin moved into high gear to push the book in ads and publicity. With its condensation in the *Saturday Evening Post*, the book generated a news article in the *New York Times* and a three-page article in *Newsweek*. These organs of the print media responded judiciously with the usual "on the one side we have this, on the other side we have this" kind of coverage. John Updike was fascinated by "the Umbrella Man" and wrote a "Talk of the Town" piece about him in *The New Yorker*. He also described the book as "absolutely fascinating. It convinced me who's never been a conspiracy man at all that the whole thing must be rethought." Max Lerner devoted the entirety of his syndicated column in the *New York Post* to *Six Seconds*, describing it as "more careful and more powerful than the Warren Report. It was not until this book that I became clear in my mind about some kind of collaborative shooting."

The *Los Angeles Times* said it was "infuriating, for it suggests the kind of analytical study the Warren Commission failed even to attempt. [It is] the most forceful, graphic, and well-organized argument for a reopening of the assassination investigation." The *Denver Post* said it "presents clear evidence to demand a re-opening of the Warren Commission investigation."

These reviews were echoed in other papers across the country, and the initial sales were more than brisk. The *Denver Post* highlighted exactly what we were hoping to bring about—a new investigation. With that end in mind, I came to see the national book tour that Letty Pogrebin put together as a lobbying effort for a new investigation. I can't remember what radio and TV stations we hit on the East Coast, but I do remember Chicago, Denver, Seattle, Los Angeles, and San Francisco. This all happened in late December and early January while Haverford was on Christmas break. We had put together a few visuals from the book that I could use over and over again with TV hosts.

While this was going on, I kept wondering if using the actual Zapruder photos in the book would have pushed public attitudes beyond the breaking point and set in motion a call for a new investigation. Now, when I look at photos taken during that book tour, I recognize that I had another disability. In my regimental tie and tweed sport coat, I looked about twelve. Why would anyone believe what this bland-looking kid of thirty-one was spouting?

Everything had been running at such a fast pace since early November that I longed for the book tour to be over. I quickly tired of the glamour of going to TV studio after TV studio to be asked the same questions by uninformed anchors. By the time I got to San Francisco, the last city on the tour, I was dead tired and had a cold. The TV spot for the evening was an interview before a live audience. After the host did whatever he was supposed to do, members of the audience could ask questions. One middle-aged guy got up and said in a kind of hectoring tone, "I have heard reports that you are a CIA agent. Would you tell us whether or not that is true?" I'd prepared no good answer to such a question, so I simply gave him a flat denial. However, the instant I heard the question, I knew its origin. Of all people, it was coming from Vince Salandria.

The grumbling from the buffs started as soon as the December 2, 1967, issue of the *Saturday Evening Post* hit the newsstands. Ray Marcus immediately accused me of plagiarism regarding his discovery of the collapse of Connally's right shoulder in frame 238. *Six Seconds* carried a footnote saying, "Raymond Marcus of Los Angeles first discovered this shoulder collapse in the spring of 1965." Since the *Saturday Evening Post* didn't use footnotes, my attribution was dropped from the condensation. I wrote a letter to the *Post*, which was published in the next issue, pointing out that it was "not I, but Raymond Marcus who first noticed the buckle of the Governor's shoulder at Z frame 238."

Marcus and Salandria began discussing my work and possible motivations.[3] Their apparent assessment: Given my background (Yale) and my break with Salandria over how to interpret the throat wound, it was obvious that I was a CIA asset. They began circulating their suspicions to the community of buffs and were roundly rejected. In a private letter to Salandria, M. S. Arnoni, the editor of *Minority of One*, who had published Salandria's original articles on the case, said Salandria's claim said more about him and his "frame of mind" than about me.[4] In a letter of her own to Salandria on the issue, Sylvia Meagher wrote, "I cannot take seriously the suggestion that Tink is a CIA plant. Nor can I honestly agree that he has committed deliberate or inadvertent plagiarism."[5]

Sylvia's enormously acute book, *Accessories after the Fact*, was published virtually simultaneously with *Six Seconds* in November 1967. That December, our two books were the subject of a joint review in the *New York Times* by law-yer-journalist Fred Graham. He knocked *Accessories* unfairly and gave back-handed compliments to *Six Seconds*.

In early 1968, Sylvia and I found ourselves in close agreement over an out-of-the-blue development when New Orleans District Attorney Jim Garrison indicted a local businessman, Clay Shaw, for conspiring to murder the pres-ident. From the outset, Garrison's case against Shaw seemed preposterous, larded with strained logic and marginal witnesses who lacked credibility. Notwithstanding, the assassination underground quickly took up Garrison's cause. In the months that followed, Sylvia ended up breaking off personal relationships with many of the critics who had trooped to Garrison's side. I trusted her judgment and readily agreed to issue a joint broadside with her against our friends' embrace of Garrison's investigation, which by now had become a circus. Months later the case went to trial, and a jury unanimously acquitted Shaw after less than an hour's deliberation.

Sylvia and I remained close friends until her death many years later.

By the summer of 1968, I was becoming increasingly discouraged about *Six Seconds* and the whole effort of the last few years. Berney Geis had been won-derful to me, and I had repaid that trust by getting him involved in a lawsuit with Time Inc. Vince Salandria, my mentor and guide in all this, was behav-ing like a wigged-out conspiracy theorist, rethinking raw facts to make them mean whatever he wanted them to mean. I had bent over backward to observe all the scholarly niceties about who had discovered what, and Ray Marcus was still screaming that I had plagiarized his work. The New Orleans circus had finally ended in the fiasco that it had been from the beginning, but in the aftermath, it felt as if Jim Garrison's unproven claims and dubious tactics had undermined and discredited—if not sabotaged—the good work so many had accomplished over four and a half years.

Then in April and again in June came the two hammer blows: the assassi-nations of Martin Luther King Jr. and Robert Kennedy. Five thousand miles away in Vietnam, the war was grinding on, with the Tet Offensive demonstrat-ing the weakness of the American position. President Johnson had declined to run, but neither Richard Nixon nor Hubert Humphrey promised any radical departure from the failed policy of the past. In 1968, US casualties increased to 14,594 killed and 87,388 wounded, an increase of almost 50 percent over the previous year.

By the beginning of classes in September 1968, I had started turning away from the Kennedy assassination. Then, on September 24, we got the good news: Judge Inzer B. Wyatt of the Southern District of New York had granted summary judgment to us in the lawsuit brought by Time Inc. In a landmark judgment that would expand first amendment rights in copyright cases—and because of that earning its place in copyright law textbooks—Judge Wyatt ruled that our use of the Zapruder film in *Six Seconds* had been a "fair use." After pointing out that the offer made by Geis and me to turn over all royalties and profits to Time Inc. "is a strong point for defendants" and after stressing that *Six Seconds* had really caused no injury to Time Inc., Judge Wyatt got to his most important paragraph:

> There is a public interest in having the fullest information available on the murder of President Kennedy. Thompson did serious work on the subject and has a theory entitled to public consideration. While doubtless the theory could be explained with sketches of the type used . . . in the *Saturday Evening Post*, the explanation actually made in the Book is easier to understand. The Book is not bought because it contained the Zapruder Pictures; the Book is bought because of the theory of Thompson and its explanation, supported by Zapruder pictures.[6]

When Time Inc. decided not to appeal, we took in the fact that we had prevailed. We had not brought about a new investigation of the case. But in a world that seemed under increasing stress, in a world where that extraordinary community of assassination buffs was sinking into internecine warfare and where the killing of political and social leaders was becoming routine, we had stood up to an enormous media organization and won.

CHAPTER 9   SHOOTING MELONS . . . AND COCONUTS, PINEAPPLES, AND WATER JUGS . . .

Winning summary judgment against Time Inc. was, I suppose, a kind of victory. It was nice to read Judge Wyatt's words, but in the grand scheme of things, it amounted to little. Much more important was the fact that *Six Seconds* had produced a plausible alternative to what the Warren Commission had been saying.

The virtually simultaneous impact of two bullets on the president's head seemed inescapable. The measurements pointing to this double impact appeared to be well established and hung together with other evidence. Impact debris—skull fragments, blood, and brain matter—was thrown in two directions, matching the double movement of his head and body. In addition, the medical evidence seemed to point to separate exit wounds that again matched the movement. Finally, the divided witness reports concerning where the shots came from completed the picture.

Yet it was precisely the closeness in time of the two impacts that offered the clearest line of attack for critics. What were the chances that two bullets from distant gunmen would arrive on target in less than two-eighteenths of a second? Even more troubling was the fact that I was claiming that there were two bullet impacts but could produce visual evidence for only one—the explosion in frame 313. When the shutter of Zapruder's camera opened in frame 313 to catch that explosion, the president's head had already moved forward two inches from its position one-eighteenth of a second earlier. What could that explosion be but the exit of the bullet that drove his head forward? That forward movement seemed to confirm the Warren Commission's view that Kennedy was killed by a shot from behind—from the depository window. The only thing to be explained was what happened next—the left and backward snap of the president's head and body. If this backward snap could be explained as due to a shot from the rear, a critic would have restored some plausibility to what the Warren Commission had been saying all along.

It took only fifteen months for Luis Alvarez, Nobel Prize winner in physics for 1968 and professor at the University of California, Berkeley Lawrence Radiation Laboratory, to provide such an explanation. He came up with a theory that showed how—in total opposition to common sense—a bullet from the rear might have moved the president's head back toward the rifle that shot him. For a considerable length of time thereafter, Alvarez's explanation changed how a great many Americans viewed what had happened in Dealey Plaza. It is no overstatement to say that in the whole tangled history of the case, no single individual ever played a more central role in preserving a mistaken view of the shooting.

Given Alvarez's reputation as a distinguished American scientist, one might have expected his work to be objective and disinterested. One might have expected him to simply grasp how a scientific principle might be applied and then to apply it. This is the impression Alvarez left in the *American Journal of Physics* article that he later wrote about the case. As we will see, the truth was far different.

The Alvarez Scuffle

A photo that I came across a few years ago is as good a place as any to begin. I found it in the program for a day of talks and panels in 2011 honoring Luis Alvarez on the one hundredth anniversary of his birth (he died in 1988). The photo showed Alvarez holding a copy of the issue of LIFE that Ed Kern, Dick Billings, and I had worked on in 1966. You can just make out the large-print title, "A Matter of Reasonable Doubt."

The photo was originally published in the July 1967 issue of *The Magnet*, the house organ of the Lawrence Radiation Laboratory.[1] This issue showcased Alvarez as having discovered "one of the most important pieces of technical evidence ever brought to light in connection with the assassination of President John F. Kennedy." It pointed out that Alvarez "was featured in the recent CBS television four-part special report on the assassination" and described how he had made his "discovery."

According to *The Magnet*, it all started when Alvarez was having lunch in the radiation lab cafeteria with a group of graduate students. It was the day before Thanksgiving 1966, and the students were arguing heatedly about the Kennedy assassination. Alvarez went home and read the LIFE magazine issue, which featured a great number of Zapruder film frames in color. He studied

Photo 9-1. Professor Luis Alvarez at University of California, Berkeley's Lawrence Radiation Laboratory with LIFE issue of November 25, 1966.

them closely and noticed that the right-hand flag on the limousine looked different in one frame than in the others. As he later wrote in his autobiography, Alvarez measured the flag's apparent width "with growing excitement" and "applied elementary formulas to calculate the acceleration of the edge of the flag." Could it be reacting to the sudden shock wave from a bullet? No. Rather quickly, Alvarez determined that the flag's distortion was due to wind rippling through it and not to a bullet's shock wave.

But Alvarez was hooked and began to work on a different theory that started with Zapruder frame 227. Alvarez noticed that several points of sunlight reflected from the limousine were blurred into streaks in this frame. It appeared that the camera had been jogged while the shutter was open, causing a point of light to become a streak. "Might this be the key?" thought Alvarez. "Might Zapruder have been startled by the sound of a shot and his flinch been recorded on the film?" He decided to get in touch with Frank Stanton, president of CBS, whom Alvarez knew personally. Stanton reacted positively by getting Alvarez access to the slides of the Zapruder film in the National Archives, the same slides Salandria and I had studied.

This new theory was presented as part of CBS News' ambitious TV special reexamining the Warren Report. It was aired over four days in June 1967 and was narrated by news anchor Walter Cronkite, widely regarded by the public

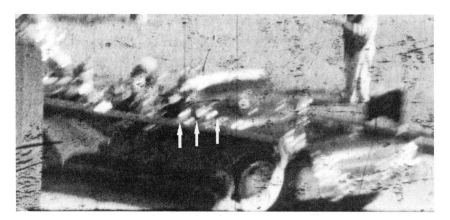

Photo 9-2. Frame 227: arrows point to the diagonal smearing of points of light.

as the most trusted man in America. Charles Wyckoff of the scientific consulting company E.G. & G. presented the gist of the theory and showed film of subjects flinching while gunshots were fired near them. Frames from these films showed blurs similar to the blurs on the Zapruder film. Alvarez appeared as the originator of the theory, presumably to lend prestige to its conclusions: three shots, just as the Warren Commission had said, and, moreover, a second and a half longer for Oswald to fire them. From the broadcast:

> CBS: What does this finding mean to those of us who simply have followed the controversy over the assassination and are not physicists?
>
> LUIS ALVAREZ: Well, to me it means there were indeed three shots fired as the Commission said. That the one that apparently didn't hit anyone in the car was fired before one that hit the President and not between the two shots that obviously hit the President.[2]

I laughed when I saw the broadcast. This was the old "jiggle theory" that we had looked into at LIFE. There were places in the Zapruder film where it looked as if the camera had been moved while the shutter was open. Pinpoints of light were changed into linear streaks of light. But there were many more of these "jiggles" than there could have been shots. Zapruder may have coughed or hiccupped, or something else may have startled him. The whole CBS program was so unconvincing that I just let it slide.[3]

Let it slide, that is, until December 1968, when I got a letter from a Dr. Walter Menaker, a Forest Hills, New York, physician with a casual interest in the assassination who, following the CBS broadcasts, had initiated a correspondence with

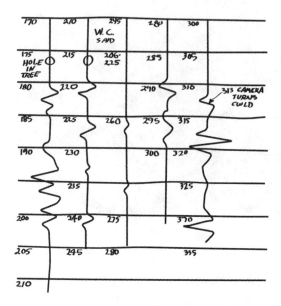

Figure 9-3. Alvarez's handwritten chart of jiggles. Note the oscillation beginning at frame 291 (*second chart line from right*).

Alvarez. Over the months that followed, Alvarez sent Menaker his raw data and explained how he had taken the "jiggle theory" further. By measuring the frame-to-frame changes in blur length, he had come to see that there were "trains of oscillations," and he explained to Menaker that every time Zapruder flinched, it took some time for the flinch to die out. He sent Menaker charts of the raw data he had recorded, a copy of which Menaker included in his letter to me.

The problem was that the data did not match what Alvarez had told a national audience on CBS. The raw data showed that there were not just three markers of shots in the data but certainly *four* and perhaps more. Dr. Menaker was no dummy and had asked Alvarez about this, inviting him to come up with an explanation for the fourth train of jiggles occurring after Zapruder frame 290. Alvarez replied that a siren in the Secret Service car had been actuated at this time, and the siren had startled Zapruder and caused the jiggles after frame 290.

The more I thought about this, the loopier it seemed. CBS had not mentioned anything about a fourth set of oscillations, yet there it was in Alvarez's own chart. If that was what the data showed, why hadn't Alvarez mentioned it? Furthermore, the siren as the explanation for the fourth set was pure nonsense. I remembered sitting with Marilyn Sitzman in the offices of Zapruder's clothing firm that afternoon in Dallas in November 1966 and thinking how odd her recollection was. She recalled the siren as being the loudest sound she heard that day and that it came after President Kennedy's head had opened up before her eyes.

I did some quick checking and found that the Warren Report itself concluded that the siren in the follow-up car was actuated "immediately after the head shot." Samuel Kinney, the Secret Service agent who actuated the siren, said in two separate documents that he hit the siren only after seeing the president's head explode.[4] Indeed, the timing of the siren going on after the impact on President Kennedy's head is one of the few facts about the shooting accepted by everyone. Had Alvarez heard somewhere about the siren and just assumed without checking that it had gone off around frame 290? Or had he knowingly moved the siren from *after* the head shot to *before* it?

Haverford was on Christmas break, so I had free time. I wrote Alvarez a letter on January 1, 1969, telling him that I had received the chart with his raw data from Dr. Menaker as well as copies of their correspondence. I typed the letter myself, and admittedly, it was sloppy—filled with cross-outs and words added via carets—and decidedly lacking in tact.[5] I quoted chapter and verse from the twenty-six volumes with the appropriate references. I pointed out that literally all the evidence showed that the siren was actuated after the head impact and that his explanation seemed like a post hoc attempt to explain data that did not fit his theory. As it happened, my letter was written shortly after Alvarez had received the Nobel Prize for Physics.

Alvarez's response stands out as one of the oddest, if not the funniest, letters I have ever received. He sent back my letter with a handwritten reply added to the last page.[6] He pointed out that, having just won the Nobel Prize, he had hundreds of congratulatory telegrams and letters on his desk. By scrawling on the back of my letter, he was slipping my letter "in ahead of its place in line." He ignored all the points I had made, implying that my letter with its quotations and references was beneath his notice. Instead, he said he was "quite pleased" (underlining his) that his efforts "have done the most to persuade the public that the assassination critics are a bunch of nuts and that the Warren Report is essentially correct." He went on to say that he was pleased with his role in "helping to restore some sanity to the American public."

I figured that was the end of it. A Nobel Prize winner in physics had better things to do than argue with an assassination researcher about jiggles. Alvarez might want to expose critics of the Warren Commission, but there was not enough skin in the game for him to continue a correspondence with a cheeky assistant professor of philosophy.

But I was wrong. My comical scuffle with Alvarez had only just begun. In early February, I received a letter from Paul Hoch, a Harvard-educated graduate student in physics who worked under Alvarez at the Lawrence Radiation Laboratory and who coincidentally was part of the assassination underground.[7] The letter began by saying that "Dr. Alvarez, who is (as you know) extremely busy," had asked him to add comments to Alvarez's earlier handwritten reply to me. Hoch corrected one mistake in my letter to Alvarez where I had confused "angular velocity" with "angular acceleration" and then, to my surprise, moved on to disagree with Alvarez on the central issue. He wrote, "I feel that your argument against the 'siren' explanation for the oscillation starting about frame 290 is basically valid. . . . I feel that a fourth shot is a quite reasonable possibility."

I immediately saw that it was quite gutsy of Paul Hoch to disagree with Alvarez in a letter written at Alvarez's behest. I wrote Alvarez back on February 5, 1969.[8] This time I had the letter typed by the department secretary. Not only was it perfectly typed, but I boiled my argument down to a single paragraph and a single point: either Alvarez had to admit that he had no explanation for one of his four data points, or he had to admit that the fourth data point was a shot. Turning the knife—which in retrospect I can attribute only to the brash confidence of youth—I pointed out that his associate "had agreed that my criticism of his 'siren' explanation was 'basically valid.'"

"You may have felt you had an explanation for the fourth period of oscillation," I wrote, "but what notion of scientific responsibility is it that justifies the misrepresentation of the data itself?"

Alvarez was apparently so disturbed by what I had written that nine days later, on February 14, 1969, he sent me a six-page single-spaced letter with copies to Dr. Menaker and Paul Hoch.[9] He began by criticizing "the very objectionable tone" of my letter and declared that "this will be absolutely my last communication on the subject."

He spent several pages describing "the history of the long search for the correct interaction for the universal weak decay." He suggested that I ask people in the Haverford Physics Department for help if I didn't understand what he was saying. I was scratching my head. Why do all this in the first place?

Alvarez said he was trying to make clear to me that "the main thing a scientist does, in my judgment, is to decide which of the evidence he sees must be wrong and must be ignored." This was what the "long search for the correct interaction for the universal weak decay" was meant to disclose to me. He emphasized that "if one can throw out the considered and often repeated work done over a period of a year or two by some of the best physicists in the world," then one is justified in throwing out "the recollections of some untrained observers under very shocking conditions." Turning to the timing of the siren, he wrote, "I am still satisfied with my conclusion since all I have to do to bring it into agreement with all other observations is to move the siren time by a few seconds."

Of course, in some powerful sense, Alvarez was correct. In the arcane world of nuclear physics, where the existence or nonexistence of a particle can be surmised only at the end of a logical chain that depends on, say, a gauge needle reading over, and not under, twenty-five units, it is critical to know what data can be disregarded.

Clearly Alvarez had a talent for doing this. But to apply the same principle to a historical event is absurd. I imagined a Monty Python skit where John Cleese appears in a scientist's lab coat, looks into the camera, smiles, and says breezily. "Now that we've gotten rid of those pesky seconds slowing down the time of the siren, we can say that our theory is just peachy keen. After all, this is science!"[10]

A decade later, the House Select Committee on Assassinations had experts retest the Zapruder film for the kind of blur described by Alvarez.[11] They found that one set of blurs at frames 158–160 had been missed by Alvarez and confirmed blurs at the other five locations indicated by Alvarez's data. In all, this made six. Alvarez's claim that he had proven that three (and only three) shots had been fired was shown to be stunningly wrong.

That Alvarez's claim was proved wrong is not in itself of much significance in the larger context of assassination research. That is, after all, how science proceeds. Various hypotheses are put forward, and we wait to see whether any survive empirical testing. What is of consequence is the degree to which the blur argument occupied Alvarez's time and energy. Why would he take the time and trouble to enter into this battle royal with an obscure young academic?

To understand why Alvarez would do this, one has to appreciate who he was in 1969. First, Alvarez was part of no conspiracy. Powerful forces did not contact Alvarez and ask him to come up with his theory. Just the opposite— Alvarez came up with his theory and then contacted Frank Stanton of CBS to publicize it. Alvarez saw himself as a gifted thinker who, by using the tools of science, could expose the fallacies of ill-informed and badly motivated critics who were bringing into question the very integrity of the US government.

At this time, Alvarez's impressive career as a scientist had been linked to the government for over twenty-five years.[12] In 1943, he made substantial progress in upgrading radar. Then he moved to the Manhattan Project, where he helped develop the detonator for the second plutonium bomb, the one dropped on Nagasaki. When the *Enola Gay* released the first atomic bomb on Hiroshima, Alvarez was in a second B-29 that dropped parachute gauges to radio information concerning the size of the blast.

It is clear from his autobiography that the war years were the happiest of his life. It was a time when his important discoveries clearly saved American and British lives. During this time, he was a member of various research teams that worked closely with the military. He enjoyed the camaraderie of the military and of flying with the Royal Air Force to test the radar system he was developing.

After the war, he supported the development of the H-bomb, and, unlike many Manhattan Project scientists, he testified against physicist J. Robert Oppenheimer during Oppenheimer's 1954 loyalty hearings.[13] In the late 1950s, he was cleared to work for several months in Washington, DC, as part of the Baker panel examining the National Security Agency. Alvarez was a longtime member of the JASON Defense Advisory Panel whose members advised the Pentagon on science-related projects.[14] In 1961, he was appointed chairman of a special Pentagon committee exploring how science could help the nation improve its capabilities to fight a limited non-nuclear war.

Meanwhile, back in the Bay Area, Alvarez had become a member of the famed Bohemian Club and would take part in its annual summer encampment of the rich and the powerful. When the Hewlett-Packard Corporation went public, he became one of its three outside directors. A lifelong Republican who made no secret of it, Alvarez said during the Berkeley campus's free-speech movement, "I find their goals are without merit, but their tactics are brilliant."

In his autobiography, Alvarez tells of visiting a submarine base in Key West, Florida, along with several fellow scientists. "The base commander," wrote Alvarez, "welcomed us as exceptional patriots." This was how Alvarez may have seen himself: a kind of patriot who, by torpedoing Kennedy assassination critics, was simply "helping to restore some sanity to the American public."

The relevance of the foregoing account is that it establishes a context for understanding Alvarez's thinking and methodology as we follow the development of his second, and far more influential, theory.

The Jet Effect Theory

Twelve days after writing me his six-page single-spaced letter, Alvarez flew off to an American Physical Society meeting in St. Louis. Several years later, he described what happened:

> Paul Hoch handed me a copy of Thompson's book as I was leaving for the
> February 1969 meeting of the American Physical Society in St. Louis. On the
> plane, I had time to study the book carefully. It is beautifully printed, with

excellent photographs and carefully prepared graphs. When I studied the graph showing the changing position of the President's head relative to the moving car's coordinate system, I was finally convinced that the assassination buffs were right; there had to be a real explanation of the fact that the President's head did not fall back, but was driven back by some real force.[15]

Alvarez went on to say that he solved the problem "to my own satisfaction and in a one-dimensional fashion on the back of an envelope as I sat in solitary splendor that the St. Louis hotel management supplied me in my capacity as President of the American Physical Society."

The essence of Alvarez's solution is to make clear that the collision between a bullet and a head is not like the collision between two billiard balls. In the billiard ball collision, the kinetic energy of the first ball is transferred to the second. The first ball stops or keeps moving, while the second moves off in a direction away from the first. When a bullet hits a human head, the collision is quite different. Some kinetic energy is transferred to the head as the bullet penetrates the thick bone of the skull. This part of the collision resembles the billiard ball collision. But there is a second part. The bullet with its shock wave continues through the semiliquid mixture of brain and blood inside the skull to make its exit out the other side. If the bullet is a military-jacketed round, it will make a small hole on entrance and a somewhat larger hole on exit. If the bullet is a dumdum or all-lead hunting round, it will deform on entrance and produce a huge exit wound, driving with it a quantity of blood and brain matter. In the latter instance, the kinetic energy of the blood and brain matter blown out may surpass the kinetic energy imparted to the head on the bullet's entry. In that case, the head will actually move backward toward the shooter.

Charles Wohl, a colleague of Alvarez at the Lawrence Radiation Laboratory, later wrote about Alvarez's back-of-the-envelope calculation.[16] "The response to this back-of-the-envelope calculation was tepid," wrote Wohl. "There is no reason to believe that a possible solution of an equation is a likely solution, especially when the equation itself comes from a simplified model of a complicated process." Paul Hoch was more pointed in what he told Alvarez. "When I showed my simple calculations to Paul Hoch," wrote Alvarez in his *American Journal of Physics* article, "he said that no one would believe my conclusions unless we could demonstrate the retrograde recoil on a rifle range, using a reasonable facsimile of a human head."

Sharon "Buck" Buckingham was a technician at the Lawrence Radiation Laboratory and an acquaintance of Alvarez. He was an avid deer hunter and had a 30.06 rifle with a hunting scope. For reasons that seem all too clear in retrospect, Alvarez suggested to Buck that a melon might be "a reasonable facsimile of a human head." On Sunday, June 29, 1969, Buckingham went to the San Leandro Large Bore Rifle Range and shot some targets.[17] He would do so on two other occasions over the next several months. The actual results of these firing tests have never before been made public. I obtained access to them only within the last two years. The details of these tests, the notes and photos, show a far different picture from the public one painted by Alvarez, the one that was widely accepted.

Because "the Range Master wanted to go home," Buckingham shot only eight targets that day. He ate targets number 3 and 9, a coconut and a small white melon. Melons six to eight inches in diameter taped with two-inch glass filament tape gave the best results for Alvarez's theory, sending spray out the exit hole and then rolling back several inches toward the rifle. Both taped and untaped green and white melons were shot. Buckingham also shot two coconuts filled with Jell-O that threw fragments as far as thirty-nine feet downrange. A one-gallon plastic jug filled with Jell-O was taped. When shot, it moved a foot to the left and seven inches downrange. An eleven-pound watermelon was taped and then shot. The notes don't make clear what happened to it. Finally, a one-gallon plastic jug was filled with water and not taped. It "sprayed water forward left and right in an arc about 25 feet. Main part of jug found forward 6 feet."

On February 15, 1970, Buckingham returned to the rifle range with Paul Hoch and Don Olson, a fellow laboratory associate. Hoch took still photos of the setup and the test results, while Olson took 8-mm movie film of the impacts. Since none of Olson's film has survived, we have only Hoch's photos and his later commentary on the event to tell us what happened.[18]

Hoch's photos of the various shootings on that date are numbered A1 through A24. He cited these photo numbers in a later commentary on the experiment. "The targets in A6 through A11," he wrote, "were rubber balls filled with gelatin; they tended to go away from the gun but not in a direct line."

Next, Hoch remarked, "A11 through A16 show plastic bottles filled with water as targets; they tended to explode." Finally Hoch pointed out, "The last target is a pineapple, taped up but not thoroughly; it shattered with the largest piece going perpendicular to the bullet path."

As far as can be determined, no melons were shot during this second test series. This series simply established that rubber balls filled with gelatin, plastic bottles filled with water, and a taped pineapple all failed to behave in accord with the Alvarez theory.[19]

On Sunday, May 31, 1970, the group assembled for a third time at the San

Leandro range to test the Alvarez theory. This time Luis Alvarez was in attendance with his wife, Jan, and their two young children. Photographs taken by Hoch show the occasion to be more like a family outing than a scientific test. Only taped-up melons were shot, and these were even a bit smaller than Hoch's earlier specifications; they weighed 1.1 to 3.5 pounds, while Hoch had earlier specified melons weighing 4 to 7 pounds. Most important, all but one of the seven melons behaved as expected when hit by a bullet. They showed some retrograde motion back toward the rifle. According to Hoch's notes, the seventh "lost spray forward, 2 smaller jet upward and back, then just slowly rolled over."

Initially Alvarez planned to submit an article on the melon experiment to *Physics Today*, a nontechnical journal for physicists. He asked Paul Hoch to look over a draft of the article. Hoch's criticism was discouraging, even devastating. In a letter dated October 21, 1970, Hoch emphasized how different were the weapons used in Dealey Plaza and for the experiment:

> The difference between the melons and a skull and between the bullets we used and Oswald's are great; sufficiently so that I do not think we can deduce that a skull would support a recoil large enough to overcome the forward impulse when struck by a single bullet under the conditions of the assassination. The principal difference, I think, is that a skull hit by a fully jacketed bullet might be driven forward by the energy lost upon impact with the bone much more than a melon, where there might be rather little energy lost as the bullet passes through the shell. . . . As long as we do not do a careful simulation—with a skull, authentic ammunition, etc.—we do not know what to expect from a skull under such circumstances.[20]

Hoch's point is obvious. A taped melon is in no way "a reasonable facsimile of a human head."

Whether a melon is taped or not, a bullet will cut through its outside like butter. A human skull is completely different. Penetrating the thick skull bone requires considerable force, and that force is deposited in the skull as momentum. The Alvarez theory requires little momentum transfer at entry and a great blowout at exit. A much closer "reasonable facsimile of a human head" is the coconut. When it was fired upon, it did not show recoil motion but was instead blasted downrange.

Then there are the wide discrepancies between Oswald's rifle and Buck Buckingham's 30.06 hunting rifle. The projectiles linked to the assassination were 6.5-mm Mannlicher-Carcano military jacketed rounds. These projectiles are jacketed in copper to give them penetrating power. Buckingham was firing "soft-nosed" hunting rounds that would balloon on impact—in short, dum-dum bullets. Although the weight of the bullets was approximately the same (160 grains for the Dealey Plaza bullets, 150 grains for Buckingham's bullets), the velocity at which they struck the target was much different. In Dealey Plaza, a bullet would have struck Kennedy's skull with a velocity of approximately 1,800 feet per second. At the San Leandro range, Buckingham's bullets struck their targets with a velocity of almost 3,000 feet per second.[21] Since the kinetic energy imparted to a target varies with the square of velocity, one of Buckingham's bullets would have struck its target with about three times the force of a bullet from Oswald's rifle striking its target.

Within a week of writing his October 21 letter to Alvarez, Paul Hoch jumped ship. He wrote to a group of critics six days later that he did not think "the work [on the melon experiments] is publishable at this point."

He pointed out that "Dr. Alvarez disagrees with me and is working on a report entirely in his own name." Given Hoch's dim view of the melon firings, Alvarez put his notes for an article away and did not publish anything until 1976. Alvarez may or may not have been aware of earlier test firings at Edgewood Arsenal that showed how correct were Hoch's reservations.

As part of its work for the Warren Commission in 1964, the army's Edgewood Arsenal carried out meticulous skull-shooting experiments with Oswald's rifle and a second Carcano. Ten skulls were filled with "gelatin tissue simulant," and the rear of the skulls was covered with goatskin to simulate Kennedy's hair and scalp. These ten skulls were then shot in the back of the skull at the point described in the Kennedy autopsy with the same ammunition used in Dealey Plaza. Larry Sturdivan, a technician from Edgewood Arsenal, later showed film of the skull-shooting experiments to the House Select Committee on Assassinations. All ten skulls were knocked forward along the bullet's path. The technician testified,

> As you can see, each of the two skulls that we have observed so far have moved in the direction of the bullet. In other words, both have been given some momentum in the direction that the bullet was going. This third one also shows momentum in the direction that the bullet was going, showing that the head of the President would probably go with the bullet. . . . In fact, all ten of the skulls that we shot did essentially the same thing.[22]

Toward the end of this discussion, Alvarez oddly defended himself against a charge that no one ever made—that he had used the Edison technique. The

Photo 9-4. A1: Preshoot. Rubber ball filled with gelatin.

Photo 9-5. A6: Postshoot. Rubber ball goes forward.

Photo 9-6. Luis Alvarez (*with melon*) and family during the test session of May 31, 1970.

Photo 9-7. Physicist Paul Hoch flipping a melon at the May 31, 1970, test session.

Photo 9-8. B16—Preshoot. Melon # 4.

Photo 9-9. Melon # 4. Postshoot showing movement of the melon toward the shooter.

term, also known as the Edison method, refers to inventor Thomas Edison's development of the incandescent light bulb. In his search for an effective filament that when energized by electricity would burn brightly for a long period of time, and lacking any systematic theoretical approach, Edison resorted to trial and error, spending many months in his laboratory patiently trying out dozens of different filaments until he finally found one with the right characteristics. Alvarez writes:

> If we had used the "Edison technique," and shot at a large collection of objects, and finally found one which gave retrograde recoil, then our firing experiments could reasonably be criticized. It is important to stress the fact that a taped melon was our *a priori* best mock-up of a head, and it showed retrograde recoil in the first test. But as the tests were actually conducted, I believe they show it is most probable that the shot in 313 came from behind the car.

You do not have to be a Nobel Prize winner to figure out in advance that a bullet going through a melon would transfer almost none of its forward momentum to the melon. Since the imbalance between forward and rearward momentum moves the melon, it is self-evident that Alvarez's theory needs the least forward momentum possible to make it work. It is not that a melon constitutes the "*a priori* best mock-up of a head." Rather, a melon constitutes the "*a priori* best mock-up up of a head" *to make the theory work.* All the other items substituted for melons—coconuts, pineapples, rubber balls filled with gelatin, plastic bottles filled with water—failed to act in the desired manner. All this contrary evidence was ignored by Alvarez in his zeal to highlight the behavior of the melons.

Alvarez's claim is, of course, true. He had not used the "Edison technique." He had done something even worse. Using his own theory, he had figured out exactly what kind of target would produce the effect he wanted to produce. He told Buckingham to use taped melons, and they behaved just as Alvarez believed they would. Then he simply failed to mention all the other targets much more like human skulls that produced no retrograde motion when shot. He describes the melon shoots as "tests" and "experiments," but perhaps his term "performances" is more accurate. In sum, Alvarez cherry-picked his results, mentioning only those that buttressed his theory. In actuality, his tests undermined his theory and highlighted its shortcomings.[23]

The results of the melon experiments were never published in The Magnet, and no article ever appeared in Physics Today. When several years had passed and there had been no publication, it seemed likely that Alvarez had taken to heart Hoch's criticism and put his notes on the melon tests in a drawer alongside notes for the unfortunate flag/shockwave theory. It would have been better if Alvarez had done this or even published his equations as simply proof of concept. But he did neither. Instead, he simply ignored Hoch's criticism, waited six years, and then published his "jet effect theory" and carefully chosen details of the melon tests in the September 1976 issue of the *American Journal of Physics*.

What seems odd is the delay. Why wait six years to publish the cherry-picked results of such obviously amateurish tests? Had something happened in the world to prompt its publication?[24]

Indeed, something had happened. As the next chapter describes, a year earlier, a single dramatic public event had occurred that overnight had changed public opinion and led to the creation of the House Select Committee on Assassinations to reopen the investigation of the case. Was Alvarez's publication of his jet effect theory his attempt to undercut this groundswell? To once again "restore some sanity to the American public"? Perhaps even to prevent the establishment of the committee? It would appear so.

What is known is that his theory was cited at several points by the committee and soon thereafter found its niche as part of the received wisdom on the case. Over time his claims slipped into the public imagination as a full explanation for what we see on the Zapruder film, becoming part of the case's folklore. Today one can turn to numerous sites on the Internet and see this folklore mentioned in citations by Warren Commission supporters. Magically, the specifics of the Alvarez shooting experiments have been generalized into the proposition that a human head will jump backward if it is hit from the rear by a bullet. None of the clear and significant differences between Dealey Plaza and the San Leandro range are recalled. All that is remembered is the extraordinary credentials of Luis Alvarez and the fact that his article was published in the much-respected *American Journal of Physics*.

From the larger historical perspective, neither Alvarez's discovery of blurs in the Zapruder film nor his largely irrelevant melon experiments would warrant any more attention than a footnote about a gadfly scientist were it not for his far more important role six years later in leading an attack by a panel of distinguished scientists on an enormously important piece of hard scientific evidence showing that the president was shot in the head from the right front. That attack had a profound and lasting impact on the case. The initial discovery of this evidence and its acceptance by the House Select Committee on Assassinations is the subject of the next three chapters.

PART II

AFTERMATH—THE 1970s

CHAPTER 10   CHANGES—AND A *GOOD NIGHT AMERICA* SHOCKER

On July 20, 1969, Neil Armstrong set foot on the moon. A few days later, our plane broke through cloud cover and began its final approach to Kastrup Airport, Copenhagen. As I looked down on the crazy quilt of Danish roofs, I could not help thinking of when Nancy and I had left the city in August 1962. We had been poor as church mice then, getting along on an American-Scandinavian Foundation scholarship, moving around Copenhagen even in the winter on a 150-cc red Vespa scooter. We had been a couple then. Now we were a family. Sleeping peacefully to my right was three-and-a-half-year-old Everson (Ev), his red hair glinting in the morning light slanting through the window. On the other side of Nancy sat Lis, who would be five in just a few days, smiling up at her mother as they talked about something.

Thanks to a Guggenheim Fellowship and half pay from Haverford, the total amounted to one-and-one-half times my yearly salary. What a difference the money made! We had already purchased a Volvo to be delivered in Copenhagen, and we had enough left over to rent a place in one of Copenhagen's nicer suburbs. Two weeks later, we had picked up the Volvo and rented a two-bedroom villa in Hellerup, just north of Copenhagen's center along the Oresund. Within another week, I had a place to set up my Underwood portable typewriter and my set of Søren Kierkegaard's *Papirer* on the second floor. Within a month of our arrival, I had started writing my critical biography of the Danish thinker.

After the political turbulence of the last few years in the United States, it was pleasant to enjoy such a quiet and comfortable world. As the days shortened dramatically that fall, only now and then would we read in the Danish papers about the Vietnam War and the protest movement. The Kennedy assassination had disappeared from view and dropped out of mind. What we had experienced in the 1960s often seemed like the sound of a disturbance that was drifting further and further away. Denmark had its own tensions, but it was a happy, fully humanized society. Our little family sank into domestic bliss, enjoying the spring flowers in the garden and the cherries on the tree when they became ripe. My writing went well. We enjoyed a simple happiness.

When we returned to Haverford in the summer of 1970, the landscape seemed to have abruptly shifted. So much had changed. On the one hand, I had been given early tenure as an associate professor, and my book on Kierkegaard had been picked up by Knopf. I was working on a second book of Kierkegaard essays for Doubleday and was able to teach exactly what I wanted to teach. In addition, we had been given a six-bedroom Victorian home that looked out on Merion Field and the Duck Pond for a monthly rent of $325. Haverford was more than living up to its billing as the stage for a drama about a small liberal arts college. Comfort was being piled on comfort.

At the same time, the national stage had changed irrevocably. That May, Nixon had invaded Cambodia and spread the Vietnam War to a third country. All the promises of secret plans for peace had proved empty. The political landscape had become darker and more desperate. Among our friends in the protest movement, dissent had shifted to resistance. In March 1971, the Media, Pennsylvania, office of the FBI was broken into and files stolen.[1] Later release of the files showed documentary proof of the Counterintelligence Program (COINTELPRO) and its recruitment of a Haverford athletic trainer and various administrative personnel at nearby Swarthmore College.

Was I happy? Perhaps so, perhaps not. Jean-Paul Sartre wrote in one of his novels that "we live our lives as if we are telling ourselves a story, and we live surrounded by the stories of others."[2] Sartre argued that each life has its own story and that it is endlessly repeated, like echoes reverberating from a single sound. I wanted to find the right story, one that was engrossing, and it was becoming clearer that the story of living at Haverford in this picture-perfect small college world was not going to be it.

Time passed. My two books were favorably reviewed. Classes were going well, and it became easy to teach much the same course year after year. Lis and Ev were flourishing in the campus environment of safe fields and playmates only doors away. Nancy was not happy being a faculty wife but found other jobs—first as a substitute teacher, then working for a motorcycle dealer, next working for a wealthy art collector—that had some interest.

I found myself looking for something quite different from this comfortable but undemanding life. In the summer of 1972, I rode my BMW motorcycle to San Francisco and back. The next year, we spent the summer with friends in Berkeley. The following spring, Haverford underwrote my attending a

German-language class in a small Bavarian village for two months. Nancy came over, and we toured on a new BMW bike. The following summer, I rode the bike to San Francisco and back. In retrospect I realized these were attempts to introduce something more demanding, more adventurous, into the lineaments of a life that had become too comfortable.

The Kennedy assassination had virtually disappeared from press accounts. As for the assassination underground, what in the 1960s had been a selfless community of inquiry became in the 1970s a swamp of competing conspiracy theories and warring factions. Sylvia Meagher and I remained friends, but I drifted away from the others. The collapse of the Garrison prosecution of Clay Shaw had cast a deep shadow over the whole enterprise. During these years, I would occasionally be called for a press interview or to make a cameo appearance on a TV show, but it often seemed as if we were stirring a soup that had long ago become tepid. All the questions we had asked in the 1960s still remained unresolved, waiting for answers that never seemed to come.

On November 22, 1973, the tenth anniversary of the shooting, I took the train down to Washington to attend a conference devoted to the event. Its organizer was Bud Fensterwald, a Harvard-trained lawyer and an old Washington hand. Bud had worked in the State Department in the 1950s, defending employees accused by Senator Joseph McCarthy of being Communist Party members. In the 1960s, he was chief counsel to the Senate Judiciary Committee under Senator Edward Long. In 1969, he cofounded the Committee to Investigate Assassinations, principally to continue the investigation of the John Kennedy assassination.

One evening during the conference, Bud held a party at his brownstone in Georgetown. A few notables—Norman Mailer and author and journalist Robert Blair Kaiser among them—were there as well as some friends from the old days. The buzz that evening came from a showing of the Zapruder film by a young man in his twenties, Robert Groden. This was not just any copy of the Zapruder film. It was infinitely better than the muddy copies circulating out of the Garrison trial, and it combined several runs (some close-up, some full-frame) of the Zapruder film intercut with footage from films taken by Dealey Plaza bystanders Marie Muchmore and Orville Nix.

The film highlighted what appeared to be the back of an individual's head and what looked like the outline of a rifle hidden in a clump of bushes just below Zapruder's pedestal. "Well, that's crapola," I thought. "No one could have fired from there and gotten away with it since the spot was no more than a few feet from Abraham Zapruder and Marilyn Sitzman." But the resolution and quality of the film were extremely high, so much so that after the film had been screened at the conference, someone had accused Groden of being a CIA plant since no one else had been able to get such a good copy.

Afterward I introduced myself to Groden and mentioned that because of Vince Salandria and Ray Marcus, we were part of the same fraternity. Dressed in full 1970s garb—sport coat, turtleneck, and long sideburns, everything but bell-bottom trousers—Groden, who was about ten years younger than I, seemed like an interesting guy. He said a few nice things about Six Seconds, and I got him talking about his film. He explained how the close-up run of the film had been "stabilized." He had rephotographed each frame, centering it on JFK's right ear. This made the frames flow together and the whole film much clearer to watch. The head-shot sequence, as it always does, drew a gasp from the audience. Groden told me that this was the first public showing of the film, which he had obtained years before and had been working on since. He also mentioned that he had been born on November 22. I thanked him for all he had done and told him I thought his copy of the film was quite wonderful.

Later that night, I asked myself, "Who is Robert Groden, and how did he get his copy of the Zapruder film?" Eventually, when our paths again crossed, I got the answer from Bob himself.

In 1969, Groden was working for A-1 Record Sales in Manhattan.[3] In June, he lost his job and went to the New York State Employment Office, where a counselor asked him if he knew anything about photography. He told her he knew his way around a darkroom and had done some still photography, but he didn't know anything about film. She said a friend of her boyfriend had something to do with an optical effects firm and that they were looking for a trainee. That firm was EFX Unlimited, owned by a man named Moses Weitzman. It did motion-picture optical effects (dissolves, fade-outs, titles) for the film and TV industry. Groden applied and was hired immediately.

It turned out that Moses Weitzman and Groden shared an interest in the Kennedy assassination. Weitzman pointed out that back in 1967 or 1968, he had been asked to do some work on the Zapruder film by Time-Life. They wanted their 8-mm original blown up to 35 mm, and EFX was the only shop in New York City that could do this. Weitzman had kept both a 35-mm color negative and a 16-mm color negative of the film. He showed these to Groden and a few months later gave them to him. Weitzman may or may not have had other copies. For his part, Groden gave Weitzman a copy of Six Seconds that he had purchased for $1.98.

In the early 1970s, he worked on the film using his stabilization technique and the skills he had learned from Weitzman. Also in the early 1970s, cigarette commercials were banned from television, and Weitzman lost about 40 percent of his business. Groden was laid off. He went on to other jobs but kept working on the film. Before showing it publicly, he'd gotten permission from Weitzman. Weitzman asked Groden only to make sure he was not connected in any way to the showing, as it would be bad for his business.

That was where things stood when Bob Groden and I met for the first time in November 1973. Two years would pass before our paths would cross again just prior to an extraordinary moment of national significance that Groden helped bring about.

Fifteen months after Bud Fensterwald's conference in Washington, Groden showed the film for only the second time, this time at the Assassination Information Bureau conference in Boston. The event turned out to be a big occasion, with thousands attending. The press covered it in detail. When Bob showed the film, some reporters photographed it off the screen, and clips of it were shown on local news programs.

Interest in the film was now building. The CBS affiliate in Washington, DC, wanted Groden to show it in Washington. He did so and then flew to California with Dick Gregory to show it on comedian Mort Sahl's TV program, *Both Sides Now*. These showings were only on local stations, but word of Groden's film was becoming a groundswell.

Then, in early February 1975, a producer from Geraldo Rivera's late-night ABC TV program, *Good Night America*, called. He expressed interest in having Groden appear on Rivera's show to screen the film as part of a series of program segments that week devoted to the John Kennedy assassination. This development was momentous. *Good Night America* was the prize inasmuch as the film would be shown to a national audience. Finally, after twelve years, the American people would get to see it.

I was also recruited to participate in one of the *Good Night America* segments. My cameo appearance was hardly worth mentioning. By this time, the appearance of defenders and critics of the Warren Report had become so ritualistic as to resemble a kind of Kabuki theater enacted over and over. The arguments raged, but the televised format was never able to reduce the complexity of the event and the arguments surrounding it to an acceptable level of simplicity. Former Commission Counsel David Belin was there, defending the report, all in the service of "fair and balanced." Everything Belin and I said turned out to be eminently forgettable.

The only interesting part for me was when Nancy and I visited Geraldo Rivera in his apartment on the upper West Side. At that point, he had only recently burst onto the national media scene. He had made his TV reputation with an exposé of how mentally retarded patients at Willowbrook Hospital were being neglected and sometimes abused. His work won him a Peabody Award, and his career was on an upward trajectory with *Good Night America*.

Sitting in his living room, we could see Central Park out the window in the fading afternoon light. Rivera appeared at ease and made us feel welcome. He struck me as a sharp, engaged professional journalist very much in command of his role as a major network host in a high-pressure environment. As Rivera and I discussed the Kennedy assassination show planned for a few days later, Nancy's eyes took in the paintings on several walls. At the time, Rivera was married to novelist Kurt Vonnegut's daughter Edith. She was not present, but her paintings were. They were very good, Nancy thought, not amateurish at all, and with subjects that were strange and vaguely mythic.

I showed Rivera photos of some exhibits I could use, and we talked about whether I should bring along my rifle, a duplicate of the 6.5-mm Mannlicher-Carcano found in the depository. Rivera mentioned Bob Groden, but I don't recall him saying Bob would be showing the Zapruder film. He did ask about the film, and I told him what I knew, including LIFE's lawsuit against us that had ended in a summary judgment defeat for LIFE. That seemed to interest him.

A few days later, Bob Groden, his Zapruder film in hand, arrived in New York to tape the show. At this juncture, the Time-Life lion roared once again. Groden, who was present during the behind-the-scenes drama, recently told me the story.

On the *Good Night America* set a few hours before the taping, Geraldo Rivera asked Groden if he had the right to broadcast the film. Groden said no, he did not, and explained what had happened regarding Time-Life's 1967 lawsuit against *Six Seconds*. A lawyer for ABC who was present on the set and who heard this exchange abruptly announced, "We're not going to show it." Rivera looked at the lawyer, paused a beat, and then said, "Then you can get yourself a new boy." The impasse was bucked upstairs to ABC's top management. Time-Life's lawyers had become aware of ABC's plans and threatened to sue for copyright infringement. It was also clear that Geraldo Rivera from the outset had every intention of showing the film, and he was willing to put his career on the line to make it happen. As the minutes passed, tension on the *Good Night America* set grew. Finally the word came down: screen the film. Rivera had prevailed. He had made a gutsy, high-stakes move that made possible a truly historic moment.

Groden's showing of the film, sandwiched between segments starring actress Raquel Welch and an author hawking a book on the Bermuda Triangle, was broadcast on March 6, 1975, and was a bona fide shocker. For the first time, a stunned national audience saw clearly the evidence of the Zapruder film. The characteristic intake of breath when an audience sees the president's head explode and his body slammed backward was heard from coast to coast. What ordinary viewers could see with their own eyes made no sense given the orthodox account of a single gunman firing from the rear. Arbitron ratings for the show trumped Johnny Carson's *Tonight Show* ratings for the first and only time in *Good Night America*'s history.

The effect was electric. Literally overnight the center of gravity shifted toward empaneling a new investigation of the event. Just days after the screening, Congressman Thomas Downing of Virginia introduced into Congress a resolution establishing a select committee to reinvestigate the Kennedy assassination. Bob Groden later learned from Geraldo Rivera's staff that the morning after the broadcast, ABC received from Time-Life a onetime license to show the film backdated to before the screening. A month later, Time-Life gave the film back to the Zapruder family for $1.00. It is tempting to suggest that senior management had realized that continuing to guard the Zapruder film as a revenue-generating asset would subject it to ridicule and embarrassment.

Over the following months, I worked with Bob to lobby various members of Congress. It would be nearly a year before the House Select Committee on Assassinations (HSCA) was established. The HSCA was given until the end of 1978 to produce its findings.

From a historical perspective, the creation of the HSCA was just one more dramatic event during a wild decade of national tumult. The 1972 burglary of the national Democratic Party headquarters in the Washington, DC, Watergate office complex had enmeshed President Nixon in a scandal that led to his resignation in August 1974. And less than a month after the Zapruder film's screening on *Good Night America*, Saigon fell to the North Vietnamese, ending America's disastrous twelve-year war in Vietnam that had cost more than a million lives, including those of fifty-eight thousand American servicemen and -women.

Those years were a time of change for me as well. In July 1976, I started a year of sabbatical leave, this time living in Bolinas, a small coastal village in rural West Marin County about forty-five minutes north of the Golden Gate Bridge. Nancy and I and the kids settled into a rustic redwood home that looked down the long curve of Stinson Beach to San Francisco beyond. I was plugging away on what I hoped would be a critical biography of Friedrich Nietzsche. My previous book on Søren Kierkegaard, published by Knopf, had assured my promotion to full professor. But things back at Haverford had become more than a little too comfortable. True, the college provided the kind of academic life that I had looked forward to back in graduate school, but now that it was real, it seemed more than a bit suffocating. In addition, my Nietzsche book was going nowhere. I was restless. I needed to get out of the house and do something else.

Sometime that fall, I met a woman in a nearby café who a few years earlier had gone through a vicious divorce. Her ex-husband had stolen their child and fled to Canada. She had hired Hal Lipset, a renowned San Francisco private investigator (PI) who was widely regarded as the dean of American private detectives, to steal back her child. He had managed to do so with panache, and they had become friends. She set up a dinner for the three of us at an upscale restaurant in San Francisco. When we got to dessert, acting on impulse, I hit up Lipset for a job. Oddly, he didn't turn me down on the spot, and a few days later, he agreed to hire me as an operative. The pay was $5 an hour. I think in the back of his mind, he must have chuckled over the idea of hiring a leftist professor to work for management in a violent strike, tailing union people around the Oakland docks.

I worked on that case for two months, operating out of the elegant Victorian mansion in San Francisco's wealthy Pacific Heights neighborhood that served as Lipset's home and office. The days were long. Still, I loved the work and its challenges—staying unnoticed, tracking the "subject," knowing right away whether I had blown the tail or succeeded. In the beginning, I was terrible. Then, chastened by failure, I got better at it. Just as my case expired, Lipset's junior partner, David Fechheimer, resigned to go off on his own. He asked if I wanted to work for him as his operative.

I jumped at the chance, and in February 1977, I entered a world as distant from the comforts of Haverford as one could imagine. The irony was not lost on me that my career track as a sleuth had begun at the very highest level, as a decently paid consultant for Time-Life investigating arguably the greatest unsolved crime in American history, and now I was on the bottom rung—an unlicensed, unsung, entry-level operative working long hours for minimum wage.

Fechheimer had a distinguished reputation in his own right, so our cases were never run-of-the-mill. One of our first cases involved Paul Skyhorse and Richard Mohawk, two American Indian Movement organizers charged with the murder of a cab driver in southern California. The lead defense counsel was Leonard Weinglass, a legendary attorney of the left. That case and most of those that followed were fascinating. Fechheimer's clientele was varied:

well-heeled private individuals, insurance companies, entertainers, and—because a principal area of his expertise was criminal defense—accused smugglers, drug dealers, and murderers, to name a few.

My apprenticeship passed quickly. On paper at least, I was still a full professor, but my Nietzsche book languished. My year of sabbatical leave was at half pay, but when the time came in the spring of 1977 to order books for next fall's classes, I couldn't pick up the phone. Instead, I wrote a letter to Haverford asking for a second year off, this time without pay. The leave was granted. I hoped I could make it on $15/hour or $150/day, but I wasn't sure.

That summer of 1977—out of the blue—came an invitation from the HSCA to come to Washington, DC, for a two-day conference with a group of assassination researchers to offer advice to the committee's chief counsel, Robert Blakey. I had given little thought to the Kennedy assassination since my work two years previously, lobbying Congress to create the HSCA, but I was happy to accept the invitation. Thus, on a hot Saturday morning in September, I walked into room 3618 of the House Annex Building, just down the hall from where the HSCA had its home—and within the first minute knew for a certainty that I was never going back to Haverford.

It was the table that did it. With its broad Formica top and oval shape, it was like the table in Hall Building 211 on the Haverford campus. If I had returned to Haverford, there would have been fifteen or sixteen students sitting around it. There were roughly the same number here, only these people were not students. They were a lot older than students, and the table was not at Haverford, and this was not a class.

In my bones, I knew that my former life was over and that something completely new had begun. Less than a month before, I had been in New England on a drug case. I'd picked up a can of drugs in the fog outside the house on which the Drug Enforcement Agency had been sitting. Nancy had then come east, and we had ended up renting the house (posing as a vacationing Haverford professor and his wife) and recovering $30,000 in hundreds from under the floorboards of the attic. That was after another drug case in Florida where I'd met a pimpled kid at the Miami airport and turned over clips from the New Orleans *Times-Picayune*.

No, I couldn't go back. I had always felt strange posing as a "philosopher" because I knew in my heart I was no more a philosopher than Donald Duck. I had never believed in philosophy because I had never believed you could figure the whole thing out. So when I looked at the Formica gray of the tabletop and it took me back to Haverford, it was not with a sense of longing. It was just something I remembered from the past, a kind of reference point.

I looked around the room. The table was in the middle with windows on one side. Across the table sat Robert Blakey, the committee's chief counsel. As the meeting got underway, he described the rest of us as those "who have labored in the vineyard . . . [as] voices crying in the wilderness" and said that "but for people like you, this investigation would not have been reopened." He also asked us to sign a nondisclosure agreement that, he said, "was tougher than the one they [the CIA] ask their people to sign."

I didn't think of myself as a voice crying in the wilderness, and when Blakey got down to business, it became clear that our voices would be tightly controlled. The basic idea was that the flow of information would run in only one direction—from us to him. Since the critics had been studying this case longer than anyone else, Counsel Blakey wanted to know what suggestions we might have for his investigation. He wanted to hear what questions we wanted answered. None of us had any difficulty with this approach.

Across the table was Paul Hoch, whom I'd known since 1967 and who had never bent during the Luis Alvarez scuffle.[4] Peter Dale Scott was another friend from Berkeley who pursued what he called the "deep structure" of the case. And over there was my good friend Sylvia Meagher. Mary Ferrell, Larry Harris, and J. Gary Shaw were all from the Dallas area. Mary had accumulated remarkable files on the shooting. The other two were unknown to me. Jim Kostman represented the Assassination Information Bureau, which organized meetings and teach-ins around the country. And there was Kathy Kinsella, who had helped in the lobbying to set up this House committee.

The discussion veered into various claims of conspiracy, of which I had little interest and even less knowledge. As the discussion droned on, I found my mind wandering. Little did I know that in attending this conference, I would be present at one of the pivotal moments in the history of the whole case.

There was a short break for lunch, and then we were back at it. Maybe it was the lunch or maybe it was the heat, but at one point I caught myself nodding off to sleep. I laughed inwardly. Here we had finally achieved what we had been working on for years. A new investigation had been started, and we were being asked what to investigate. And you, Thompson, you fall asleep! I got up, walked to the window. and looked out on D Street. As it was a Saturday, there was little traffic. I went back to my seat and sat down.

Larry Harris was talking about Patrolman Joe Marshall Smith, who was directing traffic in front of the depository. After the shooting, Smith ran down to the knoll area and felt silly that he had drawn his revolver. A guy in a sports shirt and slacks appeared out of the bushes and showed him Secret Service credentials. The only problem was that all the Secret Service people in Dealey

Plaza followed protocol and stayed with the motorcade. So who was this guy Joe Marshall Smith encountered?

I spoke up and pointed out that our LIFE magazine team had wanted to talk to Smith, but the Dallas police wouldn't permit it. The discussion veered off in another direction. Then, rather abruptly, Mary Ferrell spoke:

> MS. FERRELL: I wanted to drop one thing in. Gary Shaw recently took my copy of the police tapes . . . and Gary took that to a broadcasting man . . . and they have taken it now to about three studios. . . . Anyway, they have, by blocking out sound—I don't know, the sound waves—it's foreign to me . . .
>
> MR. BLAKEY: Stripping it.
>
> MS. FERRELL: Stripping it. They have heard eight distinct gunshots. . . .

Gary Shaw interjected that not eight but seven gunshots were apparent.

> MR. SHAW: Well, I wouldn't say eight distinct; I would say probably seven. You— maybe with the mike button depressed on the motorcycle in Dealey Plaza at the time of the shots, by stripping out the sound of the motorcycle and such as that, they were able to pinpoint certain sounds of the gunfire as it occurred, and it has gone from two studios with fine equipment and it is above my head.
> . . .

The portion of the police tapes that Shaw referenced was a period of about five and a half minutes on channel 1 (the main Dallas-wide police channel) during which a mic button on one of the police motorcycles had become stuck in the on position, causing the constant noise of its engine to drown out almost all radio traffic on that channel. It was during this time that the assassination took place. The Warren Commission knew about this incident but regarded it as inconsequential, given that malfunctioning mic buttons were a fairly common problem with Dallas Police Department motorcycle radios. Commission transcripts of channel 1 did not include any transmissions from the period of interruption. Gary Mack, the "broadcasting man" who worked for a Dallas radio station, was intrigued by the possibility that the stuck mic button may have been on a motorcycle in Dealey Plaza that had mistakenly been tuned to channel 1, not channel 2, the special event channel used for the motorcade. If so, even with the constant drone of the cycle engine, the mic might have picked up come indication of shots fired, even if nothing sounding remotely like shots could be heard by simply listening.

Either that day or the next, I mentioned to Counsel Blakey that the committee ought to track down the original or a first copy of the Dallas police transmissions and send it to Bolt, Beranek and Newman (BBN), the sound lab in Cambridge, Massachusetts, that had analyzed the eighteen-and-a-half-minute gap in the infamous Nixon tape made during the height of the Watergate scandal.

No one present at our two-day meeting could have imagined that Mary Ferrell's suggestion would lead to the discovery in March 1978 of Dallas police recordings covering the crucial five-minute period during which the assassination occurred. The acoustic information it yielded would constitute powerful new evidence destined to have a profound impact on the deliberations of the HSCA.

CHAPTER 11   ACOUSTICS

The remarks Mary Ferrell made to Chief Counsel Robert Blakey and the rest of us that summer Saturday in 1977 were not lost on Blakey. Within a few days, HSCA investigators visited her in Dallas and picked up her reel-to-reel copy of the tape. They also obtained the reel-to-reel copy of Dallas radio station staffer Gary Mack, the "broadcasting man" who had actually discovered the gunshots. Both were copies of assassination radio transmissions that had begun appearing around Dallas as souvenirs in the weeks and months following the event. Mary Ferrell's copy came from a Dallas journalist and researcher, Judith Bonner, who in turn had received it from a DPD dispatcher.

Now, who would do the analysis of these copies?

Blakey contacted the Society of American Acoustics (SAA) and requested a short list of candidates to undertake the analysis.[1] Not surprisingly, the SAA put the Cambridge, Massachusetts, firm of BBN at the top of its list. BBN was ideally suited to the task.[2] In addition to its world-class reputation and previous analysis of the suspect eighteen-and-a-half-minute gap in the Watergate tapes, BBN scientist James Barger had carried out a brilliant analysis of the 1970 Kent State shootings that traced the first gunshots to where several national guardsmen were standing. It was hoped that he could apply a similar technique to the Dealey Plaza shooting.

In his book on the HSCA investigation and hearings, Blakey's own description of his first contact with Barger makes clear that the BBN testing was meant to be simply due diligence. If tests showed that there were no gunshots on the tape, Blakey would be free to pursue more important questions. He wrote, "Dr. Barger recognized that it was as important to us to find nothing on the tape as it was to find any set number of gunshots. He suggested, therefore, that after he had made an effort to clean it up, he would conduct a series of tests that would prove that there were no gunshots recorded on it."[3]

If that proved to be the case, it would not be necessary to do an acoustical reconstruction in Dallas, and the committee would be saved both time and money. Barger would provide Blakey with a cheap and quick way to prove that the tape contained no gunshots.

Shortly thereafter, in October 1977, BBN declared the material provided by Ferrell so far down the line of multigenerational copies that it could not be used for analysis.

Moriarty's Find

That was where matters stood until one day in early March 1978 when HSCA investigator Jack Moriarty visited the offices of a Dallas private investigation firm. Blakey had wisely chosen Moriarty because he was a former Washington, DC, homicide detective who could speak cop to cop to members of the Dallas police. By 1978 the hostility of the DPD to the media and outside assassination investigators was both total and intense. From the weekend of November 23 on, the DPD had been a target of the national press corps. The department's failure to record the many hours of its interrogation of Oswald, plus Oswald's murder on national TV inside DPD headquarters, made the Dallas police look like Keystone Cops—if not something more sinister. By the time the HSCA arrived on the scene in the late 1970s, the Dallas police were not cooperating with anyone from out of town. Moriarty's task was to investigate but also to make friends with present and former DPD officers. The approach worked. Over time, many DPD officers came to trust him. On March 10, 1978, Moriarty's presence in Dallas bore fruit.[4]

On this trip—one of fifty Moriarty made to Dallas—he interviewed a retired Dallas police detective, Morris Brumley. Their meeting took place in the offices of Brumley's employer, Paul McCaghren Associates, a private investigation firm founded by ex-assistant DPD chief Paul McCaghren.

In 1963, McCaghren was a lieutenant in the burglary and theft division. Following the assassination, he looked into how Jack Ruby got into the Dallas police building to murder Oswald. By 1969, McCaghren had become head of police intelligence. Chief Jesse Curry had retired in 1966 and been replaced by Chief Charles Batchelor. Batchelor had found a locked filing cabinet outside his office filled with Kennedy assassination material and assigned the material to McCaghren. McCaghren kept these materials in the Intelligence Division until 1971 or 1972 and then took them home "for safekeeping." He stored them in a trunk in his attic.

On the morning of Moriarty's interview with Brumley, the materials were resting in a Permafile banker's box in McCaghren's office. At one point, while McCraghren was sitting in on the interview of Brumley by Moriarty, his secretary interrupted to tell him he had a phone call. McCaghren rose and paused for a moment.

"Before you leave," he said to Moriarty, "I'd like you to step down the hall to my office. In the meantime, this will give you an idea what I have to offer." He handed Moriarty an envelope in which he said were "the three original tapes of channels 1 and 2," adding, "There's more—much more."

Moriarty recounted this incident when I called him in 1979. By that time I was a licensed PI, which made a difference with him. He was comfortable and expansive. He said that he quickly wrapped up his interview of Brumley and went to McCaghren's office. McCaghren was on the phone but pointed to a cardboard box sitting on the floor in the corner. As Moriarty sifted through the contents of the box—photographs, transcripts, interviews, and documents on the assassination—he became excited. Its contents appeared to date from shortly after the assassination and had remained undisturbed since. In the envelope McCaghren had given him were transcripts and three reels of tape. One was labeled "Channel 2, 10 AM–5:12 PM" and other two "Channel 1, 9:45 AM–2:15 PM."

"I recognized the importance of it," Moriarty told me, "but I didn't realize how far it would go."

Like many of the big breaks in my own cases, it had appeared unannounced, almost incognito. I mentioned my similar experiences, and we shared a laugh. Moriarty, following by-the-book procedure on evidence handling, left the envelope and tapes with McCaghren and returned the next morning to McCaghren's office to make an inventory of the box's contents.[5] He then flew back to Washington and picked up a subpoena for the material. Three days later, he was again flying back to Washington with the file box that contained what would prove to be what students of the assassination had been seeking for fifteen years: a break in the case—in fact, the single most important piece of assassination evidence discovered since 1963.

Upon receiving the three reels of tape that Moriarty had delivered to the HSCA, Chief Counsel Blakey transferred them to James Barger's team at BBN for analysis.

Gunshots?

To understand how Barger went about his testing, it is imperative to know the basics of how the DPD radio network operated.[6] It was described by an electrical engineer as "a push-to-talk/stop-when-there's-no-carrier" kind of system, broadcasting in FM, chosen for its superior sound quality in comparison to its AM counterpart.[7] Each radio in a patrol car or on a motorcycle included a handheld microphone attached by a coiled cord to the radio. When the push-to-talk button on the microphone was pressed, it sent out a carrier wave carrying the officer's voice. The signal from an individual microphone was picked up by relay receivers scattered around the city of Dallas. Any receiver would automatically transfer it by a leased telephone line back to the dispatcher's office at Dallas police headquarters. There it would be split into duplicate signals, with one signal going to a dispatcher monitoring the particular radio channel and the other signal going to a recorder.

The DPD system was equipped with electronic circuitry that acted as a kind of automatic volume adjustment that enhanced radio communications. Called automatic gain control (AGC), the feature was designed to instantly dampen very loud signals, such as gunshots, while amplifying weaker signals, such as diminishing gunshot echoes, in effect converting all the signals into a comfortable listening range when broadcast over the DPD net. As such, the resulting wave form of a gunshot and echoes would be somewhat distorted, showing signals of similar amplitude across its length (see the wave form of the evidence shot in Figure 11-5).

Two channels were in operation on November 22. Channel 1 was the basic channel for all police operations. Channel 2 was an auxiliary channel covering special events—in this case, President Kennedy's motorcade and visit to Dallas. Even in 1963, one might imagine a tape deck with its reels slowly turning continuously and able to log several hours of radio traffic before a reel change was required. Not so, however, with the Dallas police in 1963. Instead of a tape deck, radio traffic was logged by two dictation devices designed in the 1940s for the business world. The recording of channel 1 (the DPD's normal citywide radio net) was done by a Dictaphone that used a stylus inscribing a groove onto a blue plastic belt (called a Dictabelt) mounted on a rotating cylinder. The machine itself had been purchased a decade earlier and was regularly serviced by the Dictaphone company. (See color photo gallery, Plate 6.)

In the case of channel 2, the task was handled by a Gray Audograph with a stylus that inscribed sound on thin, flat discs roughly the size of a 45-rpm record (see color photo gallery, Plate 7). Its purchase date is unknown, and it was not regularly serviced. Both machines were old and had their eccentricities, but the Audograph was clearly less reliable. Its playback needle would often jump both forward and backward. If it jumped forward, there could be a possible loss of content; if it jumped backward, there would be a repeat of content. Both units were duplex. That is, they held a second Dictabelt or flat disk in reserve while the first one recorded.

Photo 11-1. Example of an analog clock with a digital face and flip-down numbers, circa 1963.

In the dispatcher's office at Dallas police headquarters that day, three dispatchers (radio operators) were on duty in the radio room, two monitoring channel 1 and one monitoring channel 2. According to the office supervisor, Sergeant James Bowles, the dispatchers were furnished with twelve-hour digital display clocks to facilitate their broadcast of time notations. Since the actual time notations were important not only to the dispatchers but for later review in court cases, the digital clocks were not permitted to stray more than a minute from official time, which was kept in City Hall and synchronized to a wall clock visible to the dispatchers. Once every minute and every time a dispatcher spoke to a unit, he or she would announce the time. Hence, both recordings are punctuated with dispatcher time notations such as "12:28" or "12:31."

To save on recording belts and disks, both recorders were sound-actuated to shut off after a few seconds of silence. Bowles said this "run-out time" was four seconds, but later tests showed he was wrong. The actual time was 6.5 seconds for channel 1 and 7.5 seconds for channel 2.[8] This shutoff feature was not activated on channel 1 during the five-and-a-half-minute period when the sound of the motorcycle's engine droned on continuously, preventing any auto shutoff. It was during this period that the suspected shot impulses were recorded on channel 1.

Jim Barger's team began by rounding up equipment that replicated the DPD communication setup. They got an old Motorola radio of the kind carried on DPD cycles and a Dictaphone machine similar to the one used by the Dallas police. Next, they fired test shots from a Mannlicher-Carcano rifle at various distances from a microphone that picked up the shots. Each gunshot signal was then input to a computer that displayed on an oscillograph what

the sound impulse looked like. The wave form of the gunshot had a particular shape and a particular amplitude. It had a double peak showing first
the arrival of the muzzle blast and immediate echoes followed by the arrival
of later echoes. In addition, the display showed a reduction in the gunshot
amplitude (or loudness) imposed on the signal by the radio's AGC circuitry.
Now Barger's team had what they were looking for—the distinctive wave
form of a gunshot as it would appear on the Dictabelt.

The next question to answer was where exactly on the channel 1 recording
would one expect to find gunshot impulses? Here Barger's team was helped
by transmissions recorded on channel 2, the auxiliary channel recorded on
the Audograph. There was no motorcycle noise, but on this channel DPD
Chief Curry would periodically report his position in the lead car of the
motorcade. Curry reported in a normal tone of voice that he was "at the Triple
Underpass," and twenty-eight seconds later excitedly said, "Go to the hospital!" Moreover, since a dispatcher for the channel announced "12:30" during
this twenty-eight-second interval, this indicates that the shooting happened
between Chief Curry's two reports—between 12:29 and 12:31 p.m. The BBN
scientists would focus on this same two-minute time frame on channel 1.

Initial Analysis

Barger's team began by filtering and recording the entire five-minute segment through two filters designed to reveal the presence of any transient wave
forms suggestive of gunshots that might be masked by the loud, repetitive
noise of the motorcycle. The outputs from both filters were plotted on a scale
where five inches equaled one-tenth of a second.[9]

Specifically, they searched for three indicia: (1) the loud, impulsive sound
of the muzzle blast; (2) a pattern of sounds of decreasing amplitude indicative of echoes bouncing around the plaza after the muzzle blast; and (3) the
appearance of a shock wave from the bullet. Since bullet shock waves produce
sound in the 1-kHz to 3.2-kHz frequency range, by using a filter that screens
frequencies outside that range, they could readily identify the presence of a
shock wave and a muzzle blast. The results of their analysis, even at this initial
stage, were a surprise. The plots revealed six impulse patterns that were from
a source other than the motorcycle. Closer examination showed that all but
one appeared to have the required characteristics consistent with a gunshot.

The next step was to test the hypothesis that the remaining impulse patterns were caused by gunfire. Five screening tests, in the form of yes-or-no

questions, were designed to determine whether these impulses corresponded both to the characteristics of actual gunfire and to other evidence:

1. Did the impulse patterns occur at the same time the shots were actually fired?
2. Were the impulse patterns unique?
3. Did the time span between the patterns correspond to other evidence of intervals between shots?
4. Did the shape of the wave forms resemble those generated by actual rifle fire?
5. Did the range of amplitude (loudness) of the wave forms resemble that of the echo patterns produced by the test shots?[10]

The answers to all five questions were an unequivocal yes.

At this point, the scientists well understood that the proof of gunshots they possessed was quite meager. All they had discovered thus far were five sets of oscilloscope squiggles that had passed various screening tests. Nonetheless, the big surprise was that there appeared to be five shots, not the three the Warren Report had concluded.

Still, these findings were only theoretically connected to the crime scene until some empirical testing was done to determine just what a weapon sounded like when fired there. In short, the ultimate screening test needed to be conducted at Dealey Plaza itself.

For the gunshot impulses to be confirmed as gunshots, two additional— and very stringent—conditions had to be met. First, the very complex pattern of echoes produced by a test shot bouncing off buildings around the plaza had to match an equally complex pattern of echoes (typically twenty to twenty-four) generated by the corresponding evidence shot on November 22. Second, if any of these impulses matched test shots fired in Dealey Plaza, they also had to be picked up by microphones in the plaza in a particular sequence, one that matched the topological order—the path—of a motorcycle moving through Dealey Plaza. If both of these exacting criteria were not met, the BBN team would have to reject the putative gunshots as false positives and conclude that no gunshots were recorded on November 22.

Blakey's Problem

On July 13, 1978, four months after Jack Moriarty's newly discovered tapes were delivered to the HSCA, James Barger called Blakey to tell him the results of his tests. Blakey later described the phone call:

He [Barger] said he was fully aware of the significance of what he was about to say: in fact, he even felt a little sick to his stomach, for he found himself in the embarrassing position of being unable to prove that nothing had been recorded on the tape. Further, he had not only found sounds on the tape that appeared to be recorded gunfire, but—and this was what troubled him—he had found more shots than the three that the Warren Commission had thought had been fired.[11]

Clearly, the committee's expectation had been that Barger's study would close the door on Mary Ferrell's lead. Now, the HSCA was only six months from its drop-dead deadline of January 3, 1979, when both its authority and money would run out. Up to this point, the committee's work had tended in the direction of confirming the conclusions of the Warren Commission. Barger's phone call threw a giant monkey wrench into this. What to do?

The first step was to have another expert check the work of Barger and his team. Blakey once again contacted the SAA, and it recommended the team of scientists who had appeared second on their earlier short list topped by James Barger and BBN. They were Professor Mark Weiss of Queens College, City University of New York, and his research associate Ernest Aschkenasy, who specialized in developing computer programs for handling large volumes of computer data. During the Watergate scandal, Weiss had been on the technical panel that examined the White House tape recordings at the request of Judge John Sirica. Both were hired by the committee and turned loose on Barger's study.

Quite swiftly, Weiss and Aschkenasy checked the work of Barger's team and confirmed both their methods of analysis and their conclusions. In addition, they agreed with Barger's view that an acoustical reconstruction of the assassination was of critical importance, and they approved the plan Barger had put forward for that reconstruction. Blakey agreed. After consultation with Dallas officials, the event was scheduled for Sunday, August 20, 1978.

From the perspective of the HSCA staff, the world had been flipped upside down. As Blakey himself pointed out in his book, the acoustic evidence came to be known as "Blakey's Problem."[12] In addition, Blakey went on, "More than one staffer was heard to say, 'Let's see if the professor [Blakey] can talk his way out of this one.'"[13]

Acoustic Reconstruction

It was no surprise that the committee decided to fire a 6.5-mm Carcano rifle from the sixth floor corner window of the Texas School Book Depository.[14] It

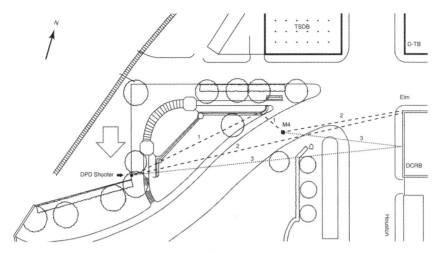

Figure 11-2. HSCA map showing the position of the test DPD shooter (*see arrow*). Dotted lines indicate three echo paths.

was somewhat of a surprise that it decided to fire both a Carcano and a .38-caliber pistol from behind the stockade fence on the knoll. That firing position matched no particular location that earlier had come under suspicion. It was not along the generally east-west section where Skinny Holland and others saw smoke and found fresh footprints and cigarette butts but instead along the generally north-south section that parallels the cement walkway.

Given that the objective of the reconstruction was to determine whether the motorcade rider whose mic button had been stuck open for five and a half minutes had also recorded gunfire, the layout of microphones in Dealey Plaza was organized accordingly. Since James Barger's recorder could process a maximum of only twelve incoming signals at a time, the test firing had to be repeated three times with the array of twelve microphones moved to new positions at eighteen-foot intervals after each firing session (see Figure 11-3).

Array 1 stretched down Houston Street in a straight line toward the corner of Elm and Houston. It was followed by array 2 with its twelve mics covering the corner of Elm and Houston. Finally, the twelve mics of array 3 stretched down Elm Street in a straight line. Within each array, the microphones were numbered in sequence from 1 to 12 as they lay along the motorcade route.

By the end of the shooting reconstruction that Sunday in late August, the scientists had recorded 432 test shots to be compared with the evidence sound impulses of November 22. Both the test patterns and the evidence impulses looked much like the pair shown in Figure 11-5. They have the general

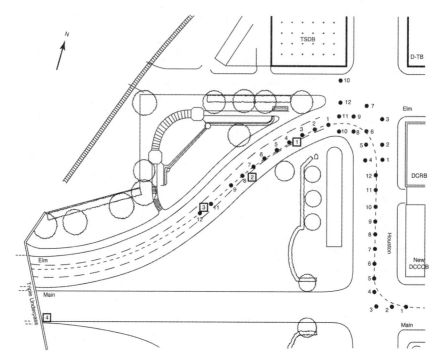

Figure 11-3. HSCA map showing the placement of targets (*numbers in squares*) and microphones (*numbered black dots*).

appearance of a comb with many teeth broken off. The length of the wave form represents about one second.

Note that the teeth of the evidence shot are significantly more pronounced than those of the test shot. This is due to channel 1's previously described AGC. The teeth sticking up are the echoes arriving after they have bounced off various structures in Dealey Plaza. The specific time of arrival shown by a tooth on the graph indicates a particular surface in the plaza from which an echo was reflected.

Still, the precision of the data is slightly limited by the scale of the map of Dealey Plaza which constrained the location accuracy of any microphone to no more than plus or minus two feet. It was decided that if a tooth on a test-shot pattern came within ±6 milliseconds of matching a similar tooth on an evidence impulse, it would be considered a match.

The Match-up

With test data now in hand, the BBN team went to work.[15] For 6 candidate impulses and 432 test patterns, a total of 2,592 calculations were carried out,

Table 11-1. Match-up of audio candidates of rifle shots

Onset Time of First Impulse	Array and (Microphone No.)	Rifle Location	Correlation Coefficient
136.20 sec	—	—	No correlations < 0.5
137.70 sec	2 (5)	TSBD	0.8
"	2 (5)	TSBD	0.7
"	2 (6)	TSBD	0.8
"	2 (6)	Knoll	0.7
139.27 sec	2 (6)	TSBD	0.8
"	2 (6)	TSBD	0.6
"	2 (10)	TSBD	0.6
"	3 (5)	Knoll	0.6
140.32 sec	2 (11)	TSBD	0.6
144.90 sec	3 (4)	Knoll	0.8
"	3 (7)	TSBD	0.7
"	3 (8)	TSBD	0.7
145.61 sec	3 (5)	TSBD	0.8
"	3 (6)	TSBD	0.8
"	3 (8)	TSBD	0.7

Note: The times listed in boldface are raw times for the appearance of gunshots on channel 1. Tests by Barger disclosed that channel 1 was running 5 percent faster than real time. Consequently, the elapsed times should be increased by 5 percent. In real time, the assassination took 8.3 seconds from the first to last shots and 4.8 seconds between the third and fourth shots. This chart may be found at 8HSCA101.

each resulting in a two-digit number representing how closely the evidence sound impulse matched its corresponding test gunshot impulse. This number, called a correlation coefficient, is a mathematical term for comparing two sets of numbers and warrants some explanation.

Let's say, for example, you know someone named Bill. Let's also say that you have many measurements of Bill's face that show the exact distance between his eyes, the exact size of his ears, the distance from the tip of his nose to his upper lip, etc. Now, say you have a photograph of an unknown person from which similar exact measurements can be made. The correlation coefficient would show how closely the metrics of the photograph match the metrics of Bill's face. A correlation coefficient of 1.0 (or 100%) would indicate a perfect match—and you would be quite certain that the photograph was of Bill.

Seldom in science do we get such a perfect match. In the case of the Dealey Plaza acoustics study, one would not expect a correlation coefficient anywhere close to 1.0 because of the uncertainty of the placement of the microphones and the position of the as yet unconfirmed knoll shooter. In addition, in all radio transmissions there is present "white noise," or static. This noise would overlie some peaks in the evidence impulses and consequently reduce any correlation coefficients. Given these uncertainties, Barger and his team determined that no correlation coefficient less than 0.6 (or 60%) would be regarded as a match.

In Table 11-1, the correlation coefficients are shown in the last column. The six evidence shots are in boldface, listed according to the time of the first impulse of each. The first impulse at 136.20 seconds—the long "pop" immediately preceding the first of the five candidates—was added to the mix out of an abundance of caution because, even though it had no echo pattern, it was so close to the others in time. Immediately it became clear that the 136.20 impulse fell below the 0.6 threshold and could be discarded.

Impressively, the remaining five candidates matched the sound impulses of one or more test shots—fifteen in all—including most notably one that matched a test shot fired from the knoll. Of those fifteen matches, however, four were eliminated because they reflected nonsensical scenarios. The fourth entry under 137.70, marked "KNOLL," was discarded, because it represented a knoll shot fired toward the underpass when the limousine was in the opposite direction, just starting its run down Elm Street. The fourth entry under 139.27, also marked "KNOLL," was discarded because it required the motorcycle to speed at fifty-five mph to reach the position where the impulse was recorded. Last, the final two entries under 145.61 were eliminated because they required the motorcycle to accelerate when its engine noise level indicated it had not.

This left the table with eleven matches between the evidence impulses and the test patterns—five shots fired in an elapsed time of 7.9 seconds. After correcting for the evidence tape speed, which was running 5 percent faster than real time, the assassination actually took 8.3 seconds.

At this point, Chief Counsel Blakey fully understood the enormity of his "problem." It had become intractable. Not only was there evidence of five shots, including one from the knoll, but the time interval between the second shot at 139.27 and the third at 140.32 was only 1.05 seconds. The FBI had determined that the rifle found in the Texas School Book Depository required a minimum of 2.30 seconds just to work the bolt and pull the trigger. Hence, the shot at 140.32 was valid evidence of a third shooter and could not be discarded.

But it was discarded by the committee's imposition on the BBN test results of a criterion of its own: if a match was shown to have occurred less than 2.3 seconds after the preceding shot, it would be discarded "because the rifle (Oswald's) cannot be fired that rapidly."[16] Thus was 140.32 made to disappear—a perfect example of flawed circular reasoning. The aim of the acoustics study was to determine whether weapons in addition to that rifle were used that day. The match of an evidence impulse to a test shot fired from the depository did not mean that the evidence impulse originated in the depository, only that it originated from the northeast end of Elm Street. To eliminate the shot at 140.32 seconds on these grounds was specious.[17]

Order in the Data

Table 11-1 also reveals an additional confirmation of the evidence developed by the BBN scientists. "Order in the data" is a phrase used to describe an important aspect of studies of this kind. Nothing in the seemingly bland, uninteresting phrase indicates its logical power. It refers to the fact that the data associated with the matches appears to be a sequentially ordered whole. This was the doing not of the scientific team but of the data itself.

Take a look at the column labeled "Array and (Microphone No.)." Note that the sound impulse of the first gunshot (137.70) matched signals received at microphones 5 and 6 in array 2. This was just south of the Houston/Elm Street corner. The next impulse, a second and a half later, was received just a few feet farther north along the motorcade route. The impulse that followed, just over a second after that, was received at microphone 11 of array 2 (this was the impulse the committee discarded). Once again this microphone was farther along the motorcade route as it turned onto Elm Street. After a pause of 4.6 seconds, two other impulses were received by microphones well down Elm Street. The entire sequence is shown on the map of Figure 11-4).

The data did not have to organize itself this way. The matching impulses for the first shot could have been picked up by one or more of the microphones farther along the motorcade route—say, somewhere in array 3, not array 1. Likewise, the matching impulses for the final, fifth shot might have

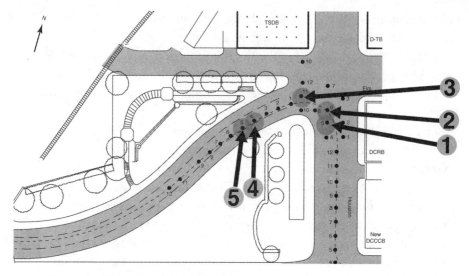

Figure 11-4. HSCA map showing the microphone positions of the matched sound impulses. The actual motorcycle positions at the time of the shots on November 22 were within a few feet of these locations.

been picked up by a microphone in array 1, not array 3. In that case, it would demonstrate that the motorcycle had run the reverse of the motorcade route—an impossibility.

In that case, we would have to conclude that our data—whatever it turned out to be—represented not the sound of shots picked up by a motorcycle's stuck microphone but something random, such as static caused by sunspots or a fault in the motorcycle's electrical system. With great exactitude, the time sequence of the different sound impulses matches the spatial progress of a motorcycle in the motorcade.

Moreover, that fit is supported by the calculated speed of the motorcycle. If we divide the distance between the first and last matching microphone by the time interval between the two, it shows that the motorcycle would have moved at an average speed of 11.7 mph. The FBI determined that the presidential limousine—which set the speed for the whole motorcade—was running on Elm Street at an average speed of 11.3 mph.

The 60-Degree Rule

There was one additional finding of the BBN tests that further reinforced the specific chronology of the shots and the placement of the motorcycle with the stuck mic when the shots were recorded. All rifle shots produce a muzzle blast and a shock wave, the latter arriving milliseconds prior to the muzzle blast. Shock waves, however, are not always detected by a microphone. Through years of empirical experimentation, acoustic science developed a principle concerning the detection of bullet shock waves based on simple geometry. Call it "the 60-degree rule." Draw a line from the gun to the target and then another line from the gun to—in this case—the microphone. If the angle formed by these two lines is greater than 60 degrees, then no shock wave will be detected by the microphone.

Of the five shots that BBN identified, only the last shot and the next-to-last shot showed shock waves due to the location of the motorcycle microphone vis-à-vis the line from gun to target. For the earlier three shots, when the motorcycle was six floors below the shooter firing down Elm Street, the critical angle was more than 60 degrees, and no shock wave was detected.

The Knoll Shot

As encouraging as the foregoing findings were, it was still not a slam dunk that a shot had been fired from the knoll. The probability was an anemic 50 percent. It was now September 1978, and the committee would expire in a little over three months. There was neither time nor money to do a definitive study of all five shots. Blakey, knowing he needed to significantly improve those odds, asked Weiss and Aschkenasy to analyze—and hopefully refine— the one shot that was the most controversial: the next-to-last shot from the knoll at 144.9 seconds.

The two scientists understood that the only way to sharpen the probability calculus for this shot was to drastically reduce the ±6-millisecond accuracy established by Barger's team—ideally down to ±1 millisecond. Technically, achieving this accuracy was possible with another shooting reconstruction, but only by using 180 microphones, at this juncture a practical impossibility. However, Weiss and Aschkenasy had dealt with greater challenges for the US Navy in designing computer programs for submarine SONAR (an acronym for sound navigation and ranging). They would apply the same principles of echo location to the data from Dealey Plaza to create a model that mathematically produced the same kind of data set embodied in the wave form of the actual rifle shot.

In the simplest terms, the knoll evidence shot during the assassination was acoustically reconstructed in Dealey Plaza and the sounds of both shots processed into echo patterns. Each pattern constitutes a kind of fingerprint unique to that shot. In their report, Weiss and Aschkenasy likened the test shot to a "clear" fingerprint, while that of the channel 1 gunshot was "badly smudged"

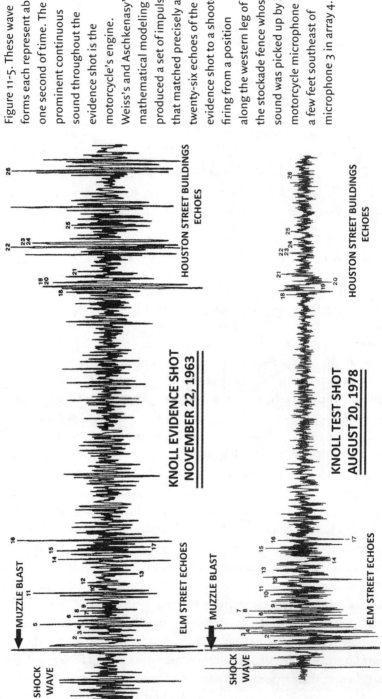

Figure 11-5. These wave forms each represent about one second of time. The prominent continuous sound throughout the evidence shot is the motorcycle's engine. Weiss's and Aschkenasy's mathematical modeling produced a set of impulses that matched precisely all twenty-six echoes of the evidence shot to a shooter firing from a position along the western leg of the stockade fence whose sound was picked up by a motorcycle microphone a few feet southeast of microphone 3 in array 4.

KNOLL EVIDENCE SHOT
NOVEMBER 22, 1963

KNOLL TEST SHOT
AUGUST 20, 1978

because of the extremely noisy environment in which the original recording was made. As a result, BBN's matching results, while very close, fell short of a perfect match because of differing conditions. The test shot was fired in August 1978, when the temperature was 90° F, while at 12:30 p.m. on November 22 it was only 65° F. In addition, the location of the microphone (array 3, microphone 4) was not at the exact point where the sound impulse was picked up on November 22, nor was the knoll evidence shot fired anywhere near the test-shot position chosen along the northern leg of the stockade fence.

To determine those two unknowns, the procedure was to begin with what was known. They knew the difference in air temperature and hence the differing speed of sound between the two shots. And they knew the locations of the echo-producing structures around Dealey Plaza. Using these knowns, it was possible to mathematically calculate the echo-delay times (and the intervals between them) characteristic of any pair of shooter and microphone locations.

Their method was both simple and ingenious. They obtained a large-scale surveyor's map of Dealey Plaza (accurate to six inches), a box of pins, and a roll of string. Next, they identified the structures in Dealey Plaza that produced the strongest direct echoes (twenty-two) and the strongest secondary echoes (four). By attaching a string from a pin placed at a shooter's position to a second pin on an echo-producing surface and thence to a third pin at a microphone position—and then measuring the resulting string length—the scientists could predict a precise echo-delay time for that echo. Doing this with all twenty-six echo-producing surfaces resulted in a sequence of sound impulses and intervals between them that was unique to the postulated shooter/microphone locations.

Through a process of shrewd trial-and-error calculations using many shooter/microphone combinations, Weiss and Aschkenasy achieved an almost exact match, to within ±1-millisecond accuracy, with the knoll evidence shot. With that, the probability that the knoll shot impulse was indeed a rifle shot jumped from 50 percent to 95 percent, or 20-to-1 odds. As robust as this figure was, later analysis by scientists, including assassination researcher Dr. Donald Thomas, revealed that Barger's team had erred in their calculations, and their odds ended up being much too conservative. When done correctly, it turns out the odds against the knoll sound impulse being random noise are about 100,000 to 1.[18]

Moreover, one is struck by two additional findings. The presence on the DPD tape of the shock wave of the evidence shot demonstrated that the shot was fired from the knoll in the direction of the limousine and the motorcycle.

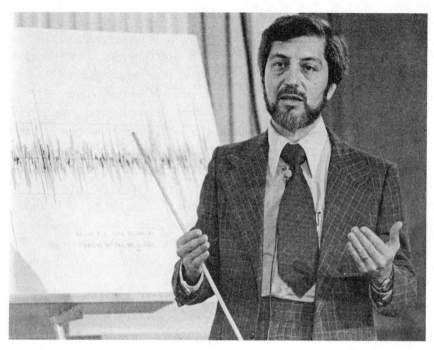

Photo 11-6. Professor Mark Weiss testifying before the HSCA on December 29, 1978.

It also shows that a rifle, not a pistol, was the knoll weapon because pistol bullet velocities are subsonic and hence do not create a shock wave.

However, probably the most important result of Weiss and Aschkenasy's study has not been mentioned. Their use of echo-location techniques ended up establishing the precise location of the unknown gunman's firing point. It was not on the northern leg of the stockade fence location used in the audio reconstruction test but a short distance away—on the southwest leg of the fence at exactly the location where the shape appears in the Moorman photo, where Lee Bowers saw the two men, and where Skinny Holland and his coworkers found fresh footprints, cigarette butts, and mud on the fence.

Mark Weiss and Ernest Aschkenasy testified publicly before the committee on December 29, 1978, only two days before the committee went out of existence. Earlier that fall, they had worked closely with Robert Groden, the committee's photo consultant, in efforts to synchronize the Zapruder film with the new acoustics evidence. As soon as their testimony was completed, Groden picked up a copy of the Moorman photo and rushed to their side. He pointed out the anomalous shape along the fence at the exact spot indicated by their study to have been the firing point.

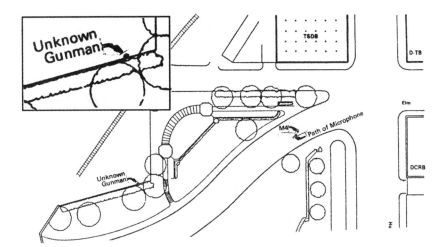

Figure 11-7. Official HSCA diagram showing the location of the motorcycle and the "unknown gunman" (*inset*) as per Weiss and Aschkenasy.

"They were amazed," Groden told me, "No one had ever told them there was photographic evidence confirming their work."

CHAPTER 12   THE HOUSE SELECT COMMITTEE ON ASSASSINATIONS

One would think I would have been excited when the news came through during the last week of 1978. All I remember is the dark, overcast skies that December and having more to do than I could possibly handle. Attorney Len Weinglass and I had just finished a habeas hearing in Sacramento for Chol Soo Lee, a Korean American immigrant wrongfully convicted of the 1973 killing of a San Francisco Chinatown gang leader and sentenced to life in prison. Lee's high-profile case had sparked the formation of a defense committee and a national coalition of Korean American activists, churches, and community groups. We had produced a breakthrough witness, and the whole thing had gone better than anyone could have expected (Chol Soo Lee was eventually freed in 1983).

Despite our professional good news, these were dark days for the Bay Area. First came the mass suicide of 920 followers of San Francisco cult leader Jim Jones at the People's Temple agricultural compound in Guyana. David Fechheimer and I had been working for attorney Charles Garry on a case involving the temple, and I had had a contact there the summer before. I wondered if she was still alive. In the summer, we had heard an ugly rumor about the settlement doctor stockpiling cyanide. Now, I guess we would have to agree that the report was true. Then the second hammer blow—Supervisor Dan White shot and killed San Francisco Mayor George Moscone and Supervisor Harvey Milk at City Hall. The city was traumatized and reeling in shock.

The news from Washington arrived first in bits and pieces and then in a few dramatic announcements. The HSCA had held open hearings in which it seemed clear that new evidence showed unequivocally that four—not three—shots had been fired. But that was not all. Apparently, one of the shots had been fired from the grassy knoll area. Even better, the shot had been fired not from just any location on the knoll but from the exact location I had pinpointed in Six Seconds—a few paces up from the corner of the stockade fence. In some quiet way, I suppose I was pleased by this development, yet I felt no excitement or elation or vindication. I had not thought of the Kennedy assassination in many months. It had slipped into the background with many things that I didn't have time to think about anymore. I was just glad I didn't have to do anything about it since I had so much else to do.

That soon changed. Shortly after I started my own detective business in June 1979, I got a call from Peter Dale Scott, a former Canadian diplomat who was now an English professor on the University of California, Berkeley faculty. We had met six years before at Bud Fensterwald's home in Washington, DC. Peter was interested in the "deep politics" behind the Kennedy assassination and had written a couple of books on it. Three years before, he, together with physicist Paul Hoch and Russ Stetler (whom I knew from my days at Haverford), had published a collection of assassination articles for Random House titled *The Assassinations: Dallas and Beyond*. The book contained a short excerpt from *Six Seconds*. Peter explained that he had just received an advance from Random House for a book on the HSCA Report to be called *Echoes of Conspiracy*, and he invited me to join him, Paul, and Russ in writing it. The four of us would split the Random House advance, and I would not have to pay for the HSCA Report and its twelve supporting volumes of testimony and exhibits.

I had few clients that summer, and I jumped at the offer. Paul Hoch and I had stayed on good terms through the Alvarez scuffle and the years that followed. Russ Stetler had been a senior at Haverford the first year I taught there, and we had become friends. He had moved on to London and ultimately became the private secretary to British philosopher, logician, and mathematician (and Nobel laureate) Bertrand Russell. In 1970, he and his son Morgan had come to Copenhagen from London and spent a week with us. Our family had spent the summer of 1972 in Berkeley living in the same house with Russ and his family. On the first night I'd spent working as a surveillance man in November 1976, I had stashed my motorcycle at Russ's home and borrowed first their VW bug and then their white van.

It was a congenial group. My job was to deal with the actual facts of the assassination, with what happened in Dealey Plaza. It was an enjoyable summer, becoming a scholar and writer again. The last few years had been filled with action and change and weirdness all around, and it was pleasant for a while just to sit back and read and write. What's more, I could satisfy my curiosity about what the committee had done. One thing I was curious about was whether it had been able to do things I had been unable to do over a decade earlier.

Photo enhancement was one of these. I had tried to get it done on the Moorman Polaroid photo with its anomalous shape the size of a human head along the stockade fence line. I had written to the Visibility Laboratory at the Scripps Institute of Oceanography in San Diego to ask if it would try to enhance prints of the Moorman photo. I had even sent along a few of my best prints. Less than two weeks later, I had received a letter informing me that Scripps "cannot undertake image processing of pictures related to the Kennedy assassination unless requested to do so by some appropriate Government organization." The HSCA was such an "appropriate Government organization."[1] I dug into the report and supporting volumes until I found an answer.

The committee's Photo Panel had asked the Rochester Institute of Technology to do what it could. First, "a high quality negative copy" of the Moorman photo was made and then printed with various contrast and brightness settings.[2] This was hardly my idea of photo enhancement. I had already done this in 1967 from copy negatives taken by a professional photographer I had hired in Dallas. In fact, since the Moorman Polaroid had decayed appreciably since 1967, I had already done what the committee had done, only with better raw material. Then I read further. This misdescribed enhancement had not even been tried on the stockade fence but had been applied only to the concrete retaining wall in front. It was no surprise that they found nothing of interest there because there was nothing there. After it became clear from the acoustic evidence that a shot had been fired from behind the fence, the Photo Panel had urged that someone else do what it had failed to do.[3] Terrific. With the authority of the federal government behind it and hence the ability to accomplish things no private party could accomplish, the Photo Panel had managed to do exactly nothing.

The acoustics evidence did not really become public until December 1978, when Weiss and Aschkenasy testified. It was easy to understand why that evidence and testimony would lead the Photo Panel to revise its report and urge others to do what it had failed to do. As I read further, I kept running into this sort of rejiggering late in the committee's tenure.

The most obvious example concerned the Forensic Pathology Panel (Medical Panel). Its report was issued in the summer of 1978, before the acoustic evidence came to light. Panel member Cyril Wecht, MD, coroner of Allegheny County, Pennsylvania, and a longtime student of the medical evidence in the case, issued a stinging dissent from the Medical Panel's conclusions. Concerning the president's head wound, Wecht wrote,

> In my opinion, the medical evidence and other physical evidence and investigative data in this case do not rule out the possibility of an additional gunshot wound of JFK's head. . . . A soft-nose bullet, or some other type of relatively frangible

ammunition, that would have disintegrated upon impact could have struck the right side of JFK's head in the parietal region. Inasmuch as there is a large defect of JFK's skull in this area, it is not possible to rule out the existence of a separate entrance wound at this site.[4]

The panel responded to Wecht's dissent with the bland comment that "the conclusions of the panel majority remain unchanged in the absence of bona fide evidence."[5] When the acoustics evidence became public in December 1978, the committee's views changed dramatically. It was too late to reconvene the Medical Panel, but its chairman, Michael Baden, MD, could be summoned from New York to testify to the same point Cyril Wecht had made in his dissent. The committee included a reference to Baden in its report: "Dr. Michael Baden, chairman of the committee's forensic pathology panel, acknowledged there was a possibility, although highly remote, that the head wound depicted in frame 312 could have been caused by a shot from the grassy knoll, and that medical evidence of it had been destroyed by a shot from the rear a fraction of a second later."[6]

Elsewhere in the report were similar responses to the eleventh-hour discovery of the acoustics evidence. Clearly it was the acoustics evidence that almost single-handedly persuaded the committee to vote that there had been a conspiracy in the Kennedy assassination, but what interested me was something else. I wanted to know why a draft of the final report, put together in early December, basically backed the Warren Commission version of events. Why, until then, had the various panels so easily dismissed out of hand the idea of a shot hitting President Kennedy from the knoll?

Many critics argued that this was just institutional bias—one could not expect an official government body such as the House committee to point a critical finger at the Warren Commission. My reading suggested that there had to be some other reason, perhaps some breakthrough in the evidence, that made any notion of a knoll shot striking the president highly unlikely.

Neutron Activation Analysis (NAA)

There was another reason, and it was not difficult to find. It was spread throughout the committee's report and the reports of its various panels and was used to backstop the Warren Commission findings in numerous areas. It concerned a series of tests run at the very start of the committee's work in September 1977. The test was neutron activation analysis (NAA). It was applied to several bullet fragments and to the intact bullet (CE 399) found on the Parkland Hospital gurney. Its results established a seemingly incontro-vertible fact of great importance.

To grasp how important this test was—and how it prepared the ground for many of the committee's conclusions—one needs to understand how the test is done and what its results establish. In NAA, a metal sample is bom-barded with neutrons in a reactor. This causes the sample to produce radio-active isotopes. The spectra of these isotopes are then studied to disclose the parts per million of the element tested. The test is an incredibly fine-grained way to discern small quantities of trace metals such as silver, copper, or anti-mony in larger samples—for example, the lead in bullets. Because the levels of various trace metals can vary from bullet to bullet, even in the same box, if one or more bullet fragments tested with NAA show the same levels of trace metals—for instance, twenty-eight parts per million of antimony and thirteen parts per million of silver—it was thought that this might demon-strate that the fragments were from the same bullet. By this reasoning, NAA made possible the assignment of what amounted to a unique fingerprint to an individual bullet.

As I read about the test, I remembered that Saturday of the HSCA-sponsored critics' conference in Washington two years before, when I had said to Chief Counsel Blakey, "In this whole area there is one experiment that has the sta-tus of the crucial experiment in science—like the Micholsen-Morley experi-ment—and that is neutron activation on Commission Exhibit 399 and . . . the fragments from Connally's wrist."[7]

Since CE 399 was a completely intact copper-jacketed bullet, the sin-gle-bullet theory required that the tiny fragments in Connally's wrist had to come from the lead base of that bullet. If they did not match, this would prove that the single-bullet theory was wrong, an opinion shared by all of us sitting there with Blakey that day. Left unsaid was that such a test would also clear up a rumor that had long circulated within the assassination research commu-nity—that the FBI in 1964 had conducted NAA testing on the whole bullet and fragments with results that were deemed inconclusive.

What I did not know when I suggested the test was that Chief Counsel Blakey had already ordered the test, and five days previously, a scientist named Vincent P. Guinn had begun NAA testing for the committee.[8] This meant that the results of Guinn's tests were available to the committee from the very beginning of its investigation.

Vincent Guinn was not your garden-variety scientist.[9] Although he had not invented NAA, he had been one of the first to refine and use it. During the late 1960s and the 1970s, he had concentrated on developing NAA as a forensic tool. In doing so, he had gained a national reputation as a pioneer in NAA forensic testing.

Guinn not only tested CE 399 and the fragments removed from Connally's wrist but also tested two small pieces of lead recovered from President Kennedy's brain, two lead fragments found in the rug under the left jump seat of the limousine, and a mashed fragment of a bullet taken from the front seat of the limousine. This mashed fragment had sufficient remaining details to be firearms-ID matched to Oswald's rifle. On the basis of some testing, Guinn argued that 6.5-mm Mannlicher-Carcano bullets were quite homogeneous in their cores as to the presence of trace metals, while individual bullets from the same box varied greatly with respect to trace metals. The logic of his tests was clear. He hoped to determine (a) whether the Connally wrist fragments came from CE 399 and (b) whether the fragments from President Kennedy's brain and from the rear rug could be linked to the large mashed fragment recovered from the limousine's front seat.

Dr. Guinn detailed his test results in three short sentences at the end of his report:

> It is highly probable that the specimen tested from Q1 (the stretcher bullet) [CE 399] and the specimen tested from Q9 (the fragments from Governor Connally's wrist) are from the same bullet. It is highly probable that Q2 (large fragment found in the limousine), Q4 and 5 (fragments from President Kennedy's brain) and Q14 (smaller fragments found in the limousine) are all from a second bullet. There is no evidence of a third bullet from any of the evidence specimens tested.[10]

When I read those words, I literally could not believe what they said. After assassination researchers had for years urged that NAA be performed on the samples Guinn had tested, those tests had finally been performed, yielding results directly counter to what we expected. My eye stuck on the term "highly probable" in the quotation above.

During his testimony before the Committee, when Guinn was asked what he meant by the phrase "highly probable," he did not offer a particular probability number, explaining, "I would not want to say how high, whether it was 99 percent or 90 percent or 99.9 percent. I can't make a calculation like that."[11] I did not understand all the science in Guinn's report to the committee, but I thought I understood enough. Guinn's eminence in his field meant that, apparently, his findings could be taken to the bank. They appeared to be beyond challenge—and they were devastating.

The match between CE 399 and the Connally wrist fragments meant that we had been wrong all these years in doubting the single-bullet theory. Guinn had proven that the wrist fragments came from the rifle found in the depository.

Just as shocking, Guinn testified that all the other small fragments came from the large fragment found in the limousine's front seat that was fire-arms-ID matched to Oswald's rifle. This meant that tiny fragments from the president's brain came from a larger fragment fired from Oswald's rifle. In short, Guinn had established a foundational fact that had to affect how one viewed other evidence in the case.

I was astonished, but I was also beginning to understand the logic of the committee's investigation. Because Guinn's results were developed very early in the HSCA's existence, their influence was felt throughout the committee's work. They amounted to a gravitational pull towards the narrative put forward by the Warren Commission. The impact of the late-developing acoustics evidence was in the opposite direction. Manifested in the last-minute actions of certain panels and experts to insert caveats or corrections to their opinions, it pulled in the direction of a multishooter narrative.

Since the assassination happened in one way rather than another, we would expect the committee to choose between the two narratives. It didn't. Instead, it chose a third alternative that attempted to honor the gravitational pull of both narratives.

Synchronizing Film and Audio

The competition between narratives would be felt throughout the core evidence in the case. Since the acoustic evidence constituted a kind of audio clock of the event, it was only natural that an immediate effort would be made to compare it with the Zapruder film. How should the audio clock of the Dictabelt be synchronized with the video clock of the Zapruder film? This seems like an apparently innocuous question, but it isn't. In answering this question, the stakes for the committee had become incredibly high.

There were really only two ways to do this. Since the president is hit in the head at Zapruder frame 313, this has to be either the last shot or the next-to-last shot. If the next-to-last shot is matched to frame 313, the consequences are momentous. If that shot blew up the president's head, then whatever Lee Harvey Oswald did or did not do on that Friday fifty years ago, he did not fire that shot. Someone else killed the president.

The committee turned first to its photo consultant, Bob Groden, who, after showing the Zapruder film on Geraldo Rivera's *Good Night America*, had been hired as a staff consultant on photographic matters. Groden also worked as a de facto staff member, solving problems as they arose. When the film/acoustics synchrony issue arose, he was asked to huddle with acoustic experts Weiss and Aschkenasy. Complicating the technical challenges posed by the analysis, both Groden and the Photo Panel were directed to proceed with the four-shot scenario the committee had accepted, not the five-shot pattern the acoustics evidence had actually revealed.

The trio came up with an ingenious technique for precisely linking the actual sounds of the test shots fired in Dealey Plaza to the magnetic sound strip of Groden's 16-mm copy of the Zapruder film and succeeded in assembling two versions of the film.

The first version synchronized the next-to-last shot on the acoustics tape with Zapruder frame 313. The second version synchronized the last shot with frame 313. Groden later told me that "when we looked at them, there was no doubt in any of our minds that the first version was the one. It matched all the shots, while the second version matched neither the blurs nor what was happening in the limousine."[12]

Chief Counsel Blakey ordered the two versions screened for committee members, and seven or eight members of Congress showed up to view the two versions. Prior to the screening, Blakey gave Groden very stern orders. He was, Blakey told him, simply the projectionist. He was not to say anything about the two versions. If he did, there would be serious consequences.

After the two versions were shown, the members started talking about how the first version seemed to synchronize the shots with what they were seeing, while the second did not. While a frustrated Groden remained silent, Blakey cautioned the members that the medical evidence indicated no impact from the right front, explaining that this tended to support the second version as probably correct.

The Startle Response and Blurs

Apart from Groden's work with Weiss and Aschkenasy, the Photo Panel pursued the same question, only with a different twist—studying individual Zapruder frames and applying Luis Alvarez's blur theory. Conducting this study were two photo experts—Dr. William Hartmann, a professor at the University of Arizona who also served as a photo analyst for the Mariner 9 mission to Mars, and Frank Scott, a photo scientist for the firm of PerkinElmer and a member of the Photography Panel.[13]

Working independently, the two measured and analyzed the blurs on the

Table 12-1. Analysis of blurs in Zapruder film

Relative magnitude of blur episode	Designation of blur episode	Shown by	Frames showing blur onset (beginning to maximum)
Largest	A_1	Alvarez	312-318 Largest
		Hartmann	313-318
		Scott	313-314
	A_2	Alvarez	330-334
		Hartmann	331-332
		Scott	331-333
2d largest	B	Alvarez	189-195 Largest
		Hartmann	191-197
		Scott	193-194
3d largest [1]	C	Alvarez	220-228 Largest
		Hartmann	227-227
		Scott	226-228
4th largest [1]	D	Hartmann	158-159 Largest
		Scott	158-160
5th largest [1]	E	Alvarez	291-293 Largest
		Hartmann	290-291
		Scott	290-292

[1] About equal.

The six blur patterns identified by Alvarez, Hartmann, and Scott. This official HSCA chart appears at 6HSCA30.

Zapruder film, each using a different method. Deliberately, they did not look at Alvarez's study until they had completed their own (see Table 12-1).

When they compared Alvarez's measurements with their own, they found that overall they agreed with Alvarez's data but not with his conclusions. Their study tended to show the opposite of what Alvarez claimed. Alvarez had asserted that there was blur evidence for only three shots. Hartmann and Scott identified six blurs.

Hartmann testified before the committee on September 11, 1978. Asked if he could deduce when the shots were fired by simply noting when the blurs occurred, Hartmann replied that things other than gunshots could have startled Zapruder or made him move his camera. "On the basis of looking just at the blur," he stated, "I would say no. However, if we then look at the photo visual evidence of what is happening in the parade, I think we can begin to identify some of them as gunshots"[14] (see Table 12-2).

As noted in an earlier chapter, the involuntary startle response had been studied by psychologists.[15] It is fairly simple to calculate how long it took for the sound of a shot fired from the depository to reach Zapruder's ears. Add to this the startle reaction time, and you know where to look in the film for something happening in the limousine.

The question then becomes: Are there places in the film just before the identified blurs where something happens in the limousine? Not surprisingly, there are, even though the restriction of synchronizing the four-shot scenario bent the results.[16]

Despite that handicap, the committee had to indicate in its report that its

Table 12-2. Match-up of sound impulses with frames and blurs if frame 313 is the next-to-last shot

Sound			Blur	Film
Sound Impulse	Tape Time	Zapruder Frame Equivalent	Zapruder Frame Blur	Zapruder Frame: Reaction in Car
Shot 1	137.7	175	181–182	194–207: JFK leans forward and raises elbows; Mrs. K. looks in his direction.
Shot 2	139.3	204	209–210	202: Shot jars Phil Willis and his finger takes picture; limousine, JBC, JFK obscured by sign after 199.
Shot 3	140.3	224	227	224: JBC's lapel flaps up and outward. 225: JBC grimaces.
Shot 4	144.9	313	313	313: Impact on JFK's head.
Shot 5	145.6	328	331–332	328: JFK's head shoots forward; his head wound changes; JBC bowled over.

Photographic Panel had reached the same conclusion as Groden had working with Weiss and Aschkenasy—the next-to-last shot of the acoustics should be matched to frame 313:

> The blur analysis conducted by the photographic evidence panel appeared to be more consistent with the grassy knoll shot striking the President. The analysis reflected no significant panning errors by Zapruder after frame 296. Such errors would have been expected if the third (grassy knoll) shot occurred 0.7 seconds before the fatal head shot. Assuming the head shot was the grassy knoll, Zapruder made significant panning errors after both the third and fourth shots.[17]

The Two-Inch Forward Head Movement

With the Photographic Panel appearing to confirm that the explosion we see in frame 313 was caused by an impacting bullet from the right front, what about the two-inch forward movement of the president's head between frame 312 and frame 313? In *Six Seconds*, I had characterized this movement as prima facie proof of the impact of a bullet from the depository window, virtually simultaneous with the shot from the knoll, while the explosion we see in frame 313 is the exit of that bullet out of the front of the president's head.

In 1976, CBS News asked the ITEK Corporation to carry out a comprehensive study of the Zapruder film.[18] ITEK was a research firm with a solid reputation and had done earlier work for both UPI and Time-Life on the Kennedy assassination. Although not part of the HSCA record, the study was clearly ancillary to the committee's work and was referenced at various points in its supporting volumes. For some reason, I had never heard of this report, although part of it rechecked the measurements of Kennedy's head movement that I had done in 1966–1967.

Francis Corbett, ITEK's senior scientist, wrote the report. Time-Life cooperated by providing the original Zapruder film plus 16-mm and 35-mm copies. The available resources and materials were breathtaking. Five photo analysts took part in the study. I thought of my own rough measurements, made on eight-by-ten-inch black-and-white copies of the relevant frames. I thought of the pinholes that I had put in by hand at the back of Kennedy's head and two fixed points on the limousine. The ITEK study was infinitely better than anything I could have accomplished in 1967 (see Table 12-3).

As to the forward movement I had measured between frames 312 and 313, I had measured the movement over thirty frames, while Corbett measured it over only seven and established limits of precision for the measurement process. He said that the movement of Kennedy's head could not be measured more accurately than ±0.20 inches in any one frame.

When I compared my charts of measurements with Corbett's, the two sets of measurements matched up remarkably well. They agreed in every case with respect to the direction of movement. The critical measurements of forward movement between frames 312 and 313 were almost identical: 2.18 inches for me and 2.26 inches for Corbett.

So here was a genuine impasse in the evidence. Measurements of head movement show that Kennedy was hit from the rear at frame 313, while comparison of the Zapruder film with the acoustics evidence shows that frame 313 must be matched to a shot fired from the knoll. Both findings cannot be correct, but both appear to be correct.

The Jet Effect and Neuromuscular Reaction

Given that the basic outlook of the committee and its panels remained pro–Warren Commission up to the final month, the various panels dealt with the violent backward movement of Kennedy's head at Zapruder frame 313 largely by ignoring it. When they actually dealt with it, the explanations usually involved some amalgam of Luis Alvarez's jet effect or a vague reference to a neuromuscular reaction.

Table 12-3. Comparison of head movement measurements, Thompson and ITEK

Zapruder Frames	Thompson	ITEK
311–312	Forward 0.16 inches	Forward 0.05 inches
312–313	Forward 2.18 inches	Forward 2.26 inches
313–314	Back 0.54 inches	Back 0.30 inches
314–315	Back 1.08 inches	Back 0.65 inches
315–316	Back 0.78 inches	Back 1.46 inches
316–317	Back 1.71 inches	Back 1.60 inches

The Medical Panel's report contains only a single mention of Alvarez and his theory (but no specifics). Still, given what the committee did know about his melon experiments, they summoned ballistics technician Larry Sturdivan of the US Army's Edgewood Arsenal to testify on September 6, 1978.

As he had done in 1964 for the Warren Commission—described earlier in Chapter 9—Sturdivan showed films of ten skulls shot with Oswald's rifle and a second 6.5-mm Mannlicher-Carcano, using the ammunition from the assassination. All the skulls were shot, Sturdivan explained, and *all ten were knocked forward along the bullet's path*.[19]

Asked if the ejection of missing skull fragments in the front would have contributed at all to the backward motion of the head, Sturdivan replied that he could not exclude this possibility, but any rearward motion would be "slight . . . [and] would not have been as dramatic as we saw [in the Zapruder film]." His answer goes to the heart of the matter. What we see at frame 313 is far from slight. It is violent and shocking.

Of the committee's panels, only the Medical Panel mentioned Alvarez, artfully commenting on his theory in words gentler than Paul Hoch had used a decade earlier but carrying the same meaning: "The panel members have critically evaluated the observations of Alvarez and the physical principles he considers in explaining the President's head movements in the Zapruder film. The panel members took note of the differences between the missile and targets (melons) in Alvarez's work and the missile and targets in this homicide."[20]

Ironically, in dismissing Alvarez's jet-effect theory, the committee ended up offering a lukewarm endorsement of an odd variant of what Alvarez himself had rejected earlier—brain trauma causing backward movement of the head. The possibility of this explanation arose after Sturdivan showed the committee a 1948 film of a goat being shot in the head while held in a harness. The goat's whole body goes into spasm as if in an epileptic seizure. The back legs splay out backward; the front legs splay out forward; the goat's back arches. Sturdivan labeled this a "neuromuscular reaction" and went on to paint its likely effect in

 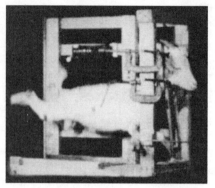

Photo 12-1. Goat before shooting.

Photo 12-2. Goat after shooting. All four legs splay outward; back arches.

John Kennedy: "Motion there [in the skull], I believe, caused mechanical stimulation of the motor nerves of the President, and since all motor nerves were stimulated at the same time, then every muscle in the body would be activated at the same time."[21] Sturdivan failed to mention that the onset of the goat's spasm was 100 milliseconds (or two Zapruder frames) after impact, while Kennedy's backward snap begins virtually simultaneously with impact.[22]

This may be what happens to a goat when shot in the head. It is clearly not what happened to John Kennedy. There is no evidence whatsoever that any muscle in his body, let alone all, was activated by the frame 313 head shot. The president's body is a rag doll dragged along by his head, not the other way around.

The Medical Panel seemed less impressed by Sturdivan's opinions and came to a more equivocal conclusion. First they pointed out that there is "a possibility of the body stiffening, with an upward and backward lunge . . . [that] might have resulted from a massive downward rush of neurologic stimuli to all efferent nerves (those which stimulate muscles)."[23] But, given this possibility, "it would be reasonable to expect" what we clearly don't see—namely, "that all muscles would be similarly stimulated."[24]

Finally, the Medical Panel punted, indicating that they really did not know why the president's head moved rearward under impact. The panel was sure (or somewhat sure since this was indicated as a conclusion of only a "majority of the panel") that the movement was not caused by the most obvious candidate—a bullet from the right front:

The majority of the panel believes that there is a possibility that this massive movement may have been caused by neurologic response to massive brain damage caused by the bullet, or by a propulsive effect resulting from the matter that exited through the large defect under great pressure, or a combination of both. Whatever the cause of the President's movement, the majority of the panel concludes that only one bullet struck the President's head and that it entered at the rear and exited from the right front.[25]

After looking into the whole question—after reviewing all the evidence and expert testimony—the Medical Panel had to admit that they really couldn't figure out why the president's head went rearward. They gave up. "Whatever the cause . . . ," they said, it didn't matter because they were sure only one bullet hit the president in the head, and it came from the rear.

A similar admission of defeat appeared in Francis Corbett's 1976 ITEK study. What Corbett got right at the start was that Kennedy's head led the body in a violent backward snap not caused by some muscle spasm. But then he went on to say, "There is strong supporting data (analysis presented here) for believing that JFK's backward motion after 313 was caused or considerably influenced by the actions of Mrs. Kennedy. The data indicates she was probably in physical contact with him through her hands at frame 312."[26]

What? Mrs. Kennedy threw him backward? This is absurd. The film shows clearly that she never touched her husband's head during this sequence. Even if she had pushed or pulled him backward, we would get the opposite effect of what Corbett observed. Kennedy's body would have moved backward first, while his head would have remained stationary and then been pulled backward by his body. A footnote to his statement added more confusion than clarity:

> The statement that Mrs. Kennedy caused the President's backward motion is not intended to mean that she was the sole cause. In fact, calculations made from the theory of jet reaction suggest that this phenomenon could explain some of the movement. Although it is beyond the scope of this report to deal with neurological reaction in a quantitative fashion, it appears plausible that this effect too could have influenced the backward motion. The data presented here does suggest that she was a strong or the dominant causal factor of the backward motion.[27]

What leaps out is that after an exhaustive study, Corbett had to admit the same thing the Medical Panel admitted: "Whatever the cause . . ."

We are returned to the same spot of official vagary. Whether due to Alvarez's jet effect, Sturdivan's neuromuscular reaction, or Mrs. Kennedy pushing the president backward, his head went backward after Zapruder frame 313.

We don't know what caused that. We don't even know if any of these theories had anything to do with why his head went backward. No matter; we'll bail this out by saying some variant of all three together caused the movement. Once again John Cleese in his white lab coat comes to mind.

Impasse

When I finished reading the HSCA Report and nearly all the volumes of supporting documentation, I was struck by the continuing duality of evidence that had bedeviled the Warren Commission. The HSCA had come up with two new and powerful pieces of evidence—the test results of neutron activation analysis and an acoustic record of the assassination—yet each pointed to completely different conclusions. In essence, the technical studies of the committee confirmed the double pattern of evidence I had noted in 1967.

The committee solved this dilemma by doing what many government panels do when faced with implacable contradictions—it papered them over. On the one hand, it concluded that a conspiracy had been involved in the Kennedy assassination since "scientific acoustical evidence established a high probability that two gunmen fired at President John F. Kennedy."[28] The committee was not happy with the facts it had uncovered, but it could neither alter these facts nor ignore them: "The committee found that, to be precise and loyal to the facts it established, it was compelled to find that President Kennedy was probably killed as a result of a conspiracy."[29]

On the other hand, it went against the results of its own studies and concluded that the next-to-last shot (the shot from the knoll) missed. The committee stated, "The Committee concluded, therefore, that the shot fired from the grassy knoll was not the shot visually represented at Zapruder frame 313 [and] that the shot from the grassy knoll missed President Kennedy."[30]

Unlike the committee, I could not paper over these contradictions, which continued to reverberate through the back spaces of my mind. In some sense, I had always doubted my 1967 assertion of a double impact at 312–314. I had seen merit in what the critics pointed out. What were the chances of two bullets striking their target within less than one-tenth of a second? If Kennedy was hit twice in the head, why did the film apparently show only one impact? Now my *Six Seconds* scenario was gone, and I had nothing to put in its place. What was left was a fundamental contradiction in the evidence.

Why, after this exhaustive commitment of resources, could we not know in 1979—sixteen years after the event—what really happened in Dealey Plaza? There could be only one answer. The evidence package was contaminated.

Some of the so-called evidence did not belong there. If you don't know what is real evidence and what is not, you are blocked. You cannot proceed further.

I went ahead and wrote my chapter for Peter Dale Scott. It ran to fifty-seven pages in typescript. Ultimately, Peter's book was never published for legal reasons, and the four of us split the advance for the work we had done. I finished my chapter for Peter's book with a sentence on the last page that would prove prescient: "To put it another way, one cannot even begin solving a puzzle if one keeps doubting whether a piece belongs in the puzzle."[31] An impasse is reached.

In 1979, that was what happened. I came to see that I was trying to put together a puzzle in which some of the pieces did not belong. Since I had no way of knowing which pieces these were, there was nothing I could do.

I just turned away.

PART III

BREAKING THE IMPASSE—
THE 2000s

The Puzzle Piece That Wasn't

Two government investigations over fifteen years had created the impasse. With one major exception, they had produced as much confusion as clarity. The HSCA acoustics study is clearly that exception. No private individual could have accomplished what it achieved. Certainly, no private individual could have brought about the firing tests in Dealey Plaza that made possible Weiss and Aschkenasy's pinpoint identification of the firing point.

With this major exception, the last fifty-plus years show one overarching fact. Ever since 1964, when the Warren Commission published its twenty-six volumes and turned over the puzzle of Dealey Plaza to the rest of us, discoveries by private individuals have been the principal engine of change. It should come as no surprise, then, that the impasse was broken by the work of private individuals even though it took twenty-five years for this to happen.

The Ad Hoc Committee on Ballistic Acoustics

From 1979 to 2006, I had little to do with the Kennedy assassination. I was working as a detective, and Nancy and I were raising a family. Each new case had its own focus and intensity, and I had little curiosity left for the impasse left by the HSCA. However, one development in 1982 momentarily caught my attention. In the spring of that year, a ninety-six-page scientific study titled *Report of the Ad Hoc Committee on Ballistics Acoustics* was issued by the National Research Council, a chartered arm of the National Academy of Sciences whose role includes forming panels of experts to study scientific topics of national interest. The report had been commissioned following the HSCA's recommendation that a blue-ribbon committee be formed to evaluate the findings of the HSCA acoustic panel.

When the report came out, I read the contemporary press reports that stressed the distinguished reputations of the committee members, one of whom was physicist and Nobel laureate Luis Alvarez. They were quoted as concluding that the sound impulses of the shots came too late after the shooting to really be shots and hence were most likely random static. I wasn't particularly surprised by this pronouncement since, back in 1978–1979, when the acoustics evidence first made a splash, I had my own doubts about it. Yes, I had earlier concluded that a shot came from the same location along the stockade fence that the acoustics evidence indicated. But back then, I was also convinced that two shots were fired between Zapruder frames 312 and 314, while the acoustics evidence said only one. Further, there was some confusion since the acoustics scientists seemed to have detected a total of five shots, while the HSCA talked about only four.

Nonetheless, during the summer of 1979, when I read the HSCA Report and supplemental volumes while working on the Scott book, I was impressed by how robust the acoustics evidence was. I was struck by how closely the acoustics timing of the shots seemed to match key events shown in the Zapruder film and how precisely the many echo patterns of the evidence gunshots matched the test shots later fired in the plaza. To my unscientific mind, the probability that the acoustics evidence could be explained away as simply random static seemed extremely small. But what did I know about such things?

Purely at the level of public buzz, people seemed to believe that there was something wrong with the acoustics evidence. If you asked someone what that was, the better informed might tell you that it had something to do with timing. Most people, however, had only the vague idea that an independent committee of highly regarded experts had discovered some flaw that made it appear unreliable. In sum, the committee's findings were settled science. The acoustics had been discredited.

As the years passed and no voices from within the scientific community were raised to challenge its assertions, the committee report became the public judgment of this evidence. At one point, after I got my hands on a copy, I tried to read it, but its technical vocabulary and complexity overwhelmed me. How was a person like me supposed to understand "Except for the two outliers, marked D, corresponding to point (1, 5) all of the values of ΔF are less than 0.09 kHz in absolute value and have a sample mean of –6.92 Hz and standard deviation of 48 Hz."[1] After wading through a dozen pages, I gave up. For me, Luis Alvarez's involvement with the committee was a red flag. I filed it all in the back of my mind with all the other things that I might want to look into sometime.

What I did not realize at the time—nor would I for nearly two decades—was the enormous impact the report had on both the public's perception of the case and the establishment media's subsequent attitude toward any arguments challenging the single-shooter scenario. In one deft stroke, the *Report of the Ad Hoc Committee on Ballistic Acoustics* had removed the acoustics evidence from discussion, in effect consigning one of the two most powerful pieces of assassination evidence to the wastebasket. It should come as no surprise that the report leveraged public opinion back toward the conclusions of the Warren Commission.

The Philosopher as Gumshoe

I was running my own shop as a PI in the early 1980s, and my bread and butter was criminal cases, especially murder cases. At that time, the San Francisco Public Defender's Office could get state funds for the investigation of death-penalty cases. It made sense for that office to hand these cases over to PIs and save its own investigators for other cases. As my workload increased, I invited Russ Stetler, my old friend of fifteen years who had worked on the book project in the summer of 1979, to come into the business with me as a partner. The shift to private investigation was a natural for him—Russ had worked for several years as a journalist out of his home in Berkeley—and we opened the office of Thompson and Stetler on Union Street in San Francisco's Cow Hollow district.

Russ and I worked many of these gritty cases. In addition, the Chol Soo Lee murder case on which I had worked with attorney Lenny Weinglass came back for retrial. We won, and ABC's 20/20 did a segment on it. That broadcast in turn inspired a feature-length movie, *True Believer*. Other murder cases came along. In a few, I worked for the victim's family in close collaboration with the police. In most, I worked as a defense investigator for the accused.

Over time the variety of cases expanded beyond criminal defense. Our office was busy. If a life of adventure, variety, challenge, uncertainty, surprises, and a certain inherent risk was what I had been looking for back at Haverford, this philosopher-turned-gumshoe had certainly found his way to the right job.

My first major case had the kind of moral ambiguity that often characterizes the work of the private, not public, investigator.[2] The client was a nice young woman of about thirty whose husband, a citizen of India, had stolen their six-year-old daughter and absconded to a town named Gorakhpur in northern India. The young woman—let us call her Neva—had custody of the child in the United States as well as the child's passport. The father, call him Krishan, had simply added the child's photo and name to his passport, hopped on a plane, and flown back to his family's home. I was hired to get the child back.

Why not simply go into an Indian court, show that you have custody, and let Indian law require him to turn over the child? When subpoenaed to show cause why he should not turn over the child, Krishan would simply flee from the family home and remain at large somewhere in India. He had already won once by stepping outside the law. By enforcing Neva's legal rights, we would be giving him the opportunity to do it all over again.

In the PI business, these sorts of cases are called "seam jobs" because they hinge on finding the "seam" in adult supervision where the child is not protected. By hiring a remarkable Indian investigator named Henry Bawa, I learned that there were no seams in Krishan's hometown. We would have to lure him and the child to Bombay (as it was known in those days). And so, a few months later, I found myself sitting on a patio of the Blue Ballerina Motel in Bombay, looking out over the calm waters of the Arabian Sea. Across the table was Bawa, while in an adjacent room sat Neva and a woman companion. Not thirty-five feet away, sitting at a similar patio table, were Krishan and the girl. I got up and led Bawa into the room with the two women. With my own eyes, I had just verified that the child we were about to kidnap was the right child.

Two hours later, on my orders, three Indian goons ("goondas" in Marathi) knocked on the door of Krishan's room and said they wanted to call the police. When admitted, two of them threw Krishan on the bed, tied his feet and hands, and put duct tape over his mouth. The other picked up the child and dashed across the hall to our room. I confronted Krishan at that point and told him I was returning his daughter to San Francisco "in accordance with outstanding court orders." Henry Bawa's men held Krishan in that hotel room until the wheels of our flight cleared the tarmac the next morning. At the same time, they released our own man, an operative who Krishan believed was an architect's representative and a business contact who had accompanied him to the motel. Krishan told our man that he was going to return to the United States and kill Neva.

After returning to the United States, I got Neva and her daughter fake identification and arranged for them to live in hiding. Shortly thereafter I received a call from a woman who identified herself as Neva's psychotherapist, who had been treating her for some time. She congratulated me on our success and then added in a matter-of-fact tone, "Of course you know Neva is psychotic."

No, I didn't know. Immediately I thought, "Well done, Thompson. You have just completed a high-risk international child snatch and been patting yourself on the back about your success. Now you learn that things have worked out differently, that the sum of your labors has been to take the child from a loving father and put her in the hands of a psychotic mother. Congratulations!"

The aftermath of the Bombay adventure could have gone very badly, but it didn't. Neva was not psychotic, and a few years later Krishan died of a heart attack. Mother and child emerged from the shadows, by all accounts happy and strong.

The point is that you begin every case with only limited understanding. In exchange for the payment of money, the client buys your absolute loyalty, your commitment to work solely on behalf of his or her interests. Neva's story about what had happened and what should happen was the only narrative I had. It was her movie, and it became mine. This is the way the game is played, and you take what goes with it. Your client employs you and, as employer, constitutes the greatest danger to you. Your client assigns you a role in his or her narrative. If this is a fictitious narrative—if you have been gulled—then you will find yourself in a different narrative with unknown dangers. In detective fiction, there is no finer example of this than Sam Spade's beguiling client Brigid O'Shaughnessey in The Maltese Falcon. Spade accepts Brigid's account of the movie she wants him to be in. As a result, Spade's partner, Miles Archer, ends up dead within twenty-four hours.

My own realization occurred one evening on a flight back to San Francisco from Los Angeles. I had just worked a competent ruse to get into a guarded residential development to ascertain the whereabouts of a drug dealer. Everything had gone extremely well—no fuss, no bother. But on the way back, I began to wonder what would happen to the man I'd fingered. The attorney I had worked for wore a gold chain and assured me it had been only a minor burn; no one would get hurt. Only "some money would change hands," was how he put it. Could I believe him? Even if I could, was his client lying to him? Would I read about a murder in the paper a week or two later and know I had helped set up the victim? As I sat on that plane, it struck me that a private detective might be simply a closet criminal, or if not a criminal, something even less—the hired hand of criminals.

When I recalled past cases, they fell along a line of memorability roughly corresponding to how close I had come to the line: the house with the $30,000 in the attic; the trip Nancy and I took to Tijuana; the flight to Frankfurt, Germany, on twenty minutes' notice; the electronics job; all those meetings in airport coffee shops where only first names were used. It sometimes seemed as if danger, heightened senses, general weirdness, and extraordinary satisfaction all lay on a graph where something like criminality was the ordinate. However you cut it, the detective and the criminal share many things: an affinity for keeping secrets, paying attention, acting evasively, and seeing the noonday public world as danger, as "other." Had I traded Haverford for a column in the *Police Gazette*? I had no answer and perhaps never would. What I did know was that this work could be both physically and spiritually hazardous, that it takes place in a boundary world where the truth, if it is ever revealed, comes in 256 shades of gray, and the best I could hope for was to operate there without crossing some undefined boundary.

In 1990, Russ, who had always had a deep commitment to abolishing the death penalty, left the PI world to become chief investigator for the California Appellate Project, an organization that provides resources for attorneys representing death-row inmates. He later became the chief investigator for the New York State Capital Defender Office and has enjoyed a fine career.

Through all these years, David Fechheimer and I remained the closest of friends. Although seven years younger than I, David trained me as an investigator. Whenever I got a case that had sufficient money for both of us, I did what I could to bring him in. He was immensely experienced in cases outside the country, which made it possible for us to work together on two of my later cases—a $100 million coffee fraud in Columbia and a $100 million arson in France. David reciprocated, and we worked together as defense investigators for Timothy McVeigh in the 1995 truck bombing of the Alfred P. Murrah Federal Building in downtown Oklahoma City. That bombing killed 168, wounded 680, and destroyed or damaged over 300 buildings within a 16-block radius. The incident was the biggest domestic terrorist attack in US history until it was eclipsed by 9/11. David's focus was going after the prosecution's case against McVeigh, an American militia movement sympathizer accused of detonating a Ryder rental truck filled with explosives parked next to the building. My focus was building the defense case.

In some ways, this case exemplified the character of work in the PI's world with its detours and quirks, its black humor, even moments when you sense you are working in an alternate universe. Somehow David found a photograph in an obscure small-town Kansas paper of a Ryder truck parked near the side of Geary Lake just north of Junction City, Kansas. It was the prosecution's theory that the bomb truck had been prepared with its explosive cargo at Geary Lake. The Ryder truck in David's photo had been rented by the FBI to carry its diving unit equipment when it searched Geary Lake about ten days after the bombing. The FBI had barred all media and photographers, but one enterprising photographer from a local paper had taken the photo with a 500-mm lens from a nearby ridge.

Two days later, the FBI's crack crime-scene investigation unit came in and performed a number of measurements of tire tracks, et cetera. From what we could determine, the FBI Ryder truck appeared to be parked exactly where these agents took tread measurements and made their plaster casts of tire treads. In short, the FBI had measured its own tire tracks, not the tracks of any bomb truck. We had a few laughs over this while preparing it as a trap for the prosecution. As it turned out, Geary Lake was dropped from the prosecution's case, and with it our trap.

During the investigation, my beat covered Kansas, Oklahoma, and Nebraska, and the responses I got from ordinary people whom I met were often surprising. I thought I was working for the most hated person in the United States. Not so. I was operating in a largely rural landscape quite apart from the larger world, one whose residents appeared to share a deep distrust of the federal government and who, while not openly supportive of the militia movement, were not hostile to it either. Often a witness or a contact would ask, "Do you get to talk to Timmy?" I would reply, yes, I often did, and they would ask me to give him some encouragement. On one occasion, a lanky, sunburned Oklahoman told me, "Just tell Timmy he should have done the damn building at night when those kids weren't there."

It was around the time I ran into that Oklahoman—late March 1997—that the Kennedy assassination pulled me back from the plains of Kansas and Oklahoma to Washington, DC. After the Oliver Stone film JFK was released in the early 1990s, a tide of public sentiment hit Congress, demanding the release of any assassination materials still being sequestered. This led to the passage of the JFK Assassination Records Collection Act in 1992 and the creation of its enforcement arm, the Assassination Records Review Board (ARRB). One item on the ARRB's to-do list was the Zapruder film, then privately owned by the Zapruder family after LIFE magazine had returned the original to the family following the March 1975 national broadcast of Bob Groden's copy on *Good Night America*. Should the ARRB carry out a legal "taking" of the film that would keep it permanently in the National Archives? I was asked to come to Washington and testify about the film before the ARRB in public session at the National Archives.

In Washington, I made no prepared statement but simply outlined to the board my own experience with the film. I said that Secret Service agent Forrest Sorrels had made a mistake on November 22, 1963. As soon as Abraham Zapruder got his camera out of the office safe, I said, Sorrels should have told him, "Mr. Zapruder, I am taking that camera and that film as evidence in this homicide."[3] Had that happened, I pointed out, "we wouldn't be here with this particular problem." The ARRB finally decided to do what other witnesses and I urged it to do and carried out a legal "taking" of the film. After arbitration, the government ended up paying the Zapruder family $16 million for the in-camera original of the film.

Comparative Bullet Lead Analysis

Until February 2001, I had never heard of comparative bullet lead analysis (CBLA) or of the special FBI laboratory that performed it. The test had come up in connection with a case I was working involving Sara Jane Olson (née Kathleen Ann Soliah), a former member of the short-lived Symbionese Liberation Army (SLA), a small radical group best known for its 1974 kidnapping of California newspaper heiress Patty Hearst. A fugitive for twenty-five years, Olsen was captured in 1999. We were defending her and other SLA defendants against a murder charge growing out of an SLA robbery of Crocker National Bank in 1975 in the Sacramento suburb of Carmichael, California. During the robbery, a woman was killed. The case was now being brought back with a vengeance by the district attorney of Sacramento County and from my perspective was stumbling from one bad scene to another.

Under discovery, we had just obtained an FBI lab report that definitively linked shotgun pellets removed from the victim with shotgun pellets found in shells—eighty-nine in all—discovered at two SLA apartments. According to the FBI report, the victim pellets "were determined to be analytically indistinguishable" from pellets loaded into eight shotgun shells. The report added that the match was "consistent with [the victim pellets] originating from the same sources (melts) of lead at the manufacturing plant as the pellets loaded in those shot shells." As troubling as this new information appeared, I was not particularly worried about the alleged match since it would be difficult to connect any of my clients to specific shotgun shells.

While I had no idea what tests may have been used in the bullet lead analysis, the lab report's use of terms such as "bullet manufacturers' lead melts" and "trace elements" brought to mind the NAA that had played such a pivotal role in the HSCA deliberations in 1978. I suspected that CBLA was very likely NAA rechristened with a more forensically persuasive name, and if so, that suggested that the test had become a powerful tool in law enforcement's tool bag.

My casual observation about CBLA and NAA soon faded into the background as I moved on to new cases. Then, one summer day in 2006, I got a call from Gary Aguilar, MD, a Bay Area ophthalmologist and assassination researcher, inviting me to attend an informal one-day seminar/workshop for a dozen or so Bay Area researchers, an event he put together from time to time as developments seemed to warrant. He had reserved a conference room at the St. Francis Hospital in San Francisco. A fellow Marin County resident, Aguilar had become the preeminent expert on the medical evidence, and over time and many spirited discussions, we had become friends.

"There are two guys coming who I want you to hear," he explained. "They're scientists working at the Lawrence Livermore National Lab. They know a lot about bullet lead analysis, and they've just published a paper about the evidence in the Kennedy assassination. They couldn't give a rat's ass as to conspiracy or no conspiracy, so what they have to say should be interesting."

When Gary's seminar got underway on a Saturday morning weeks later, I was certainly curious to hear what the two scientists, Erik Randich and Patrick Grant, both PhD metallurgists, had to say. I had no idea that before the day was over, I would learn that for several years the theoretical underpinnings of CBLA and its principal testing component, NAA, had been under critical scrutiny by the scientific community. The results conclusively showed that there was no way the test could be used to match a bullet from a crime scene to a bullet linked to a suspect. In short, CBLA was junk science.

Erik Randich, whose own inquiry had begun in 1998, in particular had played a role in unraveling CBLA. In 2002, he and several coauthors published a devastating critique in the journal *Forensic Science International* challenging the validity of CBLA testing.[4] Not surprisingly, as word of these findings spread, criminal defense attorneys facing CBLA-produced evidence sought him out as an expert witness. In 2005, Randich's expert testimony before a New Jersey appeals court resulted in the reversal of a murder conviction that relied upon NAA-produced evidence of bullet matching.[5]

As CBLA came under increasing and successful challenge in court proceedings, the FBI's concern grew. Because its laboratory was the only one in the country that did such testing, the agency's scientific credibility was at stake. To resolve the issue, the FBI turned to the National Academy of Sciences (NAS), which in turn asked its National Research Council (NRC) to assemble a committee of experts to evaluate the efficacy of CBLA. The resulting NAS/ NRC study, published in 2004, confirmed the findings of Randich and his colleagues and concluded that the usefulness of CBLA in the courtroom was at best extremely limited.[6] On September 1, 2005, the FBI closed its CBLA lab and prohibited FBI agents from testifying any longer about CBLA. In a letter released the same day, the lab director explained that after twenty years, CBLA testing was being discontinued because no one could say for sure what it meant.[7] With that announcement, CBLA was formally thrown into the dust bin of junked theories and bogus methodologies.

Photo 13-1. Lead in an industrial "melt" vat at a bullet manufacturer.

As interesting as this information was, it was the just-published paper in the July 2006 issue of the peer-reviewed *Journal of Forensic Science* by Randich and Grant that really got our attention. Titled "Proper Assessment of the JFK Assassination Bullet Lead Evidence from Metallurgical and Statistical Perspectives," the paper not only destroyed the validity of the NAA-derived evidence and seriously weakened support for the single-bullet theory but concluded that "the extant evidence is consistent with any number of between two and five rounds fired in Dealey Plaza during the shooting."[8]

That meant that the fragments tested from Kennedy's head could no longer be linked to a larger fragment from Oswald's rifle. The "phantom bullet" from the knoll was no longer a phantom.

That evening, as I drove across the Golden Gate Bridge on my way home from the workshop, I finally had time to think over the significance of what I had learned. The information Randich and Grant had presented had been a revelation, one that completely demolished the foundational findings Vincent Guinn had produced in 1978 linking all the assassination projectile fragments to only two bullets, both fired from Oswald's rifle. This alone carried major ramifications, but before I could consider possibilities, other questions began swirling.

Several stemmed from learning that a rumor that had circulated within the assassination research community decades earlier was true—that in 1964 the FBI had indeed carried out NAA on the very same fragments and the whole bullet (CE 399), and the results had been inconclusive. In a letter to the Warren Commission, released much later, FBI Director J. Edgar Hoover wrote that NAA had not produced significant results. In Hoover's words, "minor variations in composition were found," but they were not sufficient to link any of the smaller lead fragments to the complete bullet or to the larger fragment from the front seat.[9]

How could Guinn's retesting in 1978 have yielded dramatically different results? And why was retesting in 1978 ordered in the first place? How could a test that was so sophisticated, so well established that it enjoyed the official imprimatur of the FBI, manage to survive unchallenged for decades? And how many otherwise innocent people had been sent to prison as a result of its courtroom use by prosecutors?

Then I remembered Nobel laureate Luis Alvarez and his singular, disruptive impact on the public's perception of the assassination—and a valuable piece of wisdom I had gained: when the science falls apart, look at the scientist. Unquestionably, the one scientist most associated with developing and promoting NAA for forensic testing was Dr. Vincent Guinn. Before I reached home that night, I had resolved that in the months ahead, as time allowed, I would do some digging into his background and career. I was reminded of a memorable comment by my friend Sylvia Meagher, author of *Accessories after the Fact*. "This is not an evidence-based investigation," she quipped. "It's eminence-based."

While Vincent Guinn first gained prominence in connection with his work for the House Select Committee, his association with NAA had begun many years previously.[10] A graduate of University of Southern California with a PhD in physical chemistry from Harvard (1943), Guinn returned to California to begin his career. From 1962 to 1970, he was a member of the research staff of the San Diego–based Gulf General Atomic, a division of the General Dynamics Corporation. During this time, he specialized in the use of NAA to examine bullet leads, gunshot residues, and other materials. In April 1962, Guinn visited the FBI Laboratory and discussed the forensic use of NAA. The day following Kennedy's assassination, he called the laboratory and said he and his staff were standing by to offer whatever help they could.

The following month, the FBI brought Guinn in as a consultant on NAA tests performed at Oak Ridge National Laboratories on the paraffin tests taken from Oswald's cheek and hands.[11] Because of various extraneous factors, the tests produced no clear result and, if anything, tended to show that Oswald had not fired a rifle on November 22.

Later in 1964, Guinn attended a conference on NAA in Glasgow, Scotland where he spoke to the press. "I cannot say what we found out about Oswald," Guinn said, "because it is secret until the publication of the Warren Commission Report. But I can tell you about activation analysis and crime."[12] He then went on to pump up his NAA test by disclosing that antimony but no barium was found on the cast of Oswald's cheek.

These remarks soon found their way onto the UPI news wire and ultimately to FBI Director Hoover's desk, where they ignited the director's ire and spawned a rash of FBI reports. One report stated, "Guinn is known to be a publicity seeker."[13] Another described Guinn as "a typical 'high pressure salesman' with a sound scientific background who is actively promoting sales of his company's nuclear reactors and services."

In 1970, Guinn joined the faculty of the University of California, Irvine as a professor of chemistry but continued to work for Gulf General Atomic well into the 1980s. By the mid-1970s, Professor Guinn was virtually alone in having pioneered the use of NAA in forensic testing. Thus, when the HSCA was launched in 1976 with a requirement to use nongovernmental scientists for its studies, Guinn was the obvious selection for studying bullet fragments.

In the early 1970s, Guinn had studied the concentration of various trace elements in a few bullets selected from relevant lot numbers of Mannlicher-Carcano ammunition. This led him to testify in 1978 before the HSCA that "you simply do not find a wide variation in composition within individual . . . Mannlicher-Carcano bullets, but you do find wide composition differences from bullet to bullet for this kind of bullet lead."[14] In other words, individual bullets were homogeneous in their composition of trace metals, but the composition varied significantly from bullet to bullet. This assumption was essential to Guinn's argument that every bullet carries its own unique fingerprint.

Why did Guinn believe that individual Mannlicher-Carcano bullets were homogeneous in their composition? Given the evidence available, it's difficult to say. First, in a scientific journal article published in 1975, Guinn and coauthor John Nichols, MD, a forensic pathologist, recounted how they had used a Freedom of Information Act (FOIA) lawsuit to pry from the FBI the actual results of its NAA tests of the assassination bullets in 1964.[15] They wanted to challenge the FBI's "inconclusive" results, in particular those from seventeen different sample points on the famous "stretcher bullet"—CE 399. In their journal article, Guinn and Nichols noted that the antimony content in this single bullet "ranged all the way from 636 to 1135 ppm."[16] In short, far below the minimal threshold of homogeneity.

If this fact did not set off alarm bells in Guinn's head, one has to wonder what would. Since homogeneity was the essential premise of Guinn's work, he tested the antimony content in three bullets pulled from different Mannlicher-Carcano lots. Each bullet was sliced into four pieces, and a test sample was taken from each cross-section and analyzed. The four pieces of the first bullet showed a range from 1,062 to 1,235 parts per million, indicating something like homogeneity. The next bullet showed antimony content of 358, 869, 882, and 988 parts per million. For this bullet, Guinn commented in his report to the HSCA, the result "is not homogenous."[17] The third bullet evidenced antimony content of 363, 395, 441, and 667 parts per million that Guinn characterized as "not so homogenous."[18] In sum, two of the three bullets Guinn studied failed to show homogeneity, yet he concluded his remarks by saying, "The background study of M-C bullet lead indicates . . . reasonable homogeneity within an individual bullet."[19]

The clearest disproof of Guinn's homogeneity assumption came from Erik Randich and his coauthors at the Lawrence Livermore National Laboratory, who laid out the elementary facts of bullet production that make homogeneity impossible.[20] Most of the lead used in bullet production comes from recycled car batteries. The recycling involves putting the lead from car batteries into a huge kettle, sometimes containing more than three hundred tons of material. Lead melts at about 340°C. Various impurities such as arsenic, tin, copper, bismuth, and silver can be boiled off, or skimmed off, by heating the kettle above this temperature and letting the mixture cool. All of this can be precisely controlled by the refiners who supply bullet manufacturers. The bullet manufacturers specify what type of lead they want, and the refiner complies.

As the cauldron cools, trace elements in the liquefied lead compose themselves in different ways. Some end up floating to the surface of the lead "melt," where they can be skimmed off. For other trace elements—such as copper and antimony—a phenomenon called microsegregation occurs. In Mannlicher-Carcano bullets, for example, the soft lead core is actually made up of single crystals or grains of metal formed during the solidification process. The solids form in a dendritic—or Christmas-tree—pattern. The first-forming solids are lowest in antimony content. As the molten mixture cools further, the antimony concentrates in the last liquid to solidify. This concentration is found around the boundaries of the individual grains. In fact, a primitive level of heterogeneity is a characteristic feature of the solid material itself. In simplest terms, this means that there can be no such thing as homogeneity in the make-up of lead bullets.

Since Guinn was not a metallurgist, and hence evidently not knowledgeable about how trace metals collect around grain boundaries in lead, he might well have been unaware of the argument against homogeneity that destroyed the plausibility of his basic premise. However, his own knowledge of Mannlicher-Carcano bullets should have alerted him to how manifestly incorrect was his claim that an individual bullet was homogeneous in its trace element composition.

Nor was the criticism of Guinn restricted solely to the scientific community. Before retiring in 1998, William Tobin was a supervisory special agent in

Photo 13-2.
Cross-section of a
Mannlicher-Carcano
bullet from lot 3000
showing the grain
structure. Antimony
tends to fall into grain
boundaries.

the FBI Laboratory. For twenty-four years, he had served as a forensic metal-lurgist there. In an article published in 2006, he was unremitting in his crit-icism of CBLA and other bogus forensic tests. He stated that the use of NAA for CBLA "shows the long-standing tendency of forensic scientists to present misleading testimony based on inadequately validated methods."[21]

Most important, regarding the intact bullet and the fragments of lead from the assassination, all one could now say was that the small amount of anti-mony present in all of them meant they were jacketed rifle ammunition and nothing more. Except for the intact bullet and the front-seat fragment, both linked to the sixth floor rifle by individual characteristics of that rifle's barrel, the remaining fragments could have come from virtually any manufacturer and be of any caliber.

In sum, the complete repudiation of Vincent Guinn's NAA tests left the evidence right where it was in 1964 after the FBI carried out its own NAA tests—"inconclusive." What had once been advertised as a scientific break-through turned out to be a scientific bust.

Just as important from my perspective, a critical piece of the assassination puzzle was not a fact at all and could be discarded. After more than a quarter century, the impasse had begun to break.

And there was more to come.

CHAPTER 14 BREAKING THE IMPASSE
The Blur Illusion

Since the 1960s I had been bothered by the fact that my measurements of President Kennedy's head movement required that two shots from different directions impacted his head within one ninth of a second and that the Zapruder film showed only one impact, not two. However, the first sign there was something wrong with the measurements themselves came in 1998 during a visit to Dallas to attend a JFK assassination conference. While there I met physicist Arthur Snyder from the Stanford Linear Accelerator in Menlo Park, California.

Art had long been interested in the physics of the assassination puzzle. Many years earlier, when Luis Alvarez's melon shootings had attracted attention, Art and his wife, Margaret, had carried out experiments shooting taped melons with a Mannlicher-Carcano rifle. Using military jacketed rounds, like those fired on November 22, they had failed to get any retrograde motion from them. When they switched to ordinary lead bullets that would balloon on impact, some of the melons came back toward the rifle.

Art shared his results with me. As our conversation continued, he told me he had done some calculations with respect to my measurement of the president's 2.18-inch forward jog between frames 312 and 313. The measurement must be wrong, he said. For Kennedy's head to move this far forward in one-eighteenth of a second meant that his head had to have absorbed 90 percent of the kinetic energy of the bullet. This was not just wildly improbable, but impossible. I thought about this for a while but then let it go when I could not figure out what to do with it.

I don't remember exactly when I first learned of David Wimp's work. He is a systems analyst from Eugene, Oregon, who in the early 2000s published on the Internet a monograph about the effects of motion blurring in the Zapruder film. Posted without fanfare on either his own or a friend's website, his study

Photos 14-1 and 14-2. Frames 405 and 409, respectively.

provoked in me a first reaction that I will always remember: "Why didn't I think of this? It is so obvious and so simple. Of course it's right!"

The three parts of Wimp's study were: (1) "The Effect of Motion Blurring on Contrast Edges," (2) "A Method for Measuring Distances in Motion Blurred Images," and (3) "Measurements of JFK's Front to Back Head Movements in the Zapruder Film." The first two parts were easy to understand. The third was more daunting because it contained a lot of math I could not understand. I knew from Haverford physics student Bill Hoffman's work for me in 1967 that translating positions in two-dimensional photos into actual positions in three-dimensional space was quite complex mathematically. From what I could understand, I was impressed by the care with which Wimp had made his measurements and then translated them into real positions in the world.

I knew enough about photography to know that the principle behind Wimp's analysis was elementary. It goes like this: if you have a bright area and a dark area right next to it, and you move the camera, the bright area will intrude into the dark area. This is because the bright area has superior light energy that has nothing to stop it moving into the dark area when the camera is moved. This is all pretty simple, but it was something that both Dr. Francis Corbett of ITEK and I had had never taken into account. To illustrate his point, Wimp discussed several frames from the Zapruder film.

At left are two frames, one Wimp's selection and one that I chose. Frame 405 shows the black light post as it actually appeared that day. It stands in the foreground partially blocking a figure on the grass and a truck beyond. Frame 409 to the right was taken four eighteenths of a second later and shows blurring throughout the frame. Points of light in the foliage at the bottom of the frame have been smeared laterally as has the street light itself, while the brightness of the highly reflective roadway has intruded into the black light post, narrowing it and virtually removing the figure beyond it. All of these effects were caused by the movement of the camera while the shutter was open.

After Art Snyder studied Wimp's work, he confirmed that, while he could not verify the measurement data Wimp used, the physics and the formulae were correct. Snyder then pointed to other frames where the same thing happens. The most important of these distortions occurs in frame 313. In the two frames in Photo 14-3, both cropped to the areas of interest, note that frame 312 is quite clear, while frame 313 is blurred horizontally.

Note how the chrome strut over the passenger compartment (ellipsis) is sharply defined in 312 and smeared laterally in 313. Much the same thing happens with the sunlit portion of Governor Connally's forehead (ellipsis).

Photo 14-3. Frames 312 (*left*) and 313 (*right*). *Larger ellipses*: chrome strut. *Smaller ellipses*: Governor Connally's forehead.

Photo 14-4. Frame 312. *White ellipses:* chrome strut and Governor Connally's forehead. *White lines:* back of Kennedy's head and fixed pints on limousine.

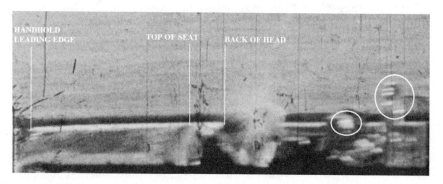

Photo 14-5. Frame 313. *White ellipses:* chrome strut and Governor Connally's forehead. *White lines:* back of Kennedy's head and fixed pints on limousine.

Of equal significance, by happenstance these same two frames also provide a basis for making accurate measurements. Viewed in nearly full frame above (Photos 14-4 and 14-5), both show a horizontally bright strip—actually the south curb of Elm Street just beyond the limousine—that provides a background for President Kennedy's head and two fixed points on the limousine.

The curb's presence made it easy to measure distances between the back of Kennedy's head and the two fixed points: the top of the rear seat and the leading edge of the left, rear hand-hold. What went unrecognized at the time was that this bright strip—like any other part of the frame—was stretched horizontally just as were the points of light on the chrome strut and the highlight on Governor Connally's temple. Since the apparent distances between the points and Kennedy's head grew between the two frames, both Dr. Corbett of ITEK and I thought that Kennedy's head had moved forward during the interval. In reality, the forward movement we measured turned out to be not movement at all but just a photo illusion produced by the blur effect.

When word of Wimp's website study subsequently reached the Assassination Archives and Research Center (AARC), the Washington, DC-based non-profit invited him to its annual conference on November 18, 2004, where he gave a talk about his discoveries. In his website study, after removing the effects of the blur, he calculated the actual movement of Kennedy's head to be approximately 0.95 inches forward between frames 312 and 313.[1] However, Wimp went on to explain that Kennedy was not the only limousine occupant who displayed this movement. He reported he had discovered that not just President Kennedy but all the occupants of the limousine tilted forward at this time due to the limousine slowing down. During the second that lasted from Z 300 through Z 318, the limousine driver turned to look in the back of his vehicle. As he did so, the speed of the limousine dropped from about 11 mph to about 8 mph.[2] With this deceleration, everyone in the limousine—Agents Greer and Kellerman in the front seat, Governor and Mrs. Connally in the jump seats, and to a lesser degree, the President and Mrs. Kennedy—pivoted forward from their hips. This forward movement began between frame 305 and 306 as the car began to slow and everyone in the limousine shifted forward. Between frames 310 and 312, Kennedy's head moved forward approximately the same 0.95 inch distance as it shifted forward between frames 312 and 313. This is critical since it shows that the apparent movement around Z 313 is not unique but is matched in earlier frames.

I wondered how accurate Wimp's measurements were. Since these measurements were also made by me in 1967 and Dr. Corbett of ITEK in 1976, we can see if they matched. A general match-up of the measurements is all we can expect here (see Table 12-3 on page 175). Remember that a frame from the Zapruder film is about the size of the fingernail on your little finger. The ITEK study asserted that the measurements, carried out from the original film and using cutting-edge technology, could be deemed accurate in real space only to the extent of ±0.2 inch.[3] By referring to other films in addition to the Zapruder film, Wimp had determined that under impact, Kennedy's head was driven somewhat downward and torqued in a counterclockwise direction. This twisting effect would give the impression that the back of Kennedy's head had moved somewhat forward. Hence, if Kennedy's head is found to move forward a fraction of an inch more than Wimp's measurements show between frames 312 and 313, this has little significance.

As Art Snyder explained to me, from a scientific perspective, it really did not matter whether any set of measurements was exactly true. Wimp had correctly demonstrated that the movement of Zapruder's camera and its resultant blurring of frame 313 had contaminated whatever measurements Dr. Corbett of ITEK and I had found in that frame. In short, the movement of JFK's head between 312 and 313 can no longer be taken as evidence of the impact of anything.

After I grasped the full significance of what Wimp had found, I had to laugh again. Almost every alleged fact about the Kennedy assassination had been challenged in some form or other. This one fact—that President Kennedy's head moved forward between frames 312 and 313 before it began its left and backward snap—had been accepted by everyone since my measurements were published in Six Seconds. I mean really everyone. Not just people critical of the Warren Report but also Warren Commission loyalists, journalists, and professional historians who had looked into the case—everyone.

This was almost the only fact that had gone through the wringer without ever being questioned. Nor was it lost on me that although I had not discovered the apparent 312–313 head movement (that distinction belonged to assassination researcher Ray Marcus), by enshrining it in Six Seconds, I had unwittingly helped validate that "fact" as a key piece of the puzzle, thereby contributing to the very impasse that had plagued the assassination inquiry for decades.

Now that any claim about Kennedy's head movement between 312 and 313 had to be discarded, everything changed and new questions arose. Was there any other evidence of a hit to Kennedy's head from behind at frames 312–313? I could not think of any. Certainly, there was abundant evidence that President Kennedy was hit in the back of the head at some time. But there was no other evidence that it happened between 312 and 313.

"How about the opposite?" I wondered. "Was there other, independent evidence that I was wrong in 1967 and that President Kennedy was not hit in the back of the head at that point?" I had long been aware that my whole scenario of a virtually simultaneous hit on Kennedy's head had been criticized from the beginning and that two of those arguments had real merit.

First, there was the sheer unlikelihood of two bullets arriving on target within that tiny sliver of time—two-eighteenths of a second out of the total 8.3 seconds of the shooting. What were the odds that two bullets would arrive on target during the same tiny interval? Very small, I had to admit—perhaps even vanishingly small. This objection, however, was minor compared to the second major argument that haunted this scenario: it requires two impacts, but only one is visible in the Zapruder film.

Photo 14-6. Frame 312

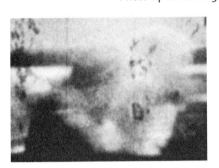

Photo 14-7. Frame 313

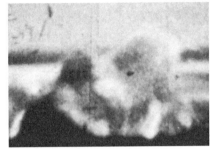

Photo 14-8. Frame 314

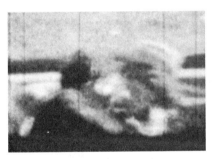

Photo 14-9. Frame 315

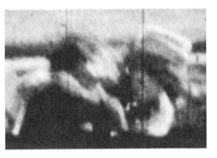

Photo 14-10. Frame 316

Photo 14-11. Frame 317

Photo 14-12. Frame 323

Photo 14-13. Moorman photo.

Photo 14-14. Moorman photo, enlarged segment.

Photo 14-15. Altgens's photo taken at frame 255. The president and Governor Connally have been wounded by body shots.

Photo 14-16. Extreme close-up of Altgens's photo, showing that the windshield is undamaged at this point.

My *Six Seconds* scenario required that probably by 314 and certainly by 315, Kennedy had taken a second bullet's impact to his head. I pulled out my good copies of the Zapruder frames immediately after 312.

While tracking the massive left and backward snap of Kennedy's head, these frames show no sign of a second impact after the one at frame 313. The same is true of relevant frames from the 8-mm color films of the same interval of time taken by witnesses Orville Nix and Marie Muchmore from the opposite side of the street. Both show the frame 313 impact but no sign of a second impact to his head. In addition, Mary Moorman's Polaroid photo (Photos 14-13 and 14-14) was taken simultaneously with frame 315 from the

Photo 14-17. Altgens's photo after the shooting was over.

Photo 14-18. Close-up of Altgens's photo. The white arrow points to windshield damage.

Photo 14-19. CE 350: photo of limousine windshield taken during the Frazier examination. The white outlined arrow points to the interior-side surface damage; white arrows point to blood spatter.

side opposite Zapruder. From that different angle, it shows exactly the same head position as Zapruder frame 315: no new impact, simply Kennedy's continuing reaction to the impact at frame 313.

Apparently, then, there was only the impact at frame 313. But, like everything else in this extraordinary case, every advance in our knowledge, every change in the fact pattern, sets up new problems for solution. In this instance, the issue was the overwhelming evidence that President Kennedy was hit in the back of the head from the rear. This fact is not based on the autopsy surgeons finding a small hole in the back of the president's head. Like almost everything in the medical evidence, this could be doubted. What cannot be doubted is all the other evidence.

Start, for example, with the windshield. AP photographer James Altgens took one of the historic photos of the assassination (see Photo 14-15). It was taken at Zapruder frame 255 and shows the limousine and its motorcycle outriders from the front. It is apparent that the windshield is undamaged at this point. Also at this point, both President Kennedy and Governor Connally have been wounded by body shots.

Altgens took a second photo as the limousine was pulling away after the shooting. That photo shows some damage to the windshield just to the left of the rearview mirror. The limousine was examined that night in the Secret Service garage by an FBI evidence collection team headed by Agent Robert

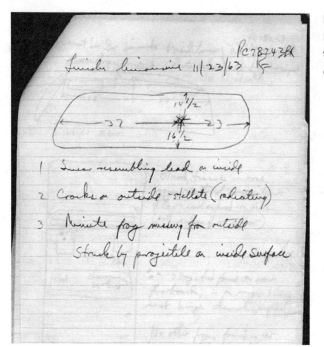

Figure 14-20. Frazier's notes from the windshield examination.

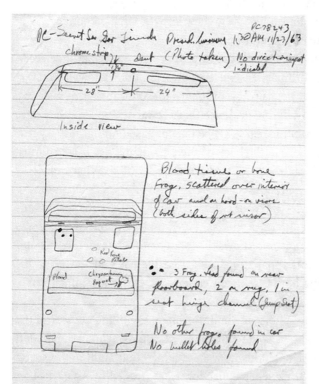

Figure 14-21. Frazier's notes from the interior inspection of the limousine.

Photo 14-22. Frame 255. Three seconds later, a shot from the right front strikes John Kennedy's head, throwing him sharply to the left rear and throwing blood and brain tissue forcefully over Clint Hill (*running to the limousine*) and the windshields, engines, and helmets of Officers Hargis and Martin.

Frazier of the FBI Laboratory, who photographed the windshield and took notes concerning what he found.

Frazier observed that the windshield had been struck on its interior surface, and a lead smear had been left.[4] He also found blood spatter on the inside of the windshield. In later testimony at the Clay Shaw trial in New Orleans, Frazier testified that he found blood and tissue as far forward as the hood ornament. His notes are informative.

Regarding the windshield, Frazier mentioned that there was a "smear resembling lead on inside" and that there were "stellate" or "radiating" cracks on the outside. He added that the windshield was "struck by projectile on inside surface." By the time Frazier and his evidence collection team got there, Secret Service agents had already recovered two fragments from the front seat of the limousine. Both were later firearms-ID matched to the rifle found on the sixth floor of the depository. One fragment was a mixture of lead and copper and hence could plausibly have caused the hit on the interior of the windshield (see color photo gallery, Plates 8a and 8b).

In his other note, Frazier wrote, "Blood, tissue or bone frag. scattered over interior of car and on hood—on visors (both sides of rt. Visor 3 frag. lead found on rear floorboard, 2 on rug, 1 in seat hinge channel (jump seat)."

In a later interview, FBI agent Francis O'Neill, who was present for the Kennedy autopsy, said he noticed blood and brain debris on the backs of the suits

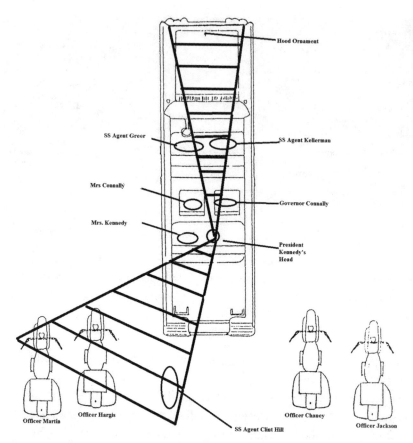

Figure 14-23. Two patterns of impact debris are forcefully thrown both forward and to the left rear.

worn by the two Secret Service agents seated in the front seat of the limousine.[5]

Where did this profusion of blood and brain debris come from?

Even more telling, where did the lead smear on the inside surface of the windshield come from? Finally, what about the bullet fragments found in the front seat that were matched to the rifle found on the sixth floor? Matched as they were to that rifle, they could not have come from the knoll shot.

That the impact debris from Kennedy's head was thrown in two distinct directions is one of the core facts of the case known since November 22 and never doubted. This bidirectional character of the debris pattern is also indicative of two shots, each fired from a different direction. But what has not been recognized is the force with which the debris was thrown in different directions. Agent Frazier noted the spray of this material as far forward as the

Photo 14-24. The limousine, follow-up car, and motorcyclists on Main Street moments before the shooting started. Minutes later, by the time of the head impact at Z frame 313, the president has moved to the center of the rear seat and the motorcyclists are no longer in this relative position to each other.

limousine's hood ornament, along with fragment impact marks on the interior of the windshield and its chrome strip, while motorcycle Officer Bobby Hargis, riding outboard to the left rear of the limousine, reported that he "was splattered with blood." "Then I felt something hit me," he stated. "It could have been concrete or something, but I thought at first I might have been hit."[6]

Sam Kinney was driving the follow-up car. He said later: "I saw it [the frame 313 head impact] and I saw his hair come out. . . . I had brain matter all over my windshield and left arm, that's how close we were to it. . . . It was the right rear part of his head."[7] Kinney's report shows how far to the rear blood and brain spatter reached.

Hargis was riding in echelon formation the inboard cycle just off the left rear fender of the limousine. To the rear and outboard of Hargis was B. J. Martin. Martin later testified that "there were blood stains on the left side of my helmet. It was just to the left of what would be the center of my forehead approximately halfway, about a quarter of the helmet had spots of blood on it

. . . and other matter that looked like pieces of flesh. . . . There was blood and matter on my left shoulder of my uniform."[8] Since Martin was riding to the left rear of the limousine and his right side was closest to the impact on Kennedy's head, why did he get blood and gore only on the left side of his helmet and the left shoulder of his uniform?

My friend and fellow buff Doug DeSalles, MD, supplied the answer recently. By studying closely the Zapruder, Nix, and Muchmore films plus the Moorman Polaroid, he was able to establish the relative positions of Hargis and Martin at the instant the bullet hit. If you get the relative positions of Hargis and Martin adjusted just right—just as they were at Z 313—Doug explained to me, you can see that Hargis and his cycle shielded the right side of Martin's helmet and uniform from the blast of brain and blood and skull. Martin was in what you might call the "rain shadow" presented by Hargis's body and cycle. This could only happen if the blast of debris was highly directional and of high velocity. The sheer power which the debris was thrown indicates the origin point of the shot. Just look in the opposite direction, look towards the corner of the stockade fence to the right front.

The Warren Commission emphasized the forward throw of head-impact debris because it was consistent with its scenario. But when it came to acknowledging and explaining the dispersion of this material backward and to the left, the commission ignored it. Nowhere in its entire 888-page report is there a single mention of this fact, just as there is no mention of the dramatic left and backward snap of Kennedy's head and body after frame 313. The vivid descriptions of Officer Hargis and his fellow rider on the limousine's left rear, Officer B. J. Martin, were relegated to volume 6 of the Warren Commission's own hearings and exhibits and left unmentioned anywhere else.

As I thought about this, it became clear to me that Wimp's discovery, while of great importance, had not come close to actually removing the impasse. His remarkable monograph had eliminated the only extant evidence that a shot from the rear hit the president in the head between frames 312 and 313. But his discovery did not eliminate the evidence that Kennedy was hit in the head from the rear because that evidence is overwhelming and persuasive. It happened. It just did not happen between frames 312 and 313.

The question then became: If the president was hit in the head from the rear, when did that happen? Until that question was answered, we had not moved beyond the impasse. It would take the work of another brilliant non-professional, Keith Fitzgerald, to answer that question.

"I'LL CHECK IT" **CHANNELS I & II**

LEAD CAR
"AT THE TRIPLE UNDERPASS"

McCLAIN'S CYCLE SLOWS
BEFORE TURN

Plate 1. The illustration above illustrates the "bird's-eye" view of Dealey Plaza when "I'll check it" was broadcast on both channels.

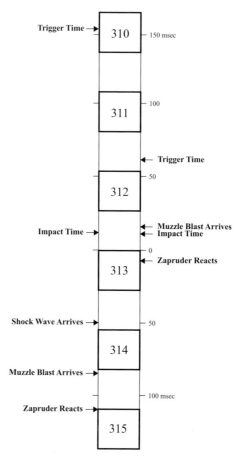

Plate 2. When Kennedy is stuck by a bullet at frame 328 and Connally is struck by a bullet at frame 224, a startled Zapruder moves his camera creating a blurred frame three frames later in frames 331 and 227. Hence it seems reasonable to expect such a lag between an impact in the car and Zapruder being startled by hearing the shot and involuntarily moving his camera. But nothing like this happens in frame 313 when a blur from Zapruder's camera movement and an impact on Kennedy's head occur simultaneously in the same frame. Why did this happen? Given numerous other facts, an answer is obvious. The shots at 224 and 328 were both fired from the Depository 6th floor window, while the 313 shot was fired from much closer in. Over a decade ago, Don Thomas ran the figures assuming the frame 313 shot originated where the acoustic scientists calculated its origin point to be, and they matched perfectly. As shown in the chart above that Thomas constructed, if the 313 shot was fired from the Depository window its shock wave and muzzle blast would not have reached Zapruder's ears until 314 and he would not have reacted until 315. For a shot from the stockade fence location, the figures match perfectly.

Plate 3a (*above left*) Frame Z 313. This original Ektachrome slide was made by the author from a 4" by 5" transparency of frame Z 313. That 4" by 5" transparency itself was made from the original film by LIFE magazine's renowned photo lab in 1966. The Ektachrome transparency has rested in my safe deposit box ever since. Plate 3b (*above right*) shows the same frame with color correction having removed the Ektachrome yellow tint.

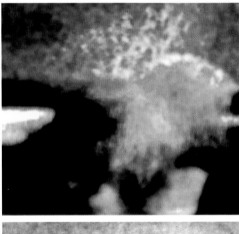

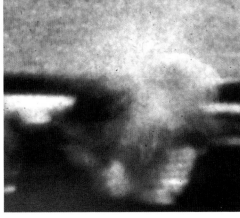

Plates 4a and 4b. Shadow-enhanced version of Frame Z 313 (*top*) derived from unenhanced version (*bottom*).

Plate 5. Frame Z 313 close-up. Arrows show direction of impact debris. The two longer arrows indicate paths of large skull fragments arcing up, forward and far to the left of the limousine direction of travel.

Plate 6. DPD Dictabelt recording.

Plate 7. DPD Audograph disk recording.

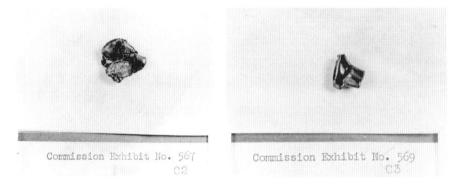

Plates 8a and 8b. These large fragments were found by Secret Service agents in the front seat area of the limousine on the evening of November 22. Later firearms identification tests showed they came from a bullet fired through the barrel Oswald's rifle.

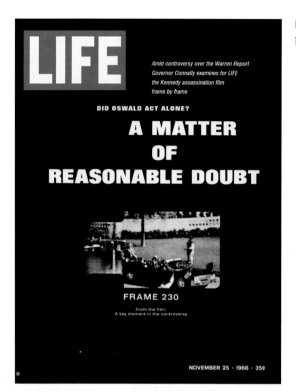

Plate 9. Cover of LIFE for November 25, 1966.

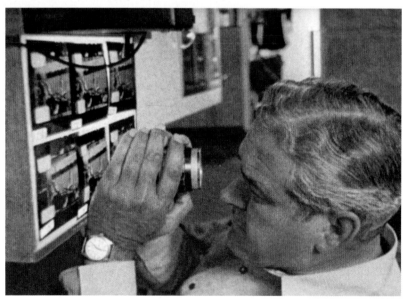

Plate 10. Governor John Connally examines LIFE magazine's frames from the Zapruder film in November 1966. These were the same frames that Ed Kern, Dick Billings and I showed Dr. Gregory a few days later.

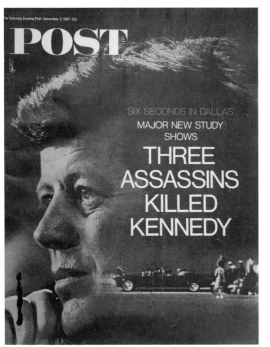

Plate 11. The *Saturday Evening Post* designed this dramatic cover for its December 2, 1967 issue.

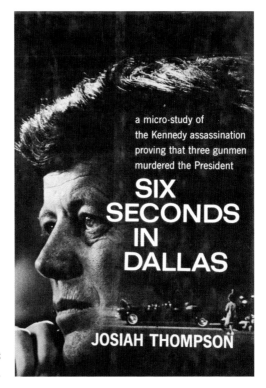

Plate 12. *Six Seconds in Dallas* published on November 17, 1967.

CHAPTER 15   BREAKING THE IMPASSE
The Crucial Piece—the Final Shot

It was November 2005, and Keith Fitzgerald had come to Bethesda, Maryland, for a conference on the Kennedy assassination that I was also attending. As I would soon learn, Keith Fitzgerald couldn't have cared less about the conference. He had come all the way from Concord, New Hampshire, to talk to me about something he had found in the Zapruder film.

Around the periphery of these conferences, there are always a few wild-eyed conspiracy theorists ready to buttonhole you with the latest skinny on how the Rosicrucians murdered the president. Yet when Keith first introduced himself to me, there was something about him that immediately signaled that he was a serious person with a serious purpose. He was a manufacturer's representative in southern New Hampshire and had spent some years earlier in the army. What I didn't know then was that he had polished his considerable analytic skills while in the army. I invited him to lunch.

We sat down at a restaurant, and the first thing he said was "You were right back then. You just didn't understand that you were right." He pointed out a fact that I had long forgotten had I ever paid any attention to it at all. Among the appendices in the back of Six Seconds was an appendix put together by Haverford physics student Bill Hoffman containing the raw data of the measurements he had done of the president's head movement under impact. Keith pulled a copy of Six Seconds out of his briefcase and opened it to page 274.

"You see right here at the end," he said, pointing to the last position measurements. "Between frame 327 and 328, his head moves forward 1.68 inches. And between frame 328 and 329, his head moves forward 1.91 inches. Then, between 329 and 330, it moves forward another 2.85 inches. That's the fastest his head moves at any point, even faster than between 312 and 313."

I interrupted him to explain that the movement in 312–313 was an illusion caused by the blur in 313. He grinned and replied, "Well, there isn't any blur here, and according to your own measurements, JFK's head moved forward 6.44 inches between frames 327 and 330."

Keith pointed out how, in the series of frames that begin with 327 and end with 337, the president's head wound changes, and his head and body accelerate forward and down.

By the time lunch was over, it seemed to me that Keith Fitzgerald might have put the last puzzle piece in place in what was becoming a revised picture of what really happened in Dealey Plaza. First came Erik Randich's acute demolition of Vincent Guinn's NAA tests. Next came David Wimp's remarkable proof of the blur illusion. Now Keith had provided the last explanation needed, a full account of just when Kennedy was hit in the head from the rear.

After that lunch in Bethesda, Keith and I began corresponding by e-mail. He would send his research, and I would ask him questions. I would challenge something, and he would meet the challenge. Finally, in October 2011, we got a chance to meet once again, this time in southern New Hampshire.

Keith has told me several times that he has no proprietary interest in what he discovered, that his only desire is that the information become public. His gesture is extraordinary in an area of historical research where pride of ownership has erupted in battles of epic silliness. Let me just say that in the following pages, I lay out what Keith has discovered over the past few years. My contributions to those discoveries have been minuscule.

The Zapruder frames show the president's body thrown violently backward and to the left until it strikes the upright back of the seat at frame 321 and bounces forward. Over the next six frames, up to frame 327, his head moves forward at an average speed of 0.945 inches per frame. Then, between frames 327 and 328, it suddenly accelerates to more than twice its earlier average speed (2.148 inches per frame) through frame 330. The measurements stop with frame 330, but the film shows the president's body continuing forward at the faster rate.

Since we know the president was not hit in the head prior to frame 313 and that he disappears from sight about frame 340, if he was hit a second time in the head, it had to be during this twenty-seven-frame sequence, or about 1.5 seconds.

What are we looking for? In frame 313, the pressure vessel of John Kennedy's head explodes. In frames after this, that pressure vessel no longer exists. Hence, any subsequent impact would cause no explosion. Instead, it would show a surge of blood and brain debris driven forward and a significant enlargement of the existing wound. Do we find indications of this in those twenty-seven Zapruder frames? Let's look at the frames from 312 to 317 (Photos 15-1 to 15-6).

These frames show no new impact after frame 313. They show the

Photo 15-1. Frame 312

Photo 15-2. Frame 313

Photo 15-3. Frame 314

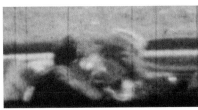

Photo 15-4. Frame 315

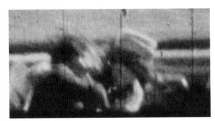

Photo 15-5. Frame 316

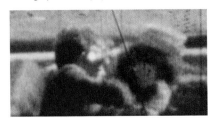

Photo 15-6. Frame 317

development of the frame 313 impact and the left and backward snap of the president's head. Note too that the blur beginning in frame 313 continues in successive frames at lesser intensity and then becomes almost clear again in frame 317. As physicist Luis Alvarez determined back in 1967, Zapruder's immediate flinch is followed by a train of movements or oscillations apparent on the film. In frames 318 and 319 (Photos 15-7 and 15-8), these oscillations become disruptive of the image as a whole.

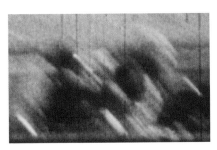

Photo 15-7. Frame 318

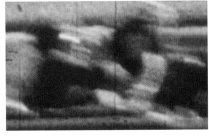

Photo 15-8. Frame 319

Could there have been an impact in these two frames that cannot be detected because of the blur? Yes, that could have happened, but when we compare the frame before and the frame after these two blurred frames, the president's head appears to be in much the same condition and in about the same position (Photos 15-9 through 15-10 below).

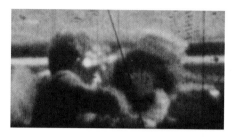 

Photo 15-9. Frame 317 (*before*)   Photo 15-10. Frame 320 (*after*)

Between these two frames, the president's head continues its backward travel, pulling along the rest of his body and raising his right elbow. Between frames 321 and 322, the president's body hits the vertical backseat cushion and bounces forward (Photos 15-11 through 15-15).

Photo 15-11. Frame 321   Photo 15-12. Frame 322

Photo 15-13. Frame 323   Photo 15-14. Frame 324

Photo 15-15. Frame 325

There is nothing in this long run of frames from 312 through 325 to suggest that the president has been hit a second time in the head after the impact shown in frame 313. Recall now the measurements and calculations that show that Kennedy's head doubled in forward speed beginning in frame 328. Does that extraordinary forward movement signal the impact from the rear for which we've been searching? Let us look closely at frame 326 and following (Photos 15-16 through 15-20).

Photo 15-16. Frame 326

Photo 15-17. Frame 327

Photo 15-18. Frame 328

Photo 15-19. Frame 329

Photo 15-20. Frame 330

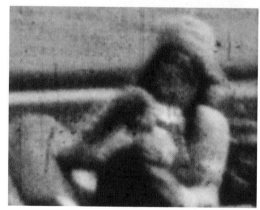

In the one-eighteenth of a second between frames 327 and 328, significant changes take place. In addition to the president's head accelerating forward at a high rate of speed, these frames show that a mass of gore has been driven out the front of his head and is hanging down before his face. But this is not the only change. Earlier frames—317 and 323 are the clearest—show that a region of scalp and hair in the upper left frontal part of his head survived the impact of the bullet at 313. After frame 328, however, this tuft of hair and scalp disappears in frame 328 to be replaced by a dark divot in the upper frontal region of the president's head. See arrows before and after (Photos 15-21 through 15-24).[1]

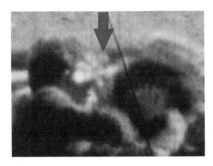

Photo 15-21. Frame 317 (*before*)

Photo 15-22. Frame 323 (*before*)

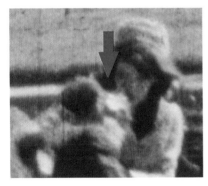

Photo 15-23. Frame 328 (*after*)

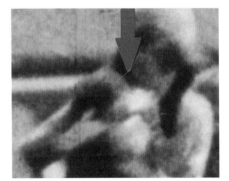

Photo 15-24. Frame 329 (*after*)

Next, right on schedule, comes a startled flinch by Zapruder in frames 331 and 332 (Photos 15-25 and 15-26).

Photo 15-25. Frame 331

Photo 15-26. Frame 332

These frames are followed by a series of frames that permit us to see how almost instantaneously the character of President Kennedy's head wound has changed. Frames 335 and 337 are enlarged because they are quite clear. First, the still somewhat blurred frames 333 and 334 are shown in Photos 15-27 and 15-28.

Photo 15-27. Frame 333

Photo 15-28. Frame 334

Photo 15-29. Frame 335

In half a second, the president's head has been driven forward and down. In addition, the wound in the right front of his head has been enlarged. Comparing frame 327 with frames 335 and 337, we see that what earlier was only a shiny surface of skull has exploded and is now a flap of bone hanging just forward of Kennedy's right ear. Whereas in frame 327 the right side of his face was visible, it is now dark in the shadow of the bone flap. In addition, it appears that a section of bone, scalp, and matted hair has been forced outward and forward. These horrific changes are the result of a shot striking Kennedy's head between frames 327 and 328 (Photos 15-30 and 15-31).[1]

Photo 15-30. Frame 327 close-up

Photo 15-31. Frame 337 close-up. This astonishing change shows that the president's head has moved forward over a foot in five-ninths of a second.

The Connally Wrist Wound

If we expand our focus to look at Governor and Mrs. Connally during the same crucial second, we will be following Keith Fitzgerald's initial discovery path. He started out trying to identify the moment when Governor Connally was hit in the wrist. Back in 1966, Connally's wrist surgeon, Dr. Charles Gregory, had made it clear to Ed Kern, Dick Billings, and me that he was convinced that Connally's wrist injury came from a bullet fragment.

The afternoon of our interview, as we were finishing our questions, I pulled Zapruder frame 230 out of the stack of four-by-five-inch transparencies. "One final question, if you don't mind, Dr. Gregory," I remember saying. "If you look here at this very clear frame, the governor looks quite composed and is holding his Stetson in his right hand. It was his right wrist that was shattered by a bullet. The government says he's already taken that bullet. Could he hold on to his hat that way if his wrist had been shattered?"

"Of course not," replied Dr. Gregory. "The government's wrong. Connally wasn't hit in the wrist with the bullet they say he was. I told them all this in my testimony down there. The bullet they're talking about has a rounded tip. He wasn't hit in the wrist with that. He took a fragment through the wrist. It must have been later."

After returning to Haverford, I went back over Dr. Gregory's testimony before the Warren Commission. It was easy to see what he had in mind. First, Dr. Gregory was an old pro with bullet wounds. He had served with the navy in the closing stages of World War II and later as a field surgeon with the First Marine Division in Korea. He estimated that as a surgeon, he had worked on more than five hundred bullet wounds.

The morning of his testimony, Dr. Gregory had been given a look at commission exhibits 567 and 569, the two fragments found in the front seat of the limousine that undoubtedly came from the shot that hit President Kennedy in the head (color photo gallery, Plates 6a and 6b). Dr. Gregory pointed out that these fragments were exactly what he had been talking about as the most likely thing to have caused Connally's wrist injury: "These distorted bits of a missile, a jacket in one case and a lead core in the other . . . these are missiles having the characteristics I mentioned earlier, which tend to carry organic debris into wounds and tend to create irregular wounds of entry. One of these, it seems to me, could conceivably have produced the injury which the Governor incurred in his wrist."

Counsel Specter asked Dr. Gregory if a fragment from the bullet that hit President Kennedy in the head could have hit Connally's wrist and caused his injury. Dr. Gregory replied,

I think it is plausible that the bullet, having struck the President's head, may have broken into more than one fragment. I think you apprised me of the fact that it did, in fact, disperse into a number of fragments, and they took tangential directions from the original path apparently. . . . I think it is possible that a fragment from that particular missile may have escaped and struck the Governor's right arm.

Back in 1966, when I read this testimony, it seemed that Dr. Gregory knew what he was talking about and that the characteristics of the wrist injury indicated that it came from a fragment thrown off by the head shot. As for the governor's assessment, he testified in 1964 that he first learned of his wrist wound when he woke up on Saturday morning and found his arm in a cast. "What's wrong with my arm?" he asked. "They told me then that I had a shattered wrist." If Connally could not throw any light on the question, perhaps the Zapruder film contained indications of when Connally was hit in the wrist.

In frame 230, we see Connally looking straight ahead, holding his Stetson upside down. As the sequence continues, we see him turning to his right

Photo 15-32. Frame 230. Connally holding his white Stetson upside down.

Photo 15-33. Frame 242. Connally holding his hat and facing the camera.

Photo 15-34. Frame 312. Connally reclining and turning forward, holding his hat to his chest.

Photo 15-35. Frame 323. Connally facing forward, holding his hat to his chest.

while showing the impact effects of a shot through his chest. By frame 242, he is facing Zapruder's camera. All the while, he holds his Stetson upside down close to his chest. He continues to hold his hat in this position through the next run of frames. By frame 312, his turn has taken him so far that his shoulders are aligned to the limousine's direction of travel. Then he begins turning back to his left, still gripping his hat with his right hand, leaning back toward his wife. By frame 323, he is looking straight ahead again while still holding his hat. Thus, for some five seconds after being wounded in the chest, he holds his hat in his right hand while turning both right and left.

There seems to be no reason to believe that Connally was hit in the wrist prior to frame 328. Now watch what happens (Photos 15-36 through 15-39).

As the president's head is driven forward and down, his head wound

Photo 15-36. Frame 328. Holding his hat in his right hand, Connally continues to collapse forward and down.

Photo 15-37. Frame 329. Connally continues to grip his hat in his right hand while collapsing forward and down.

Photo 15-38. Frame 330. Connally's fingers still grip his hat as he collapses even farther forward and down.

Photo 15-39. Frame 335. It is unclear, but Connally's right hand appears to have released his hat.

enlarging and gore streaming in front of his face, Connally's body begins a parallel trajectory down and forward. In frame 328, his right wrist is visible gripping his upside-down Stetson. Moreover, it is in precisely the correct position to have taken a bullet fragment from the president's head. The trajectory of such a fragment at this instant would have produced Connally's wrist wound, as observed by Dr. Gregory minutes later at Parkland Hospital.

Photo 15-40. Frame 328 showing the line-up of the rear impact on Connally's right wrist.

Photo 15-41. Frame 328 close-up, with bullet trajectory (red) and fragment trajectory to Connally (yellow).

The Windshield Flare

Recall the blow that the inside surface of the windshield took from a substantial lead fragment... perhaps CE 567? If the interior surface of the windshield was struck from the rear, it would bow out. That bowing would change the angle of the windshield to the noonday sun and possibly throw a flare of sunlight into Zapruder's camera. Just such a flare reflection from the windshield comes at frames 329 and 330. Note Photos 15-42 through 15-44.

Photo 15-42. Frame 328   Photo 15-43. Frame 329

Photo 15-44. Frame 330

It is difficult to know what to make of this flare. It endures for only a very short interval. Is it an indisputable sign that the windshield was struck from the rear by a fragment at this time? No. It is possible that the car's angle to the sun changed as it proceeded and this caused the flare. It would be an amazing coincidence for the car's movement to independently cause the flare at the exact moment when all the other indicia point to a hit on President Kennedy's head from the rear. But coincidences do happen.

The final shot—the ending climax to this nightmare—can be shown in a diagram overlaid on frame 328 (Photo 15-45).

Photo 15-45. Frame 328 with bullet trajectory (*red*), fragment trajectory to Connally (*white*), and windshield fragment trajectory (*yellow*).

The Acoustics Match at Frame 328

As an earlier chapter described, the 1978 discovery of the acoustics evidence presented a quandary for the HSCA. James Barger and his team at BBN in Cambridge had found a total of five shots on the DPD audiotapes. The HSCA reduced that number to four on the specious grounds that two of the shots were too close together to have been fired by Oswald's rifle. However, a match-up of the acoustics with the Zapruder film based on five shots produced by far the best alignment, particularly if the fourth (or next-to-last) shot were aligned with Zapruder frame 313.

In summarizing the evidence on December 29, 1978, the last day of the HSCA hearings, Chief Counsel Robert Blakey was acutely aware of the contradictions in the evidence. In the following, when Blakey says "third shot" and "fourth shot," read as "next-to-last shot" and "last shot":

> If Zapruder frame 313 actually reflects the time of the third shot rather than the fourth, the timing of the first, second and fourth shots would then correspond respectively with Zapruder frames 182, 313 and 328. *The possibility that the fourth shot occurred at Zapruder frame 328 would require a finding*, in light of the neutron activation analysis, the ballistics test and the medical testimony, that *both the third and fourth shots hit President Kennedy in the head* (emphasis added).[2]

In his last sentence, Blakey makes an amazing admission, compelled by the logic of the case. If frame 313 shows the next-to-last shot, then that shot obviously knocked Kennedy to the left rear and blasted blood and brains over the cyclists to the left rear. If so, then how did blood and brain tissue get thrown as far forward as the hood ornament and two large fragments fired from Oswald's rifle end up in the front seat area? How did the windshield get cracked on its interior surface and the chrome strip get dented from the rear by a bullet fragment? All these confirmed items of evidence require a second hit to Kennedy's head, this time from directly behind, from the depository's sixth floor window. The acoustic evidence says that happened at frames 327–328.

The Zapruder Film's Third Dimension: Witness Validation

I know it's an old chestnut, but it is also the truth. Time and again in various cases, I have seen it happen. You work on a case for a long, long time. Most of the work is done, and then finally a crucial piece of evidence comes in. That piece does not just fit all the other pieces, it tells you that you have it. You were right. You now know what really happened.

Something like that happened in 2009 when I got from Keith Fitzgerald his research on the witnesses close to the president along the south curb of Elm Street at Zapruder frame 328. I opened the file and read what he had put together on James Altgens, Jack Franzen, and Charles Brehm. Altgens was, of course, familiar to me from 1966–1967; the other two were not. I checked Fitzgerald's references and then called to congratulate him. It was stunning. He had filled in a new and crucial part of the puzzle.

James Altgens

I had not thought of AP photographer James Altgens for a decade or so. In 1966, he had been on our LIFE list for an interview in Dallas, but for reasons I have long forgotten, it had never worked out. Instead, I had put together a file on Altgens. It was troubling because what Altgens said he experienced did not fit with anything else we knew. He had testified to the Warren Commission that he had seen the president hit in the head and thrown forward in his seat by the shot. He was standing farther down Elm Street when this happened and had seen "flesh particles that flew out the side of his head in my direction."[3] This meant they had flown forward toward Altgens. All of this convinced Altgens that the shot to the head had come from behind the limousine, from the Texas School Book Depository. In June 1967, CBS put Altgens on television to rebut claims that the president had been shot from the right front. In that broadcast, he said,

> And as they got in close to me, and I was prepared to make the picture, I had my camera almost at eye level; that's when the President was shot in the head. And

I do know the President was still in an upright position, tilted, favoring Mrs. Kennedy. And at the time that he was struck by this blow to the head, it was so obvious that it came from behind. It had to come from behind because it caused him to bolt forward, dislodging him from this depression in the seat cushion, and already favoring Mrs. Kennedy, he automatically fell in that direction.[4]

The crucial point in all this is where Altgens was when he saw this. No one was in a better position than Altgens to observe the shot at frame 328. He had already taken photos of the presidential limousine on Main Street, again on Houston Street, and finally on Elm Street as the limousine and its motorcycle outriders headed toward him. After taking his historic photo, he later told the Warren Commission, "I had refocused [my camera] to fifteen feet because I wanted a good close-up of the President and Mrs. Kennedy and that's why I

Photo 15-46. Frame 342. The arrow points to James Altgens with his camera raised.

Photo 15-47. Frame 357

know it would be right at 15 feet because I had pre-focused in that area, and I had my camera almost to my eye when it happened and that's as far as I got with my camera"[5] (Photos 15-46 through 15-47).

Altgens appears in the Zapruder film from frames 339 through 353, standing on the south curb of Elm Street. In this sequence, we can determine what was happening in the limousine at the time that Altgens was fifteen feet from it with his camera raised to his face. As the limousine glides by Altgens, we can see that he has his "camera almost at eye level." Less than half a second earlier, Kennedy's head has been knocked forward, pulling along his body until both head and body end up in his wife's lap.

Of equal importance is Altgens's certainty that he was witnessing the last shot to be fired that day. He testified to the Warren Commission:

> There was not another shot fired after the President was struck in the head. That was the last shot—that much I will say with a great degree of certainty. . . . What made me almost certain that the shot came from behind was because at the time I was looking at the President, just as he was struck, it caused him to move a bit forward. He seemed as if at the right time—well, he was in a position— sort of immobile. He wasn't upright. He was at an angle but when it hit him, it seemed to have just lodged—it seemed as if he were hung up on a seat button or something like that. It knocked him just enough forward that he came right on down. There was flesh particles that flew out of the side of his head in my direction from where I was standing, so much so that it indicated to me that the shot came from out the left side of his head. Also, the fact that his head was covered with blood, the hairline included on the left side—all the way down, with no blood on his forehead or face—suggested to me, too, that the shot came from the opposite side, meaning in the direction of this Depository Building, but at no time did I know for certain where the shot came from.[6]

Decades ago, I had thought Altgens was describing the shot at frame 313, but I now knew that Altgens was actually describing the shot to the back of the president's head at frame 328. He had completely missed the left and backward snap at frame 313 because it occurred while he was raising the camera to his eye, and it was over in less than half a second. Everything he described we can see in the Zapruder film at frame 328. That shot caused the president to "bolt forward, dislodging him from this depression in the seat cushion." That shot "knocked him just enough forward that he came right on down."

The one thing Altgens was sure of was that he was seeing the last shot fired that day. He was right.

Jack and Joan Franzen

Some twenty to twenty-five feet farther down Elm Street from Altgens stood Jack and Joan Franzen and their six-year-old son, Jeff. Within days of the shooting, the FBI interviewed the couple, but like many FBI interviews at that time, it produced little information. Jack Franzen described hearing what he thought was a firecracker, followed by "a second and third, and possibly a fourth, explosion and recognized these sounds as shots from some firearm."[7]

In June 1997, the Franzens' daughter, Julie (who had not been born in 1963), took her father to downtown Dallas, recorded his memories of November 22,

Photo 15-48. Frame 359. Altgens and Jeff Franzen.

Photo 15-49. Frame 369. The Franzens.

and then typed out a transcript of the recording. Jack Franzen saw almost the same thing that James Altgens saw. Their reports dovetail. Franzen remembered,

> But the car kept coming and picking up a little speed. Then, we were right there at the car—maybe 25 feet from it. Connally appeared to be bending over—in retrospect, he'd probably been hit. Nell [Mrs. Connally] was looking at him. At just about that time, another explosion and, you could just see Kennedy's head—his forehead—literally explode. Whatever hit him, I would feel, hit from the back . . . for his blood and brain matter went forward. His body went forward . . . his body went forward and to his left. And he was sitting on Jackie's right. As it went forward and to the left, there was a lot of gore and he kind of fell over onto Jackie and she jumped up. Almost got her knees or feet on the seat rather than on the floor . . . At this same time, there was a relatively short Secret Service fellow kind of trotting along at the left rear of the car. . . . [He] reacted quickly, and came up to the rear of the car and jumped on the bumper.[8]

What Franzen and Altgens describe is what we see on the Zapruder film and what we described in meticulous detail, frame by frame, as it developed.

Charles Brehm

Charles Brehm, holding his five-year-old boy in his arms, was standing near the same curb farther up Elm Street, a short distance from where Mary Moorman took her famous Polaroid photo. He was too far away to witness what Altgens and the Franzens saw, but he did add a single piece to the puzzle.

Brehm had been with the US Army Ranger battalions that hit Point du Hoc on D-Day, June 6, 1944. He had been wounded later in the campaign by a bullet through the chest and had seen a lot of combat. He knew what bullets sounded like when they came close or were shot over your head.

Brehm was interviewed by two FBI agents on the Monday after the assassination.[9] He stated that the limousine was well past his position when the president "stiffened perceptibly at the same instant . . . when a rifle shot sounded." Then "another shot sounded and the President seemed to be badly hit in the head," and he saw "the President's hair fly up." He was sure Kennedy had been hit because he "recalled seeing blood on the President's face." "A third shot followed," the FBI report says. "Immediately after the third shot rang out, Brehm pushed his son down on the grass and for the moment was more concerned with the safety of his son who might be hit accidentally by any wild gunfire which might follow."

Photo 15-50. Muchmore film: Brehm and son with Hill and Moorman.

What was it about the third shot that made Brehm suddenly concerned for the safety of his son? He failed to explain this to the agents, or they failed to write it down. In a later interview, he did explain it:

> The third shot really frightened me! It had a completely different sound to it because it had really passed me, as anybody knows who has been down under targets in the Army or been shot at like I had been many times. You know when a bullet passes over you, the cracking sound it makes, and that bullet had an absolute crack to it. . . . And I grabbed the boy and threw him on the ground because I didn't know if we were going to have a "shoot-'em-up" in this area. After I hit the ground and smothered the boy, it was all over.[10]

What Brehm says fits our revised scenario: the first of two flurries of shots occurs farther up Elm Street. They did not pass over Brehm. The fourth shot, fired from the knoll, hit short of Brehm in President Kennedy's head. Only the last shot, the shot fired over Brehm, probably from the depository, could have had the distinctive sound that "really frightened" him. Only that sound could have carried him back to his days of combat in Normandy, when he had taken a bullet through the chest after hearing all the others that missed him.

S. M. "Skinny" Holland

The witnesses scattered along the south side of Elm Street found themselves inside whatever was going on. On the other hand, as we have seen earlier, for

S. M. Holland, it was like being in the audience for an outdoor stage play. His was the perfect spot to observe the assassination.

I thought of this after Keith Fitzgerald and I finished going over the witnesses along Elm Street. I pulled out my file on Holland with its interview transcript on seventy-one pages of the thin paper that we used for making carbon copies in the 1960s. I began to read.

Holland was saying that the next-to-last shot—the shot from the fence—sounded different from the others, not as loud. "It was like it came from a .38 pistol compared with a high-powered rifle."[11] Then Holland saw the president "knocked over. It was just like you'd hit somebody with your fist and knock him down."

Reading this interview after almost fifty years, I was transported back to Holland's living room with its knickknacks and signs of a life lived modestly. Back then, I believed the final two shots were fired virtually simultaneously. I remember being disappointed when he rejected my characterization:

> THOMPSON: Could you tell me—you know we speak of simultaneous and almost simultaneous—was the—was the—pardon me, were the third and fourth reports—were they "blo-om" [*Thompson indicating two sounds almost together*]? Were they like that? Or were they boom, boom?
> HOLLAND: Well, like "boom-boom" [*Holland makes two distinct but very close-together sounds*].
> THOMPSON: Pretty fast together?
> HOLLAND: Pretty fast together. They wasn't simultaneous, as we call it. They was "boom-boom."[12]

Shots fired 0.7 seconds apart at frame 313 and 328 would not be simultaneous but would be, as Holland said, not "simultaneous" but "boom-boom."

Our dialogue about the sounds of the last two shots continued:

> THOMPSON: Let me ask you, having seen this from this cockpit view, which bullet hit whom, and how—I mean, you heard the first bullet.
> HOLLAND: Well, the third and the fourth bullets hit the president.
> THOMPSON: You think both bullets hit the president?
> HOLLAND: Well, I say this: that the president fell over when the third and fourth shot was fired. Now whether he was caught in a crossfire or whether both of them hit him, I can't say.
> THOMPSON: Did you see any dust fly up from the pavement, or anything which would indicate that one of those two missed?

Photo 15-51. Less than a minute after the shooting, Holland (*ellipse*) watches press cars head under the Triple Underpass.

> HOLLAND: I didn't, and I was observing very close because that's what I was up there for.
>
> THOMPSON: Is it your opinion then—what is your opinion—that the third and fourth did hit the president?
>
> HOLLAND: My opinion is that the third and the fourth did, did hit the president.
>
> THOMPSON: In the head?
>
> HOLLAND: In the head.[13]

Twelve years before the acoustics evidence was discovered, Holland delivered the same message: the next-to-last shot was fired from near the corner of the fence on the knoll and all others from the northeast end of Elm Street, and both the next-to-last shot and the last shot hit the president in the head.

In the world of the American court system, which by design is adversarial and where dramatic courtroom battles are waged, there is one strategic advantage that attorneys prize: to be able to argue before judge and jury that based on new findings, conflicting evidence and testimony turn out instead to be confirmatory. The end result is an argument in which disparate pieces fit together with clarity and simplicity. This is precisely what has happened now with respect to earlier conflicts in evidence concerning the last shot. The Zapruder frames, the position and nature of Governor Connally's wrist injury, the windshield flare, the acoustics, the witness testimony—all are now consistent and mutually confirmative. Together, they offer a kind of climax to our narrative as the final piece of the puzzle slides effortlessly into place.

As 2011 drew to a close, I found myself for the first time in decades looking at the puzzle of the Kennedy assassination with fresh eyes and a new perspective. Thanks in great measure to the remarkable individuals whose extraordinary contributions in recent years are chronicled in these pages, the impasse had been broken. The pieces of the puzzle that never belonged there had been identified and discarded, and with their removal, the remaining pieces had fallen into place, reinforcing and validating each other as parts of a larger whole.

No better example of this process can be found than in the medical evidence, which is why I have waited until now to examine this most difficult and contentious set of puzzle pieces. As we are about to see, once one has gained full knowledge of what actually happened during the last second of the killing, the pieces of the medical evidence—as conflicting, frustrating, and indecipherable as they seem at first—fall into place with something approaching simplicity and elegance.

CHAPTER 16   THE MEDICAL EVIDENCE

U p to now, we have examined almost every aspect of what happened in Dealey Plaza during the last second of the assassination. Every aspect, that is, except one: what happened inside President's Kennedy's skull during that last second. This is by design.

Pursuing this aspect will take us deep into the medical evidence, a body of evidence sometimes described as "a swamp within a swamp." Good people have tried to figure it out and ended up wandering in circles for years before giving up in frustration. Friendships have been ended by disputes over how to make sense of the pieces. It is the most contentious and most opaque part of the case and therefore the part most subject to conspiracy theorizing. It has long been questioned whether any real clarity can be achieved with respect to evidence so riven by contradiction and doubt. Nonetheless, given the recent changes in the evidence package, it may be possible to understand at least its overall shape with greater confidence.

As mentioned in the Preface, the reader may find the president's autopsy photos in this chapter unsettling. Indeed, they are, in the same way that the gruesome frames from the Zapruder film laid out in the preceding chapter are unsettling. The emotions they produce are raw, and the cold eye of science can never quite suppress our wince when we see them. But this is a murder case, and for that reason, the details of the murder—no matter how gruesome—may hold the key to its solution.

The President's Autopsy

No part of the forensic investigation of a homicide is more important than the autopsy. Both prosecution and defense investigators count on it to provide critical information concerning the victim's murder. In the case of a shooting, it can help identify both the gun that fired the killing bullet and the trajectory of that bullet. It is performed in a formal hospital-like setting with the forensic pathologist dictating his or her observations into a tape recorder. Either the forensic pathologist or a trained autopsy technician photographs all the important wounds and features of the victim's body. This is done so that the factual underpinnings of the autopsy can be reproduced and used in any later court proceeding. If the autopsy conclusions are challenged, this careful documentation makes possible later review by experts.

At the center of all the confusion and controversy in the medical evidence is, of course, the Kennedy autopsy. Fifteen years after the event, a blue-ribbon panel of forensic medical experts was set up by the HSCA to look into the question. The chairman of that panel, Dr. Michael Baden, ex–medical examiner of the city of New York, would later write, "Where bungled autopsies are concerned, President Kennedy's is the exemplar."[1]

A central controversy is whether the autopsy was botched by simple incompetence or whether it was botched by design to cover up clear evidence of conspiracy in the shooting. Let me be clear: I opt for the former.

During the flight of Air Force One back to Washington, the president's physician, Admiral George Burkley, got up from his seat and went back to Mrs. Kennedy, who was sitting next to her husband's body in the rear of the airplane.[2] After some quiet talk, he raised the awkward question of the autopsy. At first she demurred, saying, "Well, it doesn't have to be done." They talked some more, and Mrs. Kennedy agreed to an autopsy to be done at Bethesda Naval Hospital.

Soon thereafter someone in authority radioed the White House Situation Room to say that Mrs. Kennedy wanted the autopsy performed at Bethesda. A functionary then called Admiral Calvin Galloway, the commanding officer of the Bethesda National Naval Medical Center, and told him Mrs. Kennedy had decided the autopsy should be performed at his facility. The admiral figuratively saluted and said he would get right on it. He directed the hospital's operator to call Commander James J. Humes, whose official position at Bethesda was administrative. As he later introduced himself before testifying got the Warren Commission, he was Director of Laboratories of the Naval Medical Center, Bethesda (2H348). The hospital's operator told him that he was ordered urgently to report to the hospital as soon as possible.

According to an account published years later, Dr. Humes was off call that Friday afternoon.[3] The operator's call gave him no clue that the decision had been made to perform the presidential autopsy at Bethesda rather than in Dallas. He immediately left for the hospital, only to encounter a monumental traffic jam. Reaching the hospital, Humes was informed by Admiral Galloway that the president's body would shortly arrive from Dallas and to get ready to do an autopsy that night. Humes also figuratively saluted and said he would get right on it. He asked another pathologist in a largely administrative position—Chief of Pathology at the National Naval Medical School (ZH377)—Commander J. Thorton Boswell, to assist.

Anticipating that they might be out of their depth and knowing that some of the most experienced forensic pathologists in the country were available as consultants from the medical examiner's office in either Baltimore or the District of Columbia, the two doctors asked if any of them could be called to assist. They were discouraged from doing so. They then requested that army Lieutenant Colonel Pierre Finck, a forensic pathologist with the Armed Forces Institute of Pathology, be asked to stand by. The request was granted.

While the refusal to allow the participation of civilian pathologists may seem suspicious, the context of fast-moving events suggests the absence of any dark motive. A shocked and confused country had just lost its leader, the nation's capital was on high alert, and the military—with its institutional bias against civilian intrusion—was focused on maintaining the highest level of security. Under the circumstances, the military brass were disposed to believe they needed no outside assistance.

In this whole process, no one bothered to check whether either Humes or Boswell was remotely qualified to do an autopsy on a gunshot victim. They were not. Both were board certified in anatomic and clinical pathology, but neither was board certified in forensic pathology, a specialty that requires up to five more years of experience doing medicolegal autopsies. When Humes and Boswell saw the skull with its multiple interlocking fractures, they knew they were in over their heads. Colonel Finck was called, but by the time he arrived, the autopsy was well underway, and the president's brain had already been removed from the cranial cavity.[4]

In its second paragraph, the autopsy report revealed its amateurish quality. Autopsies do not usually cite contemporaneous press dispatches, but this one did. Examination of the victim's clothes is a sine qua non of forensic autopsies, especially in gunshot cases. The president's clothes were likely in the autopsy room at Bethesda that night. For whatever reason, they were never examined.[5]

These lapses pale in comparison to more fundamental errors. No microphone was worn by Commander Humes, and no detailed notes were taken of the step-by-step procedure. A trained autopsy photographer was in the room along with his camera and his assistant, but the photos that survive seem like snapshot views of the body. Worse, the autopsy doctors and the photographer all subsequently testified that critical photos of wounds and organs were taken but did not survive.[6] Military personnel testified years later that a whole set of autopsy photos they developed had been lost.[7] Humes himself later testified that while at home on the Sunday afternoon following the autopsy, he burned in his fireplace both his notes and early drafts of the autopsy, and Finck testified that he gave his notes to Humes.[8] Since they too failed to survive, they may also have gone up the chimney of Humes's fireplace.[9] Much later it was determined by experts that the autopsy doctors had mistakenly located the position of bullet entry wounds in Kennedy's body. One entry wound in the head was off by four inches.

The consequence of these missteps on the night of November 22 is that very little in the official autopsy report can be accepted as a reliable account of the president's head wounds. If not, what can?

Here we are in luck, since the president's head wounds were examined by trained medical personnel at Parkland Hospital only minutes after the shooting. In addition, they were seen by Jacqueline Kennedy and Secret Service Agent Clint Hill as the car made its way to Parkland Hospital.

The Parkland Witnesses

Of all the medical personnel gathered around the president's body at Parkland Hospital, Dr. Kemp Clark had the most educated eye for head injuries. As chief of neurosurgery, his task was to swiftly and carefully assess the president's head injury and do what he could to save his life. Clark spent a long time observing the head wound before finally pronouncing President Kennedy dead at 1:00 p.m.

An hour and a quarter after pronouncing the president dead, Clark joined emergency-room doctor Malcolm Perry in a press conference at Parkland. At one point Perry described a small bullet entry wound in the center of Kennedy's throat. He allowed that the bullet that hit him in the throat was a bullet that "appeared to be coming at him."[10] This led to rapid-fire questions from reporters concerning whether the neck wound might be related to the head wound. Perry said he couldn't say. Clark added, "The head wound could have been either the exit wound from the neck or it could have been a tangential wound, as it was simply a large, gaping loss of tissue."[11] Two hours later, Clark wrote a brief description of the head wound in his own hand: "There was a large wound beginning in the right occiput extending into the parietal region. Much of the skull appeared gone."[12] He amplified this description in a brief summary put together the next day: "There was a large wound in the right occipito-parietal region. . . . There was considerable loss of scalp and bone tissue. Both cerebral and cerebellar tissue were extruding from the

Photo 16-1. Dr. Kemp Clark (*left, with arms crossed*) and Dr. Malcolm Perry (*right*) during the Parkland Hospital news conference, November 22, 1963.

wound."[13]Later Clark would say, "The lower right occipital bone was blown out and I saw cerebellum."[14]

In March 1964, Clark was deposed by the Warren Commission and stressed that it was his considered opinion that the head wound was "tangential":

[At the press conference] I was asked if this wound was an entrance wound, an exit wound, or what, and I said it could be an exit wound, but I felt it was a tangential wound. . . . When a bullet strikes the head, if it is able to pass through rapidly without shedding any energy into the brain, little damage results, other than the part of the brain which is directly penetrated by the missile. However, if it strikes the skull at an angle, it must then penetrate much more bone than normal, therefore, it is likely to shed more energy, striking the brain a more powerful blow.[15]

Clark is describing a tangential wound, a shot that hit Kennedy on the right side of his head high above the right temple and ranged rearward into the occipital-parietal area.

Clark's remark that the occipital bone "was blown out" is reflected in the equally vivid description of the wound given by Dr. Robert McClelland:

As I took the position at the head of the table . . . I was in such a position that I could very closely examine the head wound, and I noted that the right posterior portion of the skull had been blasted. It had been shattered, apparently, by the force of the bullet so that the parietal bone was protruded up through the scalp

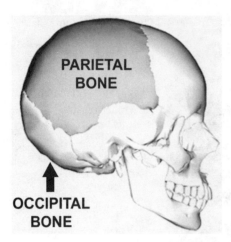

Figure 16-2. Location of parietal and occipital bones.

PARIETAL BONE

OCCIPITAL BONE

and seemed to be fractured almost along its posterior half, as well as some of the occipital bone being fractured in its lateral half, and this sprung open the bones that I mentioned in such a way that you could actually look down into the skull cavity itself and see that probably a third or so, at least, of the brain tissue, posterior cerebral tissue and some of the cerebellar tissue, had been blasted out.[16]

Other medical personnel at Parkland described the head wound in much the same way. Dr. Perry, for example, described "a large avulsive injury of the right occipitoparietal area."[17] "Avulsive" is medical language for "forcibly torn open." It recurs repeatedly in descriptions of the head wound.

During his sworn deposition, Dr. Marion Jenkins said he thought the wound in the back of President Kennedy's head was an exit wound: "Because the wound [was] with the exploded area of scalp (as I interpreted it being exploded), I would interpret it being a wound of exit."[18] On the afternoon of the shooting, Jenkins described the wound as "a great laceration of the right side of the head (temporal and occipital), causing a great defect in the skull plate so that there was herniation and laceration of great areas of the brain, even to the extent that the cerebellum . . . had protruded from the wound."[19]

Dr. James Carrico was one of the first physicians to attend President Kennedy. Later that afternoon, he wrote, "The other wound had avulsed the calvarium [skull bone] and shredded brain tissue [was] present with profuse oozing."[20] Later he expanded his description: "There seemed to be a 4 to 5 cm. area of avulsion of the scalp and the skull was fragmented and bleeding cerebral and cerebellar tissue. The wound that I saw was a large gaping wound, located in the right occipito-parietal area. I would estimate it to be about 5 to

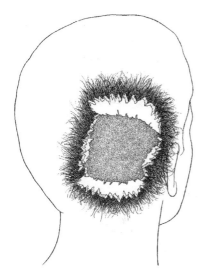

Figure 16-3. Dr. Robert McClelland's wound description as drawn by a medical illustrator. Dr. McClelland later declared the sketch to be accurate.

7 cm. in size, more or less circular, with avulsions of the calvarium and scalp tissue."[21] The head wound appeared so obviously to be an avulsive wound of exit that two other physicians thought it might well be the exit point of the bullet that entered Kennedy's throat from the front.

The list of Parkland Hospital witnesses who saw a wound in the right rear of the president's head could be greatly expanded. Gary Aguilar, MD, compiled the recollections of twenty-two Parkland Hospital witnesses who described the president's head wound. Twenty of the twenty-two described it as it was described above and located it in the right rear of the president's head.[22]

In the 1960s, only the head-wound descriptions of Parkland Hospital witnesses were known since they were included in hospital reports and Warren Commission testimony. Since that time, descriptions of the head wound from personnel who saw it during the Bethesda autopsy and afterward have surfaced. By Aguilar's count, twenty-two of twenty-four Bethesda reports describe a blow-out wound in the right rear of the head.[23] This total comprises the three autopsists as well as other physicians who attended the autopsy, two FBI agents, three Secret Service agents, five technicians, a hospital corpsman, and the morticians who prepared the body.

Jacqueline Kennedy and Secret Service Agent Clint Hill

Probably neither Jacqueline Kennedy nor Clint Hill knew what "occipitoparietal" meant. Clearly their descriptions of the head wound were less precise than those of the Parkland doctors and nurses—but also searingly vivid.

Jacqueline Kennedy was interviewed with great delicacy by the commission on June 5, 1964. She started by telling the commission that she could see the shadowed tunnel of the Triple Underpass before them as they started down Elm Street: "We could see a tunnel in front of us. Everything was really slow then. I remember thinking it would be so cool under that tunnel."[24] Then she went on to describe what happened:

I was looking this way, to the left, and I heard these terrible noises. You know. And my husband never made any sound. So I turned to the right. And all I remember is seeing my husband, he had this sort of quizzical look on his face, and his hand was up, it must have been his left hand. And just as I turned and looked at him, I could see a piece of his skull and I remember it was flesh colored. I remember thinking he just looked as if he had a slight headache. And I just remember seeing that. No blood or anything. And then he sort of did this [indicating], put his hand to his forehead and fell in my lap. And then I just remember falling on him and saying, "Oh, no, no, no," I mean, "Oh my God, they have shot my husband." And "I love you, Jack," I remember I was shouting. And just being down in the car with his head in my lap. And it just seemed an eternity.

You know then there were pictures later on of me climbing out the back. But I don't remember that at all. . . . I was just down and holding him.[25]

The transcript of Mrs. Kennedy's testimony released by the Warren Commission contained a redaction. Subsequent study of the court reporter's steno record showed that Mrs. Kennedy actually said, "I could see a piece of his skull sort of wedge-shaped, like that, and I remember that it was flesh colored with little ridges at the top. I was trying to hold his hair on. From the front there was nothing—I suppose there must have been. But from the back you could see, you know, you were trying to hold his hair on, and his skull on."[26]

It is somewhat difficult to make out clearly what she is saying here. As she held him in her lap, she was trying to "hold his hair on, and his skull on." She seems to be saying that looking at him from the front, "there was nothing" (that is, no visible damage), "but from the back you could see"—and here she breaks off.

As a Secret Service agent, Clint Hill's recollections are more specific but no less forceful than Mrs. Kennedy's. Eight days after the shooting, he put what he remembered in a written statement. He recalled that the shot that hit the president in the head "had a different sound—like shooting a revolver into something hard."[27] He went on, "I jumped onto the left rear step of the Presidential automobile. Mrs. Kennedy shouted, 'They've shot his head off!'

Photo 16-4. Clint Hill, splattered with blood and brain tissue, runs to the limousine. Note the position of the motorcycles to Hill's left, which were also splattered with impact debris.

As I lay over the back seat I noticed a portion of the President's head on the right rear side was missing and he was bleeding profusely. Part of his brain was gone. I saw a part of his skull with hair on it lying in the seat."[28]

On March 9, 1964, Hill was deposed by Arlen Specter before the commission in Washington. Once again, Hill mentioned the odd sound of the shot that hit the president in the head but this time was careful to point out that, unlike an earlier shot that clearly came from the rear, the killing shot "was right, but I cannot say for sure that it was rear."[29] Once again Hill remembered the noise of this shot and the fact that it "had removed a portion of the President's head."[30] As Mrs. Kennedy turned toward him on the trunk of the limousine, "I grabbed her and put her back in the back seat [and] crawled up on top of the back seat and lay there."[31] Hill continued,

The right rear portion of his head was missing. It was lying in the rear seat of the car. His brain was exposed. There was blood and bits of brain all over the entire rear portion of the car. Mrs. Kennedy was completely covered with blood. There was so much blood you could not tell if there had been any other wound or not, except for the one large gaping wound in the right rear portion of the head. . . . I removed it [my coat] and covered the President's head and upper chest.[32]

Photo 16-5. Frame 334. Note the creamy red spot on Hill's right forehead.

In 2012, Clint Hill published a book coauthored with Lisa McCubbin on his years in the White House in which he expanded his description of the shooting:

I was almost there and then I heard the shot. The third shot. The impact was like the sound of something hitting something hollow . . . like the sound of a melon shattering onto cement. In the same instant blood, brain matter and bone fragments exploded from the back of the President's head. The President's blood, parts of his skull, bits of his brain were splattered all over me in my face, my clothes, in my hair. . . . As I peered into the back seat of the car, I saw the President's head in her lap. His eyes were fixed, and I could see inside the back of his head. I could see inside the back of the President's head.[33]

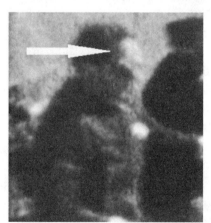

Photos 16-6 and 16-7. Frames 335 and 337. These clearer frames in the sequence show the spot on Hill's forehead.

Fifteen pages later, Hill described being taken in to see the president's body after the autopsy. The idea was that he could tell Mrs. Kennedy the nature of her husband's wounds if she wanted to know. According to Hill, looking at the wound in the back of the president's head at Bethesda Hospital brought back his experience of the afternoon:

> The image of what I saw when I was up above the back seat came flashing back into my mind. The head wound was exposed and I could see into his brain, part of which had exploded outward. It looked like somebody had flipped open the back of his head, stuck in an ice-cream scoop and removed a portion of the brain then scattered it all over Mrs. Kennedy, the car, and myself.[34]

Although expressed more dramatically, Hill's book adds only one fact to his recollections of 1963–1964: John Kennedy's blood and brains "were splattered all over me." And Mrs. Kennedy? After the horror of seeing her husband's head explode only inches from her, after climbing out on the trunk to retrieve part of his brain, she was pushed back into her seat by Hill, and her husband's body came to rest in her lap. From his perch spread-eagled on the trunk, Hill could see "inside the back of the President's head."

Commander J. Thornton Boswell

In December 1966, LIFE magazine editor Ed Kern and I drove out through the Maryland suburbs to the home of Dr. Thornton Boswell. It was early evening, and we could make out a dusting of snow in the suburban yards we passed. For unknown reasons, Boswell had agreed to give LIFE the first interview any of the autopsy doctors had given to the press. What we did know was that the autopsy doctors and their autopsy had already come in for sharp criticism.

One alarm bell was the report of the two FBI agents, Sibert and O'Neill, who attended the autopsy.[35] They told of the doctors' consternation when they found a bullet hole in the president's back. Full body X-rays had shown that no bullets remained in the body. According to Sibert and O'Neill, the hole "was below the shoulders" and two inches to the right of the spinal column. The bullet had penetrated at a downward angle of "45 to 60 degrees."

According to the FBI agents' report, this wound was neither probed nor dissected, as proper autopsy procedure would dictate. Instead, Dr. Humes stuck his little finger in the wound and commented that it ended after an inch or so. The doctors' conclusion? Sibert and O'Neill said that when news of the stretcher bullet's discovery reached Bethesda, Humes "advised" that the

Figure 16-8. Painting of Mrs. Kennedy cradling her husband's head at Parkland Hospital. At right is Clint Hill, removing the coat he put over President Kennedy's head.

stretcher bullet must have caused the back wound and then fallen out under "external cardiac massage." Nothing like this is found in the official autopsy report. Instead, it concludes that a bullet passed from an entry in the upper back to an exit in the front of the president's throat.

Kern and I talked about this in the darkened car as we neared Boswell's home. He asked what I thought of the speculation that the autopsy physicians had been part of a plot to conceal the fact that the president had been shot from the front. "Ever been in the military?" I asked. When he answered no, I told him that while in the navy, I'd heard an old World War II acronym, JANFU. When he looked perplexed, I told him, "It means Joint Army-Navy Fuckup.

Photo 16-9. (*left to right*) Commander Boswell, Commander Humes, and Lieutenant Colonel Finck.

That's what we've got here, not a sinister plot. The autopsy report itself tells you that these guys did an autopsy on the president of the United States and let the body pass through their hands without ever examining one of his bullet wounds. Need anyone say more? They keep getting in trouble because they keep trying to cover up the fact that they botched the autopsy. But let's see. Maybe Boswell can explain all this."

We were told not to bring tape recorders. When I started to take notes, I got a glance from Boswell indicating that this might not be such a good idea. Kern was largely quiet during the interview because this was an unfamiliar area for him. Later that night, I took some time to write in my red spiral notebook several pages that I titled "Highlights of Boswell Interview." The notes only now and then offer direct quotations. Most indicate the question raised and then paraphrase Boswell's answer.

I started the interview on fairly innocuous ground. The autopsy mentioned "subsequent conferences" of the doctors. I asked when they were held. Boswell replied, as my notes show,

Several conferences. Stayed with body to 4 a.m. At 8 a.m., assembled to bring together their conclusions. Dr. Humes called Dr. Perry at this meeting. Stayed together for rest of day discussing their findings. That night he "went home and died." Sunday morning worked on rough draft prepared by Dr. Humes.

Worked on histological slides. Earlier in contact with Armed Forces Institute of Pathology. Finck was standing by. Saw body and destruction. Called Pierre Finck who then came over. Denied that he and other doctors were either hurried or harried. Autopsy was performed with all due care.[36]

I knew that the autopsy face sheet had been made out by Boswell. I showed it to him. He confirmed that he had done all the writing on the sheet and then said there was another face sheet. In my notes, I put his reply in quotation marks: "I feel very sure there must have been another piece of paper with other things written down not listed here."[37] I asked him to explain what was on the sheet that we had with respect to the head wound, and he complied:

Looking down on top of skull. Defect in skull extended quite a bit into left [cerebral] hemisphere. Brain was removed without additional skull surgery.

   3-cm. area? Not in temple but in an interior bone communicating with nasal and vomer bone. There was no hole in left temple. Communicating with vomer (crushed) and globe fracture at rt. eye. Damage in frontal, parietal, occiput regions; in rt. hemisphere but also extending into left hemisphere.[38]

Boswell went on to say that "the defect in the scalp was not as large as the defect in the skull." I asked him about the left and backward snap of the president's head. He said it "had never come up in their discussions and view-ings of the film." He said he "thought 'decerebrate rigidity' might explain this phenomenon."[39] Although Boswell was clearly uneasy, his answers to these questions were direct and seemingly candid. Then I turned to the problem set by the Sibert-O'Neill report.

Was the bullet course from back to front ever dissected? Work in thoracic cavity was part of normal autopsy region. Removal of larynx. Done as part of orthodox procedure, not as part of an attempt to trace by dissection the bullet's course. B. denied in general terms that the doctors had failed to consider a transit through the neck on Nov. 22nd. To the direct question "Did you or any of the doctors observe a bullet wound in the front of President Kennedy's throat?" he answered, "No."[40]

He had to answer no because the first time any of them knew a bullet wound underlay the tracheotomy incision was when they opened their copies of the *Washington Post* the next morning and learned what Dr. Perry had done. That was why they called Perry. They had been given the job of determining just

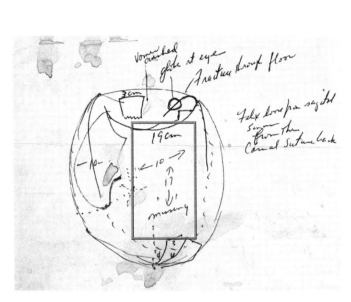

Figure 16-10. Skull diagram marked up by Boswell during autopsy, looking down onto the top of the head (as in Photo 16-15). The black rectangle shows 17 cm length of skull marked "missing." Note: The red stains are from blood on the surgical gloves Boswell wore while marking the diagram.

what had happened to President Kennedy. His body had rested in their hands for many hours without them ever examining one of his bullet wounds. Perhaps that was why I find in my notes alongside these later answers the words "Very sensitive, equivocal, evasive in this area."[41]

As we pulled away into the Maryland darkness, I released some of the frustration I had felt during the interview. After all these years, I don't remember the exact words but what I vented to Kern ran something like this: "Do you think these guys looked at the Zapruder film, saw Kennedy bowled over backward, smiled, and then said knowingly, 'Decerebrate rigidity'? They must have looked at that film and seen their worst nightmare realized. His head was an incredible mess at autopsy, and they were in way over their heads. Cyril Wecht told me that a double hit to the head like this would challenge even the very best forensic pathologist. He said you have to do a very slow and meticulous workup, and even then you shouldn't make quick judgments. Everything is provisional. You fix the brain in formalin and then wait days before doing coronal sections. You use these sections to trace fragment paths. It's all very complicated, and it takes time. These guys had no time. Upstairs at Bethesda, Jackie Kennedy and the attorney general desperately wanted to get out of there. So now Boswell and

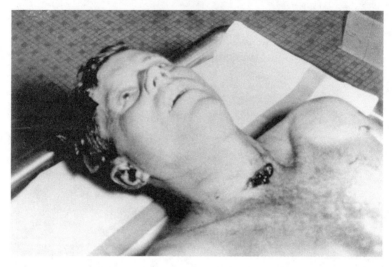

Photo 16-11. The tracheotomy incision at the base of the throat overlies a bullet wound not discovered by the autopsy team. All the Bethesda witnesses agreed that the president's wounds had left his face intact.

the others are stuck with a botched autopsy and the necessity of covering their asses professionally. Like I said, Ed, just another example of JANFU."

The Autopsy Conclusions

The obvious purpose of the autopsy was to determine what bullets struck the president and from what direction. In its summary, the autopsy report declared that the president was struck by two bullets and that they were "fired from a point behind and above the level of the deceased."[42] With regard to the president's head wounds, the report stated,

> The fatal missile entered the skull above and to the right of the external occipital protuberance. A portion of the projectile traversed the cranial cavity in a posterior-anterior direction (see lateral skull roentgenograms) depositing minute particles along its path. A portion of the projectile made its exit through the parietal bone on the right carrying with it portions of cerebrum, skull and scalp. The two wounds of the skull combined with the force of the missile produced extensive fragmentation of the skull, laceration of the superior sagittal sinus, and of the right cerebral hemisphere.[43]

The bullet's course through the head is based on three specific findings:

1. An inwardly beveled wound less than an inch (2.5 cm) "to the right and slightly above the external occipital protuberance" was found low in the back of Kennedy's skull.
2. A trail of small lead fragments led from this entry wound above to a point high in the front of the skull above Kennedy's right eye.
3. An outwardly beveled hole was found in a parietal bone fragment found in Dallas and delivered to the autopsy.

These three findings describe a trajectory from back to front through the president's head. Subsequent examination of the autopsy photos and X-rays has shown that the first two points are clearly wrong, while the third remains indeterminate as to position. Let's take a closer look.

First Finding

The first finding states that an entry hole was found at a particular location on the skull. With your fingers, you can feel a knob low in the back of your skull. This is the external occipital protuberance (EOP). The entry wound of a bullet was found less than an inch to the right of this knob and an even smaller distance above it. This is a reasonably precise location, but the hole described was not through an intact bone. The top surface of the remaining bone low in the back of Kennedy's head had a semicircular groove with the coning effect of an entering bullet. Later in the autopsy, a triangular fragment of bone arrived from Dallas that had the same sort of groove. When this fragment was fitted in place, the autopsy doctors could see the full outline of an entry hole.

Such a location for a bullet entry hole seems doubtful for numerous reasons. This location is very low in the back of the head. One thing on which all the Bethesda witnesses agree is that John Kennedy's face was undamaged by the shooting. How could a bullet like this, fired from six stories above the president, not blow through the brain and out his mouth? The Warren Commission thought of this and had the wound ballistics section at the US Army's Edgewood Arsenal carry out experiments to see what happened.[44]

Oswald's rifle was used along with cartridges from the same lot number as rounds recovered on the sixth floor. Ten skulls were filled with gelatin to simulate brain contents, and the skull backs were then covered with gelatin and unclipped goat skin to simulate the scalp. A marksman fired from ninety yards away at the correct downward angle. In the test result, the Mannlicher-Carcano bullet struck the head where the autopsy determined a bullet

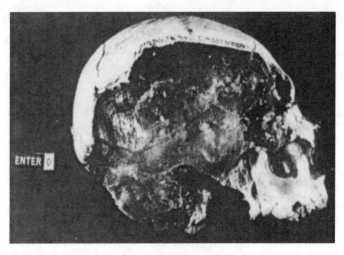

Photo 16-12. Human skull (CE 861) used in the Edgewood Arsenal experiment, showing that a 6.5 mm Mannlicher-Carcano bullet entering at the EOP blows out the right side of the skull and face.

entered. As would be expected of a military jacketed round, the bullet blew out the right side of the skull, including facial bones from the temple down almost to the mouth.

Why did this not happen in the Kennedy case? One obvious answer is that he was not hit in the back of the head at the low point described in the autopsy. In one of the most bizarre aspects of the medical evidence, this was later found to be the case. Between 1968 and 1978, various forensic experts who studied the autopsy photos and X-rays all agreed that the autopsy had mistakenly located the hole in the back of the president's head. Nor was this a minor mistake.[45] The true location was found to be over four inches above where the autopsy placed it. It was not low in the back of the head but high, near the crown. So much for the first finding.

Second Finding

According to the autopsy's conclusionary section, a bullet passed from back to front through the skull, "depositing minute particles along its path." Earlier in the autopsy report, a similar description is given of this "path" of particles: "Roentgenograms of the skull reveal multiple minute metallic fragments along a line corresponding with a line joining the above described small occiput wound and the supra-orbital ridge."[46]

"Roentgenograms" is doctor-speak for X-rays; "posterior-anterior direction" means a back-to-front direction; the "supra-orbital ridge" is the brow. Since both descriptions refer to X-rays of the skull, and in one case to the "lateral skull" X-ray, we might ask the obvious question: What does the lateral skull X-ray show?

There is a track of "multiple minute metallic fragments," but it is nowhere near either the entry hole defined in the autopsy or the other location identified later by various experts and by the HSCA Medical Panel. It begins above the right temple near the epicenter of the explosion shown in Zapruder frame 313 and then ranges upward and rearward. There is no trail of "multiple minute metallic fragments" where the autopsy said it was. If the first finding of the autopsy doctors was off by four inches, the second finding is simply mistaken.

Third Finding

The third finding of the autopsy concerned the exit of a large portion of the bullet that struck the rear of the president's head. The autopsy located this as an "exit through the parietal bone."[47] The parietal bone runs fore and aft along the top of the skull (see Figure 16-2). In the rear, it connects with the occiput bone. In the front near the top of the skull, it connects with the frontal bone. Where along the parietal bone did this "portion of the projectile" exit John Kennedy's head?

The defect in the president's head was huge. As noted above, Dr. Boswell drew a sketch of the head on the autopsy face sheet and indicated that a large section of the president's skull was missing. His notes show a seventeen-centimeter gap. On a normal male, seventeen centimeters would run rearward from the hairline in front to the EOP in back. Recall that Boswell told Ed Kern and me that the "defect in skull extended quite a bit into left [cerebral] hemisphere. Brain was removed without additional skull surgery." The actual description of the head wound in the autopsy report matched Boswell's sketch and notes: "There is a large irregular defect of the scalp and skull on the right involving the parietal bone but extending somewhat into the temporal and occipital regions . . . The complexity of these features and fragments thus produced tax satisfactory verbal description and are better appreciated in photographs and roentgenograms which are prepared."[48]

Even the rather poor, almost snapshot-quality photos we have show the devastation to the president's head. Given the extent of the damage, how were the autopsy doctors able to complete their trajectory analysis of the head?

Three small fragments of skull bone arrived from Dallas during the autopsy.

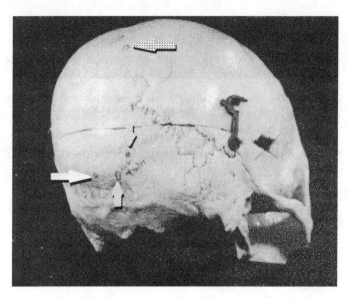

Photo 16-13. EOP (*filled-in white arrow*). Entry locations marked by Humes, Boswell, and Finck (*cross-hatched arrows*). Entry location (*top arrow*) determined by the HSCA Medical Panel in 1978. Note: There are only two marks for three people. Humes and Boswell together made one mark. Finck made his mark without knowing where Humes and Boswell had made theirs.

One of the fragments had outer-side beveling around a roughly semicircular hole. Although the autopsy report does not say so explicitly, this bone must have appeared to be parietal since (as quoted above) "the projectile made its exit through the parietal bone on the right." But where in the parietal bone? It is a large bone that covers the top and sides of the skull from about the midpoint back. Given the description of the massive damage to President Kennedy's head, it would seem that large sections of the parietal bone were marked "missing" in Boswell's sketch of the skull. A fragment of bone could go almost anywhere in that gap. Since any way to locate that bone fragment was lacking, it may have come from near where the parietal bone joins the occiput. This would put it at the extreme rear of the skull. It might just as well have come from near where the parietal bone joins the frontal bone, placing it near the very top center of the skull. Since Boswell made clear that "the defect in skull extended quite a bit into the left [cerebral] hemisphere," it is not even clear that the bone fragment came from the right parietal rather than the left parietal bone. The autopsy doctors had a large hole in the president's head and no way to tell just where this piece of bone fitted into that gap.

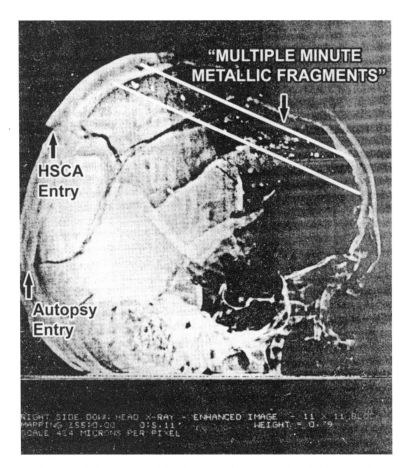

Photo 16-14. Lateral X-ray, right side, showing a trail of multiple metallic fragments and disputed bullet entry points.

The autopsy claimed to have shown that the president was struck in the head by a single bullet "fired from a point behind and above the level of the deceased." When the three detailed findings are reviewed against the background of the autopsy photos and X-rays, a quite different picture emerges. In summary, the autopsy actually determined that (1) there was a bullet hole somewhere in the back of the president's head, (2) there was an exit hole for a bullet or fragment somewhere in the top of his head, and (3) there was a trail of "multiple minute metallic fragments" with no relation to either hole that ran rearward from above the president's right temple.

How could the autopsy doctors have so bungled their central mission?

The "tell" is found in the second paragraph of the official autopsy report, where contemporary press reports are cited: "Three shots and the President

Photo 16-15. Autopsy photo of President Kennedy.

fell forward bleeding from the head. . . . According to newspaper reports (*Washington Post*, November 23, 1963), Bob Jackson, a *Dallas Times Herald* photographer, said he looked around as he heard the shots and saw a rifle barrel disappearing into a window on an upper floor of the nearby Texas School Book Depository Building."[49]

The *Washington Post* front-page story reported that "three shots reverberated and blood sprang from the President's face. He fell face forward."[50] Humes used this language almost verbatim in his handwritten draft of the autopsy report: "Three shots were heard and the president fell face downward to the floor of the vehicle."[51] These press dispatches framed a narrative of the shooting. An assassin was seen firing from a building behind the president. A rifle and three expended cases were found there. Witnesses reported three shots. Oswald, an employee of the depository, was in custody and charged with the assassination.

Only hours before, Humes and Boswell had been going about their routines as administrators in the pathology department at Bethesda. Through no fault of their own, they had been cast into the roiling sea of a presidential assassination with no preparation or lifeboat. Press dispatches made it seem as if the shooting were an open-and-shut case—a shot from the depository above and behind the president struck him in the head, killing him. Asked to carry out an examination for which they had neither training nor experience, they found it only natural to conform their observations and conclusions about what already seemed to be the basic facts of the killing.

The doctors relied on these press dispatches as if they were evidence. They were not. Some were just plain wrong, The Zapruder film, for example, shows us that the president did not "fall forward bleeding from the head." Instead, he was smashed so far left and to the rear that he then bounced forward off the rear seat cushion. Starting with the initial narrative of the shooting available in these press stories, it is not surprising that the autopsy moved to close the

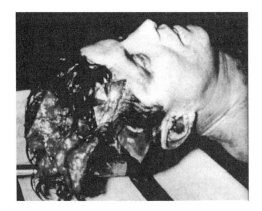

Photo 16-16. This photo conveys the great devastation to the president's head.

circle of that narrative with its observations and conclusions. The result was that the autopsy introduced into the investigation at an early point a set of influential nonfacts—not because of any conspiratorial intent but out of sheer incompetence. The mistakes of the autopsy prejudiced everything that was to follow. These mistakes also assured that the medical evidence would end up being the most contested and controversial in the case.

Because the autopsy was, in Dr. Baden's words, "bungled," there seems no way to resolve the many contradictions plaguing it. Consequently, our focus must shift more narrowly to a limited set of questions. What do the demonstrable facts of the medical evidence tell us about the scenario developed earlier? Are they consistent or inconsistent with the claim that President Kennedy was struck first in the head from the right front at Zapruder frame 313 and then from the rear 0.7 seconds later?

What the Evidence Supports

There is ample evidence in the autopsy and X-rays that the president was struck by a bullet in the back of the head. Arguments may still rage concerning whether the entry hole was high or low, but there can be little doubt that such a hole existed. In addition, the damage to the interior front of the president's head—the laceration of the superior sagittal sinus, the crushing of the vomer bone, and the fracture through the floor of the right eye socket—all point to a bullet driving forward from the rear. None of these facts indicate when that happened. As the analysis of Keith Fitzgerald shows, that impact occurred at Zapruder frame 328.

Does the medical evidence contain clues to the impact of another bullet from the right front on the president's head?

It is simply impossible to disregard the fact that almost everyone who observed the back of the president's head—whether in the car at the time of shooting, at Parkland Hospital moments later, or at Bethesda—saw an "avulsive" wound there. The person with the most educated eye for head trauma, Dr. Kemp Clark, believed that it was due to a "tangential" strike of a bullet. By "tangential," Clark meant a bullet striking tangentially high above the right temple with its force ranging upward, leftward, and rearward. It is difficult to see how a bullet fired from the rear and striking the back of the head flat-on could produce such a wound.

More evidence of such a strike may lurk in the factual details that have been, so to speak, in plain sight for a long time but whose importance has not been recognized. The trail of "multiple minute metallic fragments" beginning high above the right temple and ranging rearward connects with neither the low entry hole described by the autopsy doctors nor the higher entry hole identified by later experts. It cannot just be wished away since the lateral X-ray shows it is there. If it cannot be matched to a rear-entering bullet, what caused it?

Figure 16-17, overlaying a lateral autopsy photo on the lateral X-ray, shows the location of the fragment trail. The lower end of this trail aligns with the epicenter of the explosion high above the president's right temple in Zapruder frame 313.

Next we turn to frame 313, the impact frame. In 1967, I too believed that the president was struck in the back of the head and that the explosion was the exit of that bullet. Given the fact that the president's head moved forward over two inches in the one-eighteenth of a second prior to the explosion, it seemed inescapable that a shot from the rear caused both the movement and the explosion. In frame 313, the fact that two bone fragments can be seen arcing up and forward seemed to confirm it. What I never did was look closely at the explosion itself. But to do this now—to really see what this explosion is all about—turn to the color photo gallery, Plates 3a, 3b, 4a, 4b, and 5 to examine the best color photos we have of it.

It is true that two bone fragments arc up and forward. What is not clear in the two-dimensional frame 313 is that they are also arcing far to the left of the limousine's direction of travel. One fragment was found by Sheriff's Deputy Seymour Weitzman in the Elm Street gutter about ten feet to the left of the limousine's path, while the other was found by Texas Christian University student Billy Harper the following afternoon in the grass approximately twenty-five feet left of its origin point in the president's head.[52] This is why Douglas Jackson, the Dallas officer riding to the right rear of the limousine, said he saw the president "hit just above the right ear [and] the top of his head

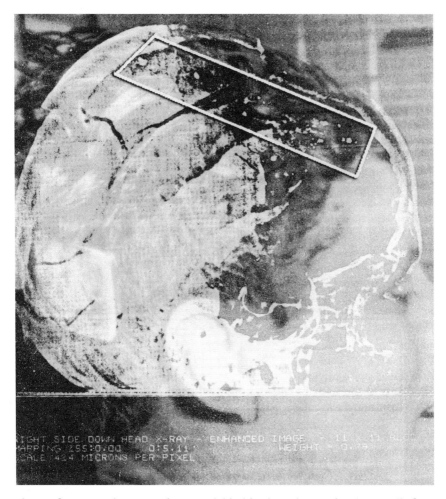

Figure 16-17. Lateral autopsy photo overlaid with a lateral X-ray showing a trail of multiple minute metallic fragments.

flew off away from me."[53] Such paths for these fragments are consistent with the impact of a bullet from the right front striking the skull above the right temple on a tangent and throwing off these fragments.

Now, look more closely at how debris spreads out from the epicenter of the explosion in frame 313 (See color photo gallery, Plates 3a, 3b, and 5). First, there are the two fragments of skull arcing upward, somewhat forward, and considerably to the left of the car's path. Next is impact debris traveling on a downward and forward vector.

In addition to these vectors, and only faintly seen here, is a major debris vector going left and rearward over Mrs. Kennedy's right shoulder. It can be

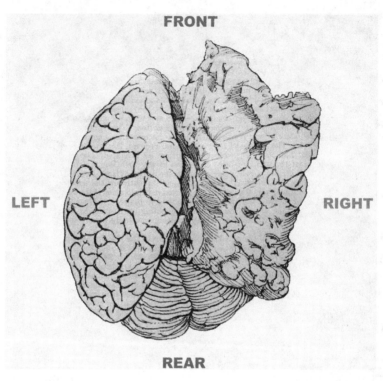

FRONT

LEFT

RIGHT

REAR

Figure 16-18. HSCA illustration of president's brain damage front to back along sagittal plane.

better seen in a shadow-enhanced version of frame 313 (See color photo gallery, Plates 4a and 4b). This blast of blood and brain tissue to the left and rear is the material that splattered the two police motorcyclists riding off the left rear fender twelve to twenty feet from President Kennedy. That vectors of impact debris are directed both up and rearward and down and rearward is consistent with what we would expect to see from the impact of a shot fired from the right front. A "tangential impact" of the sort described by Dr. Kemp Clark, striking forward of the president's right ear and ranging rearward, would produce the kind of massive damage the Zapruder film depicts.

Although no photographs of the brain have ever been released, there is a sketch of an unreleased autopsy photo that shows a front-to-back furrow in the brain. In this sketch (see Figure 16-18), the right cerebral hemisphere is disrupted from front to back along what the doctors would call the "sagittal plane." On the page opposite this sketch, the HSCA Medical Panel described the distribution of "missile dust" following this furrow along an "anterior-posterior" (front-to-back) track: "Another group of smaller, more uniform shadows, 0.1 centimeter or less in diameter, so-called 'missile dust,' forms a cylindrical pattern, with the axis directed anterior-posterior, approximately paralleling the sagittal plane, and extending toward the large bony defect in the right temporal parietal region on the right side of the head."[54]

Apparently, there is a difference between the original autopsy X-rays kept in the National Archives and the copies that have been released. David Mantik, MD, PhD, is a radiation oncologist who has studied the photos and X-rays at the National Archives on nine separate visits. In a paper delivered at an assassination symposium in 2003, Mantik pointed out "a spatially consistent, fuzzy gray cloud near the center of the fragment trail that extends across the top of the skull." Mantik went on to say that this "fuzzy gray cloud can best be seen on the x-rays at NARA [National Archives and Records Administration]."[55]

Mantik's description of a "fuzzy gray cloud" of particles was echoed in the commentary of other individuals who gained access to the original autopsy X-rays. Cyril Wecht, MD, JD, was the very first physician permitted to see them in the early 1970s. He pointed out to me that the "cloud of almost dust-like fragments" was apparent in the unenhanced later X-ray but was apparently suppressed by the enhancing process and not apparent in the enhanced version. Gary Aguilar, MD, observed the same effect when he viewed the X-rays twenty years after Wecht's visit to the National Archives.[56] Humes himself testified to the Warren Commission in 1964 that the X-rays "had disclosed to us multiple minute fragments of radio opaque material" in the brain. He was asked how many of these were visible and replied, "I would say between 30 or 40 tiny, dust-like particle fragments of radio-opaque material."[57] Secret Service Agent Roy Kellerman testified that he too saw on the skull X-ray what "looked like a little mass of stars; there must have been 30, 40 lights where these pieces were so minute they couldn't be reached."[58]

Two experts were asked to examine the skull X-rays and report their observations. Named after Ramsey Clark (the sitting attorney general in 1968), the Clark Panel was chosen by the Justice Department to reexamine the medical evidence in the case, specifically the autopsy. One of its four members was Russell H. Morgan, MD, head of the Radiology Department at Johns Hopkins University, who functioned as the panel's consulting radiologist. "Distributed through the right cerebral hemisphere," wrote the panel, "are numerous, small irregular metallic fragments which are less than 1 mm. in maximum dimension. The majority of these fragments lie anteriorly and superiorly. None can be visualized on the left side of the brain."[59] Over two decades later the Assassination Records Review Board (ARRB) asked forensic radiologist

John Fitzpatrick to review the skull X-rays. He reported, "There is a 'snow trail' of metallic fragments in the lateral skull x-rays which probably corresponds to a bullet track through the head."[60]

We must be clear that the track of small to medium-sized metal fragments shown in the enhanced lateral skull X-ray is not the "snow trail" that Humes, Kellerman, Wecht, Aguilar, Morgan, and Fitzpatrick all described. Specifically, Wecht and Aguilar made clear that what we see on the enhanced lateral X-ray is not what is visible only in the National Archive's original of the unenhanced lateral X-ray. Most important is that such a "cloud," "snow trail," or "snow storm" is present in the unenhanced X-ray of the skull. Eminent forensic pathologist Vincent Di Maio explained why in his book *Gunshot Wounds*:

> X-rays of individuals shot with hunting ammunition usually show a characteristic radiologic picture that is seen almost exclusively with this form of rifle ammunition. This is the so-called "lead snowstorm". As the expanding bullet moves through the body, fragments of lead break off the lead core and are hurled out into the surrounding tissues. Thus the X-ray shows scores of small radiopaque bullet fragments scattered along the wound track (the lead snowstorm) (Figure 7-14).[61]

Di Maio went on to explain why military bullets do not leave "lead snowstorms": "Military bullets, by virtue of their full-metal jackets, tend to pass through the body intact thus producing less extensive injuries than hunting ammunition. Military bullets do not fragment in the body or shed fragments of lead in their path." With one notable exception—the 5.56-mm round fired from the M-16 and notoriously unstable in the body—Di Maio bluntly concluded that the production of a "snowstorm" is just "not seen with pistol bullets or full metal jacketed rifle bullets."[62] All the bullets fired from Oswald's rifle were full-metal-jacketed military rounds.

As noted at the outset of our exploration of the medical evidence, the botched autopsy and its appalling absence of trustworthy findings has generated decades of controversy over issues that will likely never be resolved.

But as our assessment shows, once one has finally determined precisely what happened outside in Dealey Plaza, the pieces of the medical puzzle inside Kennedy's skull take on a coherent order. That in turn brings the larger puzzle into clearer focus.

PART IV

THE SIGNAL IN THE NOISE—2013–2017

CHAPTER 17 THE AD HOC COMMITTEE ON BALLISTIC ACOUSTICS

B y the fall of 2013, the end was in sight. I had only one chapter left to write, a summation and closing thoughts. As with earlier books, I looked forward to a sense of ease and satisfaction—even excitement— as the end approached. But this time was different. I didn't feel any of that. Instead, I found myself in a funk. Something important seemed to be missing. I had no clue what it was, even as I knew on a deeper level what was happening. The book was speaking to me.

Socrates sometimes spoke of what he called his *daimon*—an inner voice that spoke to him but never told him what to do. Rather, it just let him know that something was wrong. Likewise, the book was telling me that it lacked something essential. It needed something like "glue" that would bind all the forensic discoveries of the last decade together into a single, clear, and compelling answer to the most elementary question in the case: Was there more than one shooter?

The fall of 2013, of course, was the fiftieth anniversary of the assassination. By late November, the news coverage appeared to be little more than pro forma anniversary entertainment, a reprise of decades-old disputes and unresolved questions presented in superficial formats. Then, too, there was the pervasive impression that the establishment had long ago concluded that the Warren Commission's findings, though flawed, were essentially correct. That fall, Jill Abramson, executive editor of the *New York Times*, expressed this when she wrote, "The historical consensus seems to have settled on Lee Harvey Oswald as the lone assassin, but conspiracy speculation abounds."[1]

All this was brought home to me one November day when I got a call from a producer for CNN. One of the news shows wanted to show both sides of the debate and had invited a public relations executive billed as "a presidential historian" to present the Jill Abramson view. I was invited to present the counterview. After a hurried trip to San Francisco, I found myself sitting in a small room before a huge photo of the Golden Gate Bridge with an earpiece and microphone, looking into a camera. Next to the camera was a TV monitor showing the New York studio. The details of what happened aren't important. When I looked at the video the next morning, I saw how poorly I had done. Pure and simple, I had gotten my clock cleaned. It mattered not that the executive was skating on a veneer of nonfacts drawn from a superficial book.[2] The fact was that any casual viewer viewing the encounter would have believed him, not me. That hurt.

In the aftermath, I also sensed I hadn't been beaten simply by rhetorical tricks. There was something more. Why hadn't I used any of the new evidence I had in hand? Why had I been unable to throw anything back that the ordinary viewer could recognize as decisive?

The first question was easy to answer. The new evidence was too complex to describe in sound bites for a TV audience. But the other question was not so easily answered. Why had I ended up with nothing decisive to say?

Then, one bright December morning, it came to me. I had climbed onto my vintage BMW cycle and gone for a ride on California's coastal Highway 1. I was riding between Bolinas and Stinson Beach, the twin-cylinder engine pounding smoothly, leaning from curve to curve in the bright sunlight, when I realized what the problem was. It was the acoustic evidence. Or rather, it was what had happened to it.

In all the fiftieth anniversary festivities, the acoustic evidence was never mentioned because in May 1982, it had been discredited by a blue-ribbon committee of the NRC, a subgroup of the NAS, known as the Ramsey Panel (named for its chairman, Harvard physicist Norman Ramsey). This group issued its *Report of the Ad Hoc Committee on Ballistic Acoustics*, stating that the "putative gunshot sounds" had occurred after the shooting was over and hence could not be gunshots. Since then, the supposedly flawed acoustic evidence had been disregarded in any discussion of what happened in Dealey Plaza. That ruled out the possibility of my using it on CNN. What came to me that afternoon was not the understanding that the changes in evidence since 2000 were both momentous and unidirectional—this I had known for some time—but the realization that this new evidence both confirmed the acoustic evidence and, in turn, was explained and strengthened by it.

Not only had the forensic discoveries between 2000 and 2010 turned the core evidence in the case on its head, but these discoveries also offered detailed proof of what James Barger, Mark Weiss, and Ernest Aschkenasy had discovered in 1978. In short, the acoustic evidence might well be what I'd been searching for, the glue that would bind the various elements of evidence together into a scenario of rare simplicity.

When this evidence first became public in late 1978, I was not persuaded by it. True, it seemed to confirm the firing point behind the fence that I had picked eleven years earlier, but it conflicted with my view at that time that Kennedy had been hit twice in the head between frames 312 and 315. The only evidence for this happening in that interval was the two-inch forward movement of Kennedy's head that I had measured. David Wimp's acute discovery had shown this measurement to be based on a photographic illusion caused by a startled Zapruder moving his camera. There was only the shot from the right front—at 313—and it did exactly what we would expect it to do. It slammed Kennedy backward and to the left while spraying the motorcyclists to the left rear of the limousine with blood and brain debris. This was precisely what the acoustic evidence was telling us had happened.

Linked to this discovery and supporting it was the find by Keith Fitzgerald that President Kennedy was hit a second time in the head at Zapruder frame 328. The time interval between frames 313 and 328 is 0.71 seconds, the exact interval the acoustic evidence tells us elapsed between the fourth shot from the knoll and the fifth and final shot from the Texas School Book Depository window. The two discoveries are mutually confirming.

Likewise, the interval of 4.8 seconds between shots three and four found in the acoustics evidence matches exactly what we see in the Zapruder film. If the film is seen as the video clock of the shooting, it was looking as if the acoustic evidence might very well provide its audio twin.

Finally, there was the collapse of Vincent Guinn's conclusions that bullet fragments removed from President Kennedy's head and found on the limousine's carpet all came from Oswald's rifle. We now know that these tiny fragments could have come from bullets of virtually any caliber or any manufacturer.

Hanging over all this, I realized, was the Ramsey Panel Report and its widely influential pronouncement that the acoustic evidence was mistaken. For more than three decades, it had removed the acoustic evidence from serious discussion. The panel was made up of distinguished scientists whose only task was to fairly evaluate the work of Barger, Weiss, and Aschkenasy. Who was I to say they were wrong, even if recent discoveries seemed congruent with the acoustic scientists' findings?

I remembered getting a copy of that report in 1982 and then putting it aside because of its technical complexity. Then, as now, I was apprehensive that if I ventured into it, I would be overwhelmed with arcane arguments and end up wasting a huge amount of time and energy exploring a scientific rabbit hole that led nowhere.

In the end, I made the decision on a personal level. I simply could not put aside these adverse findings after including a whole chapter on the acoustics earlier in the book. That would be misleading and intellectually dishonest.

I recognized now, in December 2013, that whatever I had thought before, I could not leave the Ramsey Panel Report untouched. To do so would be to ignore the overarching purpose of the whole endeavor. "You started this book as a piece of unfinished business," I told myself. "This piece is unfinished. You can't just leave it sitting out there."

Revisiting the Report—First Impressions

Thus, on a chilly winter morning during the first week of January 2014, I reached across my desk and picked up the ninety-six-page *Report of the Ad Hoc Committee on Ballistic Acoustics* and began to read. The writing was still intimidating, filled with technical terms and arcane mathematics. But this time around—dipping into it more than three decades after seeing it for the first time—I was no longer a stranger to giving scientific papers or reports a critical once-over. I'd be working on a case, and the attorney would pass over some scientific article or study and say, "Please take a look at this and let me know what you think. After all, Thompson, you've got the PhD." So I would take the article back to my hotel room and spend an evening or two trying to figure out what was being said and whether it made sense. Over time, I developed a certain skill in recognizing advocacy posing as science.

With this in mind, I began reading the report. It begins with a section titled "Executive Summary." In other reports I've read, such summaries begin by listing the existing evidence and supporting arguments. Not so the Ramsey Panel Report. Instead, it introduces a concept—"crosstalk"—never mentioned by Barger, Weiss, and Aschkenasy. The executive summary emphasized that a fragment of speech first transmitted on channel 2 of the Dallas police radio net ended up also appearing on channel 1. The summary stated that "sound spectrograms show conclusively" that the part of the channel 1 recording containing the shots also contained "crosstalk from Channel II of a broadcast from Channel II of a message broadcast approximately one minute after the assassination." This led the panel to conclude that the impulses came too late to be shots. The implication is that they must have been random static generated by sunspots, a fault in the motorcycle's electrical system, or some other cause.

In a later section, the report describes the "methodologies and conclusions" of the HSCA acoustic scientists, but neither in this section nor anywhere else in the report is there any attempt to indicate and discuss the evidence offered by the acoustic scientists to establish their claim. Instead, there is a lot of adjective-sprinkled argument. We are told that "desirable control tests were omitted," "some analyses depended on subjective selection of data," and "analysis methods were novel in some respects." Nowhere in the report do we get any real idea of why the acoustic experts and the HSCA thought these particular sound impulses were gunshots.

In short, a huge hole is left in the report. Missing is any examination of the core evidence the panel was charged with reviewing. Having read many legal briefs filed by prosecuting attorneys over the years, I also noticed the report's strident prosecutorial tone, characterized by dismissive, almost mocking descriptors: "conjectured shots," "hypothetical third (knoll) shot," "hypothesized motorcycle trajectory," and "conjectured grassy knoll shot." The panel's conclusions repeatedly did not "show," they "conclusively showed" or "showed conclusively," while the assertions of the HSCA acoustic experts were not "flawed" but "seriously flawed."[3]

Tickling the back of my mind was a vague recollection of something I might have read in Luis Alvarez's autobiography, published in 1987. I pulled the book off the shelf and found it. Alvarez was talking about his service on this committee:

> My second involvement in the Kennedy assassination started with a phone call from Phil Handler, the president of the National Academy of Sciences. The U.S. Department of Justice had asked the academy to set up a committee to review this evidence, and Phil in turn asked me to chair it. Since the buffs would automatically have rejected any report published under my name, I agreed to be a committee member but suggested Norman Ramsey as a competent and acceptable chairman.[4]

What? Luis Alvarez had been asked to be chairman of this committee? Alvarez, the only eminent scientist in the country who had vigorously supported the Warren Commission, whose "jet-effect theory" and bogus melon experiments were in direct conflict with the acoustics scientists' calculations that a shot had been fired from a specific location on the knoll? If Alvarez was right, that shot so meticulously examined by Barger, Weiss, and Aschkenasy never existed. Their firing tests in Dealey Plaza had shown that five shots in all had been fired, not the three Alvarez said his blur study indicated. Why offer the chairmanship of the committee to the only American scientist whose professional reputation would take a hit if the final judgment of the committee backed the work of Barger, Weiss, and Aschkenasy? Not only was Alvarez asked to be chairman, but when he declined, his recommendation for chairman was accepted. His friend and colleague, Professor Norman Ramsey, chairman of the Harvard Physics Department (and soon himself to be a Nobel laureate), was appointed chairman of the committee.

I had read enough. My initial peek suggested that beneath the smooth veneer of objective evidence-based scientific inquiry were signs of something else—unvarnished advocacy, or at the very least what scientists call "confirmation bias."[5] Therefore, I would do what I had always done in the past. I would approach the work of the panel with the wariness of an investigative reporter.

The HSCA's Requested Follow-up

When the HSCA went out of existence on January 3, 1979, it passed on to the Justice Department the job of following up on two factual discoveries made by the committee. The first sprang from the HSCA's inability to determine from the Bronson film[6] whether or not there was movement in the Texas School Book Depository behind the windows on the fifth and sixth floors. The question was passed on to the Justice Department for decision.[7]

The second request was the acoustic evidence. The committee asked the Justice Department to ensure that the National Institute of Law Enforcement, a component of the Law Enforcement Assistance Administration (LEAA), and the National Science Foundation (NSF) "make a study of the theory and application of the principles of acoustics to forensic questions, using the materials available in the assassination of John F. Kennedy as a case study."[8] This was a convoluted way to express the committee members' collective desire for simply a review of the work and conclusions of the acoustic scientists.

Many HSCA members were afraid of what one called a "rush to judgment" due to the speed with which they had learned of the acoustic evidence and its significance in December 1978. Most members first learned of Weiss and Aschkenasy's confirmation of the knoll shot in the days leading up to the final hearing. Representative Christopher Dodd pointed out that "the acoustical evidence of a gunman on the grassy knoll has enormous significance for our nation. . . . The data upon which the experts base their conclusion should, therefore, be reviewed by other noted experts in this field."[9] In a separate dissent, Representative Robert Edgar of Pennsylvania basically accused the committee of rushing to a conclusion. He included in his dissent a letter from a University of Pennsylvania professor who described the work of the acoustic scientists as "exciting" but also cautioned that it should be subject to peer review by a scientific journal.

However, it was not until August 1980—a year and a half later—that the NAS put in a grant application for NSF money to fund the study.

The Ad Hoc Committee on the September 22 Event

Over dinner one night with two of my buff friends—Gary Aguilar, MD, and Doug DeSalles, MD—I learned that Luis Alvarez had also served on an earlier ad hoc committee appointed by the NRC/NAS. It had completed its work only a few months before he moved over to the Ramsey Panel. Here, a short digression is in order since this twin ad hoc panel offers insights into the later work of the Ramsey Panel.

On September 22, 1979, one of the US government's advanced Vela satellites detected a nuclear blast 1,500 miles southeast of Cape Town, South Africa. Immediately the event was thought to be a joint Israeli–South African nuclear test blast. If confirmed, the incident would be a severe embarrassment to the Carter administration's nonproliferation policy, exposing its willful ignoring of the Israeli nuclear program. Accordingly, the president's science adviser, Frank Press, recommended the formation of a blue-ribbon panel of scientists to look into whether the detection might be a false positive.[10] In short order, the Ad Hoc Committee on the September 22 Event (hereafter the Vela Panel) was created.

As was common practice at the time, the roster of the Vela Panel was drawn from an old boys' network of national security professionals. What struck me as interesting was that three of its members—Luis Alvarez, Richard Garwin, and F. Williams Sarles—also served on the later Ad Hoc Committee on Ballistic Acoustics. Both committees were run by a small cadre of active members. On the Vela Panel, this consisted of Alvarez, Garwin, and a young physicist from Alvarez's lab named Richard Muller. On the Ramsey Panel, it consisted of Alvarez, Garwin, Chairman Norman Ramsey, and a young physicist from Ramsey's department named Paul Horowitz.[11]

Nor did the similarities end there. The Vela Panel's subsequent report made no mention of the Vela satellites' track record. The satellite that detected the nuclear blast—one of the advanced Vela 6911 series first launched in 1967— carried sophisticated instruments configured to detect the unique signature of a nuclear blast in the atmosphere—an extremely short but high-intensity flash of light followed by a second less intense and more prolonged emission. The 6911 series enjoyed a perfect record for detecting nuclear explosions. Of

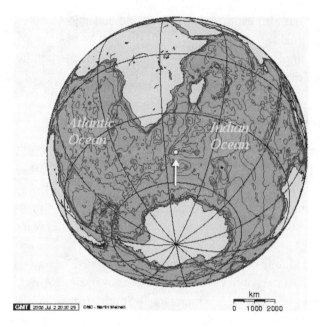

Figure 17-1. The arrow indicates the approximate position of the suspected nuclear explosion.

forty-one events detected since 1967, all were later confirmed to be nuclear by additional tests or government announcements.[12]

The Vela Panel paid no attention to this record or to other government reports confirming the blast. The first came from Arecibo, Puerto Rico, where a radar station picked up a traveling ionospheric disturbance (TID) at the same time and place as the blast. A second confirmation came from the US Navy's Sound Surveillance System (SOSUS) program designed to track Soviet submarines. Hydrophones near Ascension Island in the South Atlantic had earlier picked up signs of a French nuclear blast in the Pacific. On September 22, these hydrophones picked up a trifecta of signals (time, direction, and seabed conditions under the blast) pointing to the blast detected by the satellite.[13]

Much material concerning the detection, including top-secret CIA reports, was declassified after 2000. One of these CIA reports indicated that the South African naval base at Simonstown had been declared "off limits" to foreign personnel for the period of September 17–23. In a bizarre twist, the South African commander of Simonstown at the time was Commodore Dieter Gerhardt, who in 1983 was arrested in the United States as a Russian spy. Gerhardt was returned to South Africa, where he was imprisoned for ten years. He described to reporter Jeffrey Richelson how a group of Israeli ships made a port call at Simonstown just before the detection on September 22. He also told Richelson "that the flash was the result of a joint Israeli-South African test, Operation Phoenix."[14]

Photo 17-2. South African Naval Base at Simonstown.

In 1991, Seymour Hersh, the Pulitzer Prize–winning journalist who earlier had exposed the My Lai massacre in Vietnam, disclosed what he had been told by sources within the Israeli nuclear program. In the early-morning hours of September 22, 1979, two Israeli ships, in company with other units from the South African navy, were deployed far southeast of Cape Town. Two tests of nuclear-armed artillery projectiles were fired successfully in overcast conditions and were not picked up by the Vela 6911 satellite. Not so the third test. It "was a fuck-up," one of these officials told Hersh.[15] "There was a storm and we figured it would block Vela. But there was a gap in the weather—a window—and Vela got blinded by the flash."

For its part, the Vela committee offered the suggestion that the detection might be a false positive produced by a meteoroid striking the satellite. In addition, Luis Alvarez persuaded the committee to examine the records of "zoo events" pertaining to Vela 6911. The term came from Alvarez's research in particle physics, where irregular events with no obvious cause were branded as "coming from the zoo." None of the satellite's zoo events had the signature of a nuclear explosion, and the Defense Intelligence Agency (DIA) in June 1980 estimated that the probability of a single meteoroid causing such a double flash was less than one in one hundred billion.[16] But this did not prevent the committee from concluding officially that "although we cannot rule out the possibility that the signal was of nuclear origin, the panel considers it more likely that the signal was one of the zoo events, possibly a consequence of the impact of a small meteoroid on the satellite."[17]

On May 23, 1980, the Vela Panel issued its report, and a significant sigh of relief swept through Washington's corridors of power. None of the reporters who received the press release and the *Report of the Ad Hoc Committee on the September 22nd Event* knew anything about the committee's work. Instead, they focused on a single thirteen-word sentence that read, "The panel concludes that the signal was probably not from a nuclear explosion."[18] Within a day or so, the report and its supporting documents disappeared into the national security archives, and the whole question of what the Vela satellite had discovered could be forgotten. The Vela Panel, having successfully prevented severe discomfort to the US government, had done its job.

The Ad Hoc Committee on Ballistic Acoustics

Within a year, Frank Press, the presidential science adviser who had originated the idea of the Vela Panel, would move over to become the president of the NAS. Weeks later, that same organization would send a grant application to the NSF for money to fund a second ad hoc committee to reexamine the President Kennedy acoustic evidence.

That grant application is part of a collection of 367 pages of documents obtained from the NRC of the NAS in 1982, copies of which quite unexpectedly came into my hands in March 2014. I was having lunch in Berkeley with longtime assassination researcher Paul Hoch. Paul and I have been friends since the late 1960s and had been part of a book-writing project in 1979. He knew that I was looking into the Ad Hoc Committee on Ballistic Acoustics and had kindly photocopied a complete set of what appears to be committee documents. At one point during the meal, he handed them across the table to me. I had never seen any of them or known they even existed.

Paul explained that he had obtained the documents in 1982 from Mark Allen, another buff who lived in the Washington, DC, area. Allen had visited the NRC and picked up copies of what the NRC then called "the Public Access File." Apparently, this file had been put together to satisfy inquiries from the press and public after the *Report of the Ad Hoc Committee on Ballistic Acoustics* was released in May 1982. Upon receiving the documents from Allen, Paul had constructed a several-page table of contents. Since then, he had seldom looked at them.[19]

Over the next few days, I spent hours reading the file. Initially I couldn't determine what exactly, if anything, I had in my hands. The documents were not organized in any particular order, either chronologically or by subject. I imagined that some NRC staffer had assembled them rather hurriedly under the circumstances. Here and there I came upon tantalizing bits and pieces, but they appeared out of context, so I stopped reading and turned to sorting the documents into chronological order and putting them into three-ring binders. When I finished, I picked up the first binder and began reading.

It was a revelation. Organized chronologically, these files immediately came into focus. I spent days reading, fascinated. They seemed to offer an unparalleled glimpse into the workings of the panel. Included was correspondence between the panel and the acoustic scientists, letters from third parties to the panel, internal documents concerning the panel's work, and the grant application and associated documents. Threads of discussions began and were concluded; issues emerged and were debated. Read against the background of the final report, the documents provided a vivid picture of how the panel actually operated.

At one point during the weeks that followed, I contacted the NRC/NAS to inquire whether there were other documents available from their files on the Ramsey Panel. I learned that even the documents I had were no longer available.[20] In the late 1980s, they had become mixed with other material and hence lost their status as "accessible."

Among these documents is the August 12, 1980, grant proposal to the NSF for funds to organize the Ad Hoc Committee on Ballistic Acoustics.[21] The proposal, budgeted at $23,360, envisioned a time line of roughly five months with a provision to extend the deadline if circumstances warranted. Under this schedule, the committee would report its findings to the Justice Department by January 31, 1981.

The four-page proposal presented a smart, well-informed rendering of the issues to be studied. In addition to several paragraphs detailing specific questions to be asked concerning the work of Barger, Weiss, and Aschkenasy, the committee was charged with "reviewing the methodology employed in the evaluation of the acoustic data . . . and the rationale for the conclusions presented to the House Select Committee on Assassinations." In short, this proposal was designed to give the acoustic evidence precisely the review requested by many members of the HSCA. With equal intelligence, the proposal offered a list of the experts to make up the committee.[22] First on the list was "an acoustician." What was envisaged was a blue-ribbon panel of experts in acoustics and associated disciplines, just as the HSCA congressional members had requested.

The committee that actually came into being under this proposal was quite different from what the members of congress had envisaged. Although "acoustician" was first on the list of experts recommended in the grant application, neither an acoustics expert nor a ballistics expert ended up serving on the Ad Hoc Committee on Ballistic Acoustics. Although "physicist" was not on the list of recommended experts, fully half of the twelve members of the committee were physicists, many with long-standing personal relationships to Luis Alvarez. Harvard physicist Norman Ramsey and Alvarez had known each other for over four decades.[23] Alvarez himself pointed out that physicist "Dick Garwin and I had previously served as members of many committees involved in matters of national security."[24] Along with Alvarez and Garwin, Harvard physicist Paul Horowitz had served on the JASON[25] Advisory Group.

Why Alvarez? True, he was a Nobel Prize–winning physicist, but his specialty was particle physics. Even more relevant was the fact that Alvarez was the only major scientific figure to have taken a public position on the Kennedy assassination, claiming that there had been no shooter on the knoll. It should come as no surprise that Alvarez's first reaction to press reports of the acoustic evidence was to say he was "simply amazed that anyone would take such evidence seriously."[26]

Perhaps the oddest indication of bias on the part of the persons running this investigation was the makeup of two briefing books distributed to the members prior to their first meeting with Weiss, Aschkenasy, and Barger.[27] One might expect such books to hold copies of reports filed by the three scientists and their testimony before the HSCA. Instead, there was no material at all showing what the acoustic scientists were claiming or what others were saying in support of their work. In its place was a complete copy of Alvarez's journal article containing his "jet-effect theory" and an undergraduate paper by Shanin Specter, son of Warren Commission Counsel Arlen Specter, criticizing the acoustic evidence. The paper had been written for an undergraduate class at Haverford College, where I had taught for twelve years.

The Public Access File documents show that from the start, Alvarez played a dominant role on the Ad Hoc Committee on Ballistic Acoustics (also referred to as the Ramsey Panel). From November 1980 through January 1981, Chairman Ramsey submitted a number of written questions to Barger, Weiss, and Aschkenasy in advance of a scheduled meeting. The great majority of these questions were drafted by Alvarez. Of special interest is a series of questions and remarks authored by Alvarez and sent to the acoustic scientists by Ramsey just days before their first meeting together.

Ramsey began his letter to Barger by saying that "the member of our

Committee who raised many of the questions in my November 20, 1980, memorandum has made the following comments pertaining to your response on December 17, 1980."[28] Then Ramsey turned his letter over to that "member of our Committee," who went on for four pages. We know that member to be Alvarez since that same day, Ramsey wrote Alvarez to tell him that he had softened some of Alvarez's points "to diminish the danger that he [James Barger] would feel the Committee was prejudging the issue before his presentation."[29] The points made by Alvarez were exceedingly arcane, but his accompanying commentary was incendiary. He made remarks like these:

I find it [Barger's reply] not very responsive to the points I brought up. I was carefully sidestepped on several different occasions. . . .

. . . Now I'll return to the "second invalid assumption" which will lead to the disclosure of two separate, and I believe, quite devastating faults in Barger's analysis. . . .

. . . I believe that what I have just found in Barger's own data should convince anyone that the data analysis techniques are seriously flawed. . . .

. . . This discrepancy seems to me to be so serious as to convince one that Barger's own data analysis methods involve, to a large extent, the improper pairing of atmosphere pressure pulses in Dealey Plaza. And since these terribly serious flaws have turned up in a calibration run under almost laboratory conditions, I can't believe that the analysis of the crude Dictabelt data should be given any credence at all.[30]

These internal Ramsey Panel documents inescapably create the impression that Alvarez as concert master had taken over such a dominant role in the panel discussions that the conductor (Ramsey) was reduced to observing the formalities as a kind of master of ceremonies.

Finally, during a two-day weekend meeting between the panel and the acoustic scientists on January 31 and February 1, 1981, the atmosphere was tense and confrontational. Barger recalled that during one of the breaks, Luis Alvarez told Barger that "he didn't care what I said, he would vote against me anyway."[31] That Sunday evening, Ernest Aschkenasy was so outraged by the treatment Alvarez and the panel had given him and his colleagues that he called Paul Hoch to get HSCA Chief Counsel Robert Blakey's home telephone number[32] Three days later, HSCA Chairman Louis Stokes wrote to Chairman Ramsey, noting that a tape recording of the meeting had been running and requesting that a transcript of the meeting be made a part of the panel report.[33] Three weeks later, Ramsey wrote back, acknowledging that a tape had been made but saying it could not be transcribed, as it was merely an informal recording used by a staff member to compile summary meeting notes. Chairman Stokes was invited to come to the NAS to listen to the tape if he so desired.[34]

Chairman Ramsey's refusal to make a transcript of the meeting part of the panel's documented proceedings is echoed in the heavy-handed way he later tried to get James Barger to sign off on the panel report. On November 12, 1981, he sent Barger a draft of this report along with a prepared statement from Barger agreeing with it. The statement said that the sound impulses of the grassy knoll shot contained "crosstalk from Channel II that occurs approximately one minute after the assassination." Barger, of course, refused to comply.

Somewhat later, Ramsey went from Harvard to Barger's lab at BBN in Cambridge and had a private talk with Barger. According to Barger, they were alone when Ramsey told him that "I cannot expect to receive any recognition for my scientific work unless I change my conclusions about my study of the DPD recordings. I didn't ask whether this was a threat or an opinion. In any case, I replied, 'I cannot lie.'"[35]

Aside from Alvarez's ill-tempered brickbats, the only real work being done was carried out by MIT mathematician Herman Chernoff, who in mid-December sent his panel colleagues a thirteen-page memorandum on statistics.[36] Neither this memo from Chernoff nor later work could be considered broad-based mathematical assaults on the validity of the acoustic evidence as a whole. Instead, it was part of a persistent effort to whittle away at the probability figure for the knoll shot provided in testimony before the HSCA.

It is true that Barger, Weiss, and Aschkenasy made some minor errors in their probability computations. They were too conservative. Their errors led them to report the probability of a shot fired from the knoll to be 95 percent, but when their computations were later corrected, the probability turned out to be higher still. Mistakes were also made by the Ramsey Panel, but in the opposite direction as it tried to reduce the probability figure from 95 percent to 78 percent. Moreover, the Ramsey Panel's mistakes were of a different character.

Probability equations and their rationale are arcane. Briefly, a probability figure is spun out of a calculus that links together a number of data points. These data points are made up of "free variables" (where a value is unknown) and empirical facts (where a value can be established by research). In the present case, for example, the estimated position of a motorcycle was a free variable, while, in contrast, the temperature of the air (65°F) was an empirical fact. The more free variables in any calculus, the greater the uncertainty of the resultant probability. This is because a free variable permits the experimenter to pick any value he or she wants and therefore does not have the same status as an empirical fact with a given value. The rules of the probability calculus require that free variables be subtracted from the equation and the other factors be left as multipliers. In this particular case, such factors as motorcycle speed, air temperature, and tape recorder speed are empirical facts. The Ramsey Panel discovered an ingenious method for reducing the 95 percent probability figure. By simply calling certain factors "free variables" when they were not, they could degrade the resulting probability figure. The actual work on this can be found in a blizzard of mathematical formulae in Appendix A of the panel report.[37]

As 1980 drew to a close, the panel had come up with no significant criticism of the acoustic evidence. The evidence thus far would suggest that the Ad Hoc Committee on Ballistic Acoustics was clearly a hanging jury. However, the same committee documents that show this also show that after several months of work, the panel had failed to come up with any evidence to justify the hanging.

I n early January 1981, the Ramsey Panel's cupboard was bare. After several months of investigation, all it had to show for its efforts was a shaky statistical argument that failed to touch the central claim of the acoustic scientists. No promising ideas on how to proceed were under consideration.

It was at this point that crucial help arrived from an unlikely source. The appointment letters to panel members explained that their names would be kept secret "because of the intensity of feelings on the part of some individuals." Although *New Yorker* writer Calvin Trillin's term "buff" was not used, these were the "individuals" the letter's author had in mind. It was understood that panel members should not alarm the buffs or reveal to them their identity.

At NRC headquarters, a buff's correspondence file was created in which staff saved all communications regardless of how harebrained they might be. One such letter, carefully handwritten, languished for several months in that file before it was discovered by panel member Paul Horowitz. By itself, that letter completely revolutionized the course of the Ramsey Panel's investigation.

One version of what happened was related many years later by another panel member, Richard Garwin, during an interview on NPR:

> Luis Alvarez and I and Paul Horowitz were some of the members of the
> Committee and we began to study the statistics—how likely is it that all the noise
> on the tape could by accident conspire to give you nice results. In the middle of
> this we heard by letter—before the days of email and faxes—from Steve Barber,
> a rock musician in Mansfield, Ohio. He had a report of the House Committee on
> Assassinations published in Parade or something like that, with a little flexible
> plastic disk of the relevant five minutes of each channel of the police department
> recordings. And he says, where the shots are supposed to be, just in those few
> seconds, "I hear a little faint voice saying 'Hold everything secure.'" And when
> I listen to the other channel I hear very clearly, 'Hold everything secure until
> homicide and other detectives can get there. . . .'" Obviously, if somebody is

broadcasting 'Hold everything secure' as a result of the assassination, it can't be at the time of the shots." So we dropped our statistical efforts and we worked on trying to determine whether there was in fact this imprint of the "Hold everything secure" there.[1]

What Garwin got right was that he, Luis Alvarez, and Paul Horowitz were the heavy lifters on the Ramsey Panel and, at the very beginning, focused on statistics. What he also got right was that this work continued for only a short time before Steve Barber's discovery dropped into their midst. From that time on, as Garwin made clear, the Ramsey Panel was a one-issue committee, its investigation limited to confirming Barber's finding and his explanation of what it meant. I soon learned, however, that Garwin had gotten wrong almost everything else about Steve Barber.

In early May 2014, I searched through my contact files of assassination researchers, found Barber's e-mail address, and wrote to him. Barber immediately answered, saying he'd be happy to talk. During our phone calls and email exchanges in the weeks that followed, Barber proved to be affable, unpretentious, and knowledgeable—and still in touch with his contacts within the buff community. The story of his experience with the Ramsey Panel provides intriguing insights into the panel's inner workings.

First, the magazine was not *Parade* but *Gallery*, a girly magazine that, like *Playboy*, sprinkled serious articles in between photo spreads, contests, and sports interviews.[2] In July 1979, it published a feature-length article supporting the HSCA results that included a small 33⅓-rpm disk containing relevant recordings of Dallas police radio channel 1. It was bound into the magazine right next to the centerfold for Deborah M., winner of the *Gallery* "Girl Next Door" contest for July 1979.

Nor was Steve Barber "a rock musician," as Garwin had portrayed him, or "a rock drummer from Ohio," as CBS news anchor Walter Cronkite described him in 1988. He was twenty-four in the summer of 1979 and worked at a local department store in Shelby, Ohio. Prior to that, he had worked for several years at the American Machine and Foundry (AMF) plant that made bowling equipment.

Barber was also the percussionist in a local band, Sound Chaser, a four-piece ensemble fronted by a female vocalist that played parties, wedding receptions, and occasionally fancier bars around Shelby and nearby Mansfield. "There wasn't any real money in it," Barber told me. "You might pick up $20 of an evening."

By that summer of 1979, Steve Barber was also a full-fledged Kennedy

Photo 18-1. *Gallery* magazine for July 1979.

assassination buff.[3] He had established communication with Dealey Plaza witness Charles Brehm and had even visited Brehm in Dallas.

Garwin was also mistaken about when Barber first contacted the Ramsey Panel. The documents show that it wasn't "in the middle of this" but earlier, when the panel itself was being formed. Barber kept a small notebook, and its entries show that he kept listening to the *Gallery* disk for over a year, discussing it every now and then with his buff friends before discovering the "Hold everything" transmission on September 12, 1980. Barber recounted his experience:

> It was a Friday night. I was just sitting by my stereo—what a piece of junk it was. I said to myself, "I'm going to see if I can figure out what this talking is." I'm right at the point where the shots are heard. And I'm sitting there playing it over and over—and finally I heard just two words: "Hold everything." I thought, "Hmmm." Then I thought I picked out the next word, "secure," and thought, "Oh, my God. This can't be right. I think I've heard this before." . . . I got out my cassette player because I'd been sent a terrible copy of channel 2 by Robert Cutler. I put the tape in and let it play. I kept thinking, "I heard this on this tape." I'm just sitting there intently listening, and then it got to where he says that [". . . Hold everything secure . . ."] on channel 2 . . . I ran in and got on the phone with my friend Todd Vaughan, who was sixteen years old at the time. And he listened and said, "Yeah. You're right."[4]

From his local library, Barber got the phone number for the NRC. On October 4, he telephoned, and two days later, he mailed the Ramsey Panel a letter detailing his discovery.[5] Since appointment letters were sent out to panel members that same week, Barber's discovery was communicated to the panel just as it was being formed.[6]

Barber's October 6 handwritten letter to the panel complained of not receiving a callback after his earlier phone inquiry.[7] He wrote, "Enclosed are transcripts of the Dallas Police tape of Channel 1—the portion that includes BBN's 'gunshots'—and Channel 2 that shows it is impossible for there to be gunshots on Channel 1." Why? Because, Barber explained, "there is only a three second gap between that last [shot] impulse and the statement made by Sheriff Decker," while channel 2 shows us that Decker "didn't get to this portion of his transmission . . . until a minute after the shooting of President Kennedy." In this way, Barber did not just tell the panel what he had discovered; he also told them what it meant.

It was not until November 17 that Barber received a boilerplate reply from NRC employee C. K. Reed thanking him for his letter and assuring him that his "analysis" would be "made available to members of our committee" and that "when we have completed our report I will send you a copy."[8]

Although disappointed, Barber assumed that was the end of it. Then, in early January 1981, he received a bizarre phone call from a man whose name he had never heard: "I wish I could remember the name he gave me, but I do remember the company he said he worked for was something called 'Triconics.' This is up in Massachusetts."[9]

The caller asked Barber to send him a clip from channel 2 containing Sheriff Decker's full statement, "Hold everything secure," explaining that he would be reimbursed for the postage. Barber thought about it for a while and asked for advice from his buff friends Vaughan and Cutler. He finally decided to do nothing because he had no idea who this person was.

Two weeks later, on January 19, the Triconics caller called again, this time using a different name, one known to Barber: Paul Horowitz. According to Barber, Horowitz told him, "I'm really sorry. I should have been up-front with you."[10] Barber pointed out that had Horowitz used his real name the first time, he would have sent him the clip immediately. Asked why he had used a fake name, Horowitz answered, "We're afraid we're going to get swamped by letters and phone calls. We're trying to keep things on the QT." On the phone with me, Barber paused for a moment and then added, "He or they seemed to be afraid of the buffs, and here I am a buff."[11]

Barber recorded the channel 2 clip and mailed it to Horowitz. On Janu-

Photo 18-2. Barber's 33⅓-rpm disk from *Gallery* magazine.

THE HISTORIC
RECORDING OF THE
JFK ASSASSINATION
"GUNSHOTS" EVIDENCE
THAT DESTROYED
THE LONE ASSASSIN THEORY!

A Gallery EXCLUSIVE

With a narrated explanation by Gary Mack,
the researcher who brought this evidence
to the attention of the U. S. Congress
House Select Committee on Assassinations.

PRODUCED BY GALLERY MAGAZINE
COPYRIGHT 1979

33⅓ RPM

ary 26, the physicist called to thank him and to report that the panel was "very impressed" with it. After the fiery meeting with the acoustics scientists on the weekend of January 31/February 1, Horowitz again called Barber to report that the panel had listened to the two clips and were convinced that the two voices were Sheriff Decker. "He told me that I 'had made their job easy,' and then he said, 'You're going to be the hero of all this. I won't be surprised if I see you on the Johnny Carson show.'"[12]

Once spectrograms of the two voice patterns were made, Horowitz sent copies to Barber, cautioning him "not to discuss anything. Just keep it under your hat." Later Barber talked to journalist Ron Rosenbaum about what he knew of the panel's findings. Afterward, feeling that he had broken a confidence, he got in touch with Professor Ramsey to report it. Ramsey reassured him, "Steve, don't worry about it. You can't keep stuff like this secret."

If this account of the Ramsey Panel's history is correct, Paul Horowitz should be commended for his tenacity. Just how important the panel regarded Barber's discovery to be is reflected in a letter to panel members that Luis Alvarez wrote several months later. "All he [BBN's James Barger] has to do," wrote Alvarez, "is show how an imprint of the 'Hold everything secure' recording that appears for a reasonable purpose on the CH II tape, a minute or so after the shooting, came to exist on the CH I tape, a minute or so earlier in near coincidence with the shooting. If Jim Barger can do this, then we will have to go back to our original job of examining the properties of the 'shots' he identifies."[13]

Put another way, the Ramsey Panel, having declined repeatedly to examine

Photo 18-3. Steve Barber in Dallas, August 1979.

the evidence and analysis that had led Barger, Weiss, and Aschkenasy to their conclusions, had been given precisely what it needed—a silver bullet to undermine those conclusions.

What exactly was the significance of Barber's discovery?[14]

Barber had discovered a timing problem. Right where the HSCA's acoustic scientists had identified the shot impulses, one can just barely make out the words "Hold everything secure." He believed these words had crossed over from the other police channel when they were broadcast after the shooting, and their speaker, Sheriff Decker, was directing his men. According to Barber, this meant that whatever the so-called shot impulses are, they could not be shots since Decker spoke those words at least a minute after the shooting was over. The Ramsey Panel agreed.

Barber never used the term "crosstalk" in his letter to the Ramsey Panel or in later communications. The panel introduced the term "crosstalk" and applied a specific meaning to it. The dictionary definition of crosstalk is "interference heard on a telephone or radio because of unintentional coupling to another communication channel."[15] It's a common problem in the world of radio and electronics and can occur through a legion of different causes, especially with multichannel electronics, where care must be taken to shield circuits to prevent the migration of signals. This generic definition of crosstalk requires no particular time relationship between the original transmission and its leaked appearance on a second circuit or channel. In contrast, crosstalk that occurs simultaneously in real time on two channels is called time-synchronous, or simultaneous, crosstalk.

It is the latter definition that the Ramsey Panel used in its report, explaining that crosstalk "is quite naturally explained by assuming that the motorcycle with the open microphone (Channel I) was near another police radio receiving a transmission from Channel II, so that transmissions over Channel II would issue from its loud speaker and be picked up by the open microphone and rebroadcast on Channel I."[16] In short, an open mic on a police vehicle picked up a fragment of speech broadcast from a nearby police loudspeaker tuned to another channel.

While this scenario is technically feasible, a closer look suggests that it is far from "quite naturally" occurring. First, two different police units have to be within hearing of each other. Second, their radios have to be tuned to different channels. Third, the speaker volume of the second unit has to be set abnormally loud for it to be heard by the first unit's mic. Fourth, no other ambient sound—including the collective noise of the crowd and police motorcycles along the parade route—can be so loud as to mask what is coming out of the second unit's loudspeaker.

Notwithstanding the problematic likelihood of this scenario, there was no dispute that there had been a stuck-open mic during the shooting. Testimony before the HSCA had revealed that the malfunction of mic buttons was a common problem for the Dallas police. On November 22 alone, five different instances of motorcycle motor noise were recorded.[17] The committee learned that the brake cable near the mic button on the motorcycle might catch and switch the mic on. In addition, there was often wear and tear on a mic switch gasket that could itself make the button stick in the open position. H. B. McClain, the motorcade officer riding the motorcycle that the BBN team determined had the stuck button, testified that his particular mic button often stuck in the open position because points in the switch relay held it open.[18]

Listening to the stuck-mic segment of channel 1 and a parallel segment from channel 2 makes clear their difference. On channel 2, one can easily hear intervals of silence, while on channel 1, there is continuous engine noise. Both channels show a cacophony of voice messages, static, and other sharp noises. From time to time to time on channel 2, a phrase or sometimes a sentence is repeated, a result of the Audograph needle skipping backward. On channel 1, one can hear the shrill insistence of beeps and similar electronic interruptions (called heterodyning) caused by others on the channel keying their mics to talk while trying to transmit on the channel.

The dispatcher's time announcements establish a kind of time grid. The last announcement before the stuck button dominates channel 1 is "12:28."

Twelve seconds after this announcement, the stuck button takes over and runs for seventeen seconds, then stops for a second or two, then resumes for the next five and one-half minutes. Over this dominant engine noise, one hears a stream of static, pops, beeps, screeches, and, several times, both intelligible and unintelligible human speech.

From time to time, a voice other than that of the dispatcher will penetrate the drone. Some of these instances may or may not be crosstalk from channel 2, while others owe their existence to the party-line character of the Dallas police radio net, configured so that if two transmissions were keyed at the same time on the same channel with about the same signal strength, they would be broadcast simultaneously. Not surprisingly, these so-called party-line interruptions often resulted in unintelligible garble.

Toward the end of the channel 1 segment, sirens can be heard, and it is clear that the sirens were approaching and then leaving the microphone that picked up and transmitted their sound. At the very end of this interval, one can make out the dispatcher announcing "12:34."

On the other frequency, channel 2, the dispatcher announces, "12:26" and then "12:28." Twenty-nine seconds later, Deputy Police Chief Fisher—whose radio call sign is the number 4 (the call signs of the participants are shown hereafter in parentheses)—replies to Captain Lawrence (125) with the words "Naw, that's all right. I'll check it."[19] Two seconds later, Dallas Police Chief Curry (1), who has been periodically announcing the motorcade's position as it moves through downtown Dallas, says, "At the Triple Underpass." Eight seconds after that, one can hear the dispatcher announce, "12:30," followed eighteen seconds later by a transmission from Chief Curry saying, "Go to the hospital! . . . We're going to the hospital. . . . Parkland Hospital. Have them stand by. . . . Get men on top of that over . . . underpass. See what happened up there. Go up to the overpass."

Seconds later, Dallas County Sheriff Decker (Dallas 1), riding in the same car as Chief Curry, follows with this transmission:

DALLAS 1: 1 . . . Dallas 1 . . .

DISPATCHER: Go ahead, Dallas 1.

DALLAS 1: Tell my men to empty the jail, and up on the railroad, uh, right-of-way there . . . I'm sure it's going to take some time for you to get your men in. Pull every one of my men in there.

DISPATCHER: Repeat, 1. I didn't quite understand all of it.

DALLAS 1: Have Station 5 move all men available out of my department, back into the railroad yard there in an effort to try to determine . . . just what and where it happened down there, and *hold everything secure* until the homicide and other investigators can get there (emphasis added).

On the Audograph recorder, part of the last message is repeated twice when the machine's needle skips backward, repeating the phrase "secure until the homicide and other investigators can get there." Because of this malfunction, plus the on-and-off sound activation feature and the Audograph's propensity to simply stop recording for a few seconds when its needle skips forward, the recorded time interval between events on channel 2 are not an accurate reflection of precisely when the events occurred in real time.

As for when the shots were fired, since no microphone in Dealey Plaza was open on channel 2 to record the shots, no shots at all appear on that channel. Shots were recorded on channel 1, but given the steady drone of the motorcycle engine and the effect of AGC (described in chapter 11), the ear cannot distinguish them from noise and static. Barger, Weiss, and Aschkenasy, however, produced strip charts of sound impulses that defined exactly the position of the gunshot impulses relative to the voiced transmissions on channel 1. The 8.3-second segment containing the two flurries of gunshots begins two minutes and twenty-two seconds after the onset of the long interval of motorcycle engine noise. The Ramsey Panel, while disputing the sound impulses as shots, used the BBN team's determination of the position of the impulses for its own data set.

And the three words found by Steve Barber, where do they appear on channel 1?

It is virtually impossible to hear the words "Hold everything secure" or "Hold everything secure until" on channel 1. Electrical engineer and panel member Charles Rader later pointed out that if someone told you what you would hear and you listened very carefully, you could probably hear the words.[20]

Could someone else at some other time have spoken the words "Hold everything secure"? Was it really Sheriff Decker's voice on both channels? In acoustics science, these sorts of question are addressed by various techniques of speaker identification. The panel made spectrograms of Decker saying these words on channel 2 and compared them with spectrograms of "Hold everything secure" on channel 1. For this task, Luis Alvarez came up with an ingenious way to analyze the spectrograms, showing that they matched, which in turn became what Barber and the Ramsey Panel came to call "the double-Decker."

Given the overlap of "Hold everything secure" with the last two shots, the argument put forward by Steve Barber and the Ramsey Panel was both simple and seemingly unanswerable: Because of the overlap, the so-called gunshot sound impulses were recorded at the same time as "Hold everything secure." But this is a minute too late. Therefore, they must be something else— random static, human speech . . . anything but shots.

To support its conclusion, the panel included in its report a lengthy appendix on the timing of events that demonstrated how several automatic stoppages in the channel 2 recorder could have dropped out the time necessary to bring the two occurrences of "Hold everything" into synchrony. Still another appendix asserted the impossibility of the "Hold everything" crosstalk having been imposed on channel 1 by copying or overdubbing, either accidentally or deliberately.

Finally, the panel presented an independent and supporting argument against the acoustics evidence based on the sirens heard on channel 1 as the motorcade rushed to Parkland Hospital—notably the gradual rise and fall of the sirens' pitch and loudness over several seconds. Reasoning that this distinctive rise-and-fall pattern was best explained as sound picked up by a stationary microphone in the vicinity of the passing motorcade, not by a mic on a motorcycle with the motorcade, the panel argued that the stuck-open mic was not on a motorcycle with the motorcade but rather on one of the many motorcycles parked at the command post near the Trade Mart. If true, declared the panel, then the so-called shot impulses were picked up by a motorcycle that was never in Dealey Plaza.

The principal argument, however, was always "the double-Decker." Repeatedly in its report, the Ramsey Panel reiterated its conclusion that "the acoustic impulses attributed to gunshots were recorded about one minute after the President had been shot and the motorcade had been instructed to go to the hospital." Parenthetically, it took thirty years before a very smart private researcher named Michael O'Dell figured out that the panel had made a mistake and that in reality, the shot impulses were only about thirty seconds too late.[21]

Thirty seconds too late or sixty seconds too late, the consequences are the same: the acoustics evidence had been shown to be groundless because the "shots" were recorded at the same time Sheriff Decker said, "Hold everything."

On May 14, 1982, the Ramsey Panel Report was released. As with the Vela Panel Report two years previously, the press reception was subdued and approving. Ironically, at that same moment, the national media was focused on the trial of John Hinkley Jr., who less than a year earlier had attempted to assassinate President Ronald Reagan. That evening, all three networks punctuated their evening news programs with brief reports. ABC reported that the new study "does not support the conclusion there was a second gunman involved" and rather showed that "the sounds in question were recorded about one minute after the shots that killed President Kennedy."[22] On CBS News, Dan Rather said, "The NAS panel . . . concluded that the four pulses thought to be the gunshots were recorded more than a minute after Kennedy was shot."[23] NBC ran a short clip of Dr. Norman Ramsey saying the panel's work "shows that the shots or the impulses previously studied were approximately one minute after the assassination was over."[24]

Official Washington—and much of the rest of the country—went to sleep that night thinking this was one more loose end it did not have to worry about. Like the report of the Vela Panel, this report sank out of sight almost as soon as it was released.

Sinking into obscurity with it was a curious footnote to history. The blue-ribbon panel of scientists that had swung public opinion back towards the Warren Commission had done so by advancing the discovery of an earnest young man from Ohio. Because of this, they owed much to the buff who not only had made the crucial discovery but had explained to them what it meant. Steven Barber was quickly forgotten. He never got his call from a producer with the Johnny Carson show.

CHAPTER 19

THE RESURRECTION OF THE ACOUSTICS

Reaction to the Ramsey Panel Report within the scientific and academic community was muted. There was no spirited defense of the work of Barger, Weiss, and Aschkenasy. Privately, all three firmly stuck to their guns while making modest suggestions as to what additional testing should be done to confirm their original studies. After this, they declined any further public involvement in the issue.[1]

Among the establishment cognoscenti, the results of the Ramsey Panel seemed to confirm the perspective of the HSCA, whose members, before the late arrival of the acoustics evidence, had been ready to agree with the Warren Commission's single-shooter finding. The acoustics evidence could now be viewed as a scientific aberration, a regrettable mistake exposed by the distinguished scientists of the Ramsey Panel.

This was the settled judgment on the acoustics evidence during the last two decades of the twentieth century, decades during which I had precious little to do with the assassination. I was too busy making my living as an investigator. The defenses of Stephen Bingham and Chol Soo Lee in the Bay Area and of Timothy McVeigh in the Oklahoma City bombing, a long-lasting $100 million fraud case in Columbia, South America, and an equally long-lasting $100 million arson case in northern France—these occupied my time and attention, leaving hardly a thought for the Kennedy assassination.

That was, until the spring of 2001, when I picked up a copy of the March 26 *Washington Post* while on a case in Baltimore. It was not a front-page story, appearing instead on page 3 under the byline of the *Post*'s veteran investigative reporter George Lardner Jr.[2] The title was nonetheless dramatic: "Study Backs Theory of Grassy Knoll—New Report Says Second Gunman Fired at Kennedy." Apparently Britain's leading forensic journal, *Science & Justice*, had just published a peer-reviewed article by a US government scientist alleging significant errors in the Ramsey Panel Report. Lardner pointed out that the NRC panel had concluded that the sounds identified as gunshots "were recorded about one minute after the president was shot" on the basis of the "Hold everything" crosstalk. According to Lardner, the government scientist had simply used another instance of crosstalk and found a match to "the exact instant that John F. Kennedy was assassinated." Apparently, too, the NRC panel had bungled the probability calculations and the odds that the "gunshots" were shots were much higher than the panel had thought. The *Post* article concluded, "The House Assassinations Committee may well have been right after all."

Since I had never taken the time to understand what the NRC panel had earlier announced, none of this made much sense to me, but what registered was that the *Science & Justice* article had revived the debate over the Kennedy assassination. What I could not know was that this was the opening salvo in a series of critiques to be launched over the first decade of the twenty-first century that would undermine the scientific basis for critical facts in the assassination of President Kennedy.

Nine months later, in December 2001, I found myself in Dallas having breakfast in a hotel coffee shop with "the government scientist" mentioned in the Lardner article. His name was Don Thomas, and he was a PhD senior research entomologist with the Department of Agriculture research station on the Rio Grande River in Weslaco, Texas. He had driven up from there, and I had flown in from somewhere, both of us to do interviews in Dealey Plaza for a film by documentary filmmaker Chip Selby.[3] Selby's previous credits included writing and directing the 1988 documentary *Reasonable Doubt: The Single Bullet Theory and the Assassination of JFK.*

Thomas was about fifty and had the relaxed air of a college professor. He was even wearing a corduroy jacket. He didn't talk much. When asked a question, he answered very precisely in few words. Over the years, I had met numerous expert witnesses in the sciences and had developed the rule of thumb that the less an expert talks, the more likely he or she is to be right. True scientists, it seemed to me, kept their own counsel. Although I was fifteen years older than Thomas, we were about the same height and weight and both had retained our dark brown hair. Because of his quiet modesty, I liked him immediately.

When I asked what an expert on insects was doing in the thicket of the Kennedy assassination, he pointed out that many entomologists had attained scientific expertise outside their fields. Charles Darwin started out collecting beetles, and biologist and entomologist Alfred Kinsey had earned a ScD degree from Harvard for his wasp studies before becoming a renowned sexologist. And Cyrus Thomas, long before his groundbreaking studies in archaeology

Photo 19-1. Don Thomas in 2004.

and ethnology, was a US government entomologist attached to the Hayden Geological Survey of 1871.

As for how he had become interested in the Kennedy assassination, Thomas recalled a moment in the 1970s when he was living in Las Vegas. One evening he went to a performance of comic Mort Sahl. At one point, Sahl brought up the Kennedy assassination and began making claims about Lyndon Johnson as a conspirator and other wild tales. When several upset members of the audience got up and walked out, Thomas joined them. It was twenty years later, in the early 1990s, when he picked up a book on the assassination in a bookstore in Kingsville, Texas. The book wasn't that good, he recalled, but if only half the claims were true, he judged, there had to be something there. Rather quickly he was hooked by the puzzle.

He began reading various forensic journals to understand the science at issue in the case. Then he turned to studying the evidence contained in the Warren Commission's twenty-six volumes and the eight volumes of the HSCA. It wasn't until 1999 that Thomas turned his attention to the acoustics evidence, where he soon found significant mistakes of both fact and interpretation by the Ramsey Panel. He wrote a critique and submitted his article to the *American Journal of Forensic Sciences*. Surprisingly, the journal returned the manuscript unread, together with a letter from the editor advising him that "the journal declines to consider this manuscript" and adding that no amount of reanalysis was going to change anyone's mind. Thomas subsequently submitted the same article to the British equivalent, *Science & Justice*, the journal of the Chartered Society of Forensic Scientists. It was peer reviewed and published in March 2001.

There in the coffee shop, Thomas started to explain to me what was wrong with the Ramsey Panel's study. It all had to do with which example of crosstalk one chose to use as a tie point, but before he could elaborate further, Selby came to pick us up for our interviews in Dealey Plaza. That evening, Thomas and I were invited to the home of Gary Mack, the curator of The Sixth Floor Museum at Dealey Plaza. Gary was previously the program director of a Dallas radio station and the first assassination researcher to conduct rudimentary filtering of the Dallas police radio tapes to reveal what appeared to be the sounds of gunshots, a discovery that led to Mary Ferrell's remarks to Chief Counsel Blakey concerning the acoustics evidence.

One reason for Mack's invitation was to discuss an argument that had recently surfaced in the assassination community around claims that the Dealey Plaza films showed that it was impossible for Officer McLain's motorcycle to have been at the location where the first shots were recorded. Since Gary had video from all the assassination films, we screened them and rather quickly found the fundamental errors in the argument, had a few beers, and called it a night.

Thomas's visit to Dallas capped an eventful year marked by his emergence into the spotlight as the first and only voice from within the scientific community to publicly challenge the Ramsey Panel's nearly two-decades-old attack on the acoustics evidence. During our meeting in Dallas, what I didn't know was that a central claim of Thomas's critique had itself been shown to be mistaken. It all started with a mistake by the Ramsey Panel itself.

In any case like this, the first thing any investigator or committee of investigation should do is to obtain recorders of the same make and model used by the Dallas police on November 22, 1963. This permits multiple experiments on how the equipment actually operated. The Ramsey Panel failed to do this and consequently produced mistaken timing figures for the Audograph recorder that the DPD used for channel 2.

As described in an earlier chapter, the Audograph machine had been purchased sometime in the early 1950s for business dictation, but its design came from the 1940s. It had a fixed needle mechanically linked to a worm drive. As the worm drive turned, it drew the needle across a thin vinyl disc at a fixed speed. Since the needle on this old machine often skipped forward (thus leaving out part of the transmission) or backward (repeating part of the transmission), it was extremely difficult to compute elapsed real time for the Audograph.

The repeats were obvious, so the Ramsey Panel simply removed them in making its timing calculations. Unaware of how the recorder actually worked, it never realized that the linkage to the worm drive meant that any backward

Photo 19-2. An Audograph machine.

needle jump would be compensated for by a forward needle jump after one (or several) disk revolutions. There was nothing to subtract. Hence, the panel's timing figures were all incorrect. "Hold everything" and the gunshot impulses occurred about half a minute after the assassination, not a full minute, as the panel had announced in 1982.

It was not Don Thomas who made this discovery but Michael O'Dell, a mathematically adept and very bright independent researcher from California who figured out the panel's timing error by comparing different recorded copies of channel 2. Nonetheless, it was Don Thomas who was hurt by Odell's discovery. Instead of using "Hold everything," Thomas had used another instance of crosstalk accepted by the Ramsey Panel—the words "You want me to hold this traffic on Stemmons" spoken by motorcycle Sergeant S. Q. Bellah—to show that the gunshot impulses occurred right at the moment of the shooting. But Thomas had used the mistaken timing figures of the Ramsey Panel to reach that result. Consequently, his argument collapsed as soon as it became apparent that these figures were mistaken.

Thomas forthrightly acknowledged his miscalculation at a November 2001 assassination-related conference, saying, "To put it in lay terms, my objection to the NRC's hypothesis is largely blown away."[4] His retraction, coming as it did in the middle of a wide-ranging erudite presentation, attracted no media notice, nor did it signal an end to his inquiry about the acoustics evidence. During his spare time in the aftermath of the conference, Thomas returned to an examination of his voluminous files and correspondence on the acoustics issue.

One evening in early 2002, he went to look up something from the

Photo 19-3. Close-up of the Audograph worm gear that drives the fixed needle across the disc.

transcripts of the two DPD channel broadcasts. Instead of going to the printed version in the Ramsey Panel Report, he reached for a copy of the 1993 book *First Day Evidence* by Gary Savage with its appendix containing the complete one-hundred-page manuscript of DPD dispatch supervisor Sergeant James Bowles's monograph, "The Kennedy Assassination Tapes: A Rebuttal to the Acoustical Evidence Theory."[5]

Turning to Bowles's transcripts of channel 1 and channel 2 mere seconds before the first gunshot impulse, Thomas was surprised to discover a crosstalk pair he had never before seen: from the channel 2 transcript, "Naw, that's all right. I'll check it" and from the channel 1 transcript the snippet "I'll check it." In an accompanying footnote, Bowles specifically described this transmission as a prime example of crosstalk, identifying both the words spoken and the voice speaking them as the same on both channels. Moreover, when Thomas listened to his copies of the DPD recordings, "I'll check it" on channel 1 was strong, clear, and easily identifiable, unlike its ghostly "Hold everything" counterpart. During a conversation with me years later, Thomas recalled the moment of his discovery:

> I remember going, "Wow! How the hell did I miss this?" Basically the reason was my thought process was kind of oriented to the arguments that they [the Ramsey Panel] had made in their report, and since they hadn't included that ["I'll check it"] in their arguments, I didn't even think about looking for other crosstalk. . . . And now here was "I'll check it." It was a game changer.[6]

The importance of "I'll check it" occurring on channel 1 only three seconds before the first gunshot is that its placement also places the gunshots right where they should be and not either a minute or half a minute too late.

On March 20, 2002, just weeks after his discovery, Thomas received in the mail a copy of the rebuttal from the still-living members of the Ramsey Panel accompanied by a cover letter signed by Norman Ramsey that said simply, "For your information I am enclosing a copy of a manuscript we submitted yesterday to *Science & Justice*." The twenty-two-page rebuttal alleged a number of "errors," "misstatements," "miscalculations," and "incorrect inferences" and reasserted the validity of the Ramsey Panel's findings. In his e-mail response to the panel, Thomas offered a point-by-point defense but emphasized his discovery of "I'll check it" and its crucial importance as a robust validation of the acoustics evidence.

"My critique was pretty blunt and clear," Thomas recalled. "I told them I felt they had wanted to avoid the obvious and, more importantly, to structure their argument so the reader wouldn't pick up on 'I'll check it.' I criticized them for that."[7]

The panel's response? Silence. Thomas waited. Weeks passed. Nothing. What for him had been a collegial back-and-forth exchange of letters and e-mails reminiscent of similar intellectual duels within academia had simply ceased. The Ramsey Panel had gone dark.

After several months had gone by, still with no appearance of the panel's rebuttal in the pages of *Science & Justice*, it became apparent that they had pulled its submission and were revising it to address Thomas's new discovery. A year passed, and then another. As the silence continued, it became increasingly clear that the soft-spoken but persistent entomologist from Texas had found something for which the Ramsey Panel had no reply.

During the next few years, Thomas single-handedly faced efforts by the establishment media to denigrate or dismiss the acoustics evidence. Though it had never been his wish, the recognition of Thomas as the Ramsey Panel's only critic cast him in the role of David against the Goliath of network television. A pattern emerged. A TV broadcast about the assassination would showcase claims discrediting the acoustics evidence, following which Thomas would offer a refutation. The difference was that the TV broadcast might reach millions of viewers, while Thomas's response might be read by a few dozen. No less evident was the fact that when it comes to the Kennedy assassination, the networks are chronically disinclined to present serious scientific analysis with results peer reviewed by independent experts prior to production.

Undaunted, Thomas soldiered on, pretty much alone and largely ignored by the media.

June 5, 2014, marked five months—almost to the day—that I had been digging into the background and internal workings of the Ramsey Panel while at the same time toiling over the convoluted language of the report itself and following what Don Thomas had turned up over the past fifteen years. What I had not done during these months, however, was examine the raw evidence in the case—the recordings of DPD channels 1 and 2.

I knew that audio files had been posted on the NRC/NAS website two decades after the Ramsey Panel Report and that some copies were available from other sources. I had listened to a number of them, but what I needed now were the exact same audio files—the same data sets—that the panel had studied. This was why on that June day, I was excited to receive a priority mail envelope from Steve Barber. In that envelope were .wav files he had obtained from Ramsey Panel members Richard Garwin in 1981–1982 and Paul Horowitz in 2003. Finally, I had what I needed.

I held up the CD and looked at it. With any luck, I could determine whether a particular three-word phrase was present on the channel 1 recording and whether it was there in such a way that the Ramsey Panel could have missed it. I put the disc in the drive slot and waited for the list of tracks to come up. Almost immediately, I saw that track 1 very likely contained what I wanted. It was fifteen minutes, twenty-two seconds long and ran from 12:23 through 12:38. That interval contained the important segment from channel 1, the five-and-a-half-minute interval where the engine noise of a motorcycle dominates and where the shots appear. I pressed play, and the track began. It started out with the usual police radio patter:

231: 231 clear.
DISPATCHER: 231 clear 12:23.
606: 606 out.
DISPATCHER: 10-4, 606. 12:24.

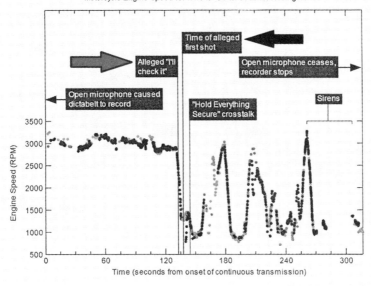

Figure 20-1. Sonalysts Corp. diagram: Note the time of "I'll check it" (*outlined gray arrow*) as the rpms drop and the time of the first shot (*filled-in black arrow*).

Then more patter and also short periods of silence lasting only a second or two. Motorcycle noise came on for seventeen seconds and then stopped. Then another "Ten-four." Finally the motorcycle noise began again and ran uninterrupted. At first I could hear only the dispatcher and someone else over the noise, but after thirty seconds, there was just noise. I kept listening, and then—two minutes, nineteen seconds into the long engine noise—I heard it, someone saying, "I'll check it." No question it was there, and no question what the words were. I went over it three times . . . four times . . . five times. It was not "I'll get it," as the still living Ramsey Panel members had mentioned in an article, nor "Alright Chaney," as Steve Barber said he had heard on the *Gallery* magazine disc. Not a shred of doubt—it was "I'll check it."[1] I let the track continue, but as expected, I could hear no shots. Nor did I really hear the ghostly "Hold everything."

Yet there *was* something else. Simultaneous with "I'll check it," the engine rpms of the motorcycle dropped off markedly. In his 1979 report to the HSCA, James Barger mentioned what I had just heard—a "single diminution of motorcycle noise about 3 sec. before the first shot is heard"—and he correlated this with a significant slowdown of the motorcycle speed.[2] A

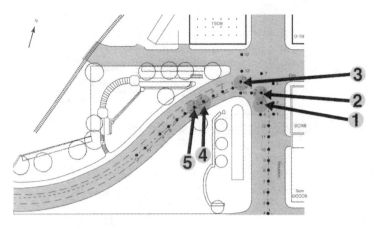

Figure 20-2. HSCA map showing motorcycle locations when shots 1 through 5 were recorded. Note that (1) on the map gives position of cycle when first shot was recorded.

later analysis in 2013 by the technology firm Sonalysts went further and constructed a graph (see Figure 20-1) showing the sudden drop-off in motorcycle rpms concurrent with other events on the channel 1 Dictabelt recording.[3]

What makes this significant is that the drop in rpms precisely matches the calculated map location of Officer McLain's motorcycle when he slowed to make a sharp 120-degree left turn onto Elm Street, three seconds before his microphone picked up the first shot. Thus, between the engine noise drop-off and the first shot, "I'll check it" is anchored to the real-time stream of Dealey Plaza by not one but two events happening in sequence.

Next, I listened to the channel 2 track for the original transmission that contained "I'll check it."[4] Like channel 1, this track begins with what sounds like police chatter—someone announcing their position as the motorcade moves through downtown Dallas: "Just at Field Street," a moment later "Crossing Lamar," and then "Just crossing Market Street."

I looked down at a transcript of this channel in front of me. It was prepared for the FBI by Sergeant James Bowles, the DPD radio dispatch supervisor, who knew and was able to recognize individual voices. I noted that the voice announcing streets was Dallas Police Chief Jesse Curry. He was driving the motorcade's lead car with Dallas County Sheriff William Decker and two Secret Service agents, staying roughly two hundred feet ahead of the presidential limousine and broadcasting his position so that other units could follow the motorcade's progress. At just about 12:30 p.m., this brief dialogue takes place between Deputy Chief Fisher and Captain Lawrence:

DISPATCHER: Go ahead, 4.

FISHER [4]: 125, this is 4. What traffic personnel do you have on Cedar Springs in the vicinity of the field here?

LAWRENCE [125]: Stand by. . . . Uh, Cedar Springs and Mocking-bird?

FISHER [4]: Yes. The traffic seems to be moving out of this lot awfully slow. What uh . . . What's your location?

LAWRENCE [125]: I'm at the Trade Mart now. I'll head back out that way.

FISHER [4]: Naw, that's all right. *I'll check it.* [emphasis added]

LAWRENCE [125]: 10–4.

CURRY [1]: *At the Triple Underpass* [emphasis added]

DISPATCHER: 10–4, 1 . . . 15 car 2 12:30 KKB364

LAWRENCE [125]: 125 to 250.[5]

Because he was familiar with Deputy Chief Fisher's voice, Bowles indicated in his transcript that the West Texas twang saying "I'll check it" on channel 1 was Fisher's voice picked up as crosstalk. When the two transmissions are compared, the voice seems to be the same. Both have the same cadence, the same rhythm as syllable follows syllable.

No less interesting was another detail that had also caught Don Thomas's attention. Lawrence followed Fisher's "I'll check it" with a perfunctory "10–4." Then, less than a second later, Chief Curry announced, "At the Triple Underpass." This closeness in time of Fisher's remark to Chief Curry's announcement reflects a real-world situation. The lead car was nearing the Triple Underpass. From numerous photos, we know where the limousine was when the lead car reached that point—just entering the "kill zone" where shots began to rain down.

Had channel 2 had a mic open in Dealey Plaza, we would have heard shots fired a second or two after Chief Curry said, "At the Triple Underpass." In sum, the utterance of "I'll check it" on each channel is independently anchored to the same moment in real time. Each channel fills in details of that moment. A bird's-eye view (see color photo gallery, Plate 1) would show Chief Curry picking up his mic as the lead car approached the Triple Underpass, while near the corner of Elm and Houston Streets, Officer McClain was slowing to make his 120-degree left turn onto Elm Street. "I'll check it" marks this moment on both channels.[6]

This is important because the time markers on both channels for "I'll check it" appear not only to meet the Ramsey Panel's requirements for being time-synchronous crosstalk, but to place it in real time—three seconds before the first shot. In contrast, the originating broadcast of "Hold everything" on

Photo 20-3. Bronson photo: The limousine enters the "kill zone" as the lead car is out of frame to the left "At the Triple Underpass."

channel 2 occurs either 30 seconds or 60 seconds after the shooting was over. In short, "I'll check it" calls into question the Ramsey Panel's enthusiastic backing of "Hold everything."

As such, we would expect the Ramsey Panel members to have recognized "I'll check it" as a lethal threat to their entire argument. We would also expect to see a section of their report devoted to it and arguing against it. There is no such section.

Could it be that the panel just missed it? Hard to imagine. First, the amplitude and clarity of "I'll check it" draws attention to it, let alone its position in a location drawing maximum scrutiny. Even Steve Barber mentioned "I'll check it" in his letter to the panel, although mishearing it as "Alright Chaney" while listening to it on his *Gallery* magazine copy of a copy.

For his part, Sergeant Bowles, whose unpublished monograph the panel used as a major resource (thanking him admiringly for his help), identified "I'll check it" as crosstalk, not once but five times, giving it special prominence.[7] In Chapter 4 of his paper, he identified it not just as the voice of Deputy Chief N. T. Fisher but as being the next-to-last transmission in a longer dialogue between Fisher and a traffic captain: "The first 'cross-talk' was the message 'I'll check it' at 12:31:02 (Channel I). On Channel II at this same time, the message, 'That's all right. I'll check it' was broadcast by a Deputy Chief [N. T. Fisher] to a Traffic Captain. The voice picked up on Channel I was that of the Deputy Chief."[8]

Sitting at my desk, I now felt certain of two things. One, it was impossible for me to believe the Ramsey Panel could have missed "I'll check it." Two, for the first time, I now fully grasped the enormity of Don Thomas's discovery and what he had done. He had not just tossed another argument at the Ramsey Panel survivors. He had rolled an evidence bomb under their door.

Recognizing the true importance of "I'll check it" led to another question: If the crosstalk could not have escaped the panel's notice, was there any evidence that the panel was aware of it?

I thought immediately of the audio tracks posted on the NRC/NAS site around 2005 and described as those studied by the panel in 1980–1982. Tracks 1, 2, and 3 contained the recordings cited earlier in endnotes to this chapter. It was the next track, track 4, that I remembered.[9] It was short—only one minute, thirty-eight seconds—and labeled by the panel as "miscellaneous short segments of Ch 1 and Ch 2." I put the CD in the drive slot, clicked on the track, and began to listen.

There they were: two short clips of "I'll check it" and "Hold everything" from channel 1, followed by two clips from channel 2 of "I'll check it" and one of "Hold everything." While this track was simply an assemblage of the two crosstalks, their appearance together indicated that the panel had known about "I'll check it."

Intrigued, I dug deeper. In the report, the panel described four crosstalks that are discussed at length. A fifth ("I have a witness") is mentioned in the appendix. None was "I'll check it." The panel made spectrograms of the four to permit further close study. In so doing, various possibilities opened up. A test called pattern cross-correlation (PCC) could be run on a mainframe computer to compare the spectrograms of each crosstalk pair. Software runs one clip by the other at various increments of speed. If there is a match, an obvious peak appears, a strong indication that the speech recorded on both channels is the same. One would think that if the panel had been interested enough in "I'll check it" to assemble clips of it with clips of "Hold everything," they would also have made spectrograms of "I'll check it."

I got in touch with Michael O'Dell, the remarkable young analyst who had found the flaw in the panel's timing calculations. With admirable collegiality, within a few days he sent me by e-mail copies of six spectrograms he had received from Paul Horowitz in 2001. All were identical in format and labeling, and all were made prior to the publication of the panel's report in 1982. Four were duplicates of spectrograms published in the Ramsey Panel Report, the fifth was of a crosstalk occurring after the motorcycle engine noise stopped ("I have a witness"), and the sixth was of "I'll check it."[10] As encouraging as this appeared, the six spectrograms were simply raw visual data with no accompanying descriptions. Nor did I recall ever seeing any mention of "I'll check it" anywhere in the report.

I searched my notes to see if I had ever come across the phrase "I'll check it" anywhere in the panel's report. Nothing turned up. Could I have missed it in that ninety-six-page thicket of scientific language? There was only one way to find out. I went back and began a tedious, sentence-by-sentence rereading of the report.

After several hours, I found it.

The phrase is nowhere in the body of the report but is found on page 70 at the very end of Appendix C in Table C-2, labeled "Channel I Transcript from J. C. Bowles, ~12:30 to ~12:37" (Figure 20-4).

12:31:02 ?   I'll check it (discounted by sound spectrograms)

"That's odd," I thought. "This isn't Bowles's transcript." It had been altered. He used the character "?" to mean "unknown speaker," but Bowles knew who said "I'll check it"—Deputy Chief N. T. Fisher. And he certainly did not add "(discounted by sound spectrograms)."

I went to Bowles's transcript in his monograph (Figure 20-5) and looked at his actual entry:

12:31:02   4-Ch. II   I'll check it   60

"4" refers to the DPD call number for Deputy Chief N. T. Fisher, and "Ch. II" means his transmission had crossed over from channel 2. The number "60" refers to Bowles's endnote describing this as a prime example of cross-talk. Evidently the panel had simply erased Bowles's notation and endnote number and substituted "?" to denote "unknown speaker."[11]

The next time entry—12:31:10 (motorcycle engine slowed to idle speed)—was the same in both the typescript and the Ramsey Panel version. But the time entry immediately following shows a big change. Bowles's original transcript shows:

12:31:12   91   . . . check wanted on P-Pecos   61

Bowles's endnote (61) explains that officer 91 had made a traffic stop and was following up on an earlier request for information on a license tag, "P-Pecos 4700." The Ramsey Panel removed the entry from Bowles's transcript, kept the 12:31:12 time slot, and in its place inserted the following:

Bowles' Times		
12:29:20	?	...Market Office...
12:29:27	?	...All right...
12:31:00		(Motorcycle engine slowed down.)
12:31:02	? ⬅	I'll check it. (discounted by sound spectrograms)
12:31:10		(Motorcycle engine slowed to idle speed.)
12:31:12		"Hold everything secure..." (confirmed by sound spectrograms to be Sheriff Decker in a crossover from Channel II.
12:31:20		(Single tone of a bell.)
12:31:24		(Motorcycle engine at very slow idle.)
12:31:32		("Bonk" sound-motorcycle engine revved up.)
12:31:40		(Motorcycle sound like it started moving.)
12:31:48		(Motor slowed down; perhaps another approached.)
12:31:52	?	...on the phone. (Motor slow to idle.)
12:31:56		(someone whistling a tune in background.)

Figure 20-4. Ramsey report, page 71. Bowles transcript of channel 1. Note the "?" next to "I'll check it" (*black arrow*).

12:29:20 ?⬅	...Market Office...	58
12:29:27 ?⬅	...All right...	
**(12:30:55)	(Approximate time first shot was fired.)	
12:31:00	(Motorcycle engine slowed down.)	59
**(12:31:03)	(Approximate time third shot was fired.)	
12:31:02 (4-Ch. II)	I'll check it.	(60)
12:31:10	(Motorcycle engine slowed to idle speed.)	
12:31:12 91	...Check wanted on P-Pecos...	61
12:31:20	(Single tone of a bell.)	62
12:31:24	(Motorcycle engine at very slow idle.)	
12:31:32	("Bonk" sound-motorcycle engine revved up.)	63
12:31:40	(Motorcycle sounds like it started moving.)	
12:31:48	(Motor slowed down; perhaps another approached.)	
12:31:52 ?⬅	...on the phone. (Motor slow to idle.)	64
12:31:56	(Someone whistling a tune in background.)	65

**Time shots were fired have been added for reference although shot sounds are not on the tape.

Figure 20-5. Original typescript of Bowles's transcript of channel 1 available to the Ramsey Panel in 1980–1982. Note "I'll check it" with the "4-Ch. II" (*medium ellipse*), the footnote number 60 (*small ellipse*), and "unknown speaker" references (*black outlined arrows*).

12:31:12   "Hold everything secure . . ." (confirmed by sound spectrograms to be Sheriff Decker in a crossover from Channel II)

Why was "I'll check it" mentioned only in an obscure table to an appendix? Why had Bowles's transcript been altered in such a way that the reader would never know Bowles had identified "I'll check it" as a prime example of cross-talk? I didn't know.

I turned to the report's channel 2 excerpt from the Bowles transcript to find the original transmission of "I'll check it" by Deputy Chief Fisher. It comes at the end of a long conversation by Fisher with Captain Lawrence, a traffic captain.

I looked in vain. It wasn't there. The Ramsey Panel's transcript of channel 2 begins on page 76 (as shown in Figure 20-6). When I compared the panel's version with Bowles's transcript (Figure 20-7), I saw immediately what had happened.

In Bowles's transcript, the transmission closest to the 12:30 start time occurred at 12:31:02. However, the start time the panel selected for its appendix begins fourteen seconds later, at 12:31:16. In those fourteen seconds, Deputy Fisher said "I'll check it," followed immediately by Lawrence's "10–4" and Chief Curry's "At the Triple Underpass." The portion that the panel omitted is outlined in Figure 20-7. However it happened, eliminating those fourteen seconds made it impossible for anyone reading the report to discern the presence of "I'll check it," let alone its crucial significance.

When the Ramsey Panel report was published, only two transcripts of the channels 1 and 2 recordings were available to the public. Both were published in the Warren Commission's twenty-six volumes of *Hearings and Exhibits*. However, both left out the critical five-and-a-half-minute segment on channel 1 during which motorcycle noise dominated the channel. There was no reason to believe that Bowles's private manuscript with its transcript would ever see the light of day. In short, the Ramsey Panel produced a transcript that omitted any clue to both the presence and significance of "I'll check it."

Long ago as an investigator, I learned that there are innocent explanations for almost anything that at first looks sinister or out of the ordinary. I tried to imagine such an explanation for what I had just found. Turning back to the panel's expurgated version of Bowles's transcript for channel 1, I thought about the three ways the brief one-line 12:31:02 entry for "I'll check it" had been altered. The phrase "(discounted by sound spectrograms)" had been added; the endnote reference number "60" had been deleted; and the notation "4-Ch. II" had been replaced by a question mark indicating "unknown speaker."

APPENDIX C

BOWLES TIMES

Approx. Dispatcher	12:30 KKB364.
12:31:16/17 125	125 to 250...
Approx. Dispatcher 12:31:23	15-2...(then, overriding the dispatcher...)
Channel II 12:31:08	Go to the hospital...("On our way")..Parkland
Channel I	Hospital. Have them stand by...... Get men on top of that there over...underpass. See what happenend up there. Go up to the overpass. (At least one transmitter was open for a while, now.)
?	(Unreadable-sounds like "91 Champion.")

Figure 20-6. Beginning of the Ramsey Panel's channel 2 transcript in Appendix C, page 76 of its report.

Approx. 12:31:02 (4)		Naw, that's all right. I'll check it.	(10)
	125	10-4.	
Approx. 12:31:04 (1)		At the Triple Underpass.	
	Dispatcher	10-4, 1...15-2...	
Approx. 12:31:16/17	Dispatcher	12:30 KKB364.	
	125	125 to 250...	
Approx. 12:31:23	Dispatcher	15-2...(then, overriding the dispathcer...)	
Channel II 12:31:08		Go to the hospital..("On our way").. Parkland	
Channel I		Hospital. Have them stand by... ...Get men on top of that there over...underpass. See what happened up there. Go up to the overpass. (At least one transmitter was open for a while, now.)	
	?	(Unreadable-sounds like "91 Champion."	

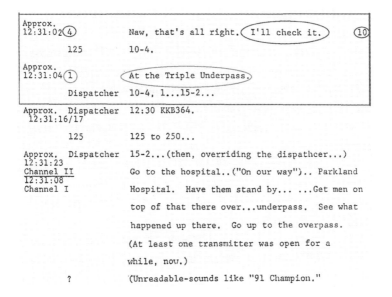

Figure 20-7. Bowles's continuous transcript of channel 2 from 12:31:02. The portion omitted by the Ramsey Panel is outlined in a black bordered rectangle with the messages from Deputy Chief Fisher (4) and Chief Curry (1) in ellipses.

As I stared at that seemingly inconsequential question mark, the hair started rising on the back of my neck. On the one hand, the "?" was only a minor mistake in an entry—a single keystroke at that—and could plausibly be excused as an innocent error, a mere typo. But three innocent mistakes in a one-line entry?

I thought back to the white-collar crime cases I'd worked on over the last thirty-five years. In these cases, the investigative process is typically tedious, in no way glamorous, let alone grist for a good mystery novel. But these cases are not without drama. Their outcomes almost always turn on documentary evidence—e-mails, memos, bank statements, bookkeeping entries, merger agreements, personal notes. Quite often the critical evidence has nothing to do with the initial crime but rather with the cover-up. The defendants are caught trying to hide what they had done with various moves they believe will be seen as ordinary, normal business practices. Good prosecutors have a nose for the thread or action that doesn't make sense. They will pull on it, end up discovering still other documents that make even less sense, and thereby tease out what had really happened.

Looking at that question mark, I felt like a prosecutor who had found the thread. Why would anyone remove the well-established identity of the speaker and substitute a question mark meaning "unknown speaker"? Why expurgate one channel and leave out fourteen seconds of the other—both changes having to do with "I'll check it"—while leaving the rest of Bowles's transcripts untouched? Given what the Ramsey Panel was supposed to be doing, all this made little sense.

Yet, from another perspective, it did. The Ramsey Panel clearly knew about "I'll check it." They prepared audio snippets of it to compare with "Hold everything" and took pains to prepare its spectrogram—no small task in those days. There the story ends. Apparently, no PCC test was done when that would have been the obvious way to show the panel that it had nothing to worry about. Simply from an investigator's point of view, the cuts and alterations of Bowles's transcripts solely with regard to "I'll check it" point toward an understanding of its importance.

As I thought more about that odd phrase—"(discounted by sound spectrograms)"—when any comparison of spectrograms for "I'll check it" was either never done or suppressed from public disclosure, and thought too of all the rejiggering of the transcript around it, a sharply etched picture popped into my mind. It was of a cop at the scene of an accident, waving away the inevitable throng of accident gawkers and saying, "Just move along, folks. There's nothing to see here."

CHAPTER 21   RAMSEY PANEL REDUX

I n October 2005—more than three and a half years after scientist Don Thomas rolled his evidence bomb under the panel's door—the surviving members of the Ramsey Panel finally broke their long silence with a lengthy rebuttal in *Science & Justice*.[1]

There had been changes in those three and a half years and even more since the release of the panel's report in May 1982. By March 2002, when it submitted its rebuttal to Thomas and then apparently withdrew it, Alvarez had died of esophageal cancer, and Norman Ramsey himself had retired from Harvard.[2] By 2005, Paul Horowitz had been replaced as "corresponding author" by Richard Garwin's colleague Ralph Linsker of the IBM Watson Research Center.[3]

The surviving panel members' draft rebuttal to Don Thomas's 2001 defense of the acoustics in *Science & Justice* was withdrawn before publication after he had raised his "I'll check it" discovery. While that draft had raised only peripheral points against Thomas, the 2005 reply was a major effort. Not only was it more than twice as long, but it frontally attacked Thomas's claim concerning "I'll check it." It had the same authoritative tone as the panel report from years earlier and was filled with technical language, replete with statements such as "The cepstrum defined here as the inverse Fourier transform of the logarithm of the magnitude of the Fourier transform of the signal, was originally devised to facilitate the detection of echoes in acoustic signals."[4]

By now I was no longer troubled by such flourishes. Given what Thomas had already shown, only one escape route from his critique was available: prove that "I'll check it" was not crosstalk. Accordingly, Linsker et al. elected to set up a kind of "shootout at the OK Corral" between "I'll check it" and two significant examples of crosstalk: "You want me . . . Stemmons" and "Hold everything."[5] By doing so, they would show that the phrase Thomas was making so much of was not crosstalk, "even if," as they put it, "the same words 'I'll check it' appear on both channels." In that case, they wrote, "we conclude that they were spoken separately, and at different times."[6]

The test they chose, described briefly in the last chapter, was PCC. It requires selecting a template or fragment of speech from one source and a target of speech from another. Software runs the template by the target at various speeds. If they match, a particular speed will produce an obvious peak on the charted results, demonstrating that the two fragments of speech are crosstalk.

Linsker et al. began their shootout with admirable directness. For each of the three crosstalk samples tested, they stated they would provide:

1. The location of the sample on the NAS/NRC posted tracks;
2. The optimum speed value for channel 1 that maximizes the PCC peak;
3. The value of that peak and the background level of noise near it, and
4. The optimal value for what they called the "d-warp."

In the first two paragraphs of their write-up for "You want me . . . Stemmons" and "Hold everything," they did all this in ten lines each. The values promised were provided directly and simply. Then, for "I'll check it," it took them seventy lines of prose to not give the same results. Nothing was provided, let alone simply or directly.[7]

Values for PCC peaks were given for the first two examples of crosstalk, along with the graphs of their peaks. But for "I'll check it," we get only the statement that the size of the maximum peak was not greater than that of some "accidental peaks." Curiously, in the accompanying graph of accidental peaks, the height is nearly the same as those of "Hold everything." Moreover, in the accompanying text, the height of the maximum peak for "Hold everything" is significantly higher than the height shown in the graph—0.320 in the text and only 0.275 in the graph.[8] Chalk it up to sloppiness.

The confusion continues when they turn to describing another test. They called it the "d-warp test," but it was actually a necessary element of the PCC test itself. D-warp in this case describes running the PCC test at various speeds (described above) to generate the highest peak. Linsker et al. described running the test on the comparison pairs "at the speed generating each pair's peak," but oddly, for "I'll check it," the test was run at "the PCC peak *near* the appropriate delay" (emphasis added).[9] Here, the critical word is "near." Is the difference between at and *near* sufficient to cause the difference between passing and failing the test? We don't know since we are never given a value for the unscientific term "near."

This 2005 article leaves a confusing impression. Its central focus defies understanding. A number of its ambiguities and non sequiturs may have stemmed from bad writing, but I was struck by the fact that the graph for the PCC test of "I'll check it" showed several peaks but no prominent standout. Perhaps this was enough to make their point: no match meant "not cross-talk." Or perhaps they really had done a credible PCC test but just botched the write-up of its results.

Don Thomas laid out many of these arguments in a sharp rebuttal to Linsker et al. published in *Science & Justice* only months after the appearance of their 2005 article. In July of the following year, *Science & Justice* published a response to Thomas from Linsker et al., which was apparently their final word on the entire matter. The response was breathtaking both for what it says and for what it doesn't say. First, consider this admission on page 2:

> The significance of the CHECK ["I'll check it"] utterances on the two channels is that, if CHECK is a valid crosstalk, it puts in doubt any conclusions drawn from the timings of the recordings. This is the case because HOLD is a valid crosstalk, and the acoustic images of HOLD and CHECK (if CHECK were also a valid crosstalk) could not both be in their proper positions on the recordings of the two channels.[10]

One could not ask for a more direct and unequivocal acknowledgment of the existential threat that Don Thomas's discovery of "I'll check it" presented. In these few lines, the authors concurred with what Thomas had been saying all along—if "I'll check it" is crosstalk, their entire analytic framework collapses.

In the very next paragraph, they went on to praise the PCC test as a kind of gold standard in signals research. They pointed out that it "is a powerful mathematical tool for comparing spectrograms" and that it works across "time and frequency automatically and can provide evidence of matches or non-matches with high precision." Given this build-up, I was expecting the next paragraph to reveal what peak the PCC test had shown for "I'll check it."[11]

Surprisingly however, after praising the PCC test, Linsker et al. said nothing more about it. Instead, they abruptly reversed, stating, "in order to resolve readers' doubts about whether CHECK is a crosstalk . . . [we] present the analysis in a way that the reader can verify and experiment with for him/herself." Without so much as a nod to Thomas's powerful rebuttal arguments, they offered a new "do-it-yourself" method to show that "I'll check it" is not crosstalk.[12]

This move is transparent. Unable (or unwilling) to defend their earlier effort, they switched the reader's attention to comparing the spectrogram of the originating transmission of "I'll check it" on channel 2 to its pickup and retransmission on channel 1. Their accompanying complex mathematical discussion only calls attention to what is readily apparent to the naked eye: the two spectrograms don't look much like each other. Because the pickup and retransmission on channel 1 is dirtied up with both engine noise and heterodyne tones, there is little similarity between the two.

Ironically, their chosen exemplar of crosstalk—"Hold everything"—shows the same thing. That is why their PCC test for it had such a low peak, a peak just about even with what may have been the peak for "I'll check it." They couldn't argue that "I'll check it" failed the crosstalk test if their own example, "Hold everything," got about the same score.

In 2015, I had seen enough. I realized now just what I had to do.

The time had come to reach out to James Barger. The entire acoustics issue had now boiled down to a simple question: In comparing PCC tests of "Hold everything" and "I'll check it," who was right: Linsker et al. or Don Thomas? I did not want to call the SAA and ask for just any expert to run a test. James Barger would certainly know the best person to call to do the test and might even be able to recommend a better test. Still, I was intimidated about contacting someone of such obvious achievement. I already knew something of Barger's work in the 1970s but nothing of what he had done since. During my foray into speech identification, I had learned something of what a towering figure in his field Barger had become.

He had spent his whole professional life at BBN. From its inception in 1948, BBN had employed a roster of science superstars who made significant discoveries. For example, in 1969, Frank Heart at BBN built the first interface message processors (IMPs) and modified Honeywell minicomputers to run them. This became the backbone of the Advanced Research Projects Agency Network (ARPANET), which became the Internet. It is no exaggeration to say that the Internet was actually born at BBN. When Congress needed to know whether or not the eighteen-and-a-half-minute gap on the Nixon tapes was a manual erasure, it went to BBN for the answer. When a court needed to know whether the US National Guard or the students had fired first at Kent State, once again BBN was called upon, and Barger ran the study.

Barger started work at BBN as a senior scientist in the 1960s. Recently, he had been given the title chief scientist. Two of the three founders of the firm, Leo Beranak and Richard Bolt, had received gold medals from the SAA in 1975 and 1979. Likewise, in 2011, the society had awarded Barger the Helmholtz-Rayleigh interdisciplinary medal. He had been made a member of the National Academy of Engineering and elected a fellow of the American Association for the Advancement of Science. His list of patents while at BBN is impressive. He designed prototypes of the Distant Thunder SONAR system

for the navy as well as doing the initial research on turbulence-induced noise that led to the design of stealth submarines.

More recently, Barger's team at BBN had designed and then constructed for the Defense Department the Boomerang antisniper system, a multi-spike array of microphones that incorporates the same analytic system that he used in the Kennedy assassination to precisely locate a sniper's location. Within one second of a shot being fired, the Boomerang will provide azimuth heading, elevation, and range to the shooter. This particular child of Barger's research was employed effectively in Iraq and Afghanistan and is now being used by numerous big-city police departments in the United States.

I was also concerned that Barger might have long ago become tired of getting inquiries about the assassination. I didn't want to approach him unless and until I myself had something to offer, which I now had. As luck would have it, I had a friend who was acquainted with Barger, and he agreed to forward my letter to Barger along with a few lines recommending me. I then drafted a long letter in which I described what I had already learned about the workings of the Ramsey Panel. I inquired if he would be willing to recommend someone to do the required tests and asked if there were other tests he might recommend.

Barger replied by letter a few weeks later.[1] His response had a tone of warmth, precision, and genuine interest. I had sent a curriculum vitae along with other items, and he pointed out various similarities between us. We were almost exactly the same age, with Barger less than a month older. In the same month and year, we had both been commissioned as ensigns in the navy. In the same month and year, we had both received our PhDs. His letter had a certain courtliness along with its clarity. I liked him immediately.

He said he had read Six Seconds after finishing his analytical work for the HSCA and found it to be "the only thoughtful early analysis of the Warren Commission's work." He referred to certain problems with the Ramsey Panel's work and to its later defense by the still-living panel members. Then he moved on to the question I had posed: Could he recommend "a capable and reliable signal processor [to] compute a meaningful comparison of the two 'I'll check it' utterances?" He first pointed out that "my lab at BBN could do it, but we would be accused of bias." He said he would get in touch with other acoustic scientists and get back to me with the names of labs "with good signal processing reputations."

This itself was a step forward since I had never grasped before that the problem here was to be solved in the subfield of signal processing rather than, say, speech identification. Then he came up with an idea of great simplicity and common sense. He suggested that he have a look at the evidence before we went to the trouble of finding a good signal processing lab. If we knew more about the evidence, we might be better able to pick the lab. With alacrity I e-mailed him the relevant tracks posted on the NAS site. He e-mailed back that he had passed the files along to "one of my engineers, Richard Mullen," who was "an important part of my team that developed our counter-sniper systems." I later learned that Richard Mullen was a veteran employee of BBN and held seven US patents in his own name. Barger cautioned that "he [Mullen] is doing this on his spare time, so it will be awhile."

Two weeks later, he e-mailed me that Mullen had spent the previous week in the hospital with "complications related to kidney stones." Poor guy. I knew how much kidney stones hurt, as I'd had them twice. The delay was understandable, but given the frustrations and dead ends I had experienced in this case over the years, it came as a blow. Sometimes it seems as if anything connected with the Kennedy assassination is snake-bitten.

I heard nothing from Jim Barger for a month. Finally, on May 29, 2015, I got an e-mail that changed everything. It started out blandly enough: "Richard Mullen is feeling better but still doesn't have a diagnosis." Then it shifted:

Nevertheless, he has analyzed "I'll check it" and "You want me. . . Stemmons."
We believe that we have found why Linsker, et al. (Science & Justice, 2005) didn't

find a significant PCC peak for "I'll check it." Rich down-sampled the data to 8820 Hz, just as Linsker did. First, Rich applied a 512-sample analysis window as used by Linsker for computing the spectrograms. Using this, he found PCC results for both crosstalks that resembled closely the results obtained by Linsker. Reasoning that the 512 sample window was too long for the very short "Check" signal, but not for the other much longer crosstalks, he tried shorter ones. Good results for both crosstalks were obtained by Rich using a 64 sample window. His analysis results obtained by using this shorter window were essentially unchanged for the "Stemmons" (rather lengthy) crosstalk. However, his results for the short "Check" signal were vastly different. A single pronounced peak with amplitude of about 0.45 now occurs in the PCC curve at the correct time. The amplitude of the surrounding noise is about 0.25, without any noticeable secondary peaks.[2]

"Wow!" I thought, laughing to myself. "This is like a movie—a scientific detective thriller."

It was clear that Rich Mullen's tests had moved us several spaces ahead in the chess game being played out in the pages of *Science & Justice*. Don Thomas had argued that the survivors of the Ramsey Panel had actually found a PCC peak for "I'll check it" and failed to admit it. I had wondered about this and threw in my chips with Thomas only when the survivors ducked any real attempt to reply to his charges. Now, that whole issue had been bypassed.

I looked up the Linsker 2005 article and found where the 512 sampling window was mentioned. Until then, I had had no clue what it meant. Now it turned out to explain everything. Apparently Linsker used the same 512 sampling window for all three crosstalks. This might make sense for "Hold everything secure" (2.1 seconds) or for "You want me . . . Stemmons?" (4.0 seconds), but it is much too long for "I'll check it" (0.6 seconds). When Mullen tried a more appropriate sampling window length of 64, "I'll check it" produced a single prominent peak around 0.45.

Nonetheless, momentous as this "vastly different" result seemed, what Mullen had yet to do was measure the peak PCC value for "Hold everything" using the same sampling window length of 64. On the results of that critical test, literally everything hung in the balance. My investigator's instincts told me this was too important to be dealt with at a distance. I made arrangements to fly to the East Coast and meet with Jim Barger and Rich Mullen at BBN in Cambridge at 10:00 a.m. on Tuesday, June 30.

The night before our meeting, I stayed in a Marriott along the Charles River in Cambridge. As the light faded that evening, I walked up Memorial

Drive along the Charles and noticed a single sculler making his way upriver. The previous night, I'd stayed in a downtown New Haven motel just around the corner from where Nancy and I had lived during the early 1960s. New Haven—really a rough kind of New England factory town—seemed ugly to me now compared to the almost European tidiness of Cambridge.

There was no doubt I was nervous about what would happen the next day. I could feel it in my bones, and it was not a new experience. How many times in how many cases had I traveled across the country to meet with a witness or an expert with the case hanging in the balance? But those were other people's cases, and this one was mine. I had been actively working it for the past four years and interested in it for almost fifty. Again and again over the decades, I had watched the evidence shift, watched the evidentiary kaleidoscope ratchet another turn and bring the whole picture into greater or lesser clarity.

Tomorrow I would learn what Mullen's results showed. If "I'll check it" did better than "Hold everything"—if it showed a higher net PCC peak than "Hold everything"—then the argument would be over. "I'll check it" would have been shown to be crosstalk, and the Ramsey Panel's findings would have collapsed. But what if "Hold everything" scored substantially better than "I'll check it"? I turned around and started walking back to the Marriott. It was almost dark now, and the Charles River was empty of scullers.

The next morning at BBN, after the receptionist gave me my security badge, I held it in my hand and looked at it. There in the lobby, it suddenly became clear to me that I was standing at a privileged place in the science of the late twentieth century. It wasn't just idle chatter that had named this place "the third university in Cambridge" (after Harvard and MIT). BBN had produced some of the most influential discoveries in acoustics and computing of the last third of that century. Near where I was standing was a Pentagon plaque on the wall honoring BBN and Jim Barger for their contributions. I smiled, thinking of how modestly Barger had told me that the receptionist was new and might not know who he was, so I should also ask for Rich Mullen. There was only one chief scientist at BBN, and everyone there knew who it was.

I saw them for the first time as they walked down the long ramp leading up from the reception desk. As they got closer, I recognized Jim Barger from his pictures. Tall and slim with white hair—a handsome guy at eighty—he had a warm manner about him, but as soon as we began talking, I understood why he was the chief scientist at BBN. Rich Mullen had brown hair and was about my size. Although I later learned he had been at BBN for almost three decades, he looked ten years younger than he must have been. Wearing a necktie and

Photo 22-2. BBN in Cambridge is now Raytheon BBN Technologies.

a short-sleeved shirt, he could have been a young professor accompanying the chairman of the department to a meeting. We made our way up the ramp to a conference room where Rich had set up a projector for his PowerPoint presentation.

The room was not unlike Hall Building 211 at Haverford, where I'd taught my last philosophy class nearly four decades earlier. There was a projection machine set up on the table next to an open laptop. Rich started his presentation by showing what happened when he used the 512 sample width specified by Linsker. Not unexpectedly, it resembled the graph Linsker et al. had published in *Science & Justice* (Figures 22-3 and 22-4). Although the time scale was different on the two graphs, both showed several peaks between 0.20 and 0.30 with no peak dominating.

Next Rich showed what happens when the 512 sample width is replaced by a 64 sample width that better fits the short 0.6-second duration of "I'll check it" (Figure 22-5).

There it was. The single peak that showed a match between the two utterances of "I'll check it" ran to 0.50 with a mean background level of 0.25. The bottom line—a net peak of 0.25.

Next, the clincher. (Figures 22-6 and 22-7) The net PCC peak for "Hold

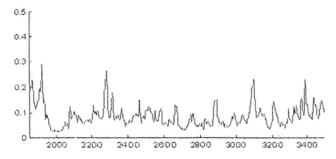

Figure 22-3. Linsker's "typical PCC plot at the correct warp" for "I'll check it" using a sampling window of 512.

everything" was lower—way lower, 0.09 or 0.16 depending on the width of the sampling window. Check . . . and mate. I sat there for a few seconds in silence, momentarily stunned—but grinning.

Later, Rich told me that he knew nothing about the Kennedy assassination and cared even less. His undramatic, factual tone as he showed the Power-Point slides made this clear. Yet for me, as graph after graph lit up the screen accompanied by his commentary, they could not have been more dramatic.

Rich's tests showed conclusively that "I'll check it" not only is crosstalk but has a higher net PCC peak than "Hold everything."[3] With this finding, the Linsker et al. argument from 2005 imploded—and with it the whole house of cards constructed by the 1982 Ramsey Panel.

We talked about the results with the PowerPoint slide still on the screen. Rich made the point that a 512 window is eight times larger than a 64 window.

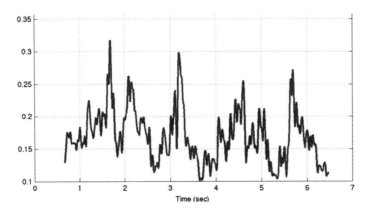

Figure 22-4. Mullen's PCC plot for "I'll check it" using a sampling window of 512.

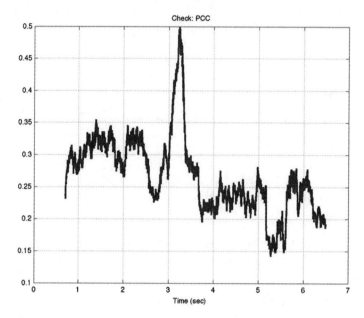

Figure 22-5. Net PCC peak of 0.25 (0.50 minus a background of 0.25) produced for "I'll check it" by using a sampling window size of 64.

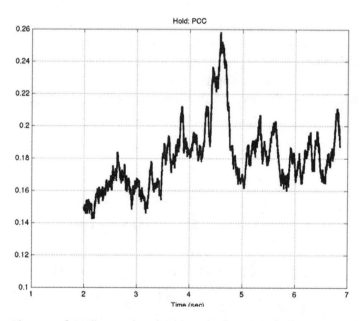

Figure 22-6. Mullen produced a net peak of 0.09 (0.26 minus a background of 0.17) for "Hold everything" using a sampling window of 64.

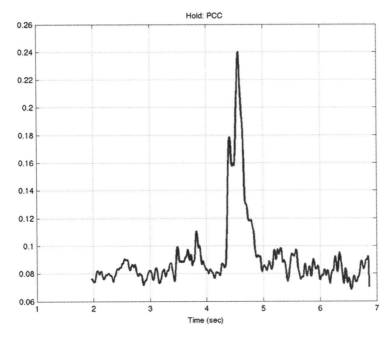

Figure 22-7. Mullen produced a net peak of 0.16 (0.24 minus a background of 0.08) for "Hold everything" using a sampling window of 512.

Jim pointed out that 512 is simply "a much coarser measurement tool" because it includes so much extraneous data. He went further and tried to explain how an actual PCC test is done, ending with a failed attempt to make me understand how "a Fourier transform" works.

I looked over at Mullen. "Rich, let me ask you something," I said. "I know there's no way to answer this short of climbing into the Ramsey Panel's skulls, and sure, I recognize it could have come from their not knowing what they were doing by blindly keeping the same sample width for all three crosstalks. But you know this test really well. So I gotta ask you the obvious question: Do you think they rigged the test?"

He just smiled.

We went to the cafeteria for lunch. During our meal, I couldn't keep my mind on what Jim or Rich was saying. I was so elated about what this all meant that the voices at the table seemed distant, as if it were all happening in a stage play, and I was part of the audience. I could hear what they were saying, but more important was the copy of Rich's PowerPoint slides that he had given me and which now resided in my briefcase. Jim mentioned that although both he and Rich were employees of Raytheon BBN, the company had nothing to do with the tests. Rich had done the work on his own at his home computer. It turns out that you must be familiar with MATLAB software, but otherwise you need only a computer and the data from the NAS website to do this work.

As we came out of the cafeteria, they pointed to a room off to the left where, they said, the first server for the Internet had been located. Jim walked me out to my car in the parking lot, and we chatted for a few moments. Then he turned toward the building, and I pressed the starter button.

I drove out of the parking lot and around the corner of a quiet street before turning back toward Fresh Pond and Concord Avenue. My cell phone rang, and I pulled over. It was my friend and editor, John Grissim, calling from Sequim, Washington. We must have been in telepathic communication. John asked hesitantly, "How did it go?" I almost exploded with excitement. "It's hard to believe, John, but it's true. Don Thomas was right all along. The tests show it. There can be no doubt. 'I'll check it' is crosstalk!"

B y the time I got back to Bolinas, it was July 4th weekend. I was still flying on a cloud of elation and relief. After nearly eighteen months of cramped, head-busting work on the Ramsey Panel and its report, we had finally caught a break. In "we," I include my editor, John Grissim, who by now had become a true collaborator with me on this task. Something else—a vague, inchoate understanding—had been bouncing around in the back of my mind since I left Cambridge. It was a sense that we could take this a lot further.

After ten minutes of hunting, I found what I was looking for. It was in the trove of Ramsey Panel internal documents given to me by Paul Hoch—a long letter written by Jim Barger to Chairman Ramsey in February 1982 after Ramsey had sent him a draft of the panel's upcoming report. Meticulously, in eight pages of single-spaced prose, Barger laid out his objections to it. On the final page, he told Chairman Ramsey that given "the possibility that your committee's results could have been produced by an artifact, we have tried intensively to visualize similarly plausible ways in which our results could have resulted from an artifact." Stating that he and his team had found none, Barger concluded his letter, "Under these circumstances, we view our scientific controversy as having shifted from a question of relative probability to a question of authenticity and integrity of data."[1]

The target of Barger's remark was, of course, "Hold everything" (HOLD). His concluding sentence essentially said that instead of debating the rules for calculating probabilities, the question now was: Is HOLD authentic evidence from November 22? As to his use of "artifact," Barger was using the word's scientific definition. In common speech, the term means "any object made by human beings"—for example, a pottery cup unearthed in an archaeological dig. In scientific parlance, an artifact is "a substance or structure not naturally present in the matter being observed but formed by artificial means, as during the preparation of a microscope slide"—a speck of dust, for example.[2]

Photo 23-1. Moorman photo with thumbprint.

A perfect illustration is the thumbprint on Mary Moorman's famous Polaroid photograph. Neither Moorman nor anyone else knows how or why this happened, only that it got there through some means extrinsic to the normal process of producing the photo.

Back in 1982, "I'll check it" (CHECK) had been so effectively veiled by the Ramsey Panel that Barger had never known that it even existed. Nonetheless, he suspected that there was something profoundly wrong with the sole piece of evidence upon which the panel had based its argument. There was no question that HOLD was identical in its appearance on both channels and thus satisfied the requirements for being common crosstalk, but the Ramsey Panel's whole argument was grounded in HOLD being the other kind of crosstalk—simultaneous crosstalk. Barger understood the absolute necessity of the panel being able to demonstrate that HOLD occurred simultaneously on both channels as the product of the normal operation of the two recorders. Anything short of that rendered HOLD an artifact.

The Panel's Central Argument

In its draft the panel acknowledged a time gap between HOLD's origination on channel 2 and its appearance 46 seconds earlier on channel 1. For HOLD to be the kind of crosstalk the panel believed it to be, this gap had to be over-come. HOLD had to be moved earlier by 46 seconds on channel 2 or later by 46 seconds on channel 1. There seemed to be no change on channel 1 that could bring this about because the constant beat of the motorcycle engine meant that no silences on channel 1 would shut off the recorder. Channel 2 was a different story. The panel asserted that the gap *might* have been caused by the operation of the channel 2 recorder's automatic shut-off feature that stopped the recorder after a preset number of seconds of recorded silence.[3] This they called "runout time," while the resulting interval of unrecorded time they termed "dropout time." Since the latter was unrecorded, its length was unknown. It lasted until someone keying a microphone turned the recorder back on. The panel asserted that hypothetically, the accumulation of dropout time from autostoppages after HOLD on channel 2 conceivably *could* have added up to 46 seconds.[4] Had this happened, it would have moved HOLD earlier in time into alignment with its channel 1 twin.

One might reasonably ask, how can adding time *after* HOLD on channel 2 move HOLD *earlier* in time? The answer, of course, is it can't, except when certain stringent requirements are satisfied. Here is a closer look at how the panel sought to satisfy those requirements.

In a lengthy twenty-page appendix[5] devoted to HOLD, the panel pointed to a second crosstalk pair, BELLAH 2, occurring more than two minutes after HOLD, that "provides a common reference point for synchronizing the Channel I and II tapes"[6]—an implicit assumption that this pair was time-synchronous. Consisting of a snippet of speech, "You want me . . . Stemmons," it is the second of two transmissions by motorcycle sergeant S. Q. Bellah, labeled BELLAH 1 and BELLAH 2.

The panel focused on BELLAH 2 for two reasons:

1. Since the panel judged BELLAH 2 to be time-synchronous crosstalk, moving BELLAH 2 either earlier or later on channel 2 would break its synchrony with its channel 1 twin. As a consequence, adding 46 seconds after BELLAH 2 would move everything after that point *later* in time, while adding 46 seconds anywhere in the two minutes after HOLD and before BELLAH 2 would move every-thing before its insertion *earlier* in time.[7] In this way, by finding a way to move HOLD earlier on channel 2, the panel satisfied the first requirement.

2. Just as important, the two minutes of time on channel 2 between HOLD and BELLAH 2 included an interval of 100 seconds immediately before BELLAH 2 that contained what the panel determined were five silences long enough to have triggered autostoppages. In this way, the panel satisfied the second requirement by identifying a source for the 46 seconds.[8]

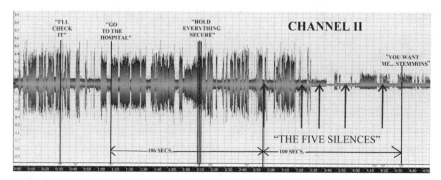

Figure 23-2. Channel 2 recording of HOLD, "You want me . . . Stemmons," and the five silences. Note that HOLD is recorded forty-five seconds *before* the first of the five silences and two minutes, twenty-three seconds *before* "You want me . . . Stemmons."

From here on it was all downhill for the panel. It "does not seem unreasonable," it noted, "that there would have been 46 seconds that Channel II was not being used during the period that the motorcade was occupied with making the trip to Parkland Hospital at high speed."[9]

Finally, the panel's principal finding, the last 18 words of which were widely quoted in the national media, was "for the two 'hold everything . . .' transmissions to coincide the recorder would have had to be inactive for 46 seconds, in which case the conjectured shots would have occurred at least 64 seconds after the chief's instruction, 'Go to the hospital.'"[10]

The Argument's Shaky Foundation

Barger understood that the panel's add-time-to-subtract-time argument, while it might be puzzling to a nonscientist, was at bottom hypothetically logical. Nonetheless, he was struck by the complete absence in the report of any evidence supporting the two principal assertions on which the panel's argument was based: (1) the BELLAH 2 crosstalks discussed were time-synchronous, and (2) the DPD recorders autostopped after a runout time of 4 seconds.

On the crosstalk issue, when the panel described BELLAH 2 "as a common reference point for synchronizing the channel 1 and II tapes," it provided no proof that BELLAH 2 was simultaneous crosstalk, simply assuming it as fact. As we saw earlier with CHECK, the test for time synchronicity involves a careful examination of the two channel recordings to ascertain whether they occurred simultaneously in the real clock time of Dealey Plaza. CHECK passed, helped by real-time event markers on both channels that confirmed its simultaneity. No such test was undertaken for BELLAH 2, nor was any other evidence presented. Thirty-five years later (as described below and in Appendix A) Barger would put in the work necessary to determine whether BELLAH 2 was synchronous in time. It wasn't, and his results would be a precursor to further discoveries.[11]

Complicating matters was the panel's mistaken confidence that the sound recordings in its possession were essentially pristine copies of the DPD's original recordings despite a growing consensus at that time that the likelihood that any of the original recordings had survived was in doubt. The panel claimed that it had worked with "tape recordings made from the original Gray Audograph and Dictaphone [sic] records."[12] Even the DPD's dispatch supervisor, Jim Bowles, asked to comment on the "original" issue, groused, "By whose authority?"[13] Ramsey Panel member Charles Rader pointed out that "nobody on our committee ever had custody of any of the Dictabelts."[14]

Since then, considerable investigation into this issue has been undertaken by respected assassination researchers, notably Chris Scally, a remarkable Irishman who spent years tracking the lack of documented provenance for the Dictabelts and Audograph disks. To date no provable original recording on any media has been found.[15] Hence, the panel's statement is most likely incorrect. Rather, as Rich Mullen's and Jim Barger's tests have shown, it was likely working with second- and third-generation copies.

As to the issue of the recorders' runout times, according to the report, the second assumption was based solely on Jim Bowles having told a panel member that both recorders had been set to automatically shut off after "approximately 4 seconds"[16] of recorded silence. Looking at this as a scientist, Barger asked an obvious question: Is there any way to determine from the recordings themselves what the actual runout times were?

There was. Measure the recorded runout times.

Barger identified about 100 recorded runout times beginning on channel 1 at 12:14 and a second set of 100 runout times on channel 2 starting at 12:22 and then measured their lengths. If Bowles was correct, the duration of the predominant number of recorded runout times on either channel should have clustered between 4 and 5 seconds.

Bowles was wrong.

The longest recorded runout times on channel 1 clustered in the 7-to-8-second range indicating a runout time of 7.5 seconds. On channel 2, the predominance was in the 6-to-7-second range, indicating a runout time of 6.5 seconds. Barger determined that these increased runout times were likely due to internal circuitry known as smoothers in both recorders designed to prevent accidental stoppage triggered by fluctuations in the carrier signal strength. Since there was no recorded runout time longer than 5.5 seconds in the roughly 100-second interval on channel 2 that the panel selected, that channel's recorder would not have automatically shut off even once. Barger communicated these findings in a long letter on March 22, 1982[17]—two months before the issuance of the panel's final report. The panel ignored the information.

In short, the panel's sole argument to prove that HOLD was simultaneous crosstalk was based upon two assumptions, each of which was mistaken.

Enter "In-buh-dustrial"

The correction of both channel recordings so that their timings reflected real time had long been a vexing challenge for both the Ramsey Panel and its critics. For months prior to my trip to Cambridge, I had examined the two tracks with this issue in mind. During our meeting in Cambridge, I gave Jim and Rich copies of the chart I had prepared. About two weeks after this meeting, Jim e-mailed me that he "had been thinking about the time-alignments of crosstalk."[18] It turned out, he said, that CHECK aligned well with the simulcast "in-buh-dustrial" (SIMULCAST)[19] but three of the remaining four crosstalks required large "stretch factors" to bring them into alignment. By "stretch factor," he meant that one must assume a significantly different tape speed for them than for the others. He said this "seems to need an explanation, and I don't have one." Nor did I. I suggested bringing Don Thomas into the e-mail discussion. "Absolutely, Tink. Please do," Jim replied.

Doubtless contributing to Barger's interest was that he apparently had not been aware earlier of the simulcast containing the mispronounced word "in-buh-dustrial" that I had included on the timing chart. Technically, a simulcast is not crosstalk because its broadcast on both channels was produced by the dispatcher flipping a toggle switch on his console, but this precise point of simultaneity between the two channels, together with the now proven CHECK crosstalk, gave him anchors to analyze other data points.

A week later, Jim e-mailed a graph illustrating the problem. It showed that CHECK and a second crosstalk, "I've got a witness" (I'VE GOT), enjoyed simultaneity across channels when "in-buh-dustrial" was chosen as the tie point, but the rest of the graph was puzzling. It showed that one had to speed up channel 2 by about 27 percent to get three of the crosstalks—HOLD, BELLAH 1, and BELLAH 2 —to align with the simulcast. It was as if these three were running on a separate tape at a much faster speed than channel 2 was ever thought to have run.

Whatever magic Barger was performing with linear regressions and least square rules was way beyond my high school algebra. Then, on August 1, Jim followed up with a refined version of his previous chart, concluding with a message to Don Thomas and me: "I hope to hear from you two on this. I suppose most of this is not new to either of you, but it surely is to me."

Immediately it occurred to me that I might be the source of the problem. Earlier Jim had remarked that "everything I have come up with hinges on your measured crosstalk times, including in particular the simulcast time." Now I was really worried. In my e-mail reply I confessed that "I'm the wrong guy for the job. I'm like your hayseed cousin from the country who knows how to stack hay but doesn't know his ass from an abscissa." Right now, what was needed for Barger's timing work was a set of unimpeachable data points—the kind that everyone can agree upon. I was pretty sure I knew where to get them.

The universe of people really knowledgeable about the acoustic evidence is vanishingly small: James Barger, Don Thomas, Chris Scally, and one other person, Michael O'Dell. Although clearly a supporter of the Ramsey Panel's findings, O'Dell is respected by both sides in the dispute as a straight shooter whose timing work was the closest thing we had to a gold standard.

Because O'Dell and I had been in touch earlier about the Ramsey Panel spectrograms, it was simple to recontact him. By e-mail I explained I wanted two tracks, one for each channel, each containing the simulcast and the five supposed crosstalks, and I wanted them both to run at the same speed in real time. In short, I needed a clean, unimpeachable apples-to-apples data set. Michael replied that channel 1 would indeed be an easy task; however, the algorithm he had written years ago for channel 2 had disappeared in a computer crash, and he would have to develop it all over again from scratch. I sensed that this would not be a trivial undertaking. I offered to commission the new study, and he set to work.

Several weeks later, he produced an algorithm for the correct timing of channel 2 and a number of cue points for the appearance of crosstalks on both channels plus dozens of previously uncharted data points in the form of dispatcher time announcements. During the months that followed, Barger, now armed with Michael O'Dell's new (and precise) charts, continued his inquiry, periodically reporting on his progress. In the meantime, John Grissim and I also devoted considerable time to studying the panel's argument for HOLD, and in the process, each of us developed our own rebuttal. In contrast to the panel's convoluted explanations, ours were simple, requiring nothing more than basic arithmetic. In fact, they were so straightforward and understandable that for a while we suspected there must be flaws in our reasoning. But none turned up. We call our two arguments "the unshrinkable 88 seconds" and "the move one, move all."

The Unshrinkable 88 Seconds Argument

Consider first what was actually recorded on channel 2 between the appearance of CHECK and HOLD. Just before 12:30 p.m., we hear the conversation between Deputy Chief Fisher and Captain Lawrence that ends with Fisher's words, "I'll check it." Less than 2 seconds later, Chief Curry announces, "At the Triple Underpass," followed a few seconds after that by the dispatcher announcing "12:30" and giving the call letters of the channel (KKB364).[20] Twenty seconds later, Chief Curry orders excitedly, "Go to the hospital. We're going to the hospital."

Then Curry and Decker, both riding in the lead car, begin telling the dispatcher to mobilize their men. This goes on for some time, as the dispatcher fails to understand Decker's instructions and asks him to repeat them.[21] There is nothing out of place about HOLD's appearance on channel 2. It comes right where we would expect it to, as shown by Figure 23-3.

Note that HOLD appears 98.7 seconds after CHECK on the chart. Also note the various squiggles that indicate speech occurring on channel 2 in addition to the static and short periods of silence. Most important, the whole 98.7 seconds, even the silences, is *recorded* time. As such, any dropouts or recorder auto shutoffs that might have occurred would have only *added* time to what is recorded here, not *subtracted* it. That interval between CHECK and HOLD is set in concrete. Nothing that happens on channel 2 can shorten it.

Now look at that same interval on channel 1 (Figure 23-4). The 98.7-second interval between CHECK and HOLD has shrunk to 10.9 seconds. The resulting

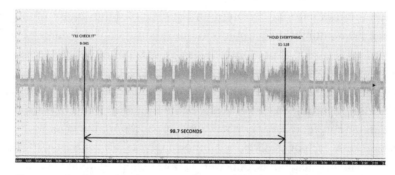

Figure 23-3. Channel 2 placement of "I'll check it" and "Hold everything."

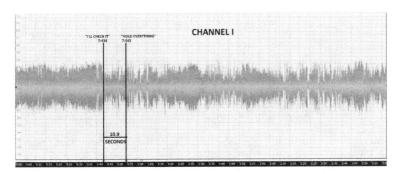

Figure 23-4. Channel 1 placement of "I'll check it" and "Hold everything." Figure 23-3 and Figure 23-4 were prepared using an edition of Goldwave based on two wave files—ch1ODELLFINAL.wav and ch2ODELLFINAL.wav provided by Michael O'Dell. The cue points for marking the dispatcher time announcements and the beginning of speech by various individuals were also provided by O'Dell.

87.8-second difference equals the amount of time shrinkage needed on channel 1 to bring the HOLD events on the two channels into real-time synchrony. Worth noting here is that the Ramsey Panel had estimated that the two HOLDS were out of synchrony by 46 seconds. It was wrong, as Michael O'Dell had pointed out in 2001. The panel had mistakenly deducted various "repeats" on channel 2 from the elapsed time when these had already been compensated for by the Audograph's worm gear. When the timing is done correctly, it turns out that 87.8 seconds are required to bring the HOLD transmissions into synchrony on both channels.

Alternatively, could something have happened on channel 1 to bring about this extraordinary shrinkage? In all the years that the DPD recordings had been studied, no one had ever observed a dropout anywhere on channel 1. All observers—including the Ramsey Panel and the panel survivors, Don Thomas, James Barger, and Michael O'Dell—agreed that the Dictabelt recorder ran continuously during this period. Any automatic shut-off mechanism was defeated by the drone of the motorcycle engine.

To believe that some process native to the operation of the two recorders caused the shrinkage, we would have to believe that during a 10.9-second interval on a recorder that had never been found to drop out or skip, a dropout of 87.8 seconds occurred when nothing like this had been known to occur on either channel—ever. In short, it is profoundly improbable that the channel 1 Dictabelt recorder caused this shrinkage. Therefore, HOLD is very likely an artifact.

Photo 23-5. The lead car and limousine on Main Street, approaching the Houston Street corner about forty-six seconds before reaching the Triple Underpass. The Ramsey Panel's argument moves channel 2 radio traffic forty-six seconds back in time, requiring Chief Curry's "At the Triple Underpass" announcement to be made at the location shown in the photograph—completely out of sync.

The Move One, Move All Argument

Given that the Ramsey Panel's entire case depended on showing that the HOLD crosstalk was time synchronous, its solution was vintage Rube Goldberg. John Grissim was the first to grasp how it failed.

Let's assume for a moment two contrary-to-fact assumptions. First, assume the Ramsey Panel's unproven claim that BELLAH 2 is time-synchronous crosstalk is correct. Second, also assume that, despite James Barger having shown the panel that that no recorded silences in its selected channel 2 time interval were long enough to shut off the recorder, those silences indeed triggered autostoppages.

If we accept all this, the panel's argument nonetheless shipwrecks on an unintended and unavoidable consequence. Not only HOLD but also everything else on channel 2 before HOLD is moved earlier in time by 46 seconds. Result: not only is CHECK thrown completely out of sync with its time-synchronous crosstalk twin, but Chief Curry in the lead car is now announcing "At the Triple Underpass" while his car is still on Main Street, having not yet turned onto Houston Street, driven a block north, and then turned onto Elm Street. Furthermore, all twenty-three of the dispatcher's time announcements before and after HOLD's new channel 2 position are likewise pushed earlier in time by 46 seconds. In fact, "At the Triple Underpass," with its solid anchor in real time and place, is itself sufficient to upend the panel's argument.

Of particular interest here, as noted in a previous chapter, is that both the CHECK and "At the Triple Underpass" transmissions contained in the first 14 seconds of Bowles's channel 2 transcript were unaccountably deleted from the Ramsey Panel Report.

As with "the unshrinkable 88-second argument" above, this shows that the time position of HOLD on channel 1 did not come about through the native and normal operations of the two recorders. Therefore, it is almost certainly an artifact. Nevertheless, "almost certainly" is not mathematical certainty.

Jim Barger's Discovery

As 2015 wound down, Jim Barger continued working away on the problem before him, aided by the new data provided by O'Dell. I was confident that no one would ever be able to produce a better data set for the two channels. Helpfully, O'Dell had also marked twenty-nine points on channel 2 and twenty-seven points on channel 1 that included not only the simulcast and the five crosstalks but also the dispatcher's time announcements. These fifty-six total data points—more than twice the number identified in 1981—were critical to the advanced analysis Barger was conducting. They provided a kind of time grid for determining when simultaneity between the two channels was achieved.

When we mentioned to Jim Barger that we were having a hard time making his method understandable to the general reader, he set about developing a more direct and less abstruse approach to the whole problem. Using this approach,[22] Barger made what he called his "single most powerful and also most straightforward discovery."

If the recorded sections were all recorded in the same "session"—that is, at the same moment in real time—then a singular rule applies: the tape speed for the audio events (the simulcast and five crosstalks) must be the same as the tape speed for the intervals between them. This firm requirement is met for CHECK, SIMULCAST, and I'VE GOT. Call these the CHECK family of crosstalks. It is not even approximately met for the HOLD family of crosstalks (HOLD, BELLAH 1, and BELLAH 2).

The fact that the requirement is met for the CHECK family of crosstalks but not for the HOLD family means that HOLD was recorded on channel 1 during a

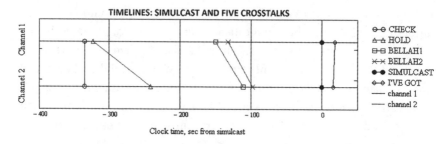

Figure 23-6. Using SIMULCAST as a zero point of simultaneity, CHECK and I'VE GOT turn out to also have been broadcast simultaneously on both channels. Not so with HOLD, BELLAH 1, and BELLAH 2.

separate session and not the November 22 session that recorded SIMULCAST, CHECK, and I'VE GOT.

It took several months for Barger to refine and check his new findings. In the spring of 2016, he sent a version of his paper with graphic presentations of what he had found. They were startling. I had still been struggling to understand the details of his discovery, but these two illustrations made clear the essence of what he had found. The first, using the simulcast as a tie point (zero clock time on Figure 23-6), shows which events occurred simultaneously and which did not:

CHECK and I'VE GOT produce essentially vertical lines across the two channels and therefore must be considered synchronous crosstalk. The other connecting lines—HOLD, BELLAH 1, and BELLAH 2—are not vertical. Not only are the errors for all three large, but—big surprise—they are exactly proportional to their time distances from the simulcast. This is clear evidence that, accidentally or intentionally, the HOLD family of crosstalks was recorded on channel 1 at some point after the assassination from the same source and running at a speed over one-third faster than the original recording of channel 1 or channel 2.

The second chart was equally dramatic, showing the same errors plotted as a function of clock time (Figure 23-7).

Barger's work constituted a sophisticated mathematical proof that the placement of HOLD on channel 1 was not due to the normal working of the two recorders, and therefore HOLD must be an artifact. Moreover, while the origin of what Barger called the "HOLD family of crosstalks" remained unknown, his calculations indicated that they all derived from the same source, a source running 34.6 percent faster than the DPD recorders. In every sense, these results appeared to be of historic importance.

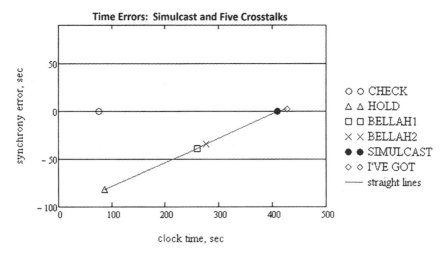

Figure 23-7. SIMULCAST, CHECK, and I'VE GOT show virtually no alignment error because they occurred simultaneously on both channels. The others show their common origin by their linked appearance on a straight line, indicating that their alignment error grows proportionally to their time-distance from the simulcast.

Further Analysis—Yet Another Discovery

With this final blow to the Ramsey Panel Report, I assumed that Barger had finally wrapped up his many months of inquiry. But I was mistaken. One morning in early 2017, he called to say he was intrigued by the possibility that a further analysis of the two channels' tapes might show that an overdub had produced the HOLD family of crosstalks on Channel 1. To this end, Barger had asked his colleague Richard Mullen to examine the various background hum frequencies on the tapes of both channels for indications of splices or overdubs. He promised to keep me posted.

To understand what Barger had in mind, a brief explanation is in order. While all recorders in those days produced a 60-Hz background hum, the DPD data recorders—the Dictabelt and the Audograph—differed from tape recorders in an important way. They were stenographic machines that turned at a fixed rate when recording, but during playback mode, they turned at variable rates at the user's option. This manual setting permitted the stenographer to slow down the machine to keep up while typing. Because of this feature, when a Dictabelt or Audograph disk was played back to a tape-recorder microphone for copying, the slightest error in its manual speed position—which almost always occurred due to the coarse control settings—generated a hum higher or lower than the primary hum. This unique hum frequency was in turn captured by the tape recorder, serving as a kind of identifying finger-print of the original recording. Just as important, that hum remained on all subsequent copies of that tape.

This same effect occurred during a copying process when, instead of a tape recorder, another DPD machine was used, for example, to create a sec-ond-generation Dictabelt or Audograph disk. To take this one step further, if a tape recorder was subsequently used to make a copy of that second-genera-tion belt or disk, it would in addition capture a second hum generated by the off-speed playback of the machine being recorded. The resulting tape would now have two secondary hum frequencies that would remain on any copies of that tape.

Evidence of precisely this occurrence turned up when Richard Mullen ana-lyzed the frequencies embedded in the tapes of both channels. Not only did he find two different secondary hums on the channel 2 tape, but those two hums were of the same frequency as two secondary hums found on the channel 1 tape.

In his e-mail report, Barger explained,

> The odds that Channel 2 would have two hum frequencies is very small. It's a strong indication that the Channel 2 tapes came from a second-generation Audograph disk. Therefore, two independent actions were responsible for those two hum frequencies. It is wholly unlikely that two additional and independent actions on Channel 1 could reproduce the exact same hum frequencies produced by two independent actions on Channel 2. The fact that both of these hum frequencies were recorded on Channel 1 is proof that the HOLD family of crosstalk was overdubbed onto Channel 1.[23]

During a later conversation, when I asked if the overdubbing was delib-erate, Barger replied that the actual overdub was "probably inadvertent." He continued, "The odd and intricate assemblage of hum frequencies Rich found was so arcane that it was impossible to see any set of purposeful actions. It was likely the result of multiple tape copies and dubs—including one splice on channel 2—made to and from multiple machines in the first days by tech-nicians at the DPD, the FBI, the Secret Service and other agencies."

He paused a moment. Then he went on, "This entire business is unusual. No trained audio technician would create such a disjointed product. Had the Ramsey Panel done a legitimate analysis of the hums they would have been horrified by all the overdubs. I guess it's just that the work was done by committee."[24]

In the aftermath of these major revelations, I now returned to the question of how best to validate them. Whom could we approach to independently replicate and therefore confirm the work done by Barger and Mullen? This problem had been there since the beginning of our work together. I had been thinking of an institution, a university or technology company, perhaps even a group of grad students led by a well-regarded professor. Conceivably any review would result in a published article in a respected peer-reviewed journal.

Then Barger suggested a new option: he and Richard Mullen would write papers documenting their work to be published in the book as appendices. They would include links to the audio files on the NAS site as well as O'Dell's new timings of channels 1 and 2. Also included would be the settings Mullen had used within MATLAB, a powerful scientific software, to produce his PCC tests and the equations Barger had employed to form his graphs. This would make all the work they did replicable by anyone sophisticated enough to follow their directions. I liked his solution. Completely public, it was a model of transparency. I readily agreed.

The Signal in the Noise

As these and other instances in previous chapters illustrate, the panel often ignored evidence contrary to the outcome it desired and used bogus assumptions in support of its arguments. On at least one occasion, it concealed powerful contradictory evidence. This is clearly not science but some form of advocacy. Calling it confirmation bias may be too generous.

What this long, sober discussion of the evidence—and the ways the Ramsey Panel treated it—fails to convey. however, is how flat-out funny parts of its investigation turned out to be. The more familiar we became with its oddball arguments, the loopier they seemed. One day I found myself literally laughing out loud.

The cause of my laughter? Recall the panel's very shaky scenario to explain the possibility—not the reality—that HOLD could be simultaneous crosstalk. If the channel 2 recorder hypothetically stopped five times over a 100-second stretch, the total time lost could conceivably total 46 seconds. What are the odds, I wondered, that the sum of five time intervals lost through five dropouts would total exactly 46 seconds? Not 48 seconds or 43 seconds but exactly 46 seconds. At the very least, they would be lottery odds. This brought to mind the earlier Vela satellite committee's conclusion that although a nuclear blast could not be ruled out, the detection signal was more likely "the consequence of the impact of a small meteoroid on the satellite." Shortly after the Vela committee announced this conclusion, the DIA went over the data and estimated that the odds of this happening were about one in one hundred billion.[25]

Another example: the panel devoted two and a half pages (Appendix E) to siren sounds from the motorcade on channel 1 a couple of minutes after the shots; the siren sounds are "heard in succession, each in turn rising and falling in intensity as would be the case if the motorcade were rapidly passing an open microphone."[26] This variable intensity, the panel claimed, could not have been recorded by a radio with a stuck-open mic button moving with the motorcade but was most likely transmitted from a stationary open mic among the more than one hundred DPD motorcycles and squad cars parked at the nearby Trade Mart awaiting the president's arrival.

This explanation was undoubtedly correct. One of the many units parked at the Trade Mart opened its mic tuned to channel 1, which transmitted the sound of the passing sirens. The sound was shared on that channel with the pounding engine sound from the cycle that earlier recorded the shots. This was possible because the DPD radio network operated like a "party line" where multiple broadcasts of the same strength could be—and were—broadcast at the same time. This was not some arcane fact but was brought up at least three times by different individuals in testimony before the HSCA on December 29, 1978.[27] Lacking any member with real knowledge of acoustics, the Ramsey Panel apparently thought only one person could transmit at a time. On this misapprehension, the panel offered the mistaken view that the motorcycle with the stuck button was never in Dealey Plaza.

Levity aside, over these many months and to our genuine astonishment, we ended up discovering something entirely unexpected, almost unimaginable. This truth emerged slowly, but once cracks in the facade were uncovered, it seemed that everywhere we looked, we found more evidence of what the report really was—an elaborate papier-mâché facade of science-as-revealed-wisdom assembled by a body of distinguished scientists, including one Nobel laureate and one soon-to-be laureate, supported in its entirety by marvelously baroque but silly arguments.

In the cold light of science, a clear gaze into the heart of the report reveals that there was nothing there to begin with. In spite of all its tables and strip charts and complex equations and multiple footnotes, it is a house of cards based on a shadowy three-word fragment of speech that quite easily could have—and should have—been recognized in 1981 as an artifact.[28]

Conspiracy?

In the summer of 2015, when I asked Richard Mullen in Cambridge, "Did they cheat?" my question had to do with a test the remaining panel members had performed on CHECK. But the same question could be asked of the Ramsey Panel's whole undertaking. Had its members conspired to discredit the validity of the acoustics evidence? Had they sat down at an initial meeting and decided to invalidate the acoustics evidence, no matter what they found out?

No. This all came about through no conspiracy. What happened here was much more complicated, more nuanced, and more human—indeed, all too human.

It was a complicity.

And this complicity had much to do with who these men were and what they had experienced earlier in their lives. By 1982, for example, Norman Ramsey and Luis Alvarez had known each other for more than forty years. Both men had come into adulthood during the crucible of World War II, and both had bent their considerable scientific talents to serving the military during wartime. They experienced science allied with government for the advancement of a righteous policy—victory in World War II. This became a paradigm for decades of service after the war. Alvarez in his autobiography recalled being welcomed with other scientists to the Key West Naval Station by its commander as "exceptional patriots."[29] This notion seemed to take root in his psyche. It likely underlay his willingness to be the only major scientist taking a public position on the Kennedy assassination. There is reason to believe that Alvarez saw his work on the Kennedy assassination as an act of patriotism that would cleanse the public arena of the confusion introduced by a "bunch of nuts" criticizing the Warren Report.

The panel members looked up to Alvarez as the one person there with any knowledge of the Kennedy assassination. Most likely, they saw themselves, like him, as patriots of a special kind called upon from time to time to do what they could for their country. Bound together by decades of association and commonality of belief, many looked back over long years of aiding their country and saw serving on the Ramsey Panel as an extension of that service. Perhaps this was why the internal documents of the panel show no internal debate whatsoever. Most of the panel members had little to do with sculpting the final conclusions but instead simply approved what Alvarez, Garwin, Ramsey, and Horowitz produced. In such an atmosphere, and in the absence of any panel member whose field was acoustics, it was easy for a powerful few to dominate.

In retrospect—whatever one may say about the Ramsey Panel—one fact is clear. If its sole objective was to discredit the acoustics evidence in the public mind—to wipe it cleanly off the table, in effect silencing one of the most powerful arguments for shots fired from multiple directions—the panel succeeded admirably. That success was reflected in the decades-long silence that followed the publication of its report and the wide acceptance of its findings that silence implied.

Up to now, no review of the Ramsey Panel Report has appeared in any peer-reviewed American journal. Not until 2001, when Don Thomas published his paper in a peer-reviewed British journal, had there been any scientific challenge to the panel's findings. This challenge, we must remember, was turned down for publication—without even being read—by the American equivalent of the British journal.

Nor have there been any lectures about it at academic conferences. No major newspaper or television network has undertaken even a cursory examination of the report. Such was the firepower of Nobel laureates Alvarez and Ramsey, and the protective chill their imprimatur cast over the report, that no scientist (other than Don Thomas), society of scientists, or university or major scientific journal has taken up the challenge of giving the report the examination it deserves.

No, not a conspiracy—but a complicity.

From the much longer perspective of history, the issue of the Ramsey Panel's intentions, steps, and machinations—its entire facade—is of no great importance. The members of the Ramsey Panel were certainly not villains. What is important is that in the end, the pseudoscience of their report be exposed and driven out by good science, leading to the emergence of a result better grounded in the facts.

And so in the end, the signal in the noise has come full circle. In 1978, through an application of long-standing principles of acoustics to a reenactment of the shooting in Dealey Plaza, the signal was confirmed by James Barger and his colleagues. In 1982, the Ramsey Panel Report consigned those same gunshot signals back to the hubbub of random noise, permitting the body politic to curl up once again in the comfort of the Warren Commission Report. But, as has happened so often in this case, the reassuring elimination of a troublesome set of facts turned out to be illusory. Now, with the comprehensive collapse of the Ramsey Panel's arguments, the assassination gunshots are heard once again above the noise.

C onsider for a moment how sheer chance defined what we can and can't know about the Kennedy assassination.

Bill and Gayle Newman left their 8-mm movie camera at home on November 22 when they left to see President Kennedy. So did Abraham Zapruder, but his assistant, Lillian Rogers, hounded him to go home and get it. Had she not done this, no Zapruder film of the assassination would ever have been taken. Zapruder himself had no professional knowledge or experience of filmmaking, yet somehow he managed to perch on the very concrete pedestal any professional film crew would have chosen had they known in advance where the shooting would take place. Perched on that pedestal and steadied by Marilyn Sitzman because of his vertigo, with bullets flying and people screaming, he kept the limousine in frame from beginning to end.

Or think of the similar dumb luck that stuck open a police motorcycle's mic button during the brief time it was in Dealey Plaza. The duration of the shooting—8.3 seconds—is a tiny fraction of the twenty-five minutes it took for the motorcade to get from Love Field to Dealey Plaza. Had the microphone button not stuck open at all during that passage—or had it stuck open and then come unstuck before the motorcade reached the plaza—we would have no recording of the shooting. Or, given the "party line" design of the Dallas police radio network, had any of the many units parked at the Trade Mart actuated their mics at the time of the shooting, their transmission could have contaminated the recording of the gunshots. Or had Dallas radio broadcaster Gary Mack not taken the trouble to run channel 1 through a series of filters on the odd chance that it might contain something new and then had the wisdom to tell Mary Ferrell about it, no acoustic evidence would have made its way to the attention of Chief Counsel Robert Blakey that afternoon in September 1977.

Perhaps the signal example of good luck was the way the shooting arranged itself. Both the Zapruder film and the acoustics evidence portray it as an event that happened in two acts—two volleys of shots separated by a pause of 4.8 seconds. The first volley produced only nonlethal wounds to the President and Governor Connally. Had the shooting ended after the first volley, the whole event would have become a mere speed bump on the way to President Kennedy's second term. But it didn't end there. The second volley killed the president with shots to the head during the final second. During this same final second, the limousine made its closest approach to Zapruder's camera. Earlier, the limousine had been two or even three times farther away from the camera. Many details visible during the last second are simply not visible earlier. It was again extremely good fortune that the climax of the film was recorded by those frames with the ability to show the greatest detail.

The final second reveals another remarkable feature. In earlier frames, when a bullet strikes a person, that person's clothes trap any dispersion of blood or tissue. Only in the last second do we have a chance to observe how elementary physics directs brain material and blood from the impact along the flight path of the bullet. The sprays of blood and brain material from both shots are quite forceful, and their different directions confirm the trajectories already indicated by the film and the acoustic evidence.

The clear result of this concentration of evidence from many sources is that almost every detail of what happened during this final second is known, while numerous details of the seconds just before remain subject to continuing argument and discussion. Given the limited image resolution of the film when the camera is much farther from the limousine and the blockage of the vehicle by a sign at a crucial time, there are questions about earlier seconds that continue to lack answers.

For example, the acoustics tell us that the second shot was fired from the general vicinity of the sixth floor window only 2.55 seconds after the first shot and 1.05 seconds before the third shot. We know that firings by the FBI lab established the "minimum mechanical firing time" of Oswald's rifle—the time between shots—to be 2.3 seconds.[1] Unambiguously, this means the first and third shots could have come from Oswald's rifle, but not the second. A third shooter must have fired it from one of the buildings near the Houston/Elm corner. However, we don't know from where he fired or what happened to the bullet.

Or take the 27-degree downward angle through Governor Connally's body that precisely matched my Abney level's upward-angle measurement to the roof of the Dallas County Records Building that Sunday morning in August so many years ago. To this day, that angle remains our best estimate of the downward trajectory through Connally. The Records Building still stands, as does the 27-degree angle to its roof from a particular point in the middle lane of Elm Street. What has changed is the evidence surrounding when Governor

Connally was shot. In 1966, it seemed virtually certain that he had been hit from back to front through the torso by a bullet as he turned. In the intervening years, that certainty gradually vanished. Both the acoustics evidence and the Zapruder film would place the impact on Connally three-fourths of a second earlier.

These new facts produce questions for which there are no persuasive answers. Was Connally hit through the chest at the earlier or later time? If he was hit earlier, could his reaction have been delayed by three-fourths of a second? Are we watching here the bullet from the famous single-bullet theory striking Connally? If so, why does he take longer to react to it than President Kennedy? If so, from where did that bullet come, and when did it hit President Kennedy?

These questions—and many others—have no easy answers. But it may be that they don't need answers. Did anything really critical happen during the first act of the shooting? Is there anything from the first act we need to know in order to understand the whole event? It is not that too many pieces of the puzzle are missing. Rather, our vision is so limited that we don't know which pieces, if any, are missing.

The critical part of the shooting is the second act . . . the last second . . . the heart of the puzzle. And here—after fifty-five years—all the pieces are finally in place. In a case where complexity grows with every passing year, its very center exhibits a quiet simplicity. No longer must we rely upon complex theories to explain away what our own eyes show so powerfully. Gone are theories such as "neuromuscular reaction" and the "jet effect" whose result was to discount and make ambiguous what had been clear. The restored acoustic evidence now provides a matching sound track to the Zapruder film. Its echo patterns of recorded gunshots track the origin of the lethal shot to a precise location to the right front of the limousine, while both theories mentioned above claim that no such shot ever existed.

Years ago, author Don DeLillo looked at the Zapruder film over and over again while writing his brilliant novel Libra. With the precision and sensitivity of a master novelist, he later spoke of how "confusion and horror" are part of the film's impact, how frame 313 and its aftermath are "like some awful pornographic moment that happens without warning in our living rooms." He points to our confusion in seeing it. "Are you seeing some distortion inherent in the film medium or in your own perception of things?" he asks. "Are you the willing victim of some enormous lie of the state—a lie, a wish, a dream? Or did the shot simply come from the front, as every cell in your body tells you it did?"[2]

Don DeLillo is right. When you look at the Zapruder film, every cell in your body tells you the shot at frame 313 came from the right front. We humans interpret the world through a host of cues that tell us what is going on around us. The cues we attend to in the Zapruder film—the inarguable way that Kennedy's head pulls the rest of his body backward and to the left, the clear signal that his body is under the sway of impact forces, his movement not self-generated but solely the result of external forces—all of these cues tell us we are witnessing the effects of a shot fired from the right front.

In the weeks and months after the shooting, the Zapruder film footage around frame 313 was treated by LIFE magazine and government investigators as "the awful pornographic moment" DeLillo described. Like pornographic magazines in Midwestern drugstores, it was never mentioned but kept under the counter. LIFE published frames from other parts of the film but declined to publish frame 313 or its neighbors due to what it called "questions of taste." Without question, frame 313 is the climax of the Zapruder film, the very second when John Kennedy is killed. It is impossible to believe that none of the hundreds of government investigators who had seen the film talked about it. Yet in the voluminous records of the FBI and the Secret Service, I have not found a single mention of it in print. Likewise, when the Warren Commission, on the first anniversary of the assassination, published its 888-page report and twenty-six volumes of hearings and exhibits, nowhere in those tens of thousands of pages[3] can you find any mention of what DeLillo truly described as "the most direct kind of statement that the lethal bullet was fired from the front."

The sequestering of the Zapruder film came to an end with the showing of it by Bob Groden on national television on March 6, 1975. When, for the very first time, the American public saw the climax of the film, the response was a tidal wave of support for the creation of the HSCA. When the existence of the acoustic evidence was made known to the committee, it in turn hired Barger, Weiss, and Aschkenasy to evaluate it. That committee's reports and this book stand in a direct line of advance that is nothing less than the unfolding over time of the raw and unequivocal meaning of these disturbing frames.

The confusion and myriad contradictions of past decades are now replaced with a fully vetted narrative of rare simplicity. Kennedy is hit from the right front, and the impact lifts and throws his body backward and to the left along the trajectory of the bullet. At the same time, bits of skull, blood, and brain tissue are blasted along that same bullet flight path, spattering the motorcyclists and their cycles as well as Clint Hill, running to the car. Seven-tenths of a second later, when the acoustic evidence predicted it would strike, a second bullet blasts into the back of Kennedy's already damaged skull. No explosion results because the pressure vessel of the cranium was ruptured by the earlier shot. Instead, the bullet blasts forward through the gore, accelerating Kennedy's head and body along its path, throwing blood and brain tissue forward while enlarging the existing wound and popping outward a flap of bone just forward of his right ear. As with the earlier shot, bits of skull, blood, and brain tissue are driven as far forward as the hood ornament, while Kennedy's head and body are catapulted forward into his wife's lap.

And so at the very end, we are returned to the beginning. But now—at least for the brutal core of the event—there are no longer any unanswered questions. The climax of the Zapruder film has not changed. After two official investigations and controversy spanning more than five decades, we return to that terrible instant, to that last second that explains all the others. It stands in stark relief. Only now we can fill in the details of the microseconds that surround it. In doing so, we answer the threshold question that has haunted every page of this book up to now: Was there more than one shooter? What other explanation can there be for two bullets to the head from opposite directions in less than three-quarters of a second?

The Final Reconstruction

It all began late that morning with the ending of the light rain and the lifting of the cloud cover. A car entered the railroad yard parking area and backed up behind the stockade fence near the corner. If S. M. Holland's memory is correct, that car was a 1960 or 1961 Chevrolet four-door sedan, "off-white" in color. Whoever was in the car left it in the lot and fell in with the crowds awaiting the presidential motorcade.

The motorcade was due to pass the corner of Main and Houston Streets at 12:25 p.m. At about that time, Lee Bowers noticed two men near the corner of the stockade fence on his side of the fence, the side away from the street. One was "middle-aged, fairly heavy-set" and wearing a white shirt but no coat. The other was "of slighter build" and was wearing "a plaid shirt or jacket." The middle-aged man remained in Bowers's sight the whole time, while the other man in the "plaid shirt or jacket . . . was walking back and forth [and] in and out of sight."

From Bowers's switching tower, it is difficult to see everything going on behind the fence, especially if cars are parked alongside it. At some point, one of the men opened the trunk and took out a rifle. We know it was a rifle because the shot fired from this location produced a shock wave, while shots from handguns don't. We know it was firing ordinary hunting ammunition, not a metal-jacketed military round like those fired from Oswald's rifle. We do not know the caliber or the brand of the weapon or whether it was semi-automatic or single-shot. The fact that numerous cigarette butts were found behind the fence along with footprints indicates that whoever was there had time to smoke several cigarettes.

The two men would have heard a ripple of shouting and applause as the limousine turned right onto Houston Street into the sunlight. This would have been the signal for taking up position behind the fence, using the top as a gun rest, the barrel of the weapon partially hidden by overlying foliage. At the end of Houston Street, Secret Service Agent Bill Greer eased the four-ton limousine through a 120-degree turn onto Elm Street. Mrs. Kennedy looked ahead towards the Triple Underpass and to the coolness of its shadow. Greer looked down the expanse of Elm Street before him with a different thought in mind. There were people there. If the need arose, Greer asked himself, could he avoid trouble by veering to a vacant section of the overpass over Elm Street?

There was a flurry of sounds. The Dictabelt indicates three shots in 2.62 seconds. Clearly, not all three could have come from the rifle found later on the sixth floor of the depository. This indicated a second shooter in the vicinity, possibly firing from the nearby Dal-Tex or Records Building. Then there was the pause that lasted almost five seconds. Toward the end of this pause, Bill Greer turned around in his seat to look back and see what was happening. He must have taken his foot off the accelerator, for the limousine slowed from twelve to eight mph. On the knoll, the gunman behind the fence may have noticed the car slowing as he squeezed the trigger.

The bullet produced the "tangential hit" high above the right temple seen minutes later by Dr. Kemp Clark at Parkland Hospital. The force of the impact ranged rearward but largely up, throwing blood and brain debris over Mrs. Kennedy's right shoulder onto Clint Hill and the motorcycle outriders. The shot first drove the president's head downward, twisting the front of his skull to the left. Then it lifted his head and body up and backward. Less than ninety-five feet away, the gunman must have recognized his success, must have seen his shot hit its mark.

Virtually at the same time, the gunman in the corner window of the depository squeezed the trigger. Ten feet below him in a fifth floor window, depository employee Bonnie Ray Williams heard another shot from above as ceiling plaster from the concussions sprinkled down. Sitting on the low wall across from the depository, Howard Brennan saw the gunman in the corner window taking his time getting off his last shot. With the rifle raised "to his right shoulder" and the barrel pointed down Elm Street, Brennan thought it took "a couple of seconds" for the gunman to take "positive aim and fire his last shot." Since his earlier shot, the gunman had had plenty of time to acquire the target in his scope, zero in the crosshairs, and squeeze the trigger. His bullet hit high up on the back of the president's head, accelerating his head forward and wounding Governor Connally for a second time. At the same time, this bullet spewed fragments and impact debris forward against the windshield and over the limousine.

In less than ten seconds, the knoll shooter pitched the rifle into the trunk of the Chevy. He either climbed in after it or walked away. Either he or his companion closed the lid and walked away from the car, where either might have become the Secret Service agent Officer Smith later encountered, the one with "the dirty fingernails."

That afternoon or evening, long after the cordon around that area had been lifted by the Dallas police, someone returned and drove the car away.

Photo 24-1. President Kennedy at Pebble Beach, California, 1960.

Three months ago, I went back to Dallas. It is hardly the city I had come to in the fall of 1966, Abney level in my suitcase, paranoia in my heart. New buildings are everywhere, fabulous in their mix of architectural styles and surfaces. Union Station still stands, but the hotel at the corner has been modernized into an upscale middle-class inn. I walk from there to Dealey Plaza in the bright light of a November morning, peering at the familiar buildings. The Criminal Courts and Records Buildings along Houston Street: How many hours had I spent peering at photographs, trying to find in their nooks and crannies something significant? Farther along, the Dal-Tex Building, gentrified now into lawyers' offices and sparkling hallways. And the depository, spruced up, the site of county offices and the Sixth Floor Museum at Dealey Plaza. On the ground floor is the gift shop. For a modest donation, you can go upstairs and tour the sixth floor sniper's nest. I heard somewhere that in 2015, Dealey Plaza passed the Alamo in San Antonio as the state's most visited tourist attraction. Leaves swirl in the clear morning light. Behind the grassy knoll, the foliage over the stockade fence has grown, and the trees near the walkway are large. The parking area has been paved, and the stockade fence is now backed by screening to discourage graffiti or souvenir hunters. But nothing has really changed. Over there is Lee Bowers's switching tower and, closer in, Zapruder's pedestal with the concrete pergola beyond.

Moving across Elm Street, I stand in the grass, looking back. As always, the setting seems so small, the distances so shrunken. Standing there, taking in the scene and the memories, all the old phrases stream back: "Zapruder frame 313," "the minimum mechanical firing time of the rifle," "commission exhibit 399," "impact debris," "the left, backward snap," "tracheostomy," "neutron activation analysis," "the Sibert-O'Neill report." For an instant, it is as if I have never been away.

But I have been away. It has been over fifty years since I first came to this spot and dodged traffic on Elm Street to take Abney level readings with those phrases sounding in my mind. It is strange to be standing in this public square on a November morning. It is like visiting the scene of an old auto accident.

This whole arduous process began with a monumental failure by the keepers of public memory—the government and the press. Their failure remains with us. Over the past half century, this case has been filled with bitter arguments and wild conspiracy theories; government bodies papering over significant failures; junk science and "eminence-based" conclusions; sober, tenacious research and trumpeting by blowhards. But over these same decades and despite many mistakes and reverses, a partial truth has been brought to light. That truth, however, leaves open many of the questions that should have been answered fifty years ago and in all likelihood cannot be answered now. Principally . . . who did it, and why?

There was a time when Dealey Plaza took on an almost mythic identity, causing little girls to pick up twigs and hand them smilingly to their mothers. Nor was it just little girls who thought of Dealey Plaza in this way. Here, we believed, was the place where it all began. If we could penetrate the layers of obfuscation and misdirection and discover what really happened here, we believed we might gain a reprieve from the world that was born here.

But no longer do we believe this, and no longer do children pick up twigs here. The parents of children who visit here now were not even born in 1963. What was a place of mystery fifty years ago is no longer. As the years slipped away, the plaza returned to its original beginnings. Now it is where hawkers sell conspiracy magazines to tourists near the Works Progress Administration–built concrete pergola. Elm Street curves downhill to the raw concrete and metal of the railroad overpass, while city government buildings line Houston Street. Above Elm Street, the redbrick Texas School Book Depository still stands guard.

Places such as Dealey Plaza can be found repeated many times over in a hundred American cities. In the crucible of the event, it took on a kind of significance that fell away from it as decade followed decade. Now, all that is left is a commonplace Texas public square. Concrete. Glass. Bricks.

Like Dealey Plaza in 2020, the case itself has been drained of its mythic resonance and, very likely, its political significance. All of that drained away as year followed year and our politics moved on. What is left is a murder case like any other where the methods of establishing truth are well-known: pay attention to the testimony of percipient witnesses. See what photos, films, and audio tapes can tell you. Give particular weight to physical evidence and its scientific testing. These are the concrete, glass, and bricks of the case, its building blocks. Cleansed of the mistakes of the past, they now create a single narrative of great simplicity.

All these are the changes that fifty years have wrought.

There is, however, one fact about the assassination that has not changed in fifty years. It is its most obvious feature—the brutal effectiveness of the crime.

The Warren Commission painted the event as an amateur assassination by glossing over its most obvious feature. Most amateur assassinations end up as "attempted assassinations." They usually fail because the assassin-to-be—the lone attacker—can never by himself bring sufficient force to the point of attack. In a professional hit—as in this case—a surplus of force is applied and almost always assures an overwhelmingly effective result.

There is no more effective ambush than a crossfire. With shots coming undeniably from two locations and likely from a third, that is what happened here. The first three shots, from high up near the corner of Elm Street, caused consternation among the president's protectors. Photos show Secret Service agents in the follow-up car looking around but, except for Clint Hill, taking no action. William Greer, driver of the limousine, turns to see what is happening, and the car slows to below ten miles per hour. While all this is going on, the limousine keeps rolling implacably down Elm Street, closer and closer to the shooter on the knoll. Finally, with the president in plain view only ninety-five feet away, he fires.

In this whole narrative, what was clear in 1966 is even clearer now. This was a highly sophisticated, devastatingly effective assassination: two bullets to the head and one to the back. Its very audacity is its most compelling feature. Any speculation as to who did it and why must at least start with that fact.

With that thought in mind, I sat down on the steps where I had sat in 1966 and watched the cars go by. For a moment, the traffic flow stopped, and there was an almost perfect silence. Perhaps it was the silence that brought it on. For sitting there in the plaza—where it is always twelve thirty—I felt, for the first time in years, a sense of calm. It was done. It was my case, and now, finally, it was finished. I could leave it.

Josiah Thompson
Bolinas, California
February 2020

Objective

The objective of this study is to find the recording histories of all five crosstalk events found between 12:30 and 12:37 p.m. in the audio files that stem from the time of President Kennedy's assassination. These files are derived from audio recordings routinely made of the two DPD radio channel transmissions. Several confounding factors acting at times between the assassination and the present combine to cause none of the crosstalk event pairs to occur synchronously in their audio files, even though they must have been synchronous when originally recorded. One of the five crosstalk events, HOLD, occurs in the channel 1 audio file during the recorded sounds of gunfire; however, it appears about 86 s later in the channel 2 audio file. An NRC committee concluded in 1982 that the gunfire sounds were very likely just random static impulses, because the context of HOLD indicated that the assassination had occurred about one minute earlier. It asserted that the cause of the HOLD asynchrony was a pause or pauses of the channel 2 data logger.

This study seeks to find the recording histories of all five crosstalk events to discover the reasons for their asynchronies and then to determine whether the NRC committee's assertion of the HOLD synchrony is compatible with a live (real-time) crosstalk process.

There are six principal factors to consider while finding the recording histories:

1. Both data loggers were fitted with recording medium savers that paused them after an idle period of "dead air" lasting 6 to 8 s.[3]

2. Both data loggers recorded on media that are difficult to play back to a tape recorder (a Dictaphone belt on channel 1 and Audograph disc on channel 2). These difficulties caused the media to be played back to tape at different speeds than their record speeds. These speed differences resulted in "time warps," whereby time intervals in the audio files are either stretched or compressed.

3. Both data loggers had recorder styli driven by vacuum-tube amplifiers, causing robust power-line hum frequencies to be imparted onto their recorded media. The audio files for each channel contain three different hum frequencies, and two of them are common to both.

4. Both DPD dispatchers announced the time showing on their individual digital-display analog clocks immediately following each voice transmission they made.

5. The channel 2 dispatcher made a simulcast on both channels that was followed by the annotation "12:36."

APPENDIX A   QUANTITATIVE ANALYSIS OF CROSSTALK FOUND IN AUDIO RECORDED DURING THE JFK ASSASSINATION

James Barger

March 24, 2019

Abstract

Five instances of crosstalk and one simulcast are heard within a period of about five minutes at the time of the JFK assassination when listening to audio records of the two Dallas Police Department (DPD) radio communication channels. However, when the two surviving audio channels are aligned in time at the simulcast, none of the five crosstalk events align in time—none are synchronous. A committee appointed by the National Research Council (NRC)[1] posited that one crosstalk event ("Hold everything" [HOLD]) did never-theless align on the basis of hypothetical channel 2 data logger pauses. More-over, the survivors of this committee concluded in 2005 that another crosstalk event ("I'll check it") was not even crosstalk.[2] This paper discovers crosstalk synchrony—i.e., recorded simultaneously in real time—by using the idea of correcting the playback times of dispatcher-voiced annotation times so that they synchronize with the corresponding original spoken clock times. Hum signal frequencies found in both radio channels, including two frequencies that are common to both, inform the deduction of recording histories of all crosstalk events. It is found that two events, "I'll check it" and "I've got" were likely recorded onto channel 1 from channel 2 audio in real time as crosstalk during the assassination. The other three events, HOLD and two others, were overdubbed onto channel 1 from channel 2 during a later session. Conse-quently, the HOLD family of crosstalks cannot be used to infer the causality of anything recorded in real time.

6. The channel 2 audio file exhibits a recording discontinuity at about 12:33, when there is a 5.3 percent change in hum frequency.

The Data

Data analysis results reported by Richard Mullen in Appendix B include both frequency analysis of hum signals in both channels and also pattern matching of all six audio image pairs. Mullen's pattern-matching technique is known as pattern cross-correlation (PCC) and is the same technique used by the authors of the Ramsey Panel survivors' report.

Richard Mullen's analysis was performed on the same audio data used by the NRC committee. These data are in the form of digital audio files created from analog tape recordings that stem from the original data logger records routinely made of both DPD radio channels' voice traffic. The original logger media were Dictaphone belts for channel 1 and Audograph disks for channel 2.

Researcher Chris Scally provides a detailed study of the provenance of the various analog tapes spawned from the belts and discs.[4] He identifies Sergeant Jim Bowles as the man mainly responsible for the creation of magnetic tape recordings taken from the original media for both channels. He describes how the original media were also given to the FBI and eventually returned. By March 1964, Bowles had created reel-to-reel magnetic tape copies of the audio for both channels. His channel 1 tape is available online[5] and is referred to here as Bowles 1. His channel 2 tape comes in two parts: data from times earlier than about 12:33 are on Bowles 2a, and data from later times are on Bowles 2b.

Audio event timing data for channel 2 used in this study are provided by Michael O'Dell.[6] His source for channel 2 audio stemmed from a magnetic tape recording of a channel 2 disc as it was being played back from a phonograph. He devised a continuous correction for the disc's constant recording groove velocity when played back at a constant rate of reducing groove velocity. His resulting file is characterized by a single prominent hum frequency at 60 Hz, indicating that the pace of the audio matches real time, and the absence of any discontinuity at 12:33. Michael O'Dell also provided audio event timing data for channel 1. His timing data for both crosstalk events and dispatcher time annotations for both channels are listed in Section 8.

Richard Mullen's pattern-matching and hum frequency calculations were performed on data from the Bowles 1 file and the Bowles 2a and Bowles 2b files. His results are consistent with possible overdubbing between the channel 1 and channel 2 audio records because both of them contain identical hum frequencies. Michael O'Dell's channel 2 audio event timing data were obtained from a single channel 2 file. Therefore, it is necessary to compute from O'Dell's event times the corresponding Bowles 2a or Bowles 2b event times. This modification of the O'Dell times is possible because the hum frequencies are known for all files. The modification makes it possible to compare the Bowles 1 to the two Bowles channel 2 audio files that were prepared shortly after the assassination, before March 1964.

The Method

Audio event times taken from the audio files are corrected in a unique way that makes their playback times match their original clock times. This procedure finds the time correction factor "B" for the audio file data that causes every dispatcher-spoken time annotation to occur at the clock time spoken, modulo one minute. The crosstalk events themselves occur at times between dispatcher-spoken clock times. Therefore, their playback times are corrected by the same factor B that is found to correct dispatcher playback times. This method for correcting audio event playback times corrects for recording time lost to original recording pauses on average, leaving random timing errors between time announcements that are to be estimated. There are two types of audio events during which there are no pauses—hum signals and crosstalk events. Time correction factors, designated B_H, are found for these events. Values of B are less than the corresponding values of B_H whenever any recorder pauses occur.

Record and playback medium effective velocities V_{rec} and V_{pb} determine the time correction factor B. These velocities incorporate both the effect of the machine's capstan and the effect of the original recorder pauses. The original time span of an audio event is equal to Δt_{orig}, and the time span of that event after it is played back is equal to Δt_{pb}.

$$\Delta t_{pb} = \Delta t_{orig} \times \frac{V_{rec}}{V_{pb}} = B \times \Delta t_{orig} \qquad (1)$$

Playback time spans obeying Equation 1 are integrated with respect to time to obtain $t_{pb} = A + B \times t_{orig}$, where A is the integration constant. The audio file time t_{pb} is modified to be zero at 12:30: $t_{pb} = C + t^{12:30}{}_{pb}$. Combining these two equations gives the required correction of playback time $t^{12:30}{}_{pb}$ to make it equal to the original clock time, Equation 2.

$$t_{clock}^{12:30} = \frac{t_{pb}^{12:30}}{B} - S \quad where \quad S = \frac{A-C}{B} \tag{2}$$

The values of parameters B and S are chosen so that all dispatcher corrected time annotations occur within the 60-s span of corrected time beginning at the first clock-time display of each new minute. B controls the slope—in this instance 45 degrees—of corrected event times so that it parallels clock time. S is chosen to place all corrected event times between the two 45-degree lines (separated by one minute) that represent real clock time; the lower line represents a new time first displayed, and the upper line represents when it is last displayed.

The time correction factor B_H is determined solely by the frequency f_H of the power-line hum signal imparted by the data logger. This factor follows from Equation 1 and the fact that frequency ratios are inversely proportional to time-span ratios.

$$B_H = \frac{60}{f_H} \tag{3}$$

The value of the time correction factor B will always be smaller than its hum-induced version B_H whenever recorder pauses occur anywhere within the time span under consideration. Equation 4 expresses the sum total of all pauses TP that occur within a clock time interval Δt_{clock}, given the two different time correction factors.

$$TP = \Delta t_{clock}\left(1 - \frac{B}{B_H}\right) \tag{4}$$

Crosstalk between the two DPD radio channels must have occurred synchronously when originally recorded by the data loggers. A crosstalk ratio β^{simul} will quantify the recording history of crosstalk events in the search to understand how the events became nonsimultaneous. A single radio broadcast made simultaneously over both channels by the channel 2 dispatcher at 12:36 serves as the reference point for synchrony. This broadcast is designated BUH owing to an odd pronunciation of the word "industrial"—"in-BUH-dustrial".

The synchrony error for an audio event is equal to the difference between the corrected time spans from BUH on both channels, where B1 and B2 are the time correction factors for channels 1 and 2.

$$error^{event} = \frac{t_{pb1}^{event} - t_{pb1}^{BUH}}{B1} - \frac{t_{pb2}^{event} - t_{pb2}^{BUH}}{B2} \tag{5}$$

Synchrony for the event requires that the event error be equal to zero. The unique value of the crosstalk ratio β^{simul} that is required for synchrony is given the crosstalk ratio.

$$\beta^{simul} = \left|\frac{B2}{B1}\right|^{simul} = \frac{t_{pb2}^{event} - t_{pb2}^{BUH}}{t_{pb1}^{event} - t_{pb1}^{BUH}} \tag{6}$$

A different crosstalk ratio, one that is completely free of data logger pause influence, is found by computation of the PCC coefficient for any crosstalk pair. A unique sample-rate correction applied to one image of the crosstalk pair results in maximum correlation. Equation 7 gives the value for the crosstalk ratio β^{PCC} when the original sample rate s_1 must be changed to equal s_2 to bring about maximum correlation.

$$\beta^{PCC} = \left|\frac{B2}{B1}\right|^{PCC} = \frac{s_2}{s_1} \tag{7}$$

This form of crosstalk ratio determines the ratio of the time spans of the two audio events, while the previous crosstalk ratio determines the ratio of the time spans *between* audio events and the simulcast event BUH. Clearly, both ratios must be the same for crosstalk events recorded during a single session.

O'Dell timing data are corrected for the known hum frequency differences between the O'Dell channel 2 and the Bowles 2a and Bowles 2b data files. The corrected times ct_k are transformed from the O'Dell times ot_k by the use of Equation 8. The O'Dell time when the Bowles file is cut is denoted Tc.

$$ct_k = if\left[ot_k < Tc, Tc + B2_{Ha}(ot_k - Tc) + D, Tc - B2_{Hb}(Tc - ot_k)\right]^7 \tag{8}$$

The Bowles 2a tape ends where it was cut from a channel 2 tape having time correction factor $B2_{Ha}$. The Bowles 2b tape begins where it was cut from a channel 2 tape having time correction factor $B2_{Hb}$. It is assumed that each tape was cut at nearly the same time Tc so that time progresses continuously at the cut. If the two tapes were not cut at exactly the same time, then there will be a time offset at time Tc that equals D.

Insights from Crosstalk Ratios and Hum Frequencies

Crosstalk ratios β^{simul}, plotted as circles on Figure A-1, are computed by Equation 6 and by using the event times provided by Michael O'Dell and listed in

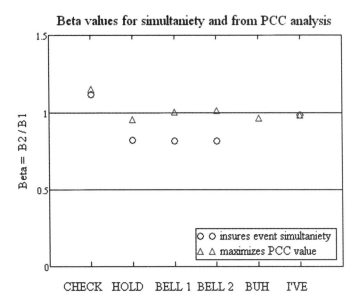

Figure A-1. Crosstalk ratios for five crosstalk events.

Section 8. Crosstalk ratios β^{PCC} are plotted as triangles on Figure A-1 using results computed by Richard Mullen, as listed in Appendix B. There is no simultaneity ratio for BUH because it is the simulcast—the reference event for all five crosstalk events.

Both crosstalk events CHECK and I'VE GOT exhibit nearly identical values of their crosstalk ratios. All three crosstalk events HOLD, BELLAH 1, and BELLAH 2, exhibit significantly different crosstalk ratios, but their differences are all nearly the same. This result identifies them as a family of crosstalk events that share the same recording history, but one that is different from the recording history of the CHECK pair. The CHECK event has uniquely large values of its crosstalk ratios, a fact that portends the discontinuity of channel 2 recording history indicated also by hum frequencies (see Section 8).

Hum frequencies found by Richard Mullen are described in Appendix B. The results are summarized in Figure A-2, where the plotting format is chosen to clarify their intricate nature.

There are two channel 2 hum tones that decrease abruptly by 5.3 percent at a discontinuity that is found to occur between the HOLD and BELLAH 1 crosstalk events. There are three channel 1 hum tones that are continuous through the discontinuity and a fourth tone that begins at the discontinuity and is exactly equal to one of the channel 2 hum tones. The lowest-frequency channel 2 hum tone is exactly equal to the lowest channel 1 hum tone after the discontinuity.

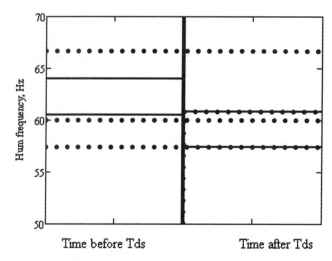

Figure A-2. Hum frequencies: channel 1 dots, channel 2 lines, before and after time Tds of channel 2 recording discontinuity.

The equality of the hum tones in the two channels is evidence of an overdub of channel 1 by channel 2.

The following section considers the recording history of the HOLD family of events, the events of prime concern because the Ramsey Panel speculated that these were originally recorded crosstalk. Section 6 considers the recording history of the CHECK family of events, of interest because the CHECK and HOLD events are mutually exclusive by the meaning of their messages.

Test of Hypothesis That HOLD Is True Crosstalk

The aim of this test is to see whether a complete set of recording parameters for both DPD dispatcher channels can be found that demonstrates the simultaneity of the HOLD family of crosstalk events and also the simultaneity of the dispatcher time annotations with the clock.

The effective value of $B1$, the time correction factor for channel 1, is found graphically on Figure A-3. The abscissa is clock time, relative to 12:30. The ordinate is corrected playback time, relative to 12:30. Corrected playback times for channel 1 time annotations are calculated by using Equation 2 and O'Dell's channel 1 event times listed in Section 8. These data are plotted as circles. The parameters used to make the plot are $B1 = 0.91$ and $S1 = 435$ sec.

These parameter choices place all twenty time annotations within the bounds defined by the two lines representing the beginning and end of the channel 1 dispatcher clock displays. The annotation data gap extending from about 12:28 until 12:34 is the period of the stuck-on motorcycle microphone. The estimate of parameter B1 = 0.91 is very robust, with less than about ±0.8 percent possible variation.

The relevant hum signal is chosen for channel 1 from the value of β^{PCC}=0.96 found by Mullen for the simulcast event and from the hum frequencies that apply to both channels after the channel 2 recording discontinuity (see Section 4). The obvious choices are $f1_H$ = 60 Hz ($B1_H$ = 1.0) and $f2_H$ = 60.8 Hz ($B2_H$ = 0.98). These choices lead via Equation 3 and Equation 7 to the value of β^{PCC} = 0.98, closer to the value of 0.96 found by Mullen than the same ratio of any other choice of hum frequencies.

Determination of the value of channel 2 time correction factor B2 is complicated by the fact that it changes in value by 5.3 percent at a clock time denoted by Tds, when the recording discontinuity occurs in the Bowles channel 2 audio record. Equation 2 is modified to account for this discontinuity by defining conditional playback correction parameters: B2a, B2b, S2a, S2b. The (a) parameters are in effect at times less than time Tds (relative to 12:30), and the (b) parameters are in effect thereafter. Values of the parameters S2a and S2b are related by the requirement that playback time shall be continuous at time Tds.[7]

The diamonds on Figure A-3 denote the twenty-two time annotations on channel 2. These diamonds are plotted at the times ct_k computed by Equation 8 (B2/Ha =60/64.0 and B2/Hb = 60/60.8) and corrected to clock time by Equation 2. The parameters used to make this plot—and that do cause HOLD to be synchronous—are B2a = 0.707, B2b = 0.730, S2a = 881.8 s, S2b = 842 s, Tc = 780 s, Tds = 226.5 s (12:33:4), and CS = 30 s, D = 0.

Crosstalk timelines that result from the use of these parameters and are plotted on Figure A-4 show that simultaneity has indeed been restored for HOLD (triangles). The simultaneity errors for the other two members of the HOLD family are small, equaling 0.1 s for BELLAH 1 (squares) and 0.1 s for BELLAH 2 (denoted by x's). The simultaneity error is 118.8 s for CHECK (circles) and −3.7 s for I'VE GOT (diamonds).

Channel synchronization on Figure A-3 is achieved by adjusting the BUH (simulcast) corrected playback time on channel 2 (denoted by a +) to have the same corrected playback time as BUH on channel 1 (denoted by an x). Next, clock synchronization is achieved by adding the amount of time CS to the channel 2 clock times that correctly positions the triangles between the same lines that represent channel 1 clock time.[8]

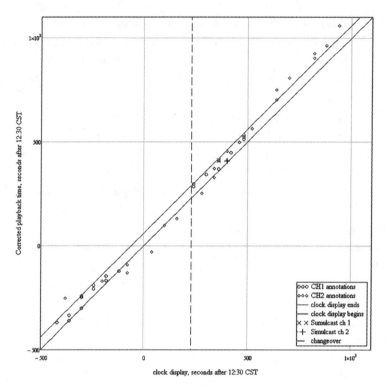

Figure A-3. Corrected announcement times vs. dispatcher clock display times for the HOLD hypothesis.

It is clearly demonstrated by Figure A-3 that the channel 2 time annotations were not made at the same time that the HOLD family of crosstalk was made. Fourteen time annotations demonstrate errors ranging from -60 to +62 s. The channel 2 time correction factors B2a and B2b that synchronize the HOLD family are very different from the near-unity values that do synchronize the voice annotations with the clock.

There are ample channel 2 pauses required to make the HOLD family time correction factor be as small as $B2 = 0.707$. For channel 1, the total pause time for HOLD is calculated (Equation 4) to equal 18.5 s. For channel 2, the total HOLD pause time is calculated (Equation 4, modified to accommodate the parameter change at time Tds) to equal 100.5 s. These channel 2 pauses are the ones that the Ramsey Panel anticipated. The panel did not anticipate the smaller but crucial pauses in the channel 1 recording.

The total channel 2 pause time of 100.5 s amounts to 31 percent of the 322.2 s between the HOLD and BUH events when HOLD simultaneity is achieved. This significant pause percentage belies the seemingly continuous and excited

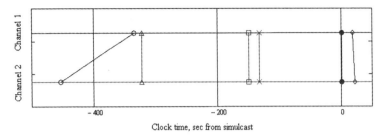

Figure A-4. Crosstalk timelines for the HOLD hypothesis.

chatter that is heard while listening to the channel 2 audio throughout this time span.

Test of Hypothesis That CHECK Is True Crosstalk

The aim of this test is to see whether a single complete set of recording parameters for both DPD dispatcher channels can be found that both demonstrates the simultaneity of the CHECK family of crosstalk events and the simultaneity of the dispatcher time annotations with the clock.

The recording parameters for channel 1 are found in section 5: channel 1 hum frequency is equal to 60 Hz, time correction factor $B1 = 0.91$, and plotting constant $S1 = 435$ s.

The set of channel 2 recording parameters that does produce simultaneity for the CHECK and I'VE GOT crosstalk events includes both "a" parameters for clock times less than Tds and "b" parameters for clock times greater than Tds. The simultaneity parameter set is: $B2a = 1.0338$, $B2b = 0.890$, $S2a = 498.1$ s, $S2b = 615$ s, $Tc = 780$ s, $Tds = 261.4$ s, $CS = 30$ s, and $D = 0$ s. The channel 2 hum frequency was chosen in Section 5 to equal 60.8 Hz., from which $B2_{Hb} = 0.99$.

The five crosstalk timelines produced with these parameters are shown on Figure A-5. Simultaneity errors are equal to zero for CHECK (circles) and for I'VE GOT (diamonds). Errors for the BELLAH family are equal to -77.4 s for HOLD

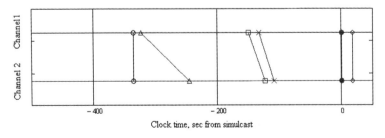

Figure A-5. Crosstalk timelines for the CHECK hypothesis.

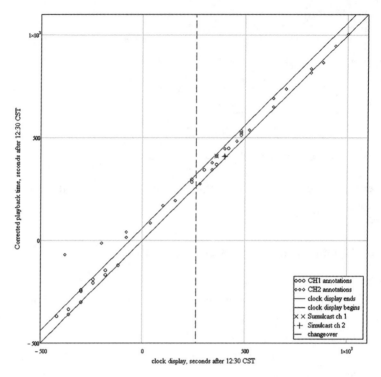

Figure A-6. Corrected announcement times vs. dispatcher clock display times for the CHECK hypothesis.

(diamonds), -26.9 s for BELLAH 1 (squares), and -23.7 s for BELLAH 2 (denoted by x's).

Figure A-6 shows the dispatcher annotations that conform to the parameter choices that produce synchrony for CHECK. The circles denoting channel 1 annotations are unchanged from those shown on Figure A-3. The diamonds denoting channel 2 annotations are computed from the corrected channel 2 times ct_k by using Equation 8 and then corrected to clock time by Equation 2.

The diamonds that represent channel 2 annotation times are all within the clock time limits throughout the entire span of time between 12:30 and 12:46, with one exception: the 12:31 annotation is 5 s late. The slope transition of diamonds that occurs at about 12:30 marks the onset of assassination-induced hectic voice traffic over the sole operational radio channel (channel 1 has been blocked since about 12:27). The lone 5-s discrepancy could be caused by an overlong pause, by a next-minute dispatcher announcement error, or by a D = 5 s cutting error between the two BELLAH channel 2 tapes. Therefore, the CHECK family is only plausibly in synchronization with the clock. This is a necessary condition for CHECK synchrony, but not a sufficient one. There are other choices of the B2 parameters that bring both equal and increasingly plausible clock synchrony for the annotations, but these cause CHECK synchrony errors as large as 12.5 s. An additional necessary condition for CHECK synchrony is met within tolerance: The value of $\beta^{PCC} = 1.15$ that was found by Mullen for CHECK is reproduced by the parameters that provide CHECK synchrony: $\beta^{simul} = $ B2a/B1 = 1.034 / 0.91 = 1.14.

Discussion

Two necessary conditions have been found that support the hypothesis that the crosstalk events CHECK and I'VE GOT were recorded onto channel 1 from channel 2 as crosstalk during the assassination event. The mechanism for this is likely to be the capture of these sounds by a channel 1 microphone that was keyed to transmit (open) at the time that the sounds were broadcast from a nearby channel 2 loudspeaker.

A sufficient condition has been found to reject the hypothesis that the HOLD family of crosstalk events was recorded onto channel 1 during the assassination event. Richard Mullen's hum frequency data, plotted on Figure A-2, show that both tapes Bowles 1 and Bowles 2b share an identical pair of non-60-Hz hum frequencies. Since non-60-Hz hum frequencies occur while recording to and playing back from the original recording media—very different machines for the two channels—it is unlikely that these two different frequencies were replicated independently during rerecording operations done on the two different tapes. Therefore, it is likely that these hum frequencies were over-dubbed from the Bowles 2 tape onto the Bowles 1 tape. It is likely that other channel 2 audio was recorded onto the Bowles 1 tape concurrently with the hum signals. It is a necessary condition for overdubbing that the hum frequencies on the donor tape will be transferred to the recipient tape.

The actual overdubbing was probably inadvertent. The HOLD family share a robust signal-to-noise ratio on channel 2. Their corresponding signals on channel 1 are very weak—HOLD itself is near hearing threshold. Therefore, the channel 2 noise level that would have been overdubbed would be well below the channel 1 noise level and cannot be identified. The effect of this overdub probably causes the presence of the HOLD family on channel 1 to be an arti-fact—the result of the multiple tape copies and dubs made to and from mul-tiple machines in the first days by technicians at the DPD and FBI and attested by the intricate and odd assemblage of hum frequencies found by Richard Mullen.

The goal of this analysis has been to find both from the timing data provided by Michael O'Dell and the pattern-matching and hum frequency calculations by Richard Mullen the recording history of all five crosstalk events. The complexity of the evidence has allowed only a partial success. For the CHECK pair of events, only a probable history that indicates it was recorded in real time has been found. For the HOLD trio of events, real-time recording has been ruled out, but a detailed overdub history has not been defined. All data and mathematical relationships are included in this appendix so that the reader's insight may further advance the goal.

O'Dell Event Times

Voiced Ch 1	Time Ch 1	Voiced Ch 2	Time Ch 2
12:23	57.76	12:23	417.2
12:24	67.27	12:26	479.2
12:24	91.01	12:28	508.7
12:25	121.39	12:28	539.3
12:25	169.22	12:30	585.25
12:25	175.95	12:31	680.89
12:26	206.4	12:32	706.18
12:26	222.14	12:34	796.77
12:27	243.31	12:35	854.01
12:27	261.49	12:35	885.22
12:28	284.3	12:36	914.77
12:34	654.61	12:36	946.45
12:34	666.79	12:37	979.93
12:35	708.38	12:38	1027.28
12:36	731.67	12:40	1130.02
12:36	769.26	12:40	1165.76
12:37	801.86	12:41	1208.43
12:38	861.15	12:43	1277.9
12:38	871.74	12:43	1294.81
12:38	879.9	12:44	1322.97
		12:45	1394.98
		12:45	1448.5
CHECK	463.41	CHECK	574.14
HOLD	474.32	HOLD	672.76
BELLAH 1	631.54	BELLAH 1	802.55
BELLAH 2	647.4	BELLAH 2	815.39
SIMULCAST	768.07	SIMULCAST	913.58
I'VE GOT	784.22	I'VE GOT	929.43

APPENDIX B SIGNAL PROCESSING RESULTS FOR BOTH DPD AUDIO FILES

Richard Mullen

August 6, 2018

Abstract

The Ramsey Panel survivors published a paper in 2005 attempting to find the synchronization of acoustic events between the two Dallas Police communication channels.[1] They analyzed several audio events common to both channels to establish that they were true copies and therefore would presumably have been originally recorded at the same clock times on both channels. They concluded that one audio pair, "Hold everything" (HOLD), does match and that its two images were originally to be found at their correct times on both channels. They concluded that another audio pair, "I'll check it" (CHECK), is not a crosstalk event because they were unable to obtain a pattern match for that pair of audio events. In this appendix, we employ the same mathematical pattern-matching technique used by the Ramsey Panel members. The technique, known as pattern cross-correlation (PCC), first calculates for each image of the pair a two-dimensional spectrogram and then cross-correlates the two spectrograms. We find that the HOLD pair is indeed made up of identical audio events and that the CHECK pair is too. The Ramsey analysis employs a wide data window that is typically used when performing speaker identification. A much narrower data window is required to obtain sufficient noise rejection to find similarity for the brief CHECK event. Inasmuch as Sergeant Bowles had no trouble identifying either the speakers or their spoken phrases on both channels for both pairs of audio events, there was no need to apply solely the wide data analysis window used for speaker identification. Doing so excluded the narrow analysis window that clearly demonstrates the cross-channel match for CHECK.

In addition to the PCC analysis, seven 0.5-Hz-resolution spectrograms were computed for 30 s of audio data situated around each of five putative crosstalk events for both channels. These spectrograms reveal two identical hum signals on both channels and one additional hum signal on channel 1. The channel 2 hum signals are discontinuous at about 30 s after the HOLD event.

Objectives

The first objective of this PCC analysis of crosstalk audio data is to find why the Ramsey Panel survivors were unable to obtain a clear peak value from their PCC calculation for the CHECK crosstalk event that would show similarity between the CHECK audio images across the two channels.

The second objective is to compute the unique ratio of channel 2 to channel 1 time-stretch coefficients that produce a peak value of the PCC calculation for each crosstalk event and for the simulcast. These quantities are designated crosstalk ratios and are denoted in Appendix A by the symbol β^{PCC}.

The third objective is to find the frequencies of all of the power line–induced nominally 60-Hz "hum" frequencies that are recorded onto the channel 1 and channel 2 and O'Dell audio files. These frequencies promote the understanding of the recording histories, and they provide a means for discovering the time-stretch coefficient for each channel.

Procedure Used for PCC Analysis

We specifically intend that any reader having access to signal processing software shall be able to reproduce exactly the results presented here. To ensure this outcome, we specify the source of the downloadable audio files that are analyzed and also the analysis software packages and all analysis parameters that were used to obtain these results.

The mathematics application is MATLAB release R2012a by Mathworks, Inc. The MATLAB functions used, in order, are wavread, resample, spectrogram, hamming, and xcorr2.

The parameters used for the first set of calculations match those used by the Ramsey survivors. They are

MATLAB spectrogram of template and target signal files
Input time series data sampled at 44100 samples/s
Down sample to 8820 samples/s
512 point FFT length (17 Hz/bin resolution)

448 sample overlap

Hamming window

Output power spectral density (PSD)

Boost data amplitude by 3 dB/kHz

Spectrogram plot output 10 log10 (PSD0.3)

MATLAB xcorr2

Input spectrogram PSD for template and target data

Frequency bound 10–3500 Hz on input PSD

Output PCC

We suspected that this 512-point sample window, used by the Ramsey survivors, was too wide to provide sufficient signal-to-noise ratio for the very short (0.6 s) CHECK crosstalk event. To test this idea, we ran a second set of PCC calculations with the much narrower window of 64 samples, overlapped by 56 samples.

In addition, we switched the template channel—that is, the channel containing the signal selected for comparison—from channel 1 to channel 2, resulting in channel 1 being the target channel on which that signal also appears. We did so because, with no competing motorcycle engine noise on channel 2, much better template data selection is possible here than on channel 1.

The source of audio data for each instance of crosstalk is given in the below table. The downloadable files are found at this site.[2]

Table B-1. Sources of audio data for each instance of crosstalk

Audio Event	Ch 1 Source	Min. into File	Ch 2 Source	Min. into File
CHECK	Track 1 of 7 P-01	3:47.7	Track 2 of 7 P-01	2:00
HOLD	Track 1 of 7 P-01	3:59.7	Track 2 of 7 P-01	3:36
BELLAH 1	Track 1 of 7 P-01	6:36.3	Track 3 of 7 P-01	0:21.0
BELLAH 2	Track 1 of 7 P-01	6:51.3	Track 3 of 7 P-01	0:32.0
SIMULCAST	Track 6B	12:53.5	Track 3 of 7 P-01	2:08.3
Fifth floor	Track 6B	13:14.5	Track 3 of 7 P-01	2:25.3

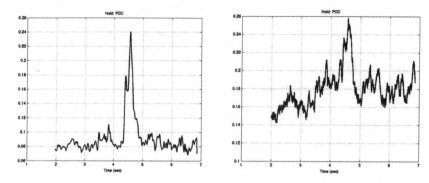

Figure B-1. PCC plots for HOLD audio event; 512 sample (*left*), 64 sample (*right*).

Confirmation of CHECK as Crosstalk

Here we show side by side the PCC output plots made with both the original wide data window (on the left) and the modified narrow window (on the right) for both HOLD (Figure B-1) and CHECK (Figure B-2) crosstalk events.

The results for HOLD are similar for both analysis windows. The peak PCC net value of 0.15 for the wider window is larger than the net value of 0.06 for the narrow window. This is a reflection of the 3-s time span of the audio signal. A time-stretch ratio $\beta^{\text{PCC}} = 0.96$ was found in both cases to produce these peak values.

The CHECK audio event produces no single peak value when using the wide data window shown at left. The peak PCC net value of 0.15 that occurs just after 3 s represents correctly the time of true pattern matching, but the

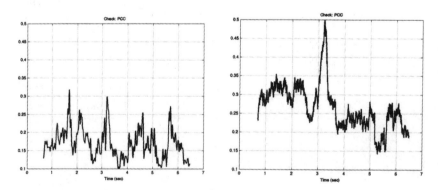

Figure B-2. PCC plots for CHECK audio event; 512 sample (*left*), 64 sample (*right*).

additional three subsidiary peaks cause ambiguity. The narrow data analysis window produces a single peak with net amplitude equal to 0.25. This increased amplitude greatly exceeds the amplitude of the HOLD event result. A time stretch ratio $\beta^{PCC} = 1.15$ was found to produce these peak values in both cases.

Now we have seen two reasons why the Ramsey team failed to show that CHECK is crosstalk. First, they used a wide data window having time resolution of 58 ms—an appropriate time resolution for doing speaker identification because the narrow frequency resolution that results (17 Hz) accurately portrays the resonance frequency of the speaker's voice. But the ear does a better job of recognizing that the speaker of both crosstalk images is the same. The wider data window produces a much lower spectrogram amplitude for the approximately 3 kHz heterodyne tone that is "noise" in the channel 1 CHECK crosstalk event. By eliminating most of this noise in this way, the very large correlation of the two CHECK crosstalk events is clearly demonstrated.

The second reason for the Ramsey team failure was their incomplete search of the time-stretch factor. It cannot be assumed that the time-stretch factors β^{PCC} are the same for CHECK as for the other crosstalk events because the stretch factors are found to change on channel 2 at a changeover time. For this reason, a wide range of stretch factors was tried in doing these PCC computations. A CHECK peak at $\beta^{PCC} = 1.15$ was found, which is more than 15 percent different than the peak for the other crosstalk items. This search with a narrow data window, combined with searching over a wide range of time-stretch factors, proved successful. CHECK is crosstalk, showing a maximum PCC value nearly as large as any of the other crosstalk instances, including the low-noise simulcast event.

Time-Stretch Factors Found for All Crosstalk and for the Simulcast

PCC plots for all six events are shown collectively in Figure B-3. The modified (narrow) time window is used for the entire set. The accompaning Table B-2 lists the net peak value for each PCC graph and the value of the simultaneity ratio β^{PCC} for each event.

Procedure Used for Spectral Analysis

To obtain sufficiently high signal-to-noise hum frequency data, 30 s of data sampled at 8820 samples/s were averaged with nonoverlapping 2-s,

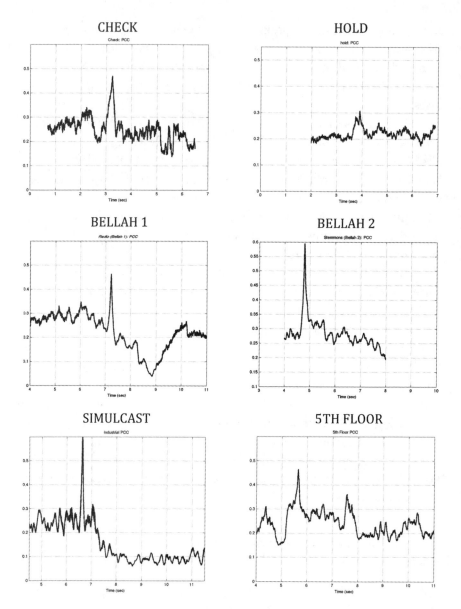

Figure B-3. PCC graphs for 6 crosstalk events.

Hamming shaded analysis windows. Prior to sampling, the data were band pass filtered to 30 Hz–300 Hz to protect them from aliasing. This process results in spectra having 0.5 Hz of resolution. There is a small variability in the hum frequencies owing to imperfect speed control of at least one of the audio machines involved in the recording and transcribing of the data on both

Table B-2. Net peak value for each PCC graph and the value of the simultaneity radio βPCC ratio for each event

Event	CHECK	HOLD	BELLAH 1	BELLAH 2	SIMULCAST	Fifth Floor
PCC net peak	0.22	0.09	0.23	0.26	0.35	0.17
β^{PCC}	1.15	0.96	1.0	1.012	0.96	0.98

channels. Measurements of a given hum frequency at different times produce variations of ±0.5 Hz. Therefore, greater resolution is expected to not produce further signal-to-noise gain.

Results Obtained by Spectral Analysis

Figure B-4 shows two spectra for each channel, one before and one after the channel 2 changeover. Seven power spectra were computed for each channel, one before CHECK, one after HOLD, one before BELLAH 1, one after BELLAH 2, one before BUH (simulcast), one after I'VE GOT, and one 2 min. after I'VE GOT. All channel 1 spectra exhibited the same hum frequency series, but with varying signal-to-noise ratios. Channel 2 spectra that occur before a changeover at about 30 s after HOLD are similar to one another, but after this changeover, they are different, though similar to one another. The frequencies of the hum signals, in Hz, are shown directly above each spectral peak representing either the fundamental frequency or one member of its harmonic series.

A distinctive harmonic series with a 15-Hz fundamental is present on all spectra. This series is judged to be the power spectrum of a pulse train having a 1/15-s period and sufficient bandwidth to exhibit overtones at 15-Hz intervals visible out to 90 Hz. This spectrum is consistent with the magnetic near field of a four-pole synchronous AC motor (the common power source for phonographs and tape recorders) that printed onto the tapes from a poorly shielded motor or its power line. This spectrum does not share the audio channel's low-frequency attenuation characteristic with the other harmonic series that originate as power-line hum. However, the fourth overtone at 60 Hz is a potential confounder of the hum signal fundamental at 60 Hz. Hum signal ambiguity is resolved by requiring at least one hum signal harmonic at 120 Hz and or 180 Hz to be present. Figure B-5, where the dominant strength of the channel 2 hum signal is shown, demonstrates this requirement.

After the changeover, there are found to be two identical harmonic series on each channel (Figure B-4a for channel 1 and Figure B-4b for channel 2),

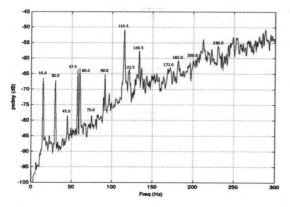

Figure B-4a. Power spectral density taken on channel 1 between HOLD and BELLAH 1. Source: Track 1 of 7, P-01, 6 minutes and 36.3 s into the file.

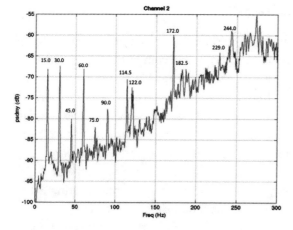

Figure B-4b. Power spectral density taken on channel 2 between BELLAH 2 and SIMULCAST. Source: Track 3 of 7, P-01, 32.0 s into the file.

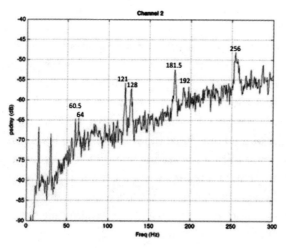

Figure B-4c. Power spectral density taken on channel 2 before CHECK. Source: Track 2 of 7, P-01, ending at 1:06 s into the file.

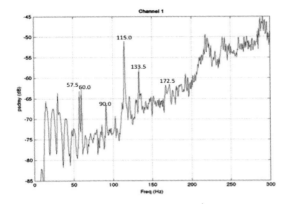

Figure B-4d. Power spectral density taken on channel 1 before CHECK. Source: Track 1 of 7, P-01, ending 5 s before CHECK.

plus an additional harmonic series on channel 1. The fundamental frequency of each series is estimated by averaging the fundamental frequencies found from each harmonic frequency divided by its harmonic number. The result of this process is channel 1 [57.5 Hz, 60.7 Hz, 66.7 Hz] and channel 2 [57.3 Hz, 60.9 Hz]. Inasmuch as the first two frequencies for both channels differ by less than the frequency resolution of the measurement, the best hum frequency estimates are channel 1 [57.4 Hz, 60.8 Hz, 66.7 Hz] and channel 2 [57.4 Hz, 60.8 Hz].

Before the changeover, the channel 2 hum signal frequencies are found to be equal to 60.5 Hz and 64.0 Hz. The power spectra taken before the CHECK event are shown in Figure B-4c.

Before the changeover, the channel 1 hum signal frequencies are found to be equal to 57.5 Hz and 66.7 Hz. The power spectra taken before the CHECK event are shown on Figure B-4d. There is also a frequency at 60 Hz, but it has

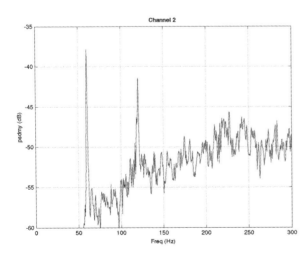

Figure B-5. Power spectral density taken on O'Dell channel 2 after HOLD. Source: O'Dell channel 2 audio file.

no visible harmonics and is therefore considered to be merely a harmonic of the overlying pulse train. Similarly, the 90-Hz signal is considered a harmonic of the same pulse train.

The O'Dell channel 2 file, made from a tape recording of the channel 2 Audograph disc being played on a phonograph machine, is corrected to a time correction factor that matches real time, as shown in Figure B-5, where the sole power-line hum frequency equals 60 Hz. The robust 17-dB signal-to-noise ratio for the fundamental frequency and the robust first harmonic at 120 Hz demonstrate how strongly the channel 2 Audograph data logger imparted its hum signal. *This strong channel 2 harmonic hum signal at 120 Hz is the key evidence that a 60-Hz spectral component is or is not present in the spectra of any channel 2 audio file.*

NOTES

CHAPTER **1.** DEALEY PLAZA

1. When *Six Seconds in Dallas* was published in November 1967, J. Edgar Hoover's FBI queried all field offices for information on Thompson. In response to a telephone call from Washington on November 27, 1967, the New Haven Field Office sent a TELEX to the director describing Thompson's visit to the New Haven Field Office on Wednesday, November 27, 1963. On that occasion, said the TELEX, Thompson had "advised a review of photographs in the then current issue of LIFE magazine which are reportedly made up of film clips from an amateur movie film indicated the President was struck first in the throat by a shot fired from somewhere ahead of the motorcade and not from the warehouse window. A memorandum was written for the file by interviewing agents and no dissemination of information was made" (aarc-fbi407-13_0001_0234; note that additional documents concerning this inquiry can be found at aarc-fbi407-13_0001_0226-0236). The relevant documents, among others, can be reviewed in the Josiah Thompson Collection at the Sixth Floor Museum at Dealey Plaza, Dallas, TX.

2. Professor Gaddis Smith was Larned Professor of History at Yale for over forty years. He chronicled President Brewster's response to Yale Professor Staughton Lynd, Yale Chaplain William Sloane Coffin, and Thompson in an essay entitled "Yale and the Vietnam War." It was presented October 19, 1999, as part of the University Seminar on the History of Columbia University and can be read at https://www.cseas.yale.edu/sites /default/files/files/GSmith_YaleandtheVietnamWar.pdf. It was to become a chapter in his forthcoming book, *Yale and the 20th Century*, to be published by Yale University Press. Although the book was scheduled to be published in 2008, it has not yet appeared.

3. On Sunday, January 9, 1966, the *Philadelphia Bulletin* published photos of the arrest but no article. One photo shows Thompson being arrested, and the other shows him continuing to hand out leaflets from the backseat of a patrol car.

4. These individuals are described in a remarkable book by John Kelin, *Praise from a Future Generation: The Assassination of John F. Kennedy and the First Generation Critics of the Warren Report* (San Antonio, TX: Wings Press, 2007).

5. Trillin's piece, "The Buffs," was published in the *New Yorker* on June 10, 1967.

CHAPTER **2.** LIFE MAGAZINE

1. On January 5, 1968, Don Preston and I met with our attorney, John Kousi, in his offices at 233 Broadway in New York City. John Kousi had been hired to defend

Bernard Geis Associates, Random House, and me from the federal lawsuit brought by Time Incorporated in mid-November 1967. As a means to learning the facts of the case, Kousi quizzed Don Preston and me about the case and my relationship to LIFE, with a court reporter taking down what was said. The total transcript of this session runs to eighty-two pages. This transcript forms the basis for the recounting in these pages of my first meeting with Kern and Billings and our return together to the Time-Life Building. A copy of this transcript (hereafter cited as Kousi transcript) can be found in the files of the Josiah Thompson Collection at the Sixth Floor Museum at Dealey Plaza, Dallas, TX.

2. Kousi transcript, page 25.

3. The Sixth Floor Museum at Dealey Plaza conducted an oral-history interview of Patsy Swank on June 11, 1996. The interview, done by Bob Porter, contains many little-known facts about Swank's early life before she went to work for LIFE. The Swank interview can be found listed under her name in the Index of the Oral History Section of the Sixth Floor Museum at Dealey Plaza, Dallas, TX.

4. On November 27, 1963, the Associated Press reported, "The man who received $25,000 for his color movie films of President John F. Kennedy's assassination gave the entire sum today to the family of Patrolman J. D. Tippit, slain by the man accused as the assassin of the President." This was an untruth that LIFE let stand.

5. On May 26, 1967, after studying X-rays of Connally's chest and wrist together with multiple close-up photos of c.e. 399, Dr. Wecht told me:

> I do not think that it could have been possible for the bullet shown as c.e. 399 to have been a bullet that transversed the bodies of both President Kennedy and Governor Connally. I think that it's something which I could not accept, that this bullet which is not fragmented, not deformed or mutilated, with just a slight defect at the tail could have inflicted this amount of damage. Particularly the damage I'm talking about to the bony structures, the rib and the right radius (just above the junction of the wrist)—I doubt that this bullet could have done it. It just does not seem to fit with any of the cases I've seen of what happens to bullets after they have struck bone.

Dr. Wecht's opinion here is buttressed by the following statement from Dr. Milton Helpern, world-renowned forensic pathologist and Chief Medical Examiner of the City of New York in the 1960s: "This bullet [c.e. 399] wasn't distorted in any way. I cannot accept the premise that this bullet thrashed around in all that bony tissue and lost only 1.4 to 2.4 grains of its original weight. I cannot believe either that this bullet is going to emerge miraculously unscathed, without any deformity, and with its lands and grooves intact." (Marshall Houts, *Where Death Delights* [New York: Coward-McCann, 1967, 62–63]).

CHAPTER 3. WITNESSES: THE BYSTANDERS

1. This chapter and the two that follow comprise not only interviews I conducted while working for LIFE magazine in 1966–1967 but also selected interviews, affidavits, and testimony available from other sources, including the Warren Commission and

the 1978 HSCA. Background material on the witnesses has been gleaned from myriad sources that have surfaced since 1966–1967.

2. Probably the most complete interview of the Newmans was done by Stephen Fagin on July 10, 2003, as part of the Oral History Project of the Sixth Floor Museum at Dealey Plaza, Dallas, TX. It runs to forty-four pages.

3. Fagin interview of the Newmans, 5.

4. WFAA-TV tape of the Newmans' interview on November 22, 1963.

5. *Warren Commission Hearings and Exhibits*, vol. 19, 490 (hereafter cited by volume and page number as, e.g., 19H490).

6. 19H488.

7. Fagin interview of the Newmans, 25.

8. 22H842–843.

9. This and successive citations from my interview of Bill Newman can be found in the nine-page transcript of the taped interview available in the Josiah Thompson Collection at the Sixth Floor Museum at Dealey Plaza, Dallas, TX (hereafter Thompson Collection).

10. WFAA-TV tape of Abraham Zapruder interview, November 22, 1963.

11. This and successive citations from the November 29, 1966, Marilyn Sitzman interview can be found in the eleven-page transcript of that interview in the Thompson Collection.

12. This citation from Emmett Hudson's affidavit, executed on the afternoon of November 22, can be found at 24H213.

13. This FBI interview was carried out by Agents Thompson and Peden on November 26, 1963. Their report can be found on pages 30–31 of CD 5 on the Mary Ferrell Foundation website, https://maryferrell.org/mffweb/archive/viewer/showDoc.do?docId =10406&relPageId=33.

14. 7H558–565.

15. In its report, the HSCA pointed out "how witnesses' memories and testimony" concerning the number, origin, and timing of the shots "may have been substantially influenced by the intervening publicity" *Report of the Select Committee on Assassinations*, US House of Representatives, 95th Cong., 2nd sess., 87 (hereafter HSCA Report). In an extended footnote that ranged over two pages, the committee used Emmett Hudson as a prime example of such a witness whose memories are changed and then confused by later press reports and questioning by government lawyers and agents. The committee pointed out that Hudson "may have been led to alter his first statement by the way he was questioned by counsel . . . and to testify in a fashion consistent with what was then generally known" (HSCA Report, 606). The committee also pointed out that "Hudson's understanding of what happened was influenced by the newspapers after he had given his November statement to the Sheriff's Department" (HSCA Report, 606). The growing confusion shown by Hudson is a familiar change undergone by witnesses whose recollections do not match the initial narrative of the event.

16. Altgens's testimony before the Warren Commission both here and in the following passages can be found at 7H515–525.

17. A transcript of the *CBS News Inquiry: The Warren Report, Part II*, June 26, 1967,

containing the Altgens interview can be found in Stephen White, *Should We Now Believe the Warren Report?* (New York: The MacMillan Company, 1968), 233–256.

CHAPTER **4.** WITNESSES: THE POLICE OFFICERS

1. Jackson went home that Friday night and recorded his memories of the day in his child's school notebook. Much later, Sergeant James Bowles of the Dallas police obtained Jackson's permission to include in his manuscript Jackson's unedited recollections of November 22. Bowles's manuscript was published by Gary Savage in *JFK: First Day Evidence* (Monroe, LA: The Shoppe Press, 1993), and Jackson's recollections as "Officer C" can be found at pages 361–364. Jackson's notes were later published on Dave Rietze's website, where they can be read as the recollections of "Officer C" at http://www.jfk-online com/bowles.html. All citations of Jackson's recollections can be found at either location.

2. Between 1970 and 1973, Douglas Jackson was interviewed over the telephone by a "John Whitney" whose real name was Gil Toft. Toft had been doing research for a book by Fred Newcomb and Perry Adams, *Murder from Within* (1974; repr., Bloomington, IN: Author House, 2011). Tyler Newcomb, Fred Newcomb's son, was kind enough to send me a digital recording of the phone call. Between six minutes, forty seconds and seven minutes, fifteen seconds, the following exchange takes place:

WHITNEY: Were you hit by any spray, by the way?

JACKSON: No. Uh-uh.

WHITNEY: You weren't hit at all?

JACKSON: No. Everything . . . everything that hit him. That's how come they know the shot came from my right rear is because all of the . . . I guess his brains and hair or what have you that came off the top of his head went towards Hargis and B. J. Martin on the left side of that car. And uh . . . the force of the bullet caused it to go that way. I didn't get anything on me until I got to Parkland Hospital. When I got out there, of course, I got some blood on me helping to get him out of the car. But that is the only blood I got on me at all.

In November 1963, Jackson apparently fell through the cracks and was never interviewed by the Dallas police, FBI or Warren Commission staff.

This was remedied on September 17, 1975, when he was interviewed by the FBI. Jackson stated, "He looked toward the Presidential vehicle and at the same time heard a third shot fired. He observed President Kennedy struck in the head above his right ear and the impact of the bullet exploded the top portion of his head, toward the left side of the Presidential vehicle." HSCA admin. folder 18, JFK Motorcycle Officers' Interviews, 14, Mary Ferrell Foundation website, http://www.maryferrell.org/mff-web/archive/viewer/showDoc.do;jsessionid=5152DCEEAAD998FA54BF5DB4681E-8DE0?docId=9965&relPageId=14

Murder from Within states that "James M. Chaney, on the right, stated that all four [motorcycle officers] were hit with the 'spray'" (60). This statement appears in a footnote to a taped interview of Chaney, carried out once again by Gil Toft ("John

Whitney") in the early 1970s. Tyler Newcomb was kind enough to send me a digital recording of this interview with Chaney. Nowhere in the interview does Chaney say that either he or other motorcycle officers were hit with a "spray" or any sort of debris from Kennedy's head wound.

3. This interview of Officer James Chaney by Lord (and Lord's later statement in his studio) can be viewed at https://www.youtube.com/watch?v=nYdB3e6yQ9E.

4. My good friend Gary Mack, original curator of the Sixth Floor Museum at Dealey Plaza and now sadly deceased, was kind enough to make available to me these outtakes from footage taken by KRLD-TV and WBAP-TV.

5. *Warren Commission Hearings and Exhibits*, vol. 25, 284 (hereafter cited by volume and page number as, e.g., 25H284).

6. HSCA admin. folder 18, JFK Motorcycle Officers' Interviews, 10–12, Mary Ferrell Foundation website, http://www.maryferrell.org/showDoc.html?docId=9965.

7. JFK Motorcycle Officers' Interviews, 26.

8. Interview of Hargis in the *New York Sunday News* carried out on November 23, 1963 and published on November 24, 1963, 1.

9. Hargis's testimony before the Warren Commission is found at 6H293–296.

10. Joe Patoki, "The Witnesses," *Texas Monthly*, November 1988, http://www.texas monthly.com/content/witnesses.

11. Martin's testimony before the Warren Commission is found at 6H289–293.

12. Ronnie Dugger, *Texas Observer*, December 13, 1963.

13. Commission Document 205—FBI Report of 23 December 1963 re Oswald, 39, Mary Ferrell Foundation website, https://www.maryferrell.org/showDoc.html ?docId=10672#relPageId=42.

14. Commission Document 205. Note that Officer Smith said "he did smell what he thought was gunpowder but stated this smell was in the parking lot by the TSBD building not by the underpass." Since at the time a mild wind—between 10 and 15 mph—was blowing in Dealey Plaza from Southwest, gunsmoke from the corner of the stockade fence would have drifted into the TSBD parking lot by the time Smith got there.

15. Joe Marshall Smith's testimony before the Warren Commission is found at 7H531–539.

16. Anthony Summers, *Conspiracy* (New York: McGraw-Hill Book Company, 1980), 81. The HSCA tried to get to the bottom of whether Smith had encountered a real Secret Service agent or perhaps another federal agent. FBI Agent James Hosty reported that Bureau of Alcohol, Tobacco, and Firearms Agent Frank Ellsworth had told him he had been in the knoll area just after the shooting. However, when Ellsworth was deposed by the committee, he denied Hosty's report. All Secret Service agents in the motorcade submitted reports indicating they had followed Secret Service procedure and stayed with the motorcade (18H722–802). One of the agents, Thomas "Lem" Johns, was spotted running on the knoll by a press photographer, Dave Weigman. According to Weigman, he saw a policeman getting off his motorcycle and running up the grass slope. In all likelihood, this was Hargis. Weigman told Richard Trask, "I figured he knows something's up there, so I ran up there. I found myself there with Lem close by, a few feet away. Then I saw the people lying on the side and I saw nothing up there.

Lem was sort of looking around." Richard Trask, *Pictures of the Pain* (Danvers, MA: Yeoman Press, 1994), 372–373. Weigman's movie camera was running during this time, and Lem Johns does not appear in the film. For his part, Johns told of jumping out of the vice-presidential follow-up car and just missing getting into the Vice-presidential car. "I jumped from the security car," wrote Johns in his report on November 22, "and started running for the Vice-President's car. . . . Before I reached the Vice-President's car, a third shot had sounded and the entire motorcade then picked up speed and I was left on the street at this point. I obtained a ride with White House movie men and joined the Vice President and ASAIC Youngblood at the Parkland Hospital" (18H774).

CHAPTER 5. WITNESSES: THE RAILROAD MEN

1. This and other material about Bowers was gleaned from the transcript of his film session with Mark Lane and Emile de Antonio during the preparation of *Rush to Judgment* in 1966. The transcript is preserved among the papers of Emile de Antonio (1919–1989) at the Archives of the Wisconsin Historical Society, Madison, WI. For information about work schedules and the daily routine of tower operators, see the interview of Gene Veal, July 12, 2001, 34, Oral History Section of the Sixth Floor Museum at Dealey Plaza, Dallas, TX. During a second Sixth Floor Museum oral history interview (this time jointly with Utah Rogers) on August 30, 2001, Veal offered this appraisal of fellow tower operator Bowers:

> Well, of course, I knew him [Lee Bowers] several years, but the man was really kind of a recluse as far as I'm concerned. He was a nice guy. I mean, I liked him and we communicated some, but he was strictly a man who was to himself. He didn't talk a whole lot. . . . Yeah, he seemed to be a real straightforward-type person. Mainly, like I said, I didn't know him personally outside of just the work, and I relieved him many times from work, but he was a straightforward kind of guy, knowing that . . . you know, he was. He told me he was a Christian . . . things like that. And as far as I knew, he was. I think he told me one time that he was a lay preacher or an assistant preacher of some church. I don't know which one. He said he was a Christian, so I don't know. I'll just have to take his word for it. I never socialized with him. (19)

2. Interview of Barney Mozley, April 19, 2002, 18–19, Oral History Section of the Sixth Floor Museum.

3. *Warren Commission Hearings and Exhibits*, vol. 24, 10 (hereafter cited by volume and page number as, e.g., 24H10).

4. Lee Bowers's testimony before the Warren Commission can be found at 6H284–289.

5. Bowers's quotations from the film can be found in the transcript of his film session with Mark Lane and Emile de Antonio.

6. In many different aspects of the assassination, Dave Perry brings the refreshing sensibility of a real investigator to answering outstanding questions. Perry's treatment of the various fantasies focusing on Lee Bowers after his death, including attempts to come up with apocryphal stories and the eagerness of TV producers to publicize

them, and specifically Perry's upending of the attempt to turn Bowers's death in a single-car auto accident into a mystery, makes Perry's work on Lee Bowers a kind of assassination classic. Under the title "Now It Can Be Told—the Lee Bowers Story," it can be found on his website at http://dperry1943.com/bowers.html.

7. The cited remarks can be found in the interview of Olan DeGaugh, February 29, 2002, 4–7, Oral History Section of the Sixth Floor Museum. DeGaugh later ended up owning the parking lot adjacent to the depository, the parking lot where Lee Bowers saw the cars circling on November 22.

8. These cited remarks can be found in the interview of Mozley, 7, 12, and 14.

9. In his November 22 sheriff's affidavit, Holland said he heard a shot and "looked over toward the arcade and trees and saw a puff of smoke come from the trees and I heard three more shots after the first shot but that was the only puff of smoke I saw" (19H480). Two days later, on November 24, Holland told two FBI agents that "simultaneously with the first shot, he stated he heard either three or four more shots fired together" (Commission Document 5, 49–50, http://www.maryferrell.org/mffweb /archive/viewer/showDoc.do?docId=10406&relPageId=52). In the spring of 1966, Holland was interviewed on film by Mark Lane and Emile de Antonio. Lane's question stimulated this exchange:

QUESTION: And did you hear any shots on November 22nd?
HOLLAND: I did.
QUESTION: How many shots?
HOLLAND: Four.
QUESTION: Is there any question in your mind that you heard four?
HOLLAND: No. No question in my mind.
QUESTION: You're certain it was four.
HOLLAND: I'm certain they were four. It is possible they could have been five, but I am certain of four because I'm familiar with firearms. I own rifles, shotguns, pistols. I've hunted all my life, and I'm familiar enough with guns to count the reports.

The transcript of this interview with Holland is preserved among the papers of Emile De Antonio (1919–1989) at the Archives of the Wisconsin Historical Society, Madison, WI.

10. Stern's examination of Holland can be found at 6H239–248.

11. Holland told us this during the first fifteen minutes of his interview. See the seventy-one-page Holland transcript, 5–7. I gave this and other transcripts to the Assassination Archives and Research Center, Washington, DC, in February 1986. I rediscovered the Holland transcript during a visit to Washington in June 2011 and was astonished by its length. It shows that after an initial period of wariness, Holland relaxed and talked without self-consciousness. He showed us photos of the three children he had adopted, one of whom had died at an early age (9). Kern ended up sitting on the floor of the living room, and Holland took off his shoes (11). This (hereafter cited as Holland transcript) and other transcripts can be found in the Josiah Thompson Collection at the Sixth Floor Museum.

12. See Holland transcript, 1–3.

13. In an FBI interview on March 19, 1964, "Simmons said he thought he saw exhaust fumes of smoke near the embankment in front of the Texas School Book Depository Building. Simmons then ran toward the Texas School Book Depository Building with a policeman. He stopped at a fence near the Memorial Arches and could not find anyone" (22H833). This description in the agent's words of what Simmons saw leaves much to be desired. Simmons clarified it years later when he testified under oath before the Clay Shaw jury in New Orleans in February 1969:

> QUESTION: Now at the time you heard the second and third shot did you notice anything unusual in the area of the grassy knoll?
> SIMMONS: Well, after I heard the shots I looked to see if I could see where they were coming from and underneath the trees up on the grassy knoll by the fence I detected what appeared to be a puff of smoke or wisp of smoke.
> QUESTION: From which direction did these noises appear to come from?
> SIMMONS: In front and to the left.
> QUESTION: Were—will you step down and point out on the aerial photograph the location in which you heard the shots coming from and the area in which you saw the puff of smoke?
> SIMMONS: I was facing this way and the sound appeared to come from this general direction over along here, and there is a row of trees along the fence and towards the end of the fence there is a small building and just this side of it a few feet is where I saw the smoke. (State of Louisiana vs. Clay L. Shaw 198-059, testimony of James L. Simmons, February 15, 1969, 8–9)

Standing next to Holland on the overpass, railroad worker Richard Dodd saw the same thing as Holland and Simmons:

> We all three—four—seen about the same thing as the shots. The smoke came from behind the hedge on—uh—north side of the Plaza. And a motorcycle policeman dropped his motorcycle in the street, with his gun in his hand and run up the embankment to the hedge. And then I went north to look around the corner to see if there was anyone behind the hedge, and met special agent of the Katy Railroad and he went down there and I walked along with him to see if there were any tracks there, and there were tracks and cigarette butts layin' where someone had been standin' on the bumper lookin' over the fence or something. (Transcript of Dodd's film session with Mark Lane and Emile de Antonio during the preparation of Rush to Judgment in March 1966, 2–3)

Also on the overpass with Holland, Simmons, and Dodd was Austin Miller. In an affidavit executed that afternoon, he said, "I saw something which I thought was smoke or steam coming from a group of trees north of Elm off the railroad tracks" (24H217).

Clemon Johnson also reported that "white smoke was observed near the pavilion" but said "he felt that this smoke came from a motorcycle abandoned near the spot by a Dallas policeman" (22H836). The Hughes, Bell, and Willis photos show that the motorcycle in question was abandoned on Elm Street at least twenty-five yards from where the smoke was seen.

Nolan Potter told the FBI that at the time of the shooting, "he recalls seeing smoke in front of the Texas School Book Depository Building rising above the trees" (22H834). From Potter's location on the overpass, the trees near the corner of the fence on the knoll would have appeared "in front of the Texas School Book Depository Building."

Two additional railroad workers—Thomas Murphy and Walter Winborn—were standing on the overpass and told Stewart Galanor in 1966 that they had seen smoke in the trees along the knoll:

GALANOR: Could you tell me where you thought the shots came from?
MURPHY: Yeah, they come from a tree to the left, of my left, which is to the immediate right of the site of the assassination.
GALANOR: That would be on that grassy hill up there.
MURPHY: Yeah, on the hill up there. There are two or three hackberry and elm trees. And I saw it come from there.
GALANOR: Well, was there anything that led you to believe that the shots came from there?
MURPHY: Yeah, smoke.
GALANOR: You saw smoke?
MURPHY: Sure did.
GALANOR: Could you tell me exactly where you saw the smoke?
MURPHY: Yeah, in that tree. (Stewart Galanor, *Cover-Up* [New York: Kestrel Books, 1998], 59)

Walter Winborn told Galanor that he saw "smoke that come out from under the trees on the right hand side of the motorcade." However, the FBI agents who earlier interviewed Winborn for the Warren Commission failed to mention this in their report. Galanor asked Walter Winborn about this omission:

GALANOR: Did you tell them about that, that you saw smoke on the grassy knoll?
WINBORN: Oh yes. Oh yes.
GALANOR: They didn't include it in their report.
WINBORN: Well.
GALANOR: Do you have any idea why they didn't?
WINBORN: I don't have any idea. They are specialists in their field, and I'm just an amateur. (Galanor, 60)

In all, it would appear that eight railroad workers observed a puff of smoke under the trees on the knoll near the corner of the fence.

14. Sheriff's Deputy L. C. Smith was standing in front of the sheriff's office on Main Street. Hearing gunshots, he ran to the plaza. There he "heard a woman say the President was shot in the head and the shots came from the fence on the north side of Elm." He went at once "behind the fence and searched also in the parking area" (19H516).

Deputy A. D. McCurley was also standing in front of the sheriff's office when the motorcade passed. Like Smith, on hearing the shots, he ran to the plaza. He "saw people running towards the railroad yards beyond Elm Street and I ran over and jumped a fence and a railroad worker stated to me that he believed the smoke from the bullets came from the stockade fence that surrounds the park area. A search was made of this vicinity and then information came to us that the shots came from the Texas School Book Depository" (19H514).

Deputy J. L. Oxford was standing with Deputy McCurley in front of the sheriff's office as the motorcade passed:

> We heard what I thought to be shots. Officer McCurley and myself ran across Houston Street on across Elm and down to the underpass. When we got there, everyone was looking towards the railroad yards. We jumped the picket fence which runs along Elm Street and on over into the railroad yards. When we got over there, there was a man who told us that he had seen smoke up in the corner of the fence. We went up to the corner of the fence to see what we could find, and searched the area thoroughly. (19H530)

15. Holland transcript, 13. Twelve years after our interview of Holland, the HSCA would consider whether the sightings of smoke by Holland and his coworkers was plausible. A section of *Report of the Select Committee on Assassinations*, US House of Representatives, 95th Cong., 2nd sess., vol. 12, 23–25 titled "Accounts of Smoke in Dealey Plaza at the Time of the Shots" is dedicated to a discussion of the smoke seen by Holland and his coworkers. Citing the opinion of Monty Lutz of the Wisconsin Crime Laboratories, the committee concluded that "smokeless powder" is not smokeless and that it would have been "possible for witnesses to have seen smoke if a gun had fired from that area":

> Based on the statements of these witnesses, if the smoke they reported was in fact the result of gunfire, it would have originated in the area of the top of the grassy knoll. There is no way of determining what type of ammunition was used in that "gunfire" so that it can be stated conclusively whether the smoke seen by the witnesses is consistent with smoke produced by the type of ammunition used in any gunfire from the knoll. Nevertheless, a firearms expert engaged by the committee explained that irrespective of the exact type of ammunition used, it would be possible for witnesses to have seen smoke if a gun had been fired from that area. According to the expert [Lutz], both "smokeless" and smoke-producing ammunition may leave a trace of smoke that would be visible to the eye in sunlight. That is because even with smokeless ammunition, when the weapon is fired, nitrocellulose bases in the powder which are impregnated with nitroglycerin may give off smoke, albeit less smoke than black or smoke-producing ammunition. In addition, residue remaining in the weapon from previous firings as well as cleaning solution which might have been used on the weapon, could cause even more smoke to be discharged in subsequent firings of the weapon.

16. Holland transcript, 23–25.

17. Holland transcript, 23–25.

18. Holland transcript, 40–41.

19. Holland transcript, 41.

20. Holland transcript, 45.

21. A fourth man, called "Mr. Cox" by Holland, heard the shot, saw the smoke, and ran with Holland, Simmons, and Dodd into the area behind the fence. "Mr. Dodd was a short fellow. He ducked under the pipe," said Holland. "Mr. Simmons is quite a large man. He jumped over the pipe and Mr. Cox jumped over right behind him, which hit Mr. Simmons on the heels and Mr. Simmons almost tripped up. He had to run about fifteen feet before he could get his balance. And we three was the first people to come around to this exact spot. Mr. Cox showed up in . . . oh about fifteen or twenty seconds, I'd say" (Holland transcript, 31, 64). Holland told us that Cox died in August 1966. I can find no mention of Cox ever being interviewed by the authorities.

22. Holland transcript, 61; see also 66.

23. 7H107.

24. In 1966 and 1967, I took extreme pains to obtain the best copy available of the Moorman Polaroid photo. I paid Mary Moorman to publish her photo, and she agreed to have her photo copied in Dallas by a professional photographer. He used a medium-format negative for the copying process that was approximately the same size as the Moorman Polaroid. I have had that negative scanned commercially at a very high resolution. This is extremely important since the Moorman Polaroid has decayed significantly since that date.

In addition, in 1967 Don Preston, my editor, obtained an eight-by-ten-inch copy of the Moorman photo used in the production of the book *Four Days in November*. This particular print shows remarkable resolution and has also been used as the basis for some of the images in this book. All in all, the resources used to produce Moorman images for this book are probably superior to any others that have survived. Many published images of this iconic photograph are seriously degraded in quality and resolution.

25. Holland offered this suggestion as to how the shooter made his escape on two occasions—first at his home on November 16 and then in Dealey Plaza when I asked him about it again on November 20. Since no tape recorder was running on the second occasion, the citation comes from his earlier remarks at his home. In substance, they were the same. See Holland transcript, 42.

CHAPTER 6. "A MATTER OF REASONABLE DOUBT"

1. Supplemented by my notes and memories, this chapter is based upon the eighty-two-page transcript of an examination of Don Preston and me by our attorney, John Kousi. The purpose of the examination was to learn as much as possible about my relationship with LIFE magazine in order to defend us against the lawsuit brought against Random House, BGA, and me by Time Inc. in November 1967. The session was held at Kousi's law firm office at 233 Broadway in New York on January 5, 1968. It took up much of the day. A copy of the transcript, titled "Taped Interview with Josiah

Thompson" (hereafter cited as Kousi transcript), is held in the Josiah Thompson Collection at the Sixth Floor Museum at Dealey Plaza in Dallas, TX.

2. *Warren Commission Hearings and Exhibits*, vol. 4, 128.

3. The text of this note as well as ancillary details can be found in the Kousi transcript, 66.

4. Contract between Josiah Thompson and LIFE magazine, signed November 23, 1966, by Richard Billings, associate editor. A copy of this contract can be found in the Josiah Thompson Collection at the Sixth Floor Museum.

CHAPTER 7. PUZZLING THE PIECES

1. This operation is described in great detail in Josiah Thompson, *Six Seconds in Dallas* (New York: Bernard Geis Associates, 1967), 89–95 and 272–276.

2. This evidence is discussed in greater detail in Thompson, 51–58.

3. The evidence surrounding this back wound is discussed in greater detail in Thompson, 146–170. The referenced and relevant Sibert and O'Neill FBI report is reproduced photographically in Thompson, 296–298.

4. Citing governmental sources, *Newsweek* (12/30/63), TIME (12/27/63), and the *Washington Post* (12/18/63) all carried stories asserting that the autopsy contained evidence that a fragment from the head shot had been deflected downward to cause the hole in the throat. The *Journal of the American Medical Association* (1/4/64) reported that "a small fragment of this bullet [the head shot] angled down and passed out through Kennedy's throat."

5. Brennan heard a crack and looked up at the depository from his position across the street. He saw "this man that I saw previous aiming for his last shot" (*Warren Commission Hearings and Exhibits*, vol. 3, 143; hereafter cited by volume and page number as, e.g., 3H143). But Brennan is clear only about hearing the first and the last shot. "The first shot and the last shot is my only positive recollection of two shots," he continued. "The first shot was positive and clear and the last shot was positive and clear, with no echo on my part" (3H154). Brennan says much the same thing in his November 22, 1963, FBI interview:

> He heard a loud report which he first thought to be the "backfire" of an automobile. He said he does not distinctly remember a second shot but he remembers "more than one noise," as if someone was shooting firecrackers, and consequently he believes there must have been a second shot before he looked in the direction of the Texas School Book Depository Building. . . . He was positive that after he observed this man in the window, he saw this person take "deliberate aim" and fire a shot. . . . He said the rifle was pointed in the direction of the President's car when he saw it fired. (Commission Document 5, 12–13, Mary Ferrell Foundation website, https://www.maryferrell.org/mffweb/archive/viewer/showDoc.do?docId=10406&relPageId=16)

The first sound drew Brennan's attention to the depository across the street. He looked up to the sixth floor window, saw the gunman take "deliberate aim," and actually saw the gun fire. In between, he remembered some additional noise, "as if someone was shooting firecrackers."

Brennan's observations match the testimony of witnesses who were deep in the depository (either at work or in hallways) during the shooting and who reported hearing fewer than three shots. Doris Burns, for example, was in a corridor on the third floor when the shooting happened. She "heard one loud noise which sounded like a shot" (22H637). At the same time, Jack Dougherty had gone back to work on the fifth floor when he "heard a shot" (24H206). See also the FBI interview of Mrs. Alvin Hopson (24H521).

6. Dillard testified before Warren Commission Counsel Joseph Ball on April 1, 1964:

MR. BALL: Did you hear anyone in your car say anything?
MR. DILLARD: Well, after the third shot I know my comment was, "They killed him." I don't know why I said that but Jackson—there was some running comment about what can we do or where is it coming from and we were all looking. We had an absolutely perfect view of the School Depository from our position in an open car, and Bob Jackson said, "There's a rifle barrel up there." I said, "Where?" I had my camera ready. He said, "It's in that open window." Of course, there were several open windows and I scanned the building.
MR. BALL: Which building?
MR. DILLARD: The School Book Depository. And at the same time I brought my camera up and I was looking for the window. Now this was after the third shot and Jackson said, "There's the rifle barrel up there." And then he said it was the second from the top in the right hand side, and I swung it and there was two figures below, and I just shot with one camera, 100-mm. Lens on a 35-mm camera which is approximately a two times daily photo twice normal lens and a wide angle on a 35-mm. Which took in a considerable portion of the building and I shot those pictures in rapid sequence with the two cameras. (6H164)

7. 24H229.
8. 3H175.
9. 3H175.
10. This evidence is discussed in Thompson, Six Seconds in Dallas, 141–146.
11. Nicol testified before the commission on the afternoon of April 1, 1964:

And it was on the basis of the match of these patterns that I would conclude that this cartridge had been introduced into a chamber at least three times prior to its final firing. So that this would represent, you might say, a practice or dry-run loading the gun and unloading it for the purpose of either determining its—how it functions, or whether it was in proper function, or just for practice. (3H509)

12. 3H509–510.

13. 26H449–450, Commission Exhibit 2968. Hoover's letter to General Counsel J. Lee Rankin was dated June 2, 1964.

14. 3H510.

CHAPTER 8. SIX SECONDS IN DALLAS

1. The correspondence between Dick Pollard and John Dowd of LIFE and Doug Hamilton and me is filed in the Josiah Thompson Collection of the Sixth Floor Museum at Dealey Plaza in Dallas, TX.

2. That is, except the Federal Bureau of Investigation. In advance of the publication of *Six Seconds*, the FBI swung into high gear. A memo dated November 15 to Deputy Director Cartha DeLoach reveals that a United Press International (UPI) wire story on the imminent publication of the *Saturday Evening Post* article set off an investigation of me. The memo summarized the UPI wire story and gave a brief sketch of my background and anti–Vietnam War activities. The next day, a *Washington Post* article was circulated, which drew Director Hoover's attention. He wrote on the article the following:

Send memo to White House on completed background of Thompson.
H [Hoover]

Two days later, an expanded background account was forwarded to the White House. This expanded account cited my arrest at the Pentagon and an earlier turn-in of my Selective Service card (along with 350 others) to a representative of the attorney general a few days before the Pentagon arrest. This memo cited the inaccurate report of an agent concerning what I had purportedly said at an antiwar "speak out" and then stated, "While Josiah Thompson has never been identified as a member of a subversive group, several of these demonstrations [that Thompson attended] were cosponsored by such groups as the W.E.B. Dubois Clubs of America, a Communist oriented youth group, and the Young Socialist Alliance, the youth affiliate of the Socialist Workers Party."

On November 22, an additional memo stated that the bureau had obtained advance copies of both the *Saturday Evening Post* article and the book itself. It cautioned that "only one copy of the book has been received, and to have a complete analysis of the book, it will have to be handled by the Laboratory Division, the General Investigative Division, and possibly the Domestic Intelligence Division."

That "complete analysis of the book" was contained in a December 7 nine-page memo titled "Book Review of *Six Seconds in Dallas* by Josiah Thompson." Like all earlier memos, it was addressed to Deputy Director DeLoach. At this time, DeLoach was the third-ranking FBI official. He was also part of Hoover's inner circle and was considered Hoover's heir apparent. When Lyndon Johnson became president, he asked that Deputy Director DeLoach be made the liaison between the FBI and the White House. DeLoach was deeply involved in the Domestic Intelligence Division, which had responsibility for the surveillance of "subversive" groups.

The documents referred to in the paragraphs above can be found in the Josiah Thompson Collection of the Sixth Floor Museum.

3. All the quotations in this and the following paragraph are taken from Kelin, *Praise*

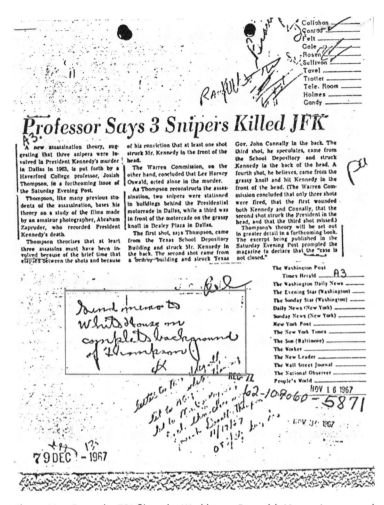

Figure N-1. From the FBI files, the *Washington Post* with Hoover's note and initial in black line bordered rectangle.

from a Future Generation: The Assassination of John F. Kennedy and the First Generation Critics of the Warren Report (San Antonio, TX: Wings Press, 2007), 431–434. I had never bothered to keep the correspondence between Vince Salandria and me dating from this time. Therefore, I was delighted to find it cited in Kelin's book as well as correspondence from Sylvia Meagher and M. S. Arnoni. Kelin's treatment of me in these pages is a model of fairness, a remarkable achievement in light of Kelin's friendship with Salandria. He and Salandria collaborated in publishing an anthology of Salandria's assassination writings in a book titled *False Mystery: Essays on the Assassination of President Kennedy.* Salandria shipped off his complete files of assassination correspondence to Kelin, and Kelin used these files as an unparalleled resource in writing his book.

4. M. S. Arnoni to Ray Marcus, December 18, 1967, quoted in Kelin, 433.

5. Sylvia Meagher to Ray Marcus, January 11, 1968, quoted in Kelin, 433. Rejection of his ideas by Sylvia Meagher and M. S. Arnoni had little effect on Vince Salandria's "mole hunt." Ten months later, on November 17, 1968, he wrote Sylvia a fawning letter complimenting her as "eloquent, brilliant, consistent, honest, brave, stubborn, self-less, tough" and ending the letter with the phrase "and I love you" (quoted in Kelin, 440). Sylvia remained adamant and did not reply. Salandria followed up with a second letter on December 14, 1968, in which he claimed that another individual who had worked with both of them two years previously had been a government agent. He looked forward to a meeting where "I will tell you what I learned and show you some supporting documents on this ugly subject" (quoted in Kelin, 440). This annoyed Sylvia sufficiently that she replied on December 17, 1968, "[Edward] Epstein, [Josiah] Thompson, Jacob Cohen, William Gurvich . . . not unnaturally, then, the cry 'wolf' may not raise any hackles even if a real one is finally in the chicken coop" (quoted in Kelin, 440–441).

6. Judge Wyatt's summary judgment ruling can be found at 293 F. Supp. 130, S.D.N.Y. 1968.

CHAPTER 9. SHOOTING MELONS . . . AND COCONUTS, PINEAPPLES, AND WATER JUGS . . .

1. *The Magnet* 11, no. 7 (July 1967), published for the employees and families of Lawrence Radiation Laboratory, University of California, Berkeley.

2. On four sequential nights in late June 1967, CBS News broadcast hourlong programs devoted to the Warren Report and its critics. Luis Alvarez appeared in the very first of the four programs. A year later, a book presenting the conclusions of the broadcasts was published by MacMillan with an introduction penned by Walter Cronkite. The book was written by Stephen White and given the title *Should We Now Believe the Warren Report?* (New York: The Macmillan Company, 1968). Its last hundred pages contain transcripts of the various broadcasts, and Alvarez's words can be found at page 228.

3. Reproduced here is the handwritten chart that Alvarez sent Menaker and Menaker sent to me. When seven years later Alvarez published his article in the *American Journal of Physics*, he reproduced the chart but somewhat changed the labeling. See Luis W. Alvarez, "A Physicist Examines the Kennedy Assassination Film," *American Journal of Physics* 44, no. 9 (September 1976): 816.

4. See *Warren Commission Hearings and Exhibits*, vol. 18, 731–732 (hereafter cited by volume and page number as, e.g., 18H731–732). Kinney was driving the follow-up car and hence controlled its siren:

> I glanced from the taillight of SS-100-X, at the President and it appeared that he had been shot because he slumped to the left. Immediately he sat up again. At this time the second shot was fired and I observed hair flying from the right side of his head. With this, simultaneously with the President's car, we stepped on the gas. I released the siren at that time. I did hear three shots but do not recall which shots were those that hit the President.

Eight days later he signed an additional statement that said, "Agent Clint Hill jumped from the follow-up car and dashed to the aid of the President and the First Lady in the President's car. I saw one shot strike the President in the right side of the head. The President then fell to the left toward Mrs. Kennedy. At this time I stepped on the siren and the gas pedal at the same time."

5. Letter of Josiah Thompson to Dr. Luis Alvarez, January 1, 1969 (misdated January 1, 1968). This letter and the additional correspondence can be found in the Josiah Thompson Collection at the Sixth Floor Museum at Dealey Plaza in Dallas, TX.

6. Thompson to Alvarez, January 1, 1969.

7. Letter of Paul Hoch to Josiah Thompson, February 2, 1969.

8. Letter of Josiah Thompson to Luis Alvarez, February 5, 1969.

9. Letter of Luis Alvarez to Josiah Thompson, February 14, 1969.

10. At the time, Alvarez clearly recognized that his theory had problems. On the morning of February 19, 1969, he was awakened by a call from Clay Shaw's attorneys in New Orleans. They asked for copies of his correspondence with CBS, and he declined to provide it. A "Memorandum to File" by Paul Hoch from that day said, "He mentioned that he had told them about Thompson's interpretation of his data (i.e. as indicating 4 shots) and apparently raised the possibility that, if he were to testify, Thompson would testify against him (or at least a counter-argument could be made. Luis, of course, believes he is right.)"

11. See chart at 6HSCA30. This chart is reproduced in Chapter 12 as Table 12-1.

12. The description of Alvarez's career that follows is drawn from his autobiography, *Alvarez: Adventures of a Physicist* (New York: Basic Books, 1987).

13. Extremely revealing is Alvarez's account of this testimony in his autobiography. He writes that in April 1954, he was working for Ernest Lawrence at the Berkeley Radiation Laboratory. Lawrence had informed the government that Lawrence, Alvarez, and others from the laboratory would all appear at the hearing when summoned. A subpoena came to Alvarez, and shortly thereafter a phone call from Lawrence, who had been Alvarez's longtime mentor. Lawrence "announced emotionally that he wouldn't testify and that I shouldn't either." Lawrence said that the radiation laboratory "would be greatly harmed if he testified and that he, Ken Pitzer, Wendell Latimer and I were viewed as a cabal bent on destroying Robert."

Alvarez immediately canceled his plane reservation and informed a government lawyer that he wouldn't be coming. That evening, Lewis Strauss, chairman of the Atomic Energy Commission, called Alvarez at home and urged him to testify. Alvarez said that he "worked for Ernest . . . and he had ordered me not to testify." Strauss insisted, wrote Alvarez:

> I had a duty to serve my country, Lewis countered. I said I had served my country during the war. Lewis' emotional intensity increased as he ran out of arguments. As a parting shot, he prophesied that if I didn't come to Washington the next day, I wouldn't be able to look myself in the mirror for the rest of my life. I had never disobeyed Ernest's direct orders, I said, and I wasn't about to start now. (Alvarez, *Alvarez*, 180)

Alvarez said that later that night, "I poured myself a stiff drink, booked a seat on the TWA midnight red-eye flight, and sent Lewis a telegram" that he was coming to testify.

14. Information in this paragraph was drawn from W. Peter Trower, *Luis Walter Alvarez, 1911–1988* (Washington, DC: National Academy of Science, 2009), 14.

15. Alvarez recounts this in "Alvarez, "A Physicist Examines the Kennedy Assassination Film," 819.

16. See Charles G. Wohl, "Scientist as Detective: Luis Alvarez and the Pyramid Burial Chambers, the JFK Assassination and the End of the Dinosaurs," *American Journal of Physics* 75, no. 11 (November 2007): 968–977. Although Wohl had no knowledge that the experimental evidence had been cherry-picked by Alvarez, he caught the informal nature of the firing tests in this description: "Pushed to somehow demonstrate the effect experimentally, Luis got a few friends together, they wrapped seven cantaloupes in filament tape to add, like a skull, some tensile strength, and they shot them with a hunting rifle" (973).

17. All the material concerning the three firing tests—the notes of Buckingham and Hoch as well as the photographs taken by Hoch during the later two tests—were graciously made available to me by Paul Hoch. He also made available his own correspondence with both Alvarez and others from that time. It is this material that provides a sharply defined account of tests that have been controversial for over forty years. Photographs and notes of the test as well as correspondence between Hoch, Thompson, and Alvarez can be found in the files of the Josiah Thompson Collection at the Sixth Floor Museum.

18. See Hoch's undated notes headed, "APPENDIX 2—THEY SHOOT MELONS DON'T THEY?," Josiah Thompson Collection at the Sixth Floor Museum.

19. On October 10, 1969, Hoch wrote a page of notes for a potential test of Alvarez's hypothesis to be published in the house organ of the Lawrence Radiation Laboratory, *The Magnet*. Hoch had talked to Judy Goldhaber of *The Magnet*, and they had agreed that the tests should be done independently and Goldhaber informed only after they were completed. Hoch specified the target as follows: "From Buck's tests [on June 29, 1969] the target should be a small melon (6"–8", 4–7 lbs.), taped with (e.g.) 2 inch glass filament tape." Of great interest is Hoch's alert suggestion of how the test should be carried out to avoid a bogus result: "To avoid complications due to possible bouncing of the target off the ground, I would suggest either or both of the following set-ups: (a) target resting on a flat surface, being shot at from the same level or below; (b) target suspended from a string." A few years later, John Lattimer, MD, ignored Hoch's suggestion and produced the exact "complications" Hoch had in mind. Consequently, Lattimer's firing tests turned out to be fatally flawed.

20. Letter of Paul Hoch to Luis Alvarez, October 21, 1970.

21. What is puzzling is why Buckingham "hot loaded" his cartridges by hand to increase their standard 2,800-feet-per-second muzzle velocity by 200 feet per second and made them more unlike the bullet that struck President Kennedy.

22. 1HSCA404. The Edgewood Arsenal results were replicated in firing experiments carried out by John M. Nichols, professor of pathology at the University of Kansas, in 1978. As a board-certified forensic pathologist, he had performed more than

one thousand autopsies during his career. He became interested in the Kennedy assas-sination in the late 1960s and performed a number of shooting experiments with a rifle similar to Oswald's Mannlicher-Carcano and ammunition from lot number 6003. In one experiment, he fired a bullet through forty-seven inches of ponderosa pine. In another, he fired through twenty-five inches of elm and produced a bullet resembling CE 399. For photos of both, see John K. Lattimer, *Kennedy and Lincoln: Medical and Ballis-tic Comparisons of Their Assassinations* (New York: Harcourt Brace Jovanovich, 1980), 272.

Nichols died before he had time to write up his most interesting shooting experi-ment. Using a rifle identical to Oswald's with the same ammunition used on Novem-ber 22, he fired at both melon targets and cadaver skulls. The skulls were suspended in slings, while the melons were either sling-suspended or placed on a stand. The results were unambiguous: (1) All target movement was in the direction of the bullet flight path. (2) There was no evidence of backward movement from the "jet effect." (3) All sling-suspended targets moved forward. (4) Movement of all cadaver specimens was away from the gun.

23. In efforts to replicate Alvarez's results, other tests using a 6.5-mm Mannli-cher-Carcano and appropriate ammunition were carried out by Doug DeSalles, MD, and Dick Hobbs in 1994 and by Art Snyder, PhD, and Margaret Snyder in 1996. DeSalles and Hobbes shot eleven tape-wrapped melons with jacketed ammunition and observed no jet-effect movement. The two Snyders used both jacketed and soft-nosed hunting ammunition to shoot melons with a 6.5-mm Mannlicher-Carcano and a 30.06 hunting rifle. They observed the same effect as did DeSalles and Hobbs: hunt-ing bullets produced a jet effect, and jacketed bullets did not (Arthur and Margaret Snyder, "Case Still Open," *Skeptic* 6, no. 4 (1998), 54).

24. Why wait until September 1976 to publish the "jet effect theory"? Why bring out the theory then? Alvarez had clearly put the theory aside after receiving devastat-ing criticism from Hoch and others in the fall of 1970. As the text makes clear, two independent and definitive tests by Edgewood Arsenal and a qualified expert using the correct ammunition and properly prepared skulls showed results contrary to those of Alvarez's tests. Given all this contrary evidence, why resuscitate the theory six years later?

It is extremely relevant that on March 6, 1975, Bob Groden showed the Zapruder film on national television, causing a firestorm of public outrage that led to the for-mation of the House Select Committee on Assassinations. That firestorm was caused specifically by the obvious question posed by the film: If Kennedy was shot in the head from the rear, why does the shot throw him violently to the left rear? Any attempt to give plausibility to the Warren Commission scenario of the shooting would have to answer that question. No matter how threadbare its underpinnings, Luis Alvarez thought he had such a theory.

CHAPTER **10**. CHANGES—AND A *GOOD NIGHT AMERICA* SHOCKER

1. In the spring of 2014, Betty Medsger published *The Burglary* (New York: Alfred A. Knopf, 2014), an account of the burglary of the Media FBI office.

2. The full quotation from Sartre's novel *La Nausee* (Paris: Editions Gallimard, 1938), 60, reads as follows: "*C'est ce qui dupe les gens: un homme, c'est toujours un conteur*

d'histoires, il vit entoure de ses histoires ad des histoires d'autrui, il voit tout ce qui lui arrive a travers elles; et il cherche a vivre sa vie comme s'il la racontait."

3. The account in the next few paragraphs is drawn from a long interview I did with Bob Groden in March 2013 as preparation for writing a preface to his latest book.

4. A 219-page transcript of what came to be called the Critic's Conference of September 17, 1977, can be found on the Mary Ferrell Foundation website at www.maryferrell.org/mffweb/archive/viewer/showDoc.do?absPageId=326491&im. The direct quotations on this and the earlier pages are drawn from that transcript. For the quotations from Mary Ferrell and Gary Shaw, see 211–212.

CHAPTER **11.** ACOUSTICS

1. The SAA publishes the *Journal of the Acoustical Society of America, Acoustics Research Letters Online*, and *Acoustics Today* plus a wide range of books and videos related to acoustics and also arranges yearly conferences where papers are presented. See also Richard N. Billings and G. Robert Blakey, *Fatal Hour: The Assassination of President Kennedy by Organized Crime* (New York, Berkley Books, 1992), 103.

2. Billings and Blakey, 103.

3. Billings and Blakey, 104.

4. As I will explain later in the text, in the summer of 1979, I agreed to write several chapters of a book on the HSCA Report. Other chapters were to be written by Peter Dale Scott, Russ Stetler, and Paul Hoch. The book was never published due to legal difficulties. However, I completed my chapters. In that capacity, I interviewed Jack Moriarty in July 1979.

When I interviewed Moriarty, I didn't know there was any uncertainty about the materials he had obtained from Paul McCaghren in Dallas. There is. The files of the HSCA contain a two-page, forty-six-item inventory prepared by Moriarty on March 11, 1978, of the materials he was taking from McCaghren's office. Of the items contained in a Permafile cardboard box, many had nothing to do with the acoustic evidence. Six channel 1 transcripts and five channel 2 transcripts were included. A "brown envelope" containing three magnetic tapes was marked "original." Tape 1 was a copy of channel 2 on November 22 from 10:00 a.m. to 5:12 p.m.. Tapes 2 and 3 contained copies of channel 1 on November 22 from 9:45 a.m. to 2:15 p.m. *There is no mention anywhere in Moriarty's inventory of any Dictabelts.*

However, the HSCA records contain a "routing slip" from April 24, 1978, showing that "Margo Jackson brought down two Dictaphone belts to be placed in Security Office." According to the slip, they were "obtained by Jack Moriarty from Paul McCaghren." See Chris Scally's very excellent study, "The Dallas Police Department's Channel I Radio Dictabelts," http://mcadams.posc.mu.edu/scally.htm. The original documents backing Scally's study can be viewed by clicking on the numbered illustrations.

The facts discussed over the next several pages were developed as part of the drafting of those chapters back in 1979. These drafts and supporting documents now reside in the Josiah Thompson Collection at the Sixth Floor Museum at Dealey Plaza in Dallas, TX. See also Billings and Blakey, *Fatal Hour*, 102–122, and Don Thomas's excellent discussion of the acoustic scientists' work in *Hear No Evil: Social Constructivism* and the *Forensic Evidence in the Kennedy Assassination* (Ipswich, MA: Mary Ferrell Foundation Press, 2010), 559–612.

5. See Scally, "The Dallas Police Department's Channel I Radio Dictabelts."

6. For a more detailed account of the facts recounted in this section, see *Report of the Select Committee on Assassinations*, US House of Representatives, 95th Cong., 2nd sess., 66–68 (hereafter HSCA Report); Billings and Blakey, *Fatal Hour*, 102–106; and Thomas, *Hear No Evil*, 559–576. The most authoritative account of these facts is surely the report of BBN on the work of James E. Barger, Scott P. Robinson, Edward C. Schmidt, and Jared J. Wolf, appendix to the HSCA Report, vol. 8, 33–127.

As the HSCA Report makes clear (65–66), the Warren Commission was also interested in a separate tape recording supposedly containing shots fired in Dealey Plaza. KBOX was broadcasting live that day from Dealey Plaza when its reporter, Sam Pate, made the famous remark "It appears as though something has happened in the motorcade route." His remark was dubbed into many films of the assassination, and this elicited the Warren Commission's interest. The commission obtained a copy of the film *Four Days That Shocked the World* and sent it to the FBI's signal analysis unit. Hoover reported in June 1964 that "no sounds which could be interpreted as gunshots" were found on the soundtrack. The commission, however, was not satisfied and had the soundtrack forwarded to Lawrence G. Kersta, a voiceprint expert at Bell Telephone Laboratories. Kersta made no determination concerning gunshots. He reported finding six "non-voiced noises" on the tape. The first was a sharp spike, followed in the next eight seconds by three more sounds of longer duration and then by two sounds similar to the former three.

The actual tape studied by Kersta could not be located. The spectrographs he produced were misfiled in the National Archives and not found by the HSCA until late 1978. The original tape of Sam Pate's broadcast could not be located and may have been overwritten for later use at KBOX. Then it was discovered that the soundtrack had been made in a studio and hence was not a copy of the original recording. All of this would seem to rule out Kersta's study as having any significance. The pattern of a loud noise, however, followed in the next eight seconds by a flurry of three sounds and then two more, matched the total time and sequence of shot sounds later verified by James Barger, Mark Weiss, and Ernest Aschkenasy. For additional details, see HSCA Report, 65–66, and Thomas, *Hear No Evil*, 560–563.

7. Charles Rader was an electrical engineer from Lincoln Laboratory at the Massachusetts Institute of Technology. He served on the Ad Hoc Committee on Ballistic Acoustics appointed by the National Research Council of the National Academy of Sciences in the fall of 1980. This committee, also called the "Ramsey Panel," is the focus of Part IV of this book. See his remarks at "The Truth about the Kennedy Assassination: Signal Processing Tells the Story," https://ieeetv.ieee.org/history/truth-about-assassination-signal-processing-tells-story.

8. These values were established experimentally by James Barger and communicated to the Ramsey Panel on March 22, 1982, by letter from James Barger to one of the panel members, Jerome I. Elkind of the Xerox Palo Alto Research Center. See Public Access File of the Ramsey Panel #9 (PAF #9) in the Josiah Thompson Collection at the Sixth Floor Museum.

9. Had the two plots been printed out in their entirety on a roll of twelve-inch-wide paper, the length would have been 1,250 feet, slightly more than the length of four football fields.

10. See HSCA Report, vol. 8, 30.

11. Billings and Blakey, *Fatal Hour*, 105.

12. Billings and Blakey, 106.

13. Billings and Blakey, 106.

14. For a more detailed account of the facts recounted in this section, see HSCA Report, 68–72; Billings and Blakey, 106–114; and Thomas, *Hear No Evil*, 576–582. As with the earlier section, surely the most authoritative account of these facts is the report of BBN on the work of Barger, Robinson, Schmidt, and Wolf.

15. Once again, see the following sources for a more detailed account of the facts reported in this section: HSCA Report, 72–79; Billings and Blakey, *Fatal Hour*, 110–119; and Thomas, *Hear No Evil*, 582–596. As with the earlier sections, the most authoritative account of these facts is the report of BBN on the work of Barger, Robinson, Schmidt, and Wolf in appendix to the HSCA Report, vol. 8, 33–127.

16. The full quotation reads, "The entry in Table II that occurred at 140.32 sec is a false alarm, because it occurred only 1.05 sec later than earlier correlations also obtained from the Texas School Book Depository. The rifle cannot be fired that rapidly. Since there are three correlations plausibly indicating the earlier shot, the one occurring 1.05 sec later must be a false alarm" (HSCA Report, vol. 8, 105).

17. In his book *Hear No Evil*, scientist and assassination researcher Dr. Donald Thomas recounts a conversation he had with Robert Blakey in May 1999 during which Blakey emphatically insisted there was no sinister intent in the decision to eliminate the fifth shot. "He confided that he knew that he would take a lot of heat for the grassy knoll shot and he didn't want to dilute his case with the weak evidence for a fifth shot" (590).

18. Thomas details the mistakes in the Barger team's calculation and lays out the correct matrix of calculations in *Hear No Evil*, 627–632.

CHAPTER 12. THE HOUSE SELECT COMMITTEE ON ASSASSINATIONS

1. Letter of James L. Harris, manager of research, Scripps Visibility Lab to Josiah Thompson, March 10, 1967. Harris wrote,

Processing of the type which would be involved would necessitate the use of image processing equipment which has been designed and constructed with funds supplied by various agencies of the U.S. Government. The use of this equipment for purposes other than those related to the research funded by these agencies would require specific authorization by the U.S. Government. The successful processing of an image involves the talents of a number of staff members of this Laboratory, and their salary could not be charged to the U.S. Government while doing processing of the type you suggest. For the reasons listed above, we believe this Laboratory cannot undertake image processing of pictures related to the Kennedy assassination unless requested to do so by some appropriate Government organization.

This letter may be found in the files of the Josiah Thompson Collection at the Sixth Floor Museum at Dealey Plaza in Dallas, TX.

2. *Report of the Select Committee on Assassinations*, US House of Representatives, 95th Cong., 2nd sess., vol. 6, 125 (hereafter HSCA Report).

3. "The Panel did not carry out any enhancement work on the Moorman photograph in the area of the stockade fence. . . . This decision, however, as well as the decision not to apply digital processing to this item, was made long before the committee's acoustic analysis was finalized. Although it is extremely unlikely that further enhancement of any kind would be successful, this particular photograph should be re-examined, in light of the findings of the acoustics analysis: (HSCA Report, vol. 6, 126).

4. HSCA Report, vol. 7, 201.

5. HSCA Report, vol. 7, 210.

6. HSCA Report, 80.

7. The Michelson-Morley experiment, first conducted in 1887, attempted to detect the existence of the so-called aether wind, a prevalent theory in physics at the time. Its negative results were considered the first powerful evidence against the concept, which in turn marked a turning point toward the development of the special theory of relativity. My remark appears on page 117 of the stenographic transcript of the critics' conference held on September 17, 1977, which can be found on the Mary Ferrell Foundation website, https://www.maryferrell.org/mffweb/archive/viewer/showDoc.do?docId=10375&relPageId=68.

8. According to Guinn, the tests were carried out between September 12 and September 14, 1977. See Guinn's report, HSCA Report, vol. 1, 507.

9. The facts recounted in this and the next two paragraphs can be found in Guinn's report (HSCA Report, vol. 1, 506–552) and in his testimony before the House Select Committee (HSCA Report, vol. 1, 491–505, 553–567).

10. HSCA Report, vol. 1, 533.

11. HSCA Report, vol. 1, 505.

12. Interview of Groden, March 2013. Groden's account from this interview stretches into the next three paragraphs.

13. The discussion here and in the next few pages can be found in HSCA Report, vol. 6, 19-32, in a section entitled "The Panning Error—Blur Analyses of the Zapruder Film."

14. HSCA Report, vol. 2, 14.

15. HSCA Report, vol. 2, 4. In his testimony, Hartmann does not cite the study he has in mind. Insofar as I can determine, it is a short book by Carney Landis, William Alvin Hunt, and Hans Strauss, *The Startle Pattern* (New York: Farrar & Rinehart, 1939). This study used gunshots to measure the startle response.

16. A far more direct and powerful way to determine which of the last two shots caused the powerful impact on Kennedy's head at frame 313 lay just below the surface. I had thought of it in 1979 but was too ignorant of math and science to figure out how to show it.

Since Alvarez first presented his theory in the 1960s, it has become apparent that each blur lags a bit behind the shot that caused it. It takes time for the sound of the shot to reach Zapruder and additional time for him to flinch and move his camera.

For shots that came from the northeast corner of Elm Street, this would appear to be three frames. (Three frames after frame 324 is 327; three frames after 328 is 331.) Frame 313, however, is different. Unlike all the others, this single frame shows both the impact of a shot and the resultant blur.

Since the acoustics evidence indicated that all but the next-to-last shot were fired from the northeast corner of Elm Street, and the next-to-last shot was fired from the fence—a location much closer to Zapruder—could this all mean that the frame itself was telling us it had to be the next-to-last shot?

Back in 1979, I wondered if this oddity of frame 313 might be due to this shot having been fired closer to Zapruder than the others. I never bothered to do anything but wonder about it, but scientist Don Thomas did. He worked out the math, which turned out not to be so complicated. Frame 313 would not have contained both impact and blur had the shot been fired from the north end of Elm Street—that is, from the depository sixth floor window. However, if the shot were fired from the knoll location defined by the acoustics (eight to ten feet from the corner of the fence), the sound would have arrived at Zapruder's ears fast enough for him to have moved the camera as the bullet hit President Kennedy.

Thus, frame 313 contained internally sufficient information to link it definitively to the next-to-last shot in the acoustics evidence. See Don Thomas, *Hear No Evil: Social Constructivism and the Forensic Evidence in the Kennedy Assassination* (Ipswich, MA: Mary Ferrell Foundation Press, 2010), 211–216. See color photo gallery, Plate 2.

17. HSCA Report, 80.

18. Titled *John Kennedy Assassination Film Analysis* and dated May 2, 1976 the report runs a bit over 100 pages. It bears HSCA Record Number 180-10001-10396 in the National Archives and may be viewed there or on the Mary Ferrell Foundation website, https://www.maryferrell.org/mffweb/archive/viewer/showDoc.do?docId=60448&relPageId=1.

19. HSCA Report, vol. 1, 404, 423. As pointed out in note 22 in Chapter 9 (page 126), the shooting experiments monitored by Sturdivan in 1964 for the Warren Commission were not the only ones carried out by scientists interested in testing what happened when a skull was hit by a 6.5-mm military jacketed bullet. In November 1978 forensic pathologist and professor John M. Nichols carried out firing tests with a duplicate of Oswald's rifle and bullets from the same lot number as used in Dealey Plaza. His results confirmed the tests monitored by Sturdivan and buried the "jet effect theory" of Luis Alvarez.

20. HSCA Report, vol. 7, 173.

21. HSCA Report, vol. 1, 415.

22. In his book *The JFK Myths* (St. Paul, MN: Paragon House, 2005), Sturdivan returned to the goat-shooting film he displayed for the HSCA during his testimony. He said, "About one-tenth of a second after the shot, the goat goes into what one Biophysics Lab colleague . . . described as a 'swan dive'" (165). One-tenth of a second is one hundred milliseconds. Years earlier in his testimony, Sturdivan had claimed that "four-hundredths of a second after that impact, then the neuromuscular reaction that I described begins to happen; the back legs go out" (HSCA Report, vol. 1, 417). Four-hundredths of a second is forty milliseconds. Since Sturdivan never indicated

how and from what he derived these figures, we cannot know which to trust. Since the "one-tenth of a second" was not made up on the spot but was part of the manuscript of a book, it seems more trustworthy.

Sturdivan had no real medical training and held no advanced degrees. As a consequence, his research on such medical phenomena as "neuromuscular reaction" is sometimes downright funny. One example is his claim that Robert Capa's famous photo from the Spanish Civil War shows a Loyalist soldier being shot in the head and then doing exactly what JFK did after frame 313. He printed the Robert Capa photo in his book and provided a long commentary: "At the moment this picture was taken, the neuromuscular spasm has already descended down the spine. . . . The neck and back are arched backward and the arms are shown fully extended and angle slightly backward . . . the rifle stayed clutched in his hand as his arm straightened" (168).

Next, Sturdivan built the bridge to what we see in the Zapruder film: "The results may be seen in the reaction of the President. Within a tenth of a second of the shot that exploded his skull, the unseen straightening of his thighs and the visible arching of his back throw his upper body violently into the back of the car" (169).

Upon reading this, I immediately looked at the photo and wondered why Sturdivan thought the Loyalist soldier had been hit in the head. I could see something extending above the man's head, but it looked like part of his cap to me. A quick search turned up a much clearer print that showed the "something" to be a kind of tassel attached to the man's cap. Then I started to research this particular photo and ended up laughing.

This photo turns out to be quite controversial. Studies of the background disclose that it was taken not at Cerro Murriano but at a small village some thirty miles away called Espejo. There was no fighting in Espejo in early September 1936, when Capa

Photo N-2. Robert Capa photo from 1936, *The Falling Soldier*.

Photo N-3. A similar photo from the Mexican suitcase.

and his girlfriend, Gerda Taro, visited the area. The initial story was that the photo showed the death of a well-known Loyalist, Frederico Borrell Garcia, who was killed at Cerro Murriano that month. Witnesses, however, pointed out that Garcia was killed by a man firing from behind a tree.

The 35-mm negative for the photo has never been found, but in 1995 an amazing trove of thousands of 35-mm negatives taken by Capa, Taro, and another photographer was found in Mexico. They had been stored in three flimsy cardboard valises and somehow had survived. They made their way to the International Center of Photography in New York in 2007 and to the Barbizon Centre in London in 2009. Several could be linked to the work of Capa and Taro in September 1936. They tell a story of how the politically committed journalists often took staged shots of Loyalist soldiers raising their rifles in supposed celebration or pointing them toward a supposed enemy. One of the photos depicts a Loyalist soldier in the exact spot occupied by the falling soldier, apparently shot and falling like the soldier in the famous photo. The cloud formations in both photos seem nearly identical, indicating that the photos were taken very close in time to each other.

The consensus is that both photos were staged and may have been taken not by Capa but by Taro. In short, not only is there no evidence that the subject of the photo was shot in the head, but there is no evidence that he was shot at all. The position that Sturdivan saw as caused by a neuromuscular spasm and that he linked to "JFK's movement in the Zapruder film" was a staged event. "Now go and look like you've just been shot," someone told the soldier, "while I take your picture!"

For additional information on the staged nature of the photo, see the Wikipedia entry for "The Falling Soldier," https://en.wikipedia.org/wiki/The_Falling_Soldier. See also "Robert Capa's Falling Soldier—Does the Evidence Stack Up?," *Ethical Martini*, https://ethicalmartini.wordpress.com/2008/11/01/robert-capas-falling-soldier-does -the-evidence-stack-up; (2) Larry Rohter, "New Doubts Raised over Famous War

Photo," *New York Times*, August 17, 2009; and Elizabeth Nash, "Shot down—Capa's Classic Image of War," *Independent*, July 21, 2009.

23. HSCA Report, vol. 7, 174.

24. HSCA Report, vol. 7, 174.

25. HSCA Report, vol. 7, 178.

26. "John Kennedy Assassination Film Analysis," ITEK Corporation, May 2, 1976, 84.

27. ITEK Report, 84n.

28. HSCA Report, 93.

29. HSCA Report, 97.

30. HSCA Report, 81.

31. Thompson manuscript for *Echoes of Conspiracy* (1979), 56. This manuscript may be found in the files of the Josiah Thompson Collection at the Sixth Floor Museum.

CHAPTER **13.** BREAKING THE IMPASSE: THE PUZZLE PIECE THAT WASN'T

1. *Report of the Committee on Ballistic Acoustics* (Washington, DC: National Academy Press, 1982), 45.

2. The many turnings in this fascinating case are described in Josiah Thompson, *Gumshoe: Reflections in a Private Eye* (New York: Little, Brown and Company, 1988).

3. Transcript of Thompson testimony before the ARRB, April 2, 1997, www.jfk -info/arrb-005.htm.

4. Erik Randich, Wayne Duerfeldt, Wade McLendon, and William Tobin, "A Metal-lurgical Review of the Interpretation of Bullet Lead Compositional Analysis," *Forensic Science International* 127 (2002): 174–191.

5. *State of New Jersey v. Michael S. Behn*, decided on appeal March 7, 2005, by Superior Court of New Jersey, Appellate Division, https://law.justia.com/cases/new-jersey /appellate-division-published/2005/a2062-03-opn.html. Similar testimony from Randich in an Alaska case brought about two hung juries.

In a Kentucky case, FBI lab examiner Kathleen Lundy testified that both bullets in question came from a batch that could have produced 280,000 units. When it turned out that this figure should have been in the tens of millions, she was indicted for misdemeanor false swearing. Lundy blamed her false testimony on "new and repeated challenges to the validity of the science associated with bullet lead comparison analysis." See Center for Investigative Journalism Report, Science Casts Doubt on FBI's Bullet Evidence," February 2, 2003, https://www.latimes.com/archives/la-xpm-2003 -feb-03-sci-bullets3-story.html.

6. See National Research Council, *Forensic Analysis: Weighing Bullet Lead Evidence* (Washington, DC: National Academies Press, 2004), https://www.nap.edu/catalog /10924/forensic-analysis-weighing-bullet-lead-evidence.

7. FBI Laboratory Director Dwight Adams wrote on September 1, 2005, that the decision to discontinue CBLA was "based primarily on the inability of scientists or manufacturers to definitively evaluate the significance of an association between bullets made in the course of a bullet lead examination." This letter was quoted in an article in the National Association of Criminal Defense Attorneys journal, *The Champion*, by William A. Tobin and William C. Thompson, "Evaluating and Challenging Forensic Identification Evidence," *The Champion* (July 2006): 12–21. Tobin and Thompson

pointed out that "because the FBI operated the only laboratory in the United States that routinely performed CBLA, its decision to [close the lab] effectively ends the technique, at least for now" (12–13). Ten years later, CBLA had disappeared from the scene.

8. Eric Randich and Patrick M. Grant, "Proper Assessment of the JFK Assassination Bullet Lead Evidence from Metallurgical and Statistical Perspectives," *Journal of Forensic Sciences* 51, no. 4 (July 2006): 717–728.

9. In a letter dated July 8, 1964, Director Hoover wrote to J. Lee Rankin, chief counsel of the Warren Commission:

> Because of the higher sensitivity of the neutron activation analysis, certain of the small lead fragments were then subjected to neutron activation analyses and comparisons with the larger bullet fragments. The items analyzed included the following: C1—bullet from stretcher; C2—fragment from front seat cushion; C4 and C5—metal fragments from President Kennedy's head; C9—metal fragment from the arm of Governor Connally; C16—metal fragments from the rear floor board carpet of the car.
>
> While minor variations in composition were found by this method, these were not considered sufficient to permit positively differentiating among the larger bullet fragments and thus positively determining from which of the larger bullet fragments any given small lead fragment may have come. (https://www.kenrahn.com/JFK/Scientific_topics/NAA/NAA_and_assassination_II/NAA_and_better_prospects.html)

In 1975, long before he was hired by the HSCA to carry out NAA tests, Guinn learned of the results of the NAA test cited by Hoover and carried out on the same materials tested by FBI Agent John F. Gallagher at the Oak Ridge National Laboratory in May 1964. See Vincent Guinn, "JFK Assassination: Bullet Analyses," *Analytical Chemistry* 51 (April 1979): 484–493.

10. The facts recounted in this paragraph are contained in an FBI report on Guinn in a memorandum from R. H. Jevons to Mr. Conrad, "Dr. Vincent P. Guinn, Neutron Activation Analysis," September 21, 1964. This document is contained in the Josiah Thompson Collection at the Sixth Floor Museum at Dealey Plaza in Dallas, TX.

11. Memorandum, "Dr. Vincent P. Guinn, Neutron Activation Analysis"; FBI memorandum from R. H. Jevons to Mr. Conrad, "President's Assassination, Lee Harvey Oswald, News Release Quoting Dr. Vincent P. Guinn," August 28, 1964. This document is also contained in the files of the Josiah Thompson Collection at the Sixth Floor Museum.

12. See an article quoting Guinn, "Radioactivity Aids Oswald," *New York World Telegram and Sun, August 28, 1964*

13. Memorandum, "President's Assassination, Lee Harvey Oswald."

14. HSCA Report, vol. 1, 505.

15. V. P. Guinn and J. Nichols, "Neutron Activation Analysis of Bullet-lead Specimens: The President Kennedy Assassination," *Transactions of the American Nuclear Society* 28 (1978): 92–93.

16. Guinn and Nichols, 93.

17. HSCA Report, vol. 1, 545.

18. HSCA Report, vol. 1, 545.

19. HSCA Report, vol. 1, 546.

20. The discussion of bullet production on this and the next two pages is drawn from Randich and Grant, "Proper Assessment of the JFK Assassination Bullet Lead Evidence."

21. Tobin and Thompson, "Evaluating and Challenging Forensic Identification Evidence," 15.

CHAPTER 14. BREAKING THE IMPASSE: THE BLUR ILLUSION

1. When the actual ITEK measurements are compared with similar measurements done by Thompson and Wimp, there is no great variation as shown below:

Z FRAMES	THOMPSON	WIMP	ITEK
301/302	+0.19"	—	—
302/303	−0.39"	—	—
303/304	−0.16"	—	—
304/305	−0.61"	—	—
305/306	+0.10"	+0.33"	—
306/307	+0.21"	+0.20"	—
307/308	+0.17"	+0.20"	—
308/309	−0.57"	+0.025"	—
309/310	+0.26"	+0.05"	—
310/311	−0.30"	+0.175"	—
311/312	+0.16"	+0.65"	+0.05"
312/313	+2.18"	+0.95"	+2.26"
313/314	−0.54"	+0.325"	−0.30"
314/315	−1.08"	−0.55"	−0.65"
315/316	−0.78"	−1.10"	−1.46"
316/317	−1.71"	−1.50"	−1.60"
318	NO DATA	NO DATA	—
317/319	−3.05"	−2.90"	—
319/320	−0.39"	−0.75"	—
320/321	−0.47"	−1.00"	—
321/322	+0.39"	+0.30"	—
322/323	+0.86"	+0.25"	—
323/324	+1.56"	+0.375"	—
324/325	+0.44"	—	—
325/326	+1.37"	—	—
326/327	+1.06"	—	—
327/328	+1.68"	—	—
328/329	+1.92"	—	—
329/330	+2.80"	—	—

The numbers above for Thompson are an average of the two measurements given on page 274 of *Six Seconds in Dallas*. The measurements were made from (a), the back of the president's head to the top of the back seat cushion, and (b) the front of the rear left handhold. (+) indicates forward movement; (−) indicates rearward movement.

The numbers above for Wimp are averages based on the two graphs he produced on pages 6 and 7 of his study, "Measurements of JFK's Front to Back Head Movements in the Zapruder Film." Measurements were made of the movement in each interval and these were averaged for the two graphs. (+) indicates forward movement; (−) indicates rearward movement.

The numbers above for ITEK are taken from Table 3.3.3 of the study produced on May 2, 1976 by the Itek Corporation entitled, "John Kennedy Assassination Film Analysis." This table can be found on page 77 of the study. (+) indicates forward movement; (−) indicates rearward movement.

Towards the close of the ITEK study, Corbett states they were able to establish parameters of precision given "the resolution limit of the film and the inherent difficulty of repeated measurements." They found this to be "0.20 inches in object space." This means that the movements of JFK could not be measured more accurately than 0.20 inches in any one frame. Corbett's point becomes important when we compare the three sets of measurements.

Frames 301–305 were measured only by Thompson and showed no significant movement in either direction. Frames 305–311 were measured by both Thompson and Wimp and showed some forward movement of JFK's head in nearly all these frames. The movement between 311 and 312 was measured by all three. All three found JFK's head to move forward a small but significant distance between these frames. Between 312 and 313, Thompson and Itek found JFK's head to move forward 3.18" and 3.26" respectively while both ignored the effect produced by Zapruder moving the camera. Wimp took this blur effect into account and found that JFK's head moved forward 0.95." Between 314 and 317, all three have JFK's head moving backward. ITEK's measurements end with 316/317, while Wimp's end with 323/324 and Thompson's with 329/330.

2. Luis Alvarez calculated the velocity of the limousine in his *American Journal of Physics* article (vol. 44, no. 9, September 1976). He writes, "The heavy car decelerated suddenly for about 0.5 sec (10 frames), centered at about frame 299, reducing its speed from about 12 mph to about 8 mph. Since the car was certainly being operated in some low gear ratio, the deceleration was no doubt caused by the driver reducing his foot pressure on the accelerator (page 825)." He went on to say that his calculations showed the car kept going at the slower 8 mph through frame 334.

3. John Kennedy Assassination Film Analysis, ITEK Corporation, May 2, 1976. 88.

4. Robert Frazier testimony in Clay Shaw trial, February 22, 1969, 8–9, Mary Ferrell Foundation website, http://www.maryferrell.org/mffweb/archive/viewer/showDoc. do?docId=1297&relPageId=12. Frazier indicated that blood and tissue had been found "on the outside of the windshield, also on the inside surface of the windshield" and over the hood "as far forward as the hood ornament."

5. William Matson Law with Allan Eaglesham, *In the Eye of History* (Southlake, TX: JFK Lancer Productions and Publications, 2005). Just prior to being interviewed by Law, Francis O'Neill showed Law a manuscript he was writing about the Kennedy

assassination. It told of Sibert and O'Neill interviewing Greer and Kellerman in Bethesda during the autopsy. Law wrote, "He [O'Neill] also wrote of the interviews of Kellerman and Greer noting that they had not had a chance to clean up after the shooting—both men had 'blood and parts of brain tissue on the backs of their coats, evidence of the force with which the President's head had, for want of a better word, 'exploded'" (157).

6. Interview of Hargis in the *New York Sunday News* carried out on 11/22/63 and published on 11/24/63, page 1. See also Chapter 4 above where Hargis's testimony before a Warren Commission lawyer is discussed.

7. Sam Kinney quoted in Vincent Palamara, *Survivor's Guilt* (Waterville, Oregon: Trine Day, 2013).

8. B. J. Martin's deposition before the Warren Commission on April 3, 1964 (6H292).

CHAPTER 15. BREAKING THE IMPASSE: THE CRUCIAL PIECE—THE FINAL SHOT

1. All these changes point to the impact of a bullet to the back of Kennedy's head between Zapruder frames 327 and 328. Using the acoustic evidence that found 0.71 seconds between the next-to-last and the last shot, one could import all the known variables (ambient temperature, time for the sound to reach the motorcycle on Elm Street, time for the bullet to reach Kennedy, etc.) and try to calculate in exactly what frame the last shot would strike Kennedy's head. Of course, as Don Thomas pointed out several years ago, both the channel 1 Dictabelt and Zapruder's camera are mechanical devices of which the speed is known only through averages. For example, Zapruder's camera was tested by the FBI and found to run at speeds ranging from 17.6 to 18.5 frames per second, depending on how fully wound the drive spring in the camera was (*Report of the Select Committee on Assassinations*, US House of Representatives, 95th Cong., 2nd sess., vol. 5, 722–723 [hereafter HSCA Report]). I suspect that no attempt to calculate the time of impact over any significant time interval using the acoustics evidence alone can be trusted to produce results more accurate than plus or minus one Zapruder frame.

2. Chief Counsel Blakey made these remarks at the close of the final hearing of the HSCA on December 29, 1978, in a section of volume 5 titled "Final Comments by Prof. G. Robert Blakey, Chief Counsel and Staff Director," HSCA Report, vol. 5, 693.

If Zapruder frame 313 actually reflects the time of the third (or next-to-last) shot, this placed the committee in a situation of great discomfort. As Blakey said unhesitatingly, this meant that the president was killed by two shots, the first from the knoll, the second from the depository sixth floor corner window, both within three-quarters of a second. To avoid this extremely inconvenient conclusion, he called upon his trajectory specialist, Dr. James Canning, a National Aeronautics and Space Administration scientist.

Canning had already produced a conclusion of stunning silliness with respect to the bullet that struck Kennedy in the back of the head. The location of in-shoot and out-shoot points established by the autopsy and then changed by the HSCA Medical Panel were extremely controversial. The panel claimed that the three autopsy doctors had mislocated the in-shoot hole by four inches, while part of the out-shoot hole was on a fragment of bone located somewhere in the parietal or frontal area of the president's skull. If that wasn't enough, there is no law of forensic pathology that says a bullet hitting the skull cannot be deflected somewhat by its initial contact with the skull so that a line between in-shoot and out-shoot may not be extended to establish the bullet trajectory before it impacted the skull. This was the method that Canning pursued, even though the distance between the in-shoot and out-shoot holes was just under six inches. Using frames 312 and 313 of the Zapruder film, Canning inferred the trajectory of the shot back several hundred feet to the southern face of the depository. "Skepticism" is far too weak a word to describe what the Medical Panel thought of Canning's method. They wrote,

> The panel is concerned as to the degree of accuracy attainable in determining the missile trajectory based on backward extension of a bullet track from within the body. The determination of the point of origin of a missile by backward extension from a bullet track through a body requires knowing, reasonably precisely, the exact position of that portion of the body at the moment it was struck. Any motion of the body, no matter how slight, would alter the extended trajectory of the missile and thereby change the point of origin. The longer the distance of the trajectory, the greater the magnification of even the smallest error in determining body position or path in the body. (HSCA Report, vol. 7, 168–169)

Canning persisted. He simply moved the limousine about a car's length farther down Elm Street and inexplicably used the supposed position of the president's head in frame 313 to once again calculate the trajectory backward over several hundred feet. It is shown below (Figure N-4) and may be found at HSCA Report, vol. 6, 61.

Canning's work had numerous flaws, but one stands out as representative of his whole effort. The out-shoot location that Canning used for his first calculation was not present at 327–328 because it had been blown away by the first shot from the knoll. For his second trajectory calculation, he had only a single point—the controversial in-shoot location. Even Canning could not calculate a trajectory from only one point.

Still, Canning's fanciful work provided what Blakey required. He wrote in the committee report at page 81, "A preliminary trajectory analysis, based on the President's location and body position at frame 328–329 failed to track to a shooter in the sixth floor southeast corner window of the Depository within a minimum margin of error radius. . . . The Committee concluded, therefore, that the shot fired from the grassy knoll was not the shot visually represented at Zapruder frame 312."

3. Altgens testimony before the Warren Commission, *Warren Commission Hearings and Exhibits*, vol. 7, 518 (hereafter cited by volume and page number as, e.g., 7H518).

4. A transcript of the broadcast containing Altgens's interview can be read in Stephen White, Stephen White, *Should We Now Believe the Warren Report?* (New York: The MacMillan Company, 1968), 238.

5. 7H518.

6. 7H518.

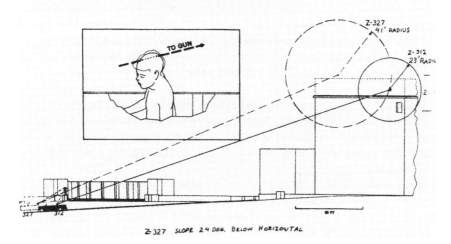

LINE OF SIGHT FROM ZAPRUDER CAMERA TO JFK/SLOPE
OF BULLET CAUSING HEAD WOUND

Figure N-4. Original exhibit by trajectory expert James Canning. Note: Scale indicator and some notations are not legible.

7. FBI interview of Jack Franzen, November 22, 1963, 22H840.

8. Part 1 of the transcript of the interview of Jack Franzen by his daughter, Julie Franzen, recorded on June 18, 1997. It is available on Julie Franzen Jackson's website at http://web.archive.org/web/20060903214950/http://www.consideritdone.cc/kennedy.html

9. 22H837–838.

10. Transcript of interview with Charles Brehm in Larry Sneed, *No More Silence: An Oral History of the Assassination of President Kennedy* (Denton, TX: University of North Texas Press, 2002), 61–62.

11. Holland transcript, 15.

12. Holland transcript, 17.

13. Holland transcript, 18–19.

CHAPTER **16.** THE MEDICAL EVIDENCE

1. Michael M. Baden, *Unnatural Death: Confessions of a Medical Examiner* (New York: Ivy Books published by Ballantine, 1989), 5.

2. On October 17, 1967, Admiral Burkley sat down for an oral history interview carried out by William McHugh for the John F. Kennedy Library. The following is an excerpt from page 9:

> When the President was on the Air Force One returning to Washington, Mrs. Kennedy, as has been noted, sat in the rear of the plane, next to the coffin bearing the President's remains. During the flight I contacted her, and stated that an autopsy would be necessary, and that I was perfectly willing to arrange to have it

done at any place that she felt it should be done. She said, "Well, it doesn't have to be done." I said, "Yes, it is mandatory that we have an autopsy. I can do it at the Army hospital at Walter Reed, or at the Navy hospital at Bethesda, or any civilian hospital that you would designate." However, I felt that it should be a military hospital, in that he had been President of the United States and was, therefore, the Commander in Chief of the Military. After some consideration she stated that she would like to have the President taken to Bethesda.

The whole oral history interview can be read at https://mcadams.posc.mu.edu/russ /testimony/burkley.htm. See also Burkley's "Report of my participation in the activities surrounding the assassination of President John Fitzgerald Kennedy," *Warren Commission Hearings and Exhibits*, vol. 22, 93–97 (hereafter cited by volume and page number as, e.g., 22H93–97).

3. Dr. James Humes and Dr. John Lattimer were acquainted. The account of Dr. Humes's actions on the afternoon of November 22 is drawn from Lattimer's book *Kennedy and Lincoln: Medical and Legal Comparisons of their Assassinations* (New York: Harcourt Brace Jovanovich, 1980), 155. With respect to the navy doctors' request to have forensic examiners from the Washington or Baltimore offices to assist them, Lattimer wrote, "Commanders Humes and Boswell inquired as to whether or not any of their consultants from the medical examiner's office in Washington or Baltimore should be summoned, but this action was discouraged."

4. Dr. Cyril Wecht, longtime coroner of Allegheny County (Pittsburgh), Pennsylvania. and ex-president of the American Academy of Forensic Sciences, told me that if Kennedy had been struck twice in the head by separate bullets from different directions, figuring out what happened would have taxed the considerable skills of the best forensic pathologists in the country (personal communication, October 18, 2013).

5. Secret Service Agent William Greer testified before the Warren Commission that he received the president's clothes in the emergency room at Parkland Hospital. "I was in the emergency room, and a nurse got two shopping bags and I held them and she put the President's suit, his belongings into the two bags including his shoes and socks, and his pants and jacket which they had torn and the shirt they had torn, they had torn it to take it off him, and the nurse put these into the two bags and I got custody of them right then from the nurse at the emergency room" (2H125).

On the next page of his testimony, Greer said, "I had this, his clothing, I kept it in my hand at all times, all the time" (2H126). Greer continued that he and Roy Kellerman remained in the autopsy room at Bethesda while it was performed: "Mr. Kellerman and I stayed permanently the whole time there" (2H127).

Lt. Col. Finck wrote a memo to the commanding officer at the Armed Forces Institute of Pathology in which he said, "I was denied the opportunity to examine the clothing of Kennedy. One officer who outranked me told me that my request was only of scholarly interest." See the Mary Ferrell Foundation website, https://www.maryferrell .org/showDoc.html?docId=609#relPageId=22&tab=page.

6. The whole purpose of autopsy photos is to preserve photographically critical elements in the autopsy for later review and proof. Since the autopsy doctors and the Warren Commission ultimately concluded that the bullet that struck Kennedy in the

back bruised the right lung before exiting where Dr. Perry made his later tracheotomy incision, photographs of this damage at the midpoint of the bullet's purported transit are important. In 1964, Humes had told the Warren Commission that "Kodachrome photographs were made in the interior of the President's chest" (2H363). Fifteen years later, Humes was even more explicit about the taking of these Kodachromes in testimony before the HSCA Medical Panel:

> That's one photograph that we were distressed not to find when we first went through and catalogued these photographs, because I distinctly recall going to great lengths to try and get the interior upper portion of the right thorax illuminated—you know the technical difficulties with that, getting the camera positioned and so forth—and what happened to that film, I don't know. (*Report of the Select Committee on Assassinations*, US House of Representatives, 95th Cong., 2nd sess., vol. 7, 253)

Even later, he told the ARRB that "we took one of the right side of the thorax. . . . I wanted to have a picture of it and I never saw it" (Humes testimony before the ARRB, February 13, 1996, 97). Humes's claim was backed by autopsy photographer John Stringer, who told the ARRB that "there were some views that were taken are missing . . . some things inside the body that weren't there" (Stringer testimony before the ARRB, July 16, 1996, 133).

There is more.

One of the most critical elements in the Kennedy autopsy was the appearance of a small bullet hole in the back of the president's head. When Humes testified before the Warren Commission, he explained the importance of the "shelving" or "coning" effect of a bullet wound to the skull. Humes explained the effect as similar to "a B-B fired by a child's air rifle when this strikes a pane of glass" (21H252). He pointed out that the B-B makes a small round hole on the side of the glass it hits and "a coned-out surface on the opposite side" (2H252). Likewise, this is often but not always the case when a bullet strikes the skull. It creates a small hole in the outer table of the skull and a "shelving" or "coning" effect on the inner table. The doctors found this effect around the hole in the back of the president's skull. Humes testified that "photographs illustrating this phenomenon from both the external surface of the skull and from the internal surface were prepared" (2H352).

Testifying before the ARRB, Finck read from the notes he had prepared around the time of the autopsy: "I help the Navy photographer to take photographs of the occipital wound (external and internal)" (Finck testimony before Testimony Before the ARRB, May 24, 1996, 88–89). During that same session before the ARRB, Finck testified that he specifically ordered photos of the inner and outer tables of the skull at the low point described in the autopsy to demonstrate the beveling effect described by Humes above. He pointed out that the scalp was reflected away from the remaining bones at this point to show the important "shelving" or "coning" effect.

Navy photographers John Stringer and his assistant, Floyd Riebe, were charged with taking photos during the autopsy. Both testified that they recalled that the scalp had been reflected away from the skull for the taking of photos. Stringer told the ARRB that he recalled taking photos after the scalp "had been pulled down or reflected" (Stringer testimony before the ARRB, July 16, 1996, 91). Riebe recalled Stringer taking photos from angles very near the inside of the cranium. He said, "Yes, I think Mr. Stringer did that when the body was on its side" (Riebe testimony before the ARRB, May 7, 1997, 39).

No photos of these two critical areas have survived, although there is overwhelming evidence that they were taken.

7. The case of Sandra Kay Spencer appears to provide proof that a whole series of autopsy photos locked away in government files have been suppressed. Somehow or other, investigators for the ARRB found her, and she was deposed at the National Archives in June 1997. Her testimony is worth considering in *extenso*.

In November 1963, Spencer had been in the navy for six years and had become a first-class petty officer in charge of the White House photo lab at Anacostia. It was a special unit that did work for the naval aide to the president. Spencer had been interested in photography since she was eleven years old, and she had attended most of the navy's photographic schools. She had bounced around before coming to the White House lab and for a while had taken autopsy photos at Pensacola "for the student pilots who didn't quite make it" (NB: Numbers in parentheses refer to the transcript page numbers of Spencer's sworn deposition. See Spencer testimony before the ARRB, June 17, 1997.) When news of the Dallas shooting came over the radio, Spencer had been "color correcting a photo of John-John in President Kennedy's office" (13).

Sometime after she finished this job and before the funeral commenced on Monday, a government agent who may or may not have been named Fox brought to her a set of "four or five" four-by-five-inch film holders, each one containing two negatives from a large-format camera (20–21). He wanted the film developed and printed and also wanted to make sure that no additional prints were made and all materials returned to him. She complied, but as the prints revolved on a drum, she had "about 15 seconds" (40) to observe each one.

Spencer was deposed at the National Archives, where she could be shown the official autopsy photos that were kept there. She was shown each of the official photos and firmly stated that none of them were the photos she had developed and printed for the agent. When shown the first color transparency of the president's head and upper body, she exclaimed that her photos had shown "none of the blood and matted hair" (44). The body had been cleaned up for her photos. The president's eyes and mouth had been shut, and there was none of the blood and gore visible in the official autopsy photos. She confirmed that "the body appeared to be clean, had been washed" (35). She herself had shot autopsy photos at Pensacola, so she knew how bloody and gory they were. The ones the agent turned over to her weren't like that. At the close of her deposition, she said she thought the photos she developed and printed "were taken after reconstruction of the body" (59). Referring to the known, official autopsy photos, she said that "between those photographs and the ones that we did, there had to be some massive cosmetic things done to the President's body" (58).

Spencer brought with her a photo of the president that had been printed by her unit "about a week or ten days before the printing of the autopsy material" (26). It showed the president with the Black Watch regiment, which had performed at the

White House before the president left for Dallas that November. She explained that paper was bought in bulk by the photography center and then cut to various sizes. This meant that all photos printed over a substantial period of time would be on the same lot of paper. She compared each of the official autopsy photos with the photo she had printed in mid-November 1963, and all were printed on different paper. Spencer concluded that none of the official autopsy photos were printed at the White House lab or the photography center at Anacostia.

Spencer described differences between the photos she worked on and the official autopsy photos. One photo she printed showed the president's brain beside his body, both lying on a pad. In the official autopsy photos, the president's eyes and mouth are open. In the photos she worked on, they are shut. Nowhere in the official autopsy photos do we see any hole in the back of the president's head. Spencer said she worked on one photo of the president's head that clearly showed a two-inch hole in the back of the head through the occiput. She drew its approximate size and location on an anatomic illustration of the back of the skull.

Spencer's testimony does not demonstrate a massive conspiracy surrounding the autopsy photos. Her suggestion that they were made after technicians from the funeral home had cleaned up the body is probably correct. However, the eight to ten photos should have been preserved because—if for no other reason—they showed a sizable hole in the back of the president's head not shown in other autopsy photos.

8. Lt. Col. Finck testified to both the HSCA and the ARRB that he had taken measurements and written notes, and these materials "were turned over to Dr. Humes" (AARB testimony of Pierre Finck, MD, May 24, 1996, 16, 20, 14–25). A colleague of Finck at the Armed Forces Institute of Pathology was having lunch in the institute dining room the week after the assassination. He heard Finck "complain that he had been unable to locate the handwritten notes he had taken during the autopsy. Dr. Finck elaborated to his companions, with considerable irritation, that immediately after washing up following the autopsy, he looked for his notes and could not find them anywhere" (AARB Medical Records #252, AARB Contact Report with Leonard D. Saslow, PhD, April 25, 1996).

9. Humes testified before the Warren Commission that "in the privacy of my own home, early in the morning of Sunday, November 24th, I made a draft of this report which I later revised and of which this [the official autopsy report] represents the revision. That draft I personally burned in the fireplace of my recreation room" (2H373).

It turned out that a draft of the autopsy report was not the only thing Humes burned in his fireplace that Sunday morning. Years later, Humes testified before the ARRB that two or three pages of handwritten notes taken by him during the autopsy were also burned that morning (Humes testimony before the ARRB, February 13, 1996, 128, 130). These notes had bloodstains on them, said Humes, and for that reason, he "burned the original notes in the fireplace of my home to prevent them from falling into the hands of what I consider inappropriate people" (128). Since all this material was being transferred to the president's physician, Admiral George Burkley, and since the bloodstained autopsy face sheet was preserved by Humes, his explanation makes little sense.

10. Transcript of press conference, Parkland Memorial Hospital, Dallas, TX, November 22, 1963, 2:16 p.m. CST, 5, http://mcadams.posc.mu.edu/press.htm.

11. Transcript of press conference, Parkland Memorial Hospital.

12. 17H10.

13. 17H3. For a better copy of the same document, see Warren Report, 517–518.

14. Interview of Clark by David Naro in 1994, cited by Dr. Gary Aguilar in "John F. Kennedy's Fatal Wounds: The Witnesses and the Interpretations from 1963 to the Present," *Electronic Assassinations Newsletter*, August 1994, 4, http://www.assassination web.com/ag6.htm; 6H21.

15. 6H21.

16. 6H33.

17. 6H11.

18. 6H51.

19. 17H15.

20. 17H5.

21. 6H3, 6.

22. Gary L. Aguilar, "John F. Kennedy's Fatal Wounds: The Witnesses and the Interpretations from 1963 to the Present," *Electronic Assassinations Newsletter*, August 1994, 16, http://www.assassinationweb.com/ag6.htm. Alfred Giesecke, M.D., thought the wound extended from the occiput to the front of the skull but got his directions mixed up and placed the wound on the left side of the head (6H74). Kenneth Salyer, M.D., saw a "gaping skull wound" in the "right temporal area" that extended both forward and rearward above the right ear (6H81).

23. Aguilar, pp. 25–26.

24. 5H179.

25. 5H180.

26. See "Warren Commission Suppressed Jackie's Testimony on JFK's Head Wound: Court Reporter's Tape Shows Additional Description Withheld," *JFK Lancer*, http://www.jfklancer.com/LNE/jbkwc.html. *Lancer* reproduces the redacted steno record.

27. 18H742.

28. 18H742.

29. 2H144. Hill seems to be describing what plausibly could have been two shots fired very close together. His full quotation runs as follows:

> It was right, but I cannot say for sure that it was rear, because when I mounted the car it was—it had a different sound, first of all, than the first sound that I heard. The second one had almost a double sound—as though you were standing against something metal and firing into it, and you hear both the sound of a gun going off and the sound of the cartridge hitting the metal place, which could have been caused probably by the hard surface of the head. But I am not sure that is what caused it.

Earlier in his testimony, Hill had said he heard the "double sound" just as he reached the presidential limousine and that it sounded "as though someone was shooting a revolver into a hard object—it seemed to have some type of an echo" (2H138).

Hill went on to say that the interval between the earlier shot he heard and the shot with the curious "double sound" was "approximately 5 seconds" (2H139). Hill's report of the shot times produces an uncanny fit with the actual time between shots, as shown by the acoustics evidence: 4.8 seconds between the third shot and the next-to-last shot (the knoll shot) and 0.7 seconds between the next-to-last knoll shot and the final shot from the depository. With the final two shots only 0.7 seconds apart, we can understand why Hill described hearing "a double sound." With the next-to-last shot coming from the right front and the final shot coming from the rear, we can understand why Hill said the last shot "was right, but I cannot say for sure it was rear."

30. 2H138. Hill says specifically that "the second noise that I heard had removed a portion of the President's head" (2H138).

31. 2H139.

32. 2H141.

33. Clint Hill and Lisa McCubbin, Mrs. Kennedy and Me (New York: Simon and Schuster, 2012), 290.

34. Hill and McCubbin, 306.

35. The Sibert-O'Neill report was published for the first time in Josiah Thompson, Six Seconds in Dallas (New York: Bernard Geis Associates, 1967), 296–298. It can be read at "FBI Agents James Sibert and Francis O'Neill Wrote this Report from Their Notes Taken during the Autopsy of President Kennedy," JFK Lancer, http://jfklancer.com/Sibert-ONeill.html.

36. Photocopies of "Highlights of Boswell Interview" can be found in the files of the Josiah Thompson Collection at the Sixth Floor Museum at Dealey Plaza in Dallas, TX.

37. "Highlights of Boswell Interview."

38. "Highlights of Boswell Interview."

39. "Highlights of Boswell Interview."

40. "Highlights of Boswell Interview."

41. "Highlights of Boswell Interview."

42. The official autopsy report is CE 387 and can be found in the Warren Report, pages 538–543, and at 16H978–983.

43. 16H983.

44. These experiments are described in the testimony of Alfred G. Olivier, director of veterinary medicine at Edgewood Arsenal, at 5H87–90. After displaying a photo of CE 861, Dr. Olivier pointed out that the bullet "blew out the whole side of the cranial cavity away. . . . It exited very close to the superorbital ridge, possibly below it" (5H89). The "superorbital ridge" is the brow above the eye. Dr. Olivier is saying that the bullet exited out the face of the skull, as shown in the photo of CE 861. Nothing like this happened to President Kennedy, whose face was undamaged. Unaccountably, Dr. Olivier went on to say that "we found that this bullet could do exactly—could make the type of wound that the President received" (5H89).

45. Gary Aguilar's excellent study, "How Five Investigations into JFK's Medical/ Autopsy Evidence Got It Wrong," discusses this fact in detail. It can be read at the Mary Ferrell Foundation website, https://www.maryferrell.org/mffweb/archive/viewer/show Doc.do?docId=368.

46. Page 6 of the official autopsy report, or 16H983.

47. Page 6 of the official autopsy report, or 16H983.

48. Pages 3–4 of the official autopsy report, or 16H980–981.

49. Page 2 of the official autopsy report, or 16H979.

50. *Washington Post*, November 23, 1963, 1.

51. The full sentence in Humes's handwritten draft of the autopsy report reads, "Three shots were heard and the president fell face forward to the floor of the vehicle while bleeding from the head" (17H30–31).

52. Weitzman testified that the found the skull fragment "8 to 12 inches from the [south] curb of Elm Street" (7H107). This is some ten feet south or left of the limousine's path in the middle lane of Elm Street.

The FBI report on Harper's finding of the bone states that he found it at around 5:30 p.m. on November 23, "approximately 25 feet south of the spot where President Kennedy was shot." Harper's uncle, Jack C. Harper, M.D., was interviewed much later by the FBI and made available photos he had taken of both sides of the bone fragment. These photos have survived and show a triangular-shaped bone fragment about three inches across. A. B. Cairns, M.D., chief pathologist at Methodist Hospital in Dallas, was also interviewed by the FBI concerning the Harper fragment. He had examined it and offered the opinion that at "it came from the occipital region of the skull." Billy Harper was interviewed by the FBI on November 26, 1963; Jack Harper, MD, on July 13, 1964; and A. B. Cairns, MD, on July 13, 1964. Photocopies of their FBI interview reports are reprinted in Thompson, *Six Seconds in Dallas*, 302–303.

With the president riding in the right rear seat of the limousine as it cruised in the middle lane of Elm Street, this three-inch bone fragment must have flown more than twenty-five feet to the south (or left) of the limousine's path.

53. See Chapter 4, where Officer Jackson's recollections are discussed. The actual quotation can be found in Sergeant James Bowles's manuscript published by Gary Savage in *JFK: First Day Evidence* (Monroe, LA: The Shoppe Press, 1993), 361–364, where Jackson's recollections as "Officer C" can be found.

54. Both the sketch shown in Figure 16-18 and commentary on it are found in *Report of the Select Committee on Assassinations*, US House of Representatives, 95th Cong., 2nd sess., appendix, vol. 7, 130–131.

55. Mantik, 17.

56. This "cloud of almost dust-like fragments" has been the focus of discussions between Drs. Wecht and Aguilar and the author for more than a decade.

57. See Humes's testimony at 2H353.

58. See Kellerman's testimony at 2H100.

59. Clark Panel Review of Photographs, X-Ray Films, Documents and other Evidence Pertaining to the Fatal Wounding of President John F. Kennedy on November 22, 1963 In Dallas Texas, 1968, 11, https://www.history-matters.com/archive/jfk/arrb/master_med_set/md59/html/Image00.htm.

60. See *Inside the ARRB: Current Section: ARRB Staff Report on Observations and Opinions of Forensic Radiologist Dr. John J. Fitzpatrick, after Viewing the JFK Autopsy Photos and X-Rays*, 2, Mary Ferrell Foundation website, https://maryferrell.org/showDoc.html?docId=145280&relPageId=225.

Photo N-5. Harper bone fragment (exterior).

61. Vincent J. M. Di Maio, *Gunshot Wounds* (New York: Elsevier Science Publishing Co., 1985), 155.

62. Di Maio, 145, 155.

CHAPTER 17. THE AD HOC COMMITTEE ON BALLISTIC ACOUSTICS

1. Jill Abramson, "Kennedy, the Elusive President," *New York Times Book Review*, October 22, 2013, 24. Abramson noted, "Even the basic facts of Kennedy's death are still subject to heated argument. The historical consensus seems to have settled on Lee Harvey Oswald as the lone assassin, but conspiracy speculation abounds—involving Johnson, the CIA, the mob, Fidel Castro or a baroque combination of all of them."

2. The guest, Nick Ragone, wrote a book describing fifteen decisions of presidents from Washington to Kennedy "that changed the nation." In 2013, he was director of the Washington office of Ketchum, a public relations firm. In May 2014, he became chief communications officer of Ascension Health.

3. *Report of the Committee on Ballistic Acoustics* (Washington, DC: National Academy Press, 1982), 2, 5, 7, 10, 13, and 35.

4. Luis W. Alvarez, *Alvarez: Adventures of a Physicist* (New York: Basic Books, 1987), 246–247.

5. For a definition of "confirmation bias," see *Science Daily* (http://www.science daily.com/terms/confirmation_bias.htm). The Wikipedia entry for confirmation bias is comprehensive: http://en.wikipedia.org/wiki/confirmation_bias. Such bias is endemic in the scientific literature and remains a /huge problem. A fuller explanation

can be found in Raymond S. Nickerson, "Confirmation Bias: A Ubiquitous Phenomenon in Many Guises," *Tufts University Review of General Psychology* 2 (1998): 175–220,
http://psy2.ucsd.edu/~mckenzie/nickersonConfirmationBias.pdf.

6. An amateur 8-mm film taken by Dealey Plaza witness Charles Bronson.

7. *Report of the Select Committee on Assassinations*, US House of Representatives, 95th
Cong., 2nd sess., 480–481 (hereafter HSCA Report).

8. HSCA Report, 481.

9. The professor was Marvin E. Wolfgang. The letter is referred to in Representative
Edgar's dissent, which can be found in the HSCA Report, 494–500.

10. Seymour Hersh, *The Samson Option: Israel's Nuclear Arsenal and American Foreign
Policy* (New York: Vintage Books, 1993), 273.

11. The last page of the committee's report lists its members: Jack Ruina, chairman (MIT), Luis Alvarez (University of California, Berkeley), William Donn (Lam-
ont-Doherty Geological Observatory, Columbia University), Richard Garwin (Thomas
J. Watson Research Center, IBM), Riccardo Giacconi (Harvard/Smithsonian Center for
Astrophysics), Richard Muller (University of California, Berkeley), Wolfgang Panof-
sky (Stanford Linear Accelerator Center), Allen Peterson (Stanford University), and F.
William Sarles (Lincoln Lab at MIT). The full report has been posted on the Internet by
the Federation of American Scientists, http://www.fas.org/rig/800717-vela.pdf.

12. Leonard Weiss, "The Vela Event of 1979 (or the Israeli Nuclear Test of 1979),"
paper presented at The Historical Dimensions of South Africa's Nuclear Weapons
Program conference, Pretoria, South Africa, December 10, 2012, 11. Weiss worked at
the Center for International Security and Cooperation at Stanford University.

The flawless track record was due to the design of the "advanced" Vela satellite.
The Vela program was launched following the signing of the Partial Test Ban Treaty
in 1963. The program name was drawn from a constellation in the southern hemisphere sometimes called "the sails" and comprised satellites launched between 1963
and 1970. Satellites in the advanced Vela series (including Vela 6911) were launched
between 1967 and 1970 and accrued a flawless record of forty-one confirmed detec-
tions out of forty-one claimed.

The satellites carried instrumentation precisely configured to detect the unique
signature of nuclear blasts in the atmosphere—an extremely short but high-intensity
flash of light followed by a second, less intense and more prolonged emission. The
first peak endures for only about one millisecond, while the second peak is much
longer. This phenomenon springs from the basic physics of a nuclear explosion in air.
The fireball produced is quickly overtaken by a shock wave that functions as an optical
curtain, obscuring the fireball behind an opaque screen of ionized material. The Vela
satellites took advantage of this fact by mounting two sensors called "bhangmeters"
that recorded the characteristic double-hump flash.

13. One month after the Vela Panel released its report, the Naval Research Laboratory forwarded to the White House a three-hundred-page report that its director of
research said "was strong enough to make the case [for a nuclear explosion] in its
own right." Still classified thirty-four years later, it is not available for study. What
is available is a letter from that director of research, Alan Berman, to a White House
official on December 11, 1980.

Berman began by saying he wanted to make clear that there was "a useful set of well-documented facts that had been somewhat obscured" in earlier discussions of the Vela 6911 incident. In 1982, after Berman had moved on to the University of Miami, he was less diplomatic in his language. He told an interviewer that he was "furious" that the Vela Panel Report had been released only a month before the NRL report was submitted and that the White House subsequently—and unceremoniously—buried the NRL report. In short, Berman asserted that a set of "well-documented facts" pointing to an unpalatable conclusion had been ignored by the Carter administration. In his letter, he laid out the nature of these "well-documented facts."

He pointed out that three wide-band hydrophones placed in the water near Ascension Island had registered a strong impulse at a time "remarkably close to the VELA time." Given the fact that the sound impulses had to travel ten thousand kilometers to reach Ascension Island, this kind of match was extraordinary. Data picked up from earlier French tests in the Pacific could be used to interpret what the hydrophones registered. Since the United States knew from the French tests that a nuclear explosion had occurred and also knew its size, this permitted a much more fine-grained and reliable analysis of the September 22 event. Both the earlier French test and the September 22 blast had a similar profiles, indicating an explosion ten to twenty meters above a thin sediment layer overlying basalt. This was in fact the situation in the vicinity of the supposed blast location near Prince Edward and Marion Islands.

These islands are located ten kilometers west of Natal Bank and one hundred kilometers west of East Bank. The signal detected was extremely strong, twenty-five decibels above background. Using the French tests as a control, this would indicate a two-kiloton blast. The existence of data from the French tests permitted the NRL not only to estimate the time of the blast (remarkably synchronous with the Vela 6911 detection) and its probable location (consistent with the Vela 6911 detection) but also to estimate the depth and underwater conditions beneath the blast (precisely identical to those conditions near Prince Edward and Marion Islands). At most, one might have hoped for hydro-acoustic confirmation of the time of the blast. Instead, there was a trifecta of confirmation by the time, direction, and underwater features of the blast location.

See the letter from Alan Berman to John M. Marcum, December 11, 1980. This five-page letter can be found in the South African Nuclear History collection at the Woodrow Wilson International Center for Scholars, Washington, DC, http://digitalarchive .wilsoncenter.org/document/116758.

14. Jeffrey T. Richelson, *Spying on the Bomb* (New York: W. W. Norton, 2006), 313. Richelson devoted a section of his book to the Vela 6911 detection. He pointed out that further press investigation had not been kind to the Vela Panel conclusions. In April 1997, the Israeli *Haaretz* newspaper reported that the South African deputy foreign minister, Aziz Pahad, had "confirmed that the double flash had resulted from a test" (Richelson, 313). Later that month, *Aviation and Space Technology* stated directly that "a South African government official has confirmed that his nation detonated a nuclear weapon in the atmosphere in September 1979" (Richelson, 314).

15. Hersh, *The Samson Option*, 271–272.

16. The DIA issued a report entitled "The South Atlantic Mystery Flash" by Dr. John

E. Mansfield and Lt. Col. Houston T. Hawkings. It is document 10 at the National Security Archive, George Washington University, 27–28. The National Security Archive is maintained by George Washington University.

17. Executive Office of the President, *Ad Hoc Panel Report on the September 22 Event*, July 17, 1980, 3 (hereafter cited as Vela Panel Report). This report may be downloaded from the Federation of American Scientists site, http://www.fas.org/rlg/800717-vela.pdf.

18. Vela Panel Report, 2.

19. The table of contents provided by Paul Hoch is preserved in the reference footnotes to these documents. "PAF #42," for example, refers to "Public Access File" (PAF) with "#42" being the number that Paul's table assigned to the document. I have provided the Sixth Floor Museum at Dealey Plaza in Dallas, TX, with scans of the 367 pages as well as Paul Hoch's table of contents and notes. The documents cited can be reviewed there in the Josiah Thompson Collection. The grant application for the Ad Hoc Committee on Ballistic Acoustics can also be seen there under the title "Grant Application to National Science Foundation for Support of the Ad Hoc Committee on Ballistic Acoustics," PAF #72,

20. What was called the "Public Access File (PAF)" no longer exists at the NAS. No written material is any longer available to the public from the NAS (telephone communication with Judith Goldblum, archivist at the NAS, May 6, 2014).

21. PAF #72, 2.

22. See PAF #72, 3. When the chief counsel of the HSCA learned that he had audio evidence on a Dallas police channel, he went to the SAA for the names of the best experts in acoustic science. At the top of the list was Dr. James Barger and his firm Bolt, Beranek and Newman (BBN). When he needed additional experts to work on Barger's results, he asked the SAA for a second recommendation and was given the names of Dr. Mark Weiss and Ernest Aschkenasy. Given the desire of Representative Sawyer for a "wholly independent expert consultant knowledgeable in the science of acoustics," one would have thought that the SAA would once again have been consulted to recommend acoustic experts. As it turned out, for unknown reasons, the SAA was never asked, and no acoustic experts were appointed to the committee.

23. Alvarez was four years older than Ramsey. Their friendship began in November 1940 when both were recruited to work at MIT with British colleagues on what Alvarez later called the "microwave committee." The idea was to use physicists' familiarity with electronic pulses from ionization chambers and Geiger counters to enable them to jump-start efforts developing pulsed radar for the British Fighter Command. Only two months before, the Fighter Command had used radar to gain a victory in the Battle of Britain.

Reading Alvarez's autobiography, one gets the impression that this time in the early 1940s working with the RAF—and even flying with it—was probably the happiest time of his life. By the fall of 1943, both Alvarez and Ramsey had moved on from this early work on radar to the Manhattan Project. Both were at Los Alamos together for over eighteen months, and then both moved on with the two completed bombs to Tinian Island in the Pacific. Alvarez, of course, had developed blast test equipment to measure the size of the Hiroshima blast. This equipment was to be parachuted from a chase plane flying with the *Enola Gay*. Alvarez was on Tinian Island to prepare the

Photo N-6. Tinian Island, August 1945: Luis Alvarez in flak jacket standing before a B-29 named *The Great Artiste*.

equipment for the mission and flew in the chase plane over Hiroshima. At Los Alamos, Ramsey led a team charged with integrating the design and delivery of the two weapons being assembled there. He supervised the modification of a B-29 to drop the weapons and arranged test drops. Ramsey went to Tinian in July 1945 to ready the planes to carry the bombs and specifically helped assemble the "Fat Man" bomb dropped on Nagasaki.

After the war, Ramsey went to Harvard and Alvarez to Berkeley, but both kept up their contacts and service for what Alvarez called "Washington-based committees." Alvarez worked on a number of committees for the Pentagon and was a longtime member of the JASON Advisory Group. Ramsey seemed to move a step farther apart from that inner circle of defense scientists. In the late 1940s, he helped found the Brookhaven National Laboratory, and, in the late 1960s and 1970s the Fermi Lab in Illinois. In the 1970s, he was an adviser to the North Atlantic Treaty Organization (NATO), where he spearheaded a program to support the training of future scientists.

In his autobiography, Alvarez pointed out that in 1961, "old physics friends on the

Photo N-7. Tinian Island, August 1945: Norman Ramsey autographs the Nagasaki bomb.

limited war committee included Norman Ramsey now at Harvard and William Shockley, the 1956 physics Nobel laureate" (Alvarez, *Alvarez*, 219). Alvarez chaired this panel, which was charged with finding ways to oppose the Soviet Union through limited wars that would not lead to a thermonuclear conflict. In that summer of 1961, it led to Alvarez leading his committee on tours throughout the world to visit armed forces bases and units. "After more briefings in Washington," Alvarez wrote, "I led most of the committee on a tour of the Far East while Norm Ramsey and Bill Shockley took the rest to the Middle East" (Alvarez, 220).

24. Alvarez, 248.

25. JASON is a thirty- to sixty-member advisory group of scientists formed in 1960 to advise the US government on matters of science and technology, mostly defense related.

26. Carl Oglesby, *The JFK Assassination: The Facts and the Theories* (New York: Signet, 1992), 250–251.

27. PAF #118 and #119. Shanin Specter's undergraduate paper is found in PAF #118, and Alvarez's "jet-effect" paper is found in PAF #119. Specter's undergraduate paper at Haverford College was titled "An Evaluation of the House Select Committee on Assassinations' Findings of Possible Conspiracy in the Assassination of President Kennedy and an Evaluation of the Utility of the Committee"; it was received at the NAS on November 11, 1980, and circulated to members of the Ramsey Panel two months later. Alvarez's article was entitled "A Physicist Examines the Kennedy Assassination Film" (*American Journal of Physics* 44, no. 9 [September 1976]: 816); it was circulated to members of the Ramsey Panel when Specter's paper was circulated.

Photo N-8. Professor Norman F. Ramsey.

28. Letter of Norman F. Ramsey to Barger, Weiss, and Aschkenasy, January 20, 1981, PAF #108.

29. Letter of Norman F. Ramsey to Luis Alvarez, January 20, 1981, PAF #109.

30. PAF #109.

31. E-mail from James Barger to Don Thomas, April 22, 1999. The full quotation reads as follows:

My view about the "political correctness problem" is that many scientists were stifled by the luster of the NRC committee members. Alvarez had a Nobel Prize in Physics and Ramsey got one soon after the NRC report. As you know, Luis had published two "scientific" papers—one purporting to prove that there was no frontal shot and the other to show there were only three shots based on Zapruder's jiggle. In fact, Luis told me at the first meeting I had with the NRC committee that he "didn't care what I said, he would vote against me anyway." I pointed out there were other jiggles just as big as the ones he cited, and he denied it—even as he looked at a copy of his paper that showed them. So I never thought I would be able to change at least his mind—no matter what.

32. Personal communication to author by Paul Hoch, May 6, 2014.

33. PAF #84.

34. PAF #83.

35. E-mail from James Barger to author, April 17, 2015.

36. PAF #127.

37. Don Thomas carried out the only independent analysis of these factors and published the results in a 2001 article in the British journal Science & Justice and in his 2010 book, Hear No Evil: Social Constructivism and the Forensic Evidence in the Kennedy Assassination (Ipswich, MA: Mary Ferrell Foundation Press, 2010). According to Thomas, a correct rendering of the probability equations yields a 1 in 100,000 chance that the knoll-shot sound impulse is not a shot. (Thomas, 632). In March 2002, Herman Chernoff admitted that he had in fact made precisely the error of confusing free variables with empirical facts charged by Thomas. Art Snyder, PhD, of the Stanford Linear Accelerator experimental group, confirmed Thomas's correction of the Ramsey Panel's probability calculus: "Don Thomas did correct the

statistics calculation made by Herman Chernoff for the Academy of Science's report and I checked Don's stats and he got them right. Chernoff also agreed he had made an error and corrected it to get a number much like Don's" (e-mail from Arthur E. Snyder to Paul Hoch's Listserv group, May 6, 2013). I write more about Thomas in a later chapter.

CHAPTER 18. THE CROSSTALK SILVER BULLET

1. "An Evening with Richard L. Garwin: Conversation with David Kestenbaum of National Public Radio," January 10, 2006, 8 (https://fas.org/rlg/060110-aaas.pdf).

2. The facts described in this and the next few paragraphs are drawn from a ninety-minute tape-recorded interview with Steve Barber carried out by the author on May 24, 2014.

3. Barber was friends with Robert Cutler and Richard Sprague, well-known researchers in the 1970s. He was also acquainted with Todd Vaughan. Vaughan was only in high school at the time but later became prominent in researcher circles. Before leaving for a visit to Dallas in August 1979, Barber had purchased his copy of Gallery magazine with its disk of the Dallas police channels. Barber's younger sister, Kathi, had been born on November 22 and accompanied Barber on the Dallas trip. During this visit, she ended up meeting and later marrying Larry Harris, one of the movers behind the founding of the Conspiracy Museum in Dallas and himself a longtime buff.

4. Interview with Barber, May 24, 2014.

5. Public Access File (PAF) #130 (the number is the one assigned to the document in Paul Hoch's table of contents; these files and Hoch's table of contents and notes may be viewed in the Josiah Thompson Collection at the Sixth Floor Museum at Dealey Plaza in Dallas, TX).

6. PAF #57, #58.

7. PAF #130, #131.

8. PAF #130.

9. Interview with Barber, May 24, 2014.

10. Interview with Barber.

11. Interview with Barber. One of the oddest features of the Ad Hoc Committee on Ballistic Acoustics was its almost hysterical fear of the private individuals making up the community of "buffs." Take, for example, the appointment letters to members of the committee sent out by Herbert Friedman on October 8, 1980 (PAF #57, #58). Friedman's letter made the point that due to the sensitivity of the Kennedy case and "the intensity of feelings on the part of some individuals with respect to the outcome of any such study," special precautions were being taken. "It has been decided, therefore, to protect the privacy of members of the Committee by withholding their names from public announcement until their report has been completed and submitted to the sponsors."

Much later, a member of the Ramsey Panel, Charles Rader, made the same point in an interview video put together by IEEE.tv called, "Uncovering the Truth about the Kennedy Assassination: Signal Processing Tells the Story." Rader was a signal processing expert at the Lincoln Laboratory at MIT in 1980. The narrator of the video introduces the Ramsey Panel by saying, "Called the Committee on Ballistic Acoustics, an obscure name chosen to help keep assassination fanatics from hounding the members with their theories, its mission was to analyze and critique the methodologies of the previous researchers." Rader then says, "It didn't work. Some of the assassination buffs found us. And it's a good thing they did because the crucial part of our work came from a hint from an assassination buff. There was this young man from Shelby, Ohio—a rock musician named Steve Barber" (https://ieeetv.ieee.org/history /truth-about-assassination-signal-processing-tells-story).

12. This and later quotations in these paragraphs are taken from the interview with Barber.

13. Letter from Luis Alvarez to members of the Ramsey Panel, July 3, 1981 (PAF #44). Apparently, at a meeting only two weeks earlier, Professor Ramsey had indicated a lack of interest in Barger's offer to him of all their "reconstruction data and analysis." According to a letter from Barger to Ramsey, dated February 2, 1982 (PAF #17),

> From the time you first talked with us regarding your committee's task, we urged you to examine the basic acoustical reconstruction data and technical details of our analysis, and in my letter of February 4, 1981, we renewed our offer to make all our reconstruction data and analysis available to you, so that you could check our pattern matching. When, in your meeting with us June 18, you said in essence, ". . . We give you all that . . . ," we appreciated your expression of confidence, but now we realize that you do not intend to examine our basic data and analysis, which, we believe, are essential to a real understanding and evaluation of our work.

In the February 4, 1981, letter cited mentioned above, Barger wrote, "We think that the committee can best determine what we did by receiving access to all our data and results, and then by repeating our analysis to any desired extent. I renew my offer to host a small subgroup of your committee to spend several days in our laboratory for this purpose" (letter from Barger to Ramsey, February 4, 1981, PAF #91). The panel continued to decline invitations to the BBN lab to review the evidence.

14. The basis for the facts recounted in the paragraphs that follow can be found in James C. Bowles's 1979 manuscript essay, "The Kennedy Assassination Tapes: A Rebuttal to the Acoustical Evidence Theory." The manuscript essay is reprinted in whole along with its appendices in Gary Savage, JFK: First Day Evidence (Monroe, LA: The Shoppe Press, 1993), 313–410. Like almost all Dallas law enforcement officers, Bowles was deeply suspicious of the HSCA and the national media. At some points, his essay reads like a screed against the work of the HSCA and its acoustics scientists.

Nonetheless, Bowles was in charge of the communications department of the Dallas police, and his detailed recounting of how the radio and recording system worked is invaluable. His essay influenced the Ramsey Panel at many points, and the committee members were unstinting in their praise of it. Bowles went on to become sheriff of Dallas County.

15. The Random House Dictionary of the English Language, 2nd ed., unabridged (New York: Random House, 1987).

16. Report of the Committee on Ballistic Acoustics (Washington, DC: National Academy Press, 1982), 18.

17. Donald B. Thomas, *Hear No Evil: Social Constructivism and the Forensic Evidence in the Kennedy Assassination* (Ipswich, MA: Mary Ferrell Foundation Press 2010), 564.

18. See *Report of the Select Committee on Assassinations*, US House of Representatives, 95th Cong., 2nd sess., vol. 5, 637.

19. In March 1964, the FBI asked Captain Bowles to prepare a transcript of both channels because the agents could not understand all the words spoken in the north Texas dialect, and they could not identify the speakers' voices. He repeated his work for his essay. In notes to his transcripts, he noted the full identity of the callers listed in this paragraph. See Bowles, "The Kennedy Assassination Tapes," in Savage, JFK, 404–405.

20. Charles Rader in IEEE.tv video, "The Truth about the Kennedy Assassination: Signal Processing Tells the Story" (https://ieeetv.ieee.org/history-truth-about -assassination-signal-processing-tells-story).

21. Michael O'Dell, "The Acoustic Evidence in the Kennedy Assassination," 3 (http://mcadams.posc.mu.edu/odell/); see also Thomas, *Hear No Evil*, 638–639. O'Dell cleverly determined that the Ramsey Panel had misunderstood how the Audograph machine worked and had consequently miscalculated the time discrepancy.

22. PAF #139.

23. PAF #138.

24. PAF #140.

CHAPTER 19. THE RESURRECTION OF THE ACOUSTICS

1. James Barger told me that BBN had to absorb $20,000 of unpaid expenses, and I have heard that Weiss and Aschkenasy were never paid for any of their work. Although I have not been able to confirm this report in detail, it is clearly true that Weiss and Aschkenasy did not write the report ascribed to them in volume 8 of the HSCA volumes. There, an odd footnote to the title page of the report states that "materials submitted for this report by the committee's acoustics panel were compiled by HSCA staff member Gary T. Cornwell" (*Report of the Select Committee on Assassinations*, US House of Representatives, 95th Cong., 2nd sess., appendix, vol. 8, 3).

2. George Lardner Jr., "Study Backs Theory of 'Grassy Knoll,'" *Washington Post*, March 26, 2001, A3, https://www.washingtonpost.com/archive/politics/2001/03/26 /study-backs-theory-of-grassy-knoll/9e9cfdod-d8b7-4cae-8317-30860999539b/.

3. Selby was working on an episode for the Travel Channel on the locations of famous murders. I don't know if the episode—or the series—ever aired.

4. Donald B. Thomas, "Hear No Evil: The Acoustical Evidence in the Kennedy Assassination," lecture presented at the Lancer Conference, Dallas, TX, November 17, 2001, 17. For the text of the whole lecture, see http://the-puzzle-palace.com/hear noevil.htm.

5. This manuscript was not published until 1993, when it appeared in Gary Savage's book *JFK: First Day Evidence* (Monroe, LA: The Shoppe Press, 1993), 313–410. In spite of its animus against the HSCA and the acoustics evidence, it remains a gold mine of information about the two Dallas police channels. Of special interest are the transcripts of both channels prepared by Bowles.

6. Don Thomas, personal communication to author, November 24, 2014.

7. Thomas, personal communication, November 24, 2011.

CHAPTER 20. "I'LL CHECK IT"

1. Listen for yourself. This particular track can be heard as track 1 on the NAS website, where it has been posted since 2005 (https://nap.edu/catalog/10264/report-of -the-committee-on-ballistic-acoustics). The crosstalk "I'll check it" can be heard quite clearly at 03:47 into the track.

2. James E. Barger, Scott P. Robinson, Edward C. Schmidt, and Jared J. Wolf, "Analysis of Recorded Sounds Relating to the Assassination of President John F. Kennedy," in *Report of the Select Committee on Assassinations*, US House of Representatives, 95th Cong., 2nd sess., appendix, vol. 8, 33–127.

3. See Charles Olsen and LeeAnn Maryeski, "Further Research, Analysis, and Commentary on the Dallas Police Department Recordings of November 22, 1963," 3, http://www.thekennedyhalfcentury.com (click on "new audio research").

4. Track 2 of the NAS tracks contains channel 2, 12:25 through 12:33 (see https:// nap.edu/catalog/10264/report-of-the-committee-on-ballistic-acoustics). The exchange between Deputy Chief Fisher and Captain Lawrence begins at 1:40 into the track. "I'll check it" is not heard until 2:07.

5. See James C. Bowles, "Transcript Channel II Dallas Police Department Communications 11:37 am to 12:40 pm November 22, 1963," in Gary Savage, *JFK: First Day Evidence* (Monroe, LA: The Shoppe Press, 1993), 404.

6. Plate 1 in the color photo gallery shows a "bird's-eye view" of Dealey Plaza when "I'll check it" was broadcast simultaneously on both channels.

7. See Savage, *JFK* (1993), 344, 348, 359, 393, and 409.

8. Savage, 344.

9. The panel described this track on the NRC/NAS site as "miscellaneous short segments of Ch 1 and Ch 2." The recording is ninety-eight seconds long. Listen to it at https://www.nap.edu/catalog/10264/report-of-the-committee-on-ballistic-acoustics.

10. See Figure N-9 on the next page for the spectrogram labeled "I'll check it" and made by the Ramsey Panel in 1981–1982. Note that the time given of 12:31:02 (ellipses on both channels) is taken from Bowles's transcript as the time of "I'll check it."

11. This copy of Bowles's monograph and the associated transcripts was given to me by Chris Scally. Scally obtained it from the National Archives while preparing his definitive studies of the provenance of both the acoustic evidence and the Zapruder film. The title page contains in typescript the legend "'THE KENNEDY ASSASSINATION TAPES: A Rebuttal to the Acoustical Evidence by James C. Bowles." The top-left corner of the title page contains Bowles's name, address, and phone number. It can be reviewed in the National Archives, record 124-10053-10354, file 62-109060-8202, or in the Josiah Thompson Collection at the Sixth Floor Museum at Dealey Plaza in Dallas, TX. Although this cannot be said with certainty, it may very well be the very copy used by the Ramsey Panel in drafting Appendix C when it was purportedly reproduced but was actually changed.

CHAPTER 21. RAMSEY PANEL REDUX

1. R. Linsker, R. L. Garwin, H. Chernoff, P. Horowitz, and N. F. Ramsey, "Synchronization of the Acoustic Evidence in the Assassination of President Kennedy," *Science & Justice* 45, no. 4 (2005): 207–226.

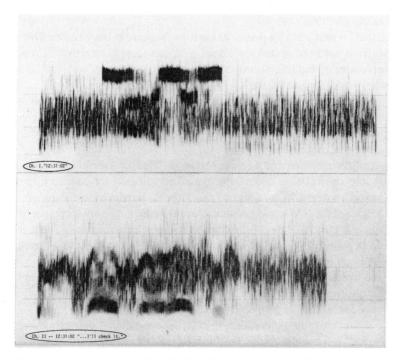

Figure N-9. Spectrograms for "I'll check it" on channels 1 (*above*) and 2 (*below*) prepared by the Ramsey Panel in 1980–1982.

2. The 2002 unpublished manuscript titled "Synchronization of the Acoustic Evidence in the Assassination of President Kennedy" ("Scientific and Technical" manuscript submission to *Science & Justice*) can be viewed in the Josiah Thompson Collection at the Sixth Floor Museum at Dealey Plaza in Dallas, TX.

3. Linsker et al., "Synchronization of the Acoustic Evidence," 207.

4. Linsker et al., 212.

5. Linsker et al., 220.

6. Linsker et al., 222.

7. Linsker et al., 220–222.

8. Linsker et al., 221.

9. Linsker et al., 222.

10. See R. Linsker, R. L. Garwin, H. Chernoff, and N. F. Ramsey, "Acoustic Synchronization: Rebuttal of Thomas' Reply to Linsker et al.," *Science & Justice* 46, no. 3 (July 2006):1–6, cited quotation on page 2.

11. Linsker et al., "Acoustic Synchronization: Rebuttal," 2–3.

12. Linsker et al., 2–3.

CHAPTER **22.** JOURNEY TO THE LAIR OF THE MASTER

1. Letter from James Barger to Josiah Thompson, March 24, 2015.

2. E-mail from James Barger to Josiah Thompson, May 29, 2015.

3. As we saw in Chapter 21, Linsker et al. stated that they had produced a peak for "Hold everything" of 0.32, while their graph showed a peak of only 0.275. These translated into net peaks for "Hold everything" of either 0.19 or 0.145 depending on whether you choose to credit the authors' text or their actual graph. See R. Linsker, R. L. Garwin, H. Chernoff, P. Horowitz, and N. F. Ramsey, "Synchronization of the Acoustic Evidence in the Assassination of President Kennedy," *Science & Justice* 45, no. 4 (2005): 207–226.

CHAPTER 23. IN THE COLD LIGHT OF SCIENCE

1. Letter from James E. Barger to Prof. Norman Ramsey, February 2, 1982, PAF #17 (the number is the one assigned to the document in Paul Hoch's table of contents; these files and Hoch's table of contents and notes may be viewed in the Josiah Thompson Collection at the Sixth Floor Museum at Dealey Plaza in Dallas, TX).

2. Entry for "artifact," *The Random House Dictionary of the English Language*, 2nd ed., unabridged (New York: Random House, 1987).

3. *Report of the Committee on Ballistic Acoustics* (Washington, DC: National Academy Press, 1982), 64 (hereafter Ramsey Panel Report).

4. Ramsey Panel Report, 65.

5. Ramsey Panel Report, Appendix C, 60–69.

6. Ramsey Panel Report, 60.

7. Ramsey Panel Report, 65.

8. Ramsey Panel Report, 65–66.

9. Ramsey Panel Report, 65.

10. Ramsey Panel Report, 66.

11. Barger's approach is fully described in his paper, "Quantitative Analysis of Crosstalk Found in Audio Recorded during JFK Assassination," included here as Appendix A. He provides a step-by-step account along with the relevant equations that he used to reach his results. The raw material for his study are the two .wav files matched in speed with events and time announcements, marked by Michael O'Dell as "ch1ODELLFINAL.wav" and "ch2ODELLFINAL.wav."

12. Ramsey Panel Report, 60.

13. Chris Scally, *The Dallas Police Department Channel 1 Radio Dictabelts: The Chain of Possession*, last page. This excellent study can be reviewed or downloaded from http://mcadams.posc.mu.edu/scally.htm.

14. Scally, 3.

15. Having carried out the definitive study, Chris Scally remains our guide. To summarize what we know of these materials, we start with the obvious fact that the reel-to-reel tapes that Jack Moriarty obtained from McCaghren were not original recordings from November 22. They couldn't be since the original recordings from November 22 were a Dictabelt and an Audograph disk, while Moriarty inventoried only reel-to-reel copies from McCaghren. Secret Service records show that what appeared to be original recordings were picked up by Secret Service Agents Roger Warner and Elmore Moore on November 29 "for transcription." The agents received the recordings from Deputy Chief Lumpkin, and no receipts were given. Agent Warner then made a reel-to-reel copy, which he sent on to the Protective Research Section in Washington.

The Warner tape was copied in Washington, but the Secret Service was unable to find either Warner's tape or copies of it when inquiries were made in 1970 and 1978. We know, however, that the tape existed because a transcript made from it was found in Secret Service records by researcher Mark Allen in 1982. Also in 1982, Scally initiated a third search of Secret Service records for the Warner tape with negative results.

For unknown reasons, the recordings picked up by Warner and Moore were not returned by the FBI to the Dallas Police until March 1964. However, as Bowles told Gary Mack, he could give no assurance that the recordings returned were the same recordings that had left the DPD on November 29. Deputy Chief Lumpkin gave the recordings to Warner and Moore, and they may or may not have been returned to Sergeant Bowles by the FBI. The FBI asked Bowles to make a transcript from the recordings and provided a Wollensak reel-to-reel recorder for the job.

The reel-to-reel tapes recorded by Bowles on the Wollensak recorder became the actual recordings of the event studied by future panels and individuals. There is no difficulty establishing what happened to the four reel-to-reel copies Bowles made. He kept one, gave a second to Chief Curry, and passed the remaining two on to the FBI. The bureau passed one of these on to the Warren Commission. Today, neither the FBI nor the Warren Commission copy can be located due to the cavalier way in which the material was treated. This left Chief Curry's copy, which was the seven-inch reel-to-reel copy Paul McCaghren passed on to Jack Moriarty that March morning in Dallas. This was also what Barger, Weiss and Aschkenasy, and the Ramsey Panel used for their studies. These tracks were posted by the remaining members of the Ramsey Panel on the NRC/NAS website in 2002 and obtained from there by Mullen and Barger for our more recent studies.

What about the materials Bowles used to make these reel-to-reel tapes? After making the reel-to-reel copies Bowles used the materials that were returned to make his transcript. Every time he dropped the needle on the Dictabelt to listen to a stretch of sound, it would (according to Bowles) "add minute dimples in the belts." It was fortunate that he had made his reel-to-reel copies first because making his transcript severely degraded the sound quality and accuracy of the materials he used.

Since no system was ever established to track the movements of particular Dictabelts or Audograph disks, we can only say that many Dictabelts and Audograph disks were making the rounds in Dallas, but it's unclear whether any were originals. In July 1964 Chief Curry gave ten Dictabelts to the FBI. But nothing indicated whether a particular belt was an original or a copy. The presumption was that all were originals. When the Dallas police provided fifteen belts to the HSCA in July 1978, the presumption again was that these were originals, but the start and end times of these belts do not match the start and end times of the ten belts provided earlier to the FBI. Somehow or other in 1990, a taped copy of DPD assassination recordings turned up in the files of the Minneapolis Public Library with indications that it had been placed there in December 1963 by a fictitious company.

Scally ended his multiple-decade study with the following observation: "Indeed, one could now reasonably ask—were *any* [emphasis in original] of the currently existing dictabelts recorded on that fateful Friday in November 1963?"

16. Ramsey Panel Report, 64.

17. Letter from James Barger to [Ramsey Panel Member] Jerome I. Elkind, March 22, 1982, PAF #9. This letter can be found in the Josiah Thompson Collection at the Sixth Floor Museum.

18. E-mails exchanged between James Barger, Don Thomas, and other members of our research team are not individually referenced. They may be reviewed in the Josiah Thompson Collection at the Sixth Floor Museum.

19. The simulcast was produced by Sergeant Gerald Henslee, a dispatcher on Channel 2, who flipped a switch on his console and broadcast on both channels simultaneously: "Attention all emergency equipment. Do not use Industrial Boulevard. Do not use In-buh-dustrial Boulevard. 12:36." Henslee's odd mispronunciation, "in-buh-dustrial," marks an exact instant shared between the two channels.

20. This announcement was made in pro forma compliance with Federal Communications Commission regulations requiring that a station's call letters be given at roughly thirty-minute intervals. The dispatcher inserted it when possible during a time of high traffic volume; hence the one-minute time discrepancy.

21. The best available transcript appears to be that done by Jim Bowles and published by Gary Savage at the end of his extremely useful book, JFK: First Day Evidence (Monroe, LA: The Shoppe Press, 1993), 371–410.

22. Barger, "Quantitative Analysis of Crosstalk Found in Audio Recorded during JFK Assassination."

23. E-mail from James Barger to John Grissim, September 18, 2019, Josiah Thompson Collection at the Sixth Floor Museum.

24. Notes from a telephone conversation on September 19, 2019, between Josiah Thompson and James Barger, Josiah Thompson Collection at the Sixth Floor Museum.

25. The Defense Intelligence Agency (DIA) issued a report titled "The South Atlantic Mystery Flash" by Dr. John E. Mansfield and Lieutenant Colonel Houston T. Hastings. It is Document 10 at the National Security Archive, http://www2.gwu.edu/ffinsarchiv/NSAEBB/NSAEBB190/index.htm. The National Security Archive is maintained by George Washington University.

26. Ramsey Panel Report, 89.

27. Ernest Aschkenasy, James Barger, and DPD Officer H. B. McLain all testified that the Dallas police radio networks would broadcast more than one transmission at the same time if the carrier waves of the transmissions were about equal. They all testified on December 29, 1978, in the final public hearing of the HSCA. Their testimony can be read in Report of the Select Committee on Assassinations, US House of Representatives, 95th Cong., 2nd sess., vol. 5, with Aschkenasy at 591–592, Barger at 672, and McLain at 640.

28. To have learned this, all the Ramsey Panel needed to do was run the battery of tests run by Rich Mullen in his study of the hums on channels 1 and 2.

29. Luis W. Alvarez, Alvarez: Adventures of a Physicist (New York: Basic Books, 1987), 164.

CHAPTER 24. THE LAST SECOND

1. The exact timing of the three shots in the first act of the shooting is important because it tells us something about their origin. Over the years, various firing tests have

been performed under various conditions not using the rifle found on the sixth floor. Since the firing speed of a bolt-action rifle depends not only on the model of the rifle but also on its state of lubrication, firing tests with other rifles prove little. The gold-standard for tests showing how fast the rifle could be fired were conducted by FBI agent Robert Frazier of the FBI Laboratory beginning on November 27, 1963, and using the rifle in evidence. Frazier was timed firing the rifle at targets at various distances. He fired three shots in 4.6 seconds, 4.8 seconds, 5.6 seconds, 5.8 seconds, 5.9 seconds, and "a little over 6 seconds" (3H410). Frazier later testified that "I would say that 4.6 seconds is firing the weapon as fast as the bolt can be operated" (3H407). The Warren Commission accepted Frazier's judgment and announced in its report (p. 97) that "tests of the assassin's rifle disclosed that 2.3 seconds were required between shots."

2. This and other quotations from Don DeLillo are drawn from an interview by Adam Begley, "Don DeLillo: The Art of Fiction No. 135," *Paris Review*, Issue 128 (Fall 1993): 1–21. The quotation is from page 17.

3. The commission, however, did publish Zapruder frames in volume 18 of its hearings and exhibits, including the sequence following frame 313. The frames were published in black and white, two to a page, and ran from frame 171 through 334. In all, 163 frames were published, but the sequence was marred by a single mistake. Frames 314 and 315 were reversed in both numbering and position. The result, of course, makes the backward movement look like a forward movement. When queried in 1965, Director Hoover stated in a letter dated December 14, 1965, that there had been a "printing error" by the Government Printing Office. See Josiah Thompson, *Six Seconds in Dallas* (New York: Bernard Geis Associates, 1967), 89n.

APPENDIX A. QUANTITATIVE ANALYSIS OF CROSSTALK FOUND IN AUDIO RECORDED DURING THE JFK ASSASSINATION

1. See *Report of the Committee on Ballistic Acoustics* (Washington, DC: National Academy Press, 1982), hereafter referred to as the Ramsey Panel.

2. R. Linsker, R. L. Garwin, H. Chernoff, P. Horowitz, and N. F. Ramsey, "Synchronization of the Acoustic Evidence in the Assassination of President Kennedy," *Science & Justice* 45, no. 4 (2005): 205–226.

3. These run-out times were found at BBN in 1978 and conveyed to Norman Ramsey by letter from James Barger. The procedure, used for both channels, was to construct histograms of about 100 recorded silent time spans as functions of their time spans in 1-s intervals. A narrow probability maximum was found for the 7–8-s span on channel 1, and a similar probability maximum was found for the 6–7-s span on channel 2.

4. Chris Scally, "The History of the DPD Channel 2 Audograph Discs—A Report for Josiah Thompson," Version 2, May 31, 2016.

5. These files are downloadable from https://www.nap.edu/catalog/10264/report-of-the-committee-on-ballistic-acoustics. The eight tracks are listed as "Podcast(s)" on the right side of the page under "Resources at a Glance."

6. Michael O'Dell, file ch2ODELLFINAL.wav and ch1ODELLFINAL.wav.

7. $S2a = Tds \times (B2b/B2a - 1) + S2b \times (B2b/B2a) + D$

8. Clock synchronization parameter; CS = Channel 2 clock time – Channel 1 clock time.

1. R. Linsker, R. L. Garwin, H. Chernoff, P. Horowitz, and N. F. Ramsey, "Synchronization of the Acoustic Evidence in the Assassination of President Kennedy," *Science & Justice* 45, no. 4 (2005): 205–226.

2. These files are downloadable from https://www.nap.edu/catalog/10264/report-of-the-committee-on-ballistic-acoustics. The eight tracks are listed as "Podcast(s)" on the right side of the page under "Resources at a Glance."

ILLUSTRATION CREDITS

Photo 2-1. CE 399 is the bullet in the middle. Image © US Government.

Photo 2-2. Polaroid photos taken at Parkland Hospital. Image © Josiah Thompson.

Photo 2-3. CE 399. Image © US Government.

Photo 2-4. .30-caliber projectile from O. P. Wright. Image © Josiah Thompson.

Photo 3-1. Newmans on the ground with their boys. Image © Josiah Thompson.

Photo 3-2. Bill Newman with news reporter Jay Watson at WFAA-TV. Image © WFAA-TV Collection. Courtesy The Sixth Floor Museum at Dealey Plaza.

Photo 3-3. Newmans on the ground after the shooting. Image © Wilma Bond.

Photo 3-4. People stream onto the grassy knoll. Image © F. W. Bell.

Photo 3-5. Abraham Zapruder with Jay Watson at WFAA-TV. Image © WFAA-TV Collection, Courtesy The Sixth Floor Museum at Dealey Plaza.

Photos 3-6 and 3-7. Muchmore frame. Image © AP Images.

Photo 3-8. Moorman photograph with shot trajectory. Image © AP Images.

Photo 3-9. Hudson remains sitting on the steps. Image © The Sixth Floor Museum.

Photo 3-10. AP photographer James Altgens's photo of the motorcade snapped at Zapruder frame 255. Image © AP Images.

Photo 3-11. Frame 342. Zapruder Film © 1967 (Renewed 1995) The Sixth Floor Museum at Dealey Plaza.

Photo 3-12. Frame 347. Zapruder Film © 1967 (Renewed 1995) The Sixth Floor Museum at Dealey Plaza.

Photo 4-1. Altgens photograph taken at frame 255. Image © AP Images.

Photo 4-2. Officer James Chaney during the ABC television interview. Image © Black Star.

Photo 4-3. Officer Hargis turns toward the knoll. Image © Wilma Bond.

Photo 5-1. Lee Bowers in 1966. Image © Wisconsin Center for Film and Theater Research.

Photo 5-2. Bowers's view from the switching tower. Image © Josiah Thompson.

Photo 5-3. S. M. "Skinny" Holland. Image © Josiah Thompson.

Photo 5-4. Holland on the overpass pointing toward the fence. Image © Josiah Thompson.

Photo 5-5. Holland on the overpass during the assassination. Image © AP Images.

Photo 5-6. Holland retraces his steps on November 22. Image © Josiah Thompson.

Photo 5-7. Holland's view from the overpass. Image © Josiah Thompson.

Photo 5-8. Area behind the stockade fence, summer of 1967. Image © Josiah Thompson.

Photo 5-9. Holland standing behind the stockade fence. Image © Josiah Thompson.

Photo 5-10. Holland's diagram of cars and footprints behind the stockade fence. Image © Josiah Thompson.

Photos 5-11 and 5-12. Holland behind the stockade fence, as seen from Moorman's position. Image © Josiah Thompson.

Photos 5-13, 5-14, and 5-15. Moorman photograph. Image © AP Images.

Figure 5-16. Holland's diagram of cars and footprints behind the stockade fence. Image © Josiah Thompson.

Figure 7-1. The possible path of a bone or bullet fragment from the head impact out the throat. Image © Josiah Thompson.

Photo 7-2. Bonnie Ray Williams and James Jarman. Image © Tom C. Dillard Collection, The Dallas Morning News, Courtesy The Sixth Floor Museum at Dealey Plaza.

Photo 7-3. Three of the four cartridge cases. Image © US Government Archives.

Photo 7-4. CE 543: Dented cartridge case. Image © US Government Archives.

Photo 9-1. Professor Luis Alvarez at University of California. Image © 2010–2019 The Regents of the University of California, Lawrence Berkeley National Laboratory.

Photo 9-2. Frame 227. Zapruder Film © 1967 (Renewed 1995) The Sixth Floor Museum at Dealey Plaza.

Figure 9-3. Alvarez's handwritten chart of jiggles. Image © Josiah Thompson.

Photo 9-4. A1: Preshoot. Rubber ball filled with gelatin. Image © Paul Hoch.

Photo 9-5. A6: Postshoot. Rubber ball goes forward. Image © Paul Hoch.

Photo 9-6. Luis Alvarez and family during the test session of May 31, 1970. Image © Paul Hoch.

Photo 9-7. Physicist Paul Hoch flipping a melon at the May 31, 1970. Image © Paul Hoch.

Photo 9-8. B16—Preshoot. Melon #4. Image © Paul Hoch.

Photo 9-9. Melon #4. Postshoot. Image © Paul Hoch.

Photo 11-1. Analog clock with digital face. Image © Josiah Thompson.

Figure 11-2. HSCA map. Image © HSCA, US Government.

Figure 11-3. HSCA map. Image © HSCA, US Government.

Table 11-1. Match-up of audio candidates of rifle shots. Image © HSCA, US Government. See the following sources for a more detailed account of the facts reported in this section: (1) HSCA Report, 72–75, and (2) Richard N. Billings and G. Robert Blakey, *Fatal Hour: The Assassination of President Kennedy by Organized Crime* (New York, Berkley Books, 1992), 11.

Figure 11-4. HSCA map. Image © Don Thomas.

Figure 11-5. These wave forms each represent about one second. Image © Josiah Thompson.

Photo 11-6. Professor Mark Weiss testifying before the HSCA on December 29, 1978. Image © HSCA, US Government.

Figure 11-7. Official HSCA diagram showing the location of the motorcycle and the "unknown gunman" as per Weiss and Aschkenasy. Image © HSCA, US Government.

Table 12-1. The six blur patterns identified by Alvarez, Hartmann, or Scott. See 6HSCA30. © HSCA, US Government.

Table 12-2. Match-up of sound impulses with frames and blurs if frame 313 is the next-to-last shot. © Josiah Thompson.

Table 12-3. Comparison of movement measurements, Thompson and ITEK. © Josiah Thompson.

Photos 12-1 and 12-2. Goat before and after shooting. Image © Edgewood Arsenal, US Government.

Photo 13-1. Lead in an industrial "melt" vat at a bullet manufacturer. Image © Josiah Thompson.

Photo 13-2. Cross-section of a Mannlicher-Carcano bullet from lot 3000 showing the grain structure. Antimony tends to fall into grain boundaries. Image © Erik Randich, PhD and Patrick M. Grant, PhD "Proper Assessment of the JFK Assassination Bullet Lead Evidence from Metallurgical and Statistical Perspectives Journal of Forensic Sciences," July 2006, vol. 51, no. 4, page 727.

Photos 14-1 and 14-2. Frames 405 and 409. These illustrations are found in part I of David Wimp's monograph "The Effect of Motion Blurring on Contrast Edges." Zapruder Film © 1967 (Renewed 1995) The Sixth Floor Museum at Dealey Plaza.

Photo 14-3. Frames 312 and 313. Zapruder Film © 1967 (Renewed 1995) The Sixth Floor Museum at Dealey Plaza.

Photo 14-4. Frame 312. Zapruder Film © 1967 (Renewed 1995) The Sixth Floor Museum at Dealey Plaza.

Photo 14-5. Frame 313. Zapruder Film © 1967 (Renewed 1995) The Sixth Floor Museum at Dealey Plaza.

Photos 14-6 to 14-12. Frames 312, 313, 314, 315, 316, 317, 323. Zapruder Film © 1967 (Renewed 1995) The Sixth Floor Museum at Dealey Plaza.

Photos 14-13 and 14-14. Moorman photo. Image © AP Images.

Photo 14-15. Altgens's photo taken at frame 255. Image © AP Images.

Photo 14-16. Extreme close-up of Altgens's photo. Image © AP Images.

Photos 14-17 and 14-18. Altgens's photo after the shooting was over. Image © AP Images.

Photo 14-19. CE 350: photo of limousine windshield taken during the Frazier examination. Image © US Government Archives.

Figures 14-20 and 14-21. Frazier's notes from the windshield examination. Image © US Government Archives.

Photo 14-22. Frame 255. Image © AP Images.

Figure 14-23. Two patterns of impact debris. Image © Josiah Thompson.

Photo 14-24. The limousine, follow-up car, and motorcyclists on Main Street. Courtesy Wikimedia Commons.

Photos 15-1 to 15-8. Frames 312 through 319. Zapruder Film © 1967 (Renewed 1995) The Sixth Floor Museum at Dealey Plaza.

Photos 15-9 and 15-10. Frames 317 and 320. Zapruder Film © 1967 (Renewed 1995) The Sixth Floor Museum at Dealey Plaza.

Photos 15-11 to 15-20. Frames 321 through 330. Zapruder Film © 1967 (Renewed 1995) The Sixth Floor Museum at Dealey Plaza.

Photo 15-21. Frame 317. Zapruder Film © 1967 (Renewed 1995) The Sixth Floor Museum at Dealey Plaza.

Photo 15-22. Frame 323. Zapruder Film © 1967 (Renewed 1995) The Sixth Floor Museum at Dealey Plaza.

Photos 15-23 and 15-24. Frames 328 and 329. Zapruder Film © 1967 (Renewed 1995) The Sixth Floor Museum at Dealey Plaza.

Photos 15-25 to 15-29. Frames 331 through 335. Zapruder Film © 1967 (Renewed 1995) The Sixth Floor Museum at Dealey Plaza.

Photo 15-30. Frame 327. Zapruder Film © 1967 (Renewed 1995) The Sixth Floor Museum at Dealey Plaza.

Photo 15-31. Frame 337. Zapruder Film © 1967 (Renewed 1995) The Sixth Floor Museum at Dealey Plaza.

Photo 15-32. Frame 230. Zapruder Film © 1967 (Renewed 1995) The Sixth Floor Museum at Dealey Plaza.

Photo 15-33. Frame 342. Zapruder Film © 1967 (Renewed 1995) The Sixth Floor Museum at Dealey Plaza.

Photo 15-34. Frame 312. Zapruder Film © 1967 (Renewed 1995) The Sixth Floor Museum at Dealey Plaza.

Photo 15-35. Frame 323. Zapruder Film © 1967 (Renewed 1995) The Sixth Floor Museum at Dealey Plaza.

Photos 15 36 to 15-39. Frames 328, 329, 330, 335. Zapruder Film © 1967 (Renewed 1995) The Sixth Floor Museum at Dealey Plaza.

Photo 15-40. Frame 328. Zapruder Film © 1967 (Renewed 1995) The Sixth Floor Museum at Dealey Plaza.

Photo 15-41. Frame 328. Zapruder Film © 1967 (Renewed 1995) The Sixth Floor Museum at Dealey Plaza.

Photos 15-42 to 15-44. Frames 328, 329, 330. Zapruder Film © 1967 (Renewed 1995) The Sixth Floor Museum at Dealey Plaza.

Photo 15-45. Frame 328. Zapruder Film © 1967 (Renewed 1995) The Sixth Floor Museum at Dealey Plaza.

Photo 15-46. Frame 342. Zapruder Film © 1967 (Renewed 1995) The Sixth Floor Museum at Dealey Plaza.

Photo 15-47. Frame 357. Zapruder Film © 1967 (Renewed 1995) The Sixth Floor Museum at Dealey Plaza.

Photo 15-48. Frame 359. Zapruder Film © 1967 (Renewed 1995) The Sixth Floor Museum at Dealey Plaza.

Photo 15-49. Frame 369. Zapruder Film © 1967 (Renewed 1995) The Sixth Floor Museum at Dealey Plaza.

Photo 15-50. Muchmore film. Zapruder Film © 1967 (Renewed 1995) The Sixth Floor Museum at Dealey Plaza.

Photo 15-51. Holland watches press cars head under the Triple Underpass. Image © Tom Dillard.

Photo 16-1. Dr. Kemp Clark and Dr. Malcolm Perry, November 22, 1963. Image © Josiah Thompson.

Figure 16-2. Diagram sketch of human skull showing locations of parietal and occiput bones. Image © BodyParts3D, © The Database Center for Life Science licensed under CC Attribution-Share Alike 2.1 Japan.

Figure 16-3. Dr. Robert McClelland's wound description as drawn by a medical illustrator. Image © Josiah Thompson.

Photo 16-4. Clint Hill, splattered with blood and brain tissue, runs to the limousine. Image © AP Images.

Photo 16-5. Frame 334. Zapruder Film © 1967 (Renewed 1995) The Sixth Floor Museum at Dealey Plaza.

Photos 16-6 and 16-7. Frames 335 and 337. Zapruder Film © 1967 (Renewed 1995) The Sixth Floor Museum at Dealey Plaza.

Figure 16-8. Painting of Mrs. Kennedy cradling her husband's head at Parkland Hospital. Image © Pieta Tempera Grassa on Canvas 5' x 7' Mark Balma 2004.

Photo 16-9. Commander Boswell, Commander Humes, and Lieutenant Colonel Finck. Image © Josiah Thompson.

Figure 16-10. Skull diagram marked up by Boswell during autopsy. Image © US Government.

Photo 16-11. The tracheotomy incision at the base of the throat. Image © US Government.

Photo 16-12. Human skull (CE 861) used in the Edgewood Arsenal experiment. Image © Edgewood Arsenal, US Government.

Photo 16-13. EOP. Entry locations marked by Humes, Boswell, and Finck. Image © HSCA, US Government.

Photo 16-14. Lateral X-ray, right side. Image © HSCA, US Government.

Photos 16-15 and 16-16. Autopsy photos of President Kennedy. Image © US Government Archives.

Figure 16-17. Lateral autopsy photo. Image © US Government Archives.

Figure 16-18. HSCA illustration of the president's brain damage from front to back along the sagittal plane. Image © HSCA, US Government.

Figure 17-1. The arrow indicates the approximate position of the suspected nuclear explosion. Image © GMT.

Photo 17-2. South African Naval Base at Simon's Town. Courtesy of Wikimedia Commons, Discott.

Photo 18-1. *Gallery* magazine for July 1979. Image © Gallery Magazine.

Photo 18-2. Barber's 33⅓-rpm disk from *Gallery* magazine. Image © Gallery Magazine.

Photo 18-3. Steve Barber in Dallas, August 1979. Image © Steve Barber.

Photo 19-1. Don Thomas in 2004. Image © Don Thomas.

Photo 19-2. An Audograph machine. Image © Michael O'Dell.

Photo 19-3. Close-up of the Audograph worm gear. Image © Michael O'Dell.

Figure 20-1. Sonalysts Corp. diagram. Image © "Further Research, Analysis, and Commentary on the Dallas Police Department Recordings of November 22, 1963" by Charles Olsen and LeeAnn Maryeski of Sonalysts, Inc. 6 June 2014, page 3.

Figure 20-2. HSCA map with motorcycle locations. Image © HSCA, US Government.

Photo 20-3. The limousine enters the "kill zone" as the lead car is out of frame to the left "At the Triple Underpass." Image © Charles L. Bronson Collection. Courtesy The Sixth Floor Museum at Dealey Plaza.

Figure 20-4. Ramsey report, page 71, Bowles transcript of channel 1. Image © Ramsey Report, US Government.

Figure 20-5. Original typescript of Bowles's transcript of channel 1 available to the Ramsey Panel in 1980–1982. Image © Ramsey Report, US Government.

Figure 20-6. Beginning of the Ramsey Panel's channel 2 transcript in Appendix C, page 76 of its report. Image © Ramsey Report, US Government.

Figure 20-7. Bowles's continuous transcript of channel 2 from 12:31:02. Image © Ramsey Report, US Government.

Photo 22-1. James E. Barger. Image © Josiah Thompson.

Photo 22-2. BBN in Cambridge is now Raytheon BBN Technologies. Image © Raytheon BBN Technologies.

Figure 22-3. Linsker's typical PCC plot at the correct warp for "I'll check it" using a sampling window of 512. Image © Science & Justice, vol. 45, no. 4 (2005), page 222.

Figure 22-4. Mullen's PCC plot for "I'll check it" using a sampling window of 512. Image © Josiah Thompson.

Figure 22-5. Net PCC peak of 0.25 produced for "I'll check it" by using a sampling window size of 64. Image © Josiah Thompson.

Figure 22-6. Mullen produced a net peak of 0.09 (0.26 minus a background of 0.17) for "Hold everything" using a sampling window of 64. Image © Josiah Thompson.

Figure 22-7. Mullen produced a net peak of 0.16 (0.24 minus a background of 0.08) for "Hold everything" using a sampling window of 512. Image © Josiah Thompson.

Photo 23-1. Moorman photo with thumbprint. Image © AP Images.

Figure 23-2. Channel 2 recording of HOLD, "You want me . . . Stemmons," and the five silences. Image © Josiah Thompson.

Figure 23-3. Channel 2 placement of "I'll check it" and "Hold everything." Image © Josiah Thompson.

Figure 23-4. Channel 1 placement of "I'll check it" and "Hold everything." Image © Josiah Thompson.

Photo 23-5. The lead car and limousine on Main Street. Image © AP Images.

Figure 23-6. Using SIMULCAST as a zero point of simultaneity, CHECK and I'VE GOT turn out to also have been broadcast simultaneously on both channels. Image © Josiah Thompson.

Figure 23-7. SIMULCAST, CHECK, and I'VE GOT show virtually no alignment error because they occurred simultaneously on both channels. Image © Josiah Thompson.

Photo 24-1. President Kennedy at Pebble Beach, California, 1961. Used with Permission by Pebble Beach Company. Photo by William C. Brooks (Anthony Grissim collection).

Figures A-1 to A-6. Image © Josiah Thompson.

Table B-1. Sources of audio data for each instance of crosstalk. © Richard Mullen.

Figures B-1 to B-5. Image © Josiah Thompson.

Table B-2. Net peak value for each βPCC graph and the value of the simultaneity radio PCC ration for each event. © Richard Mullen.

Figure N-1. From the FBI files, the *Washington Post* with Hoover's note and initial. Image © US Government Archives.

Photo N-2. Robert Capa photo from 1936, *The Falling Soldier*. Image © Robert Capa, [Death of a Loyalist militiaman, near Espejo, Cordoba front, Spain], early September 1936. International Center of Photography, © International Center of Photography/Magnum Photos (2010.86.647).

Photo N-3. A similar photo from the Mexican suitcase. Image © Robert Capa, [Death of a Loyalist militiaman, near Espejo, Cordoba front, Spain], early September 1936. International Center of Photography, © International Center of Photography/Magnum Photos (2010.86.629).

Figure N-4. Canning diagram, 6HSCA61. Image © HSCA, US Government.

Photo N-5. Harper bone fragment. Image © HSCA, US Government.

Photo N-6. Luis Alvarez in flak jacket. Image © 2010–2019 The Regents of the University of California, Lawrence Berkeley National Laboratory.

Photo N-7. Norman Ramsey autographs the Nagasaki bomb. Image © National Archives.

Photo N-8. Professor Norman F. Ramsey. Image © Harvard University Physics Department.

Figure N-9. Spectrograms for "I'll check it" on channels 1 and 2 prepared by the Ramsey Panel in 1980–1982. Image © Michael O'Dell.

Plate 1. Illustration of "bird's-eye" view of Dealey Plaza. Image © Josiah Thompson.

Plate 2. Chart constructed by Thomas. Donald B. Thomas, *Hear No Evil* (New York: Skyhorse, 2013), 216.

Plates 3a and 3b. Frame Z 313 (with and without Ektachrome yellow tint). Zapruder Film © 1967 (Renewed 1995) The Sixth Floor Museum at Dealey Plaza.

Plates 4a and 4b. Frame Z 313, shadow-enhanced version. Zapruder Film © 1967 (Renewed 1995) The Sixth Floor Museum at Dealey Plaza.

Plate 5. Frame Z 313 close-up. Zapruder Film © 1967 (Renewed 1995) The Sixth Floor Museum at Dealey Plaza.

Plate 6. DPD Dictabelt recording. Image © NARA.

Plate 7. DPD Audograph disk recording. Image © NARA.

Plates 8a and 8b. Large fragments found by Secret Service agents. Images © National Archives, photos by FBI personnel.

Plate 9. *LIFE* magazine cover from November 25, 1966. Image © *LIFE* Magazine.

Plate 10. Governor John Connally examines *LIFE* magazine's frames. Image ©
   LIFE Magazine.
Plate 11. *Saturday Evening Post* cover. © SEPS licensed by Curtis Licensing India-
   napolis, IN. All rights reserved.
Plate 12. Cover of *Six Seconds in Dallas*. Image © Josiah Thompson.

Page numbers in italics refer to pages with photos or figures.

Federal Bureau of Investigation (FBI), *continued*

comparative bullet lead analysis and, 190, 191, 413–414n7

copies of the DPD recordings and, 440n15

examination of the presidential limousine and impact debris, 207–209, 210–211

Hoover's report on the cartridges found at the depository building, 102

interview of Bill and Gayle Newman, 34–35

interview of Douglas Jackson, 390n2

interview of Emmett Hudson, 43

interview of Lee Bowers Jr., 64

interview of Officer Joe Marshall Smith, 58–59

interview of S. M. Holland, 68

interviews of Officer James Chaney, 53–54

investigations of Josiah Thompson by, 387n1, 400n2, 401

neutron activation analysis of CE 399 and other bullet fragments, 24, 192, 193–194, 413–414n7

Oklahoma City bombing and, 188–189

Josiah Thompson's visit to in 1963, 6

Zapruder frame 313 and, 354

Fensterwald, Bud, 135, 165

Ferrell, Mary, 10, 142, 143, 145, 351

Fields, Maggie, 10

final shot

acoustic evidence and, 235–236

bidirectional pattern of head-impact debris and, 210–212

Howard Brennan's account of, 398–399n5

coherence of the evidence for, 243–244

Connally's wrist wound from a fragment of, 230–233

final reconstruction of events in the assassination and, 356–357

Keith Fitzgerald's identification of, 221–229, 277

medical evidence supporting, 267, 270–272

narrative of the Kennedy assassination and, 354–355

windshield flare and, 234–235

witness validation for, 236–244

Zapruder film and (*see* Zapruder film—and the final shot)

See also double-impact theory

Finck, Pierre, 247–248, 257, 258, 264, 420n5, 423n8

First Day Evidence (Savage), 306

Fisher, N. T., 297, 310–311, 314, 316, 340

Fitzgerald, Keith

identification of Connally's wrist wound from the final shot, 231–233

identification of the final shot, 221–229, 277

identification of windshield flare from the final shot, 234–235

Josiah Thompson's introduction to, 221

witness validation in the Zapruder film for the final shot, 236–244

Fitzpatrick, John, 272

Forensic Pathology Panel (of the HSCA), 166–167, 175–178

Forensic Science International, 191

Four Days That Shocked the World (film), 407n6

Franzen, Jack and Joan, 239–240

Franzen, Jeff, 239

Franzen, Julie, 239–240

Frazier, Robert, 207, 208, 209, 210–211, 416n4, 441–442n1

Freedom of Information Act, 194

free variables, 288–289

Friedman, Herbert, 434n11

Fritz, Will, 63

Fuller, Ronnie, 24

Galanor, Stewart, 395n13

Gallagher, John F., 414n9

Gallery (magazine), 291, 292, 294

Galloway, Calvin, 246

Garcia, Frederico Borrell, 412n22

Garrison, Jim, 112, 135

Garry, Charles, 164

Garwin, Richard, 281, 290–291, 308, 349

Geis, Bernard

production and publication of *Six Seconds in Dallas* and, 11, 12, 93, 106

Josiah Thompson's entry into the LIFE magazine investigation and, 16, 17, 18

Time Inc. lawsuit and, 109–110, 112–113

Geis, Darlene, 106

General Dynamics Corporation, 193

Gerhard, Dieter, 282

Giesecke, Alfred, 424n22

goat shooting experiment, 175–176, 410–411n22

results of the initial acoustic analysis of the
DPD recordings and, 151–152
review of Kennedy's autopsy, 246
synchronization of acoustic evidence to
the Zapruder film, 170–171, 235
Warren Commission version of events
and, 167, 170, 178
HSCA. *See* House Select Committee on
Assassinations
Hudson, Emmett, 13, 29, 41–45, 48, 389n15
Humes, James J.
burning of the autopsy notes and draft
report made by, 247, 423n9
drafting of the autopsy report, 257
examination of a bullet hole in the back of
Kennedy's head, 255–256, 264, 421n6
Pierre Finck's autopsy notes and, 423n8
influence of press dispatches on the
autopsy report and, 266–267
John Lattimer and, 420n3
missteps in conducting the Kennedy
autopsy, 246–248
photos taken during the Kennedy autopsy,
420–421n6
request for forensic examiners, 247, 420n3
Hunt, George, 27

"I'll check it" crosstalk
James Barger's analysis of time
synchronicity in the crosstalks and, 338,
343–344, 345
evidence for the purposeful omission of by
the Ramsey Panel, 312–318, 326
Richard Mullen's analysis of, 325–332
responses of the Ramsey Panel to, 307,
319–322, 326
spectrograms for, 438
Don Thomas and, 305–307, 311, 313, 326,
332
Josiah Thompson's contact with James
Barger regarding the validity of,
323–326
Josiah Thompson's examination of the
DPD recordings for, 308–313
unshrinkable 88 seconds argument,
340–341
impact debris
analysis from the Zapruder frames,
268–270
bidirectional pattern of, 210–212

failure of the Warren Commission to fully
explain, 211–212
FBI examination of, 207–209, 211
final reconstruction of events in the
assassination and, 356
Robert Frazier's testimony on, 416n4
Clint Hill and, 209, 210, 254, 354
Officer B. J. Martin and, 58, 209, 210,
211–212
Officer Bobby Hargis and, 55, 56, 209,
210, 211, 212
Officer Douglas Jackson and, 52, 390n2
Officer James Chaney's account of,
390–391n2
Francis O'Neill's description of, 417n5
skull fragments, 268–269, 426n52, 427
"in-buh-dustrial" (SIMULCAST), 338, 343,
344, 345, 441n19
Inquest (Epstein), 17, 83
Israeli–South Africa nuclear test operation,
281–284, 428–429n13, 429n14
ITEK Corporation, 174, 175, 177, 199, 201,
415–416n1
"I've got a witness" crosstalk, 313, 338

Jackson, Bob, 266
Jackson, Douglas, 49, 50–52, 54, 268–269,
390–391n2, 390n1
Jarman, James, 100
Jenkins, Marion, 250
jet effect theory
Luis Alvarez and the development of,
122–130, 432n27
efforts to reproduce Luis Alvarez's results,
405n23
HSCA explanations for Kennedy's
backward head movement and,
174–175, 177–178
reasons for Luis Alvarez's delayed
publication of, 405n24
JFK (film), 189
JFK Assassination Records Collection Act
(1992), 189
jiggle theory
Luis Alvarez and the development of,
115–121, 223
analysis of the Zapruder film by the HSCA
and, 171–173
Johns, Thomas ("Lem"), 391–392n16
Johnsen, Richard, 23–24

Johnson, Clemon, 394–395n13
Johnson, Marion, 10
Jones, Jim, 164
Jones, Penn, 10
Journal of Forensic Science, 192
Journal of the American Medical Association, 98

Kaiser, Robert Blair, 135
KBOX broadcast tape, 407n6
Kellerman, Roy, 271, 417n5, 420n5
Kennedy, Jacqueline
   description of John Kennedy's head
      wound, 251–252
   final reconstruction of events in the
      assassination and, 356
   motions of John Kennedy's body when
      shot and, 177
   painting of the assassination and, 256
   permission for John Kennedy's autopsy,
      246, 419–420n2
Kennedy, Robert, 112
Kennedy assassination
   effectiveness of a crossfire ambush, 361
   final reconstruction of events in, 355–357
   final shot and (*see* final shot)
   narrative of the last second, 353–355
   portrayed by the evidence as two volleys of
      shots, 351–353
   primary narrative immediately following,
      28
   role of chance in providing evidence
      concerning, 351
   single-bullet theory and, 83–85
   Josiah Thompson's 2020 visit to Dallas
      and reflections on, 359–361
   Josiah Thompson's early independent
      investigations into, 3, 9–15
   Josiah Thompson's reconstruction of in
      Six Seconds in Dallas, 103
   the Umbrella Man and, 102–103
   Warren Commission findings, 6
"Kennedy Assassination Tapes, The"
      (Bowles), 306, 312, 314–316, 317,
      435n14, 437n11
Kennedy autopsy
   J. Thornton Boswell's account of, 94,
      255–260
   description of Kennedy's back wound, 95
   failure to examine Kennedy's clothing,
      420n5

failure to examine the back wound, 94, 95,
      255–256
   faulty conclusions of, 260–267
   on the head wounds, 97
   James Humes's examination of a bullet
      hole in the back of the head, 255–256,
      264, 421n6
   incompetency and failures of, 245–248
   influence of press dispatches on the
      conclusions on, 266–267
   Jacqueline Kennedy's permission for, 246,
      419–420n2
   lost photos from, 420–422n6
   suppression of photos from, 422–423n7
   the throat wound and, 258–259, 260
   See also medical evidence
Kennedy back wound
   autopsy doctors and, 94, 95, 255–256
   autopsy photos of, 420–421n6
   questions regarding, 94
Kennedy head shot(s)
   acoustic evidence and, 277
   James Altgens's account of, 45–48
   Luis Alvarez and the jet effect theory (*see* jet
      effect theory)
   analysis of motion blurring in the
      Zapruder film and, 197–202, 277,
      415–416n1
   James Canning's explanation of,
      417–418n2, 419
   Edgewood Arsenal skull-shooting
      experiments, 126
   final reconstruction of events in the
      assassination and, 355–357
   Keith Fitzgerald's identification of the
      final shot from the rear, 221–229, 277
      (*see also* final shot)
   S. M. Holland's account of, 70–71, 72,
      74–75
   HSCA analysis of Kennedy's forward head
      movement, 173–174, 175
   HSCA explanations for the backward head
      movement, 174–178
   Emmett Hudson's account of, 42–45
   impact debris from (*see* impact debris)
   narrative of the last second and the final
      shots, 353–355
   neuromuscular reaction hypothesis,
      174–178, 410–413n22
   the Newmans' account of, 32–38

HSCA 1977 conference with assassination
    researchers and, 142
on the Kennedy assassination
    investigation as "eminence-based," 193
Vincent Salandria and, 402n5
Six Seconds in Dallas and, 107, 111–112
medical evidence
    autopsy conclusions, 260–267
    Thornton Boswell's account of, 255–260
    challenges of, 245
    Clint Hill's account, 251, 252–255
    incompetency and failures of the autopsy,
        245–248
    Jacqueline Kennedy's account, 251–252
    number of witnesses confirming a
        blow-out wound to the right rear of
        Kennedy's head, 251
    Parkland Hospital witnesses, 248–251
    what the evidence supports, 267–272
    See also Kennedy autopsy; Kennedy head
        wound
Medical Panel. See Forensic Pathology Panel
    (of the HSCA)
melon-shooting experiments, 124, 125–126,
    128, 129–130, 197
Menaker, Walter, 117–118, 120
microsegregation, 195
Miller, Austin, 394n13
minimum mechanical firing time, 352,
    441–442n1
Minority of One, 111
"missile dust," 270–272
Mohawk, Richard, 140
Moore, Elmore, 439n15, 440n15
Moorman, Mary, 13, 41, 241, 397n24
Moorman Polaroid photo
    absence of evidence for a second head
        impact in, 204, 205, 206
    blowup of the stockade fence, 81
    description of, 41, 42
    HSCA and, 166
    Emmett Hudson and, 43
    shot trajectory superimposed on, 44
    Josiah Thompson's copy and the
        enhancement of, 165–166, 397n24
    Josiah Thompson's examination of the
        stockade fence with S. M. Holland, 79,
        81
    with thumbprint artifact, 334
Morgan, Russell H., 271–272

Moriarty, Jack, 146–147, 406n4, 439n15
Morris, Willie, 11
motion blurring
    comparison of measurements by
        Thompson, Wimp, and ITEK,
        415–416n1
    David Wimp's analysis of Kennedy's
        head wound in the Zapruder film and,
        197–202, 277
    See also jiggle theory
Mourelatos, Alex, 4–5
move one, move all argument, 342–343
Mozley, Barney, 66–67, 68
Muchmore, Marie, 135
Mullen, Richard
    analysis of crosstalk evidence, 325–332
    determination of "Hold everything"
        crosstalk as an artifact, 345, 346
    "Signal Processing Results for Both DPD
        Audio Files," 347, 377–386
Muller, Richard, 281
Murphy, Thomas, 395n13

NAS. See National Academy of Sciences
National Academy of Sciences (NAS), 184,
    191, 276, 284, 285
National Archives, 10, 99
National Institute of Law Enforcement, 280
National Research Council (NRC), 184, 191,
    276, 284, 285
National Science Foundation (NSF), 280,
    281, 284, 285
Naval Research Laboratory, 428–429n13
NBC News, 300
neuromuscular reaction hypothesis, 174–178,
    410–413n22
neutron activation analysis
    analysis of CE 399 and other bullet
        fragments for the HSCA, 167–170
    comparative bullet lead analysis and, 190,
        191
    criticism and ultimate failure of, 191,
        192–196
    FBI and, 192, 193–194, 414n9
Newman, Bill
    biographical overview, 30
    events on the day of the Kennedy
        assassination, 30–31, 351
    failure of the Warren Commission to
        interview, 30

Salandria, Vincent, *continued*
    disagreement with Josiah Thompson on
      Kennedy's throat wound, 97
    John Kelin and, 401n3
    Ray Marcus's discovery of Connally's
      wounding in the Zapruder film and,
      94–95
    Sylvia Meagher and, 402n5
    reaction to *Six Seconds in Dallas*, 111, 112
    Josiah Thompson's introduction to, 9–10
Salyer, Kenneth, 424n22
San Leandro Large Bore Rifle Range,
    124–125, 127–128
Sarles, F. William, 281
Sartre, Jean-Paul, 134
Saturday Evening Post, 107–108, 109, 111
Savage, Gary, 306
Scally, Chris, 337, 437n11, 439–440n15
Schatz, Arthur, 90, 99, 102
Science & Justice
    Linsker, et al. rebuttal to Don Thomas's
      allegations, 319–321, 325–326, 328,
      329
    Don Thomas's allegation of errors in the
      Ramsey Panel Report in, 301, 302, 303,
      433–434n37
    withdrawn Ramsey Panel Report rebuttal
      to Don Thomas's allegations, 307
Scott, Frank, 171, 172
Scott, Peter Dale, 165, 179
Scripps Institute of Oceanography, 166
SEAL Team 2, 104
seam jobs, 186
Secret Service
    DPD recordings and, 439–440n15
    William Robert Greer, 356, 361, 417n5,
      420n5
    Roy Kellerman, 271, 417n5, 420n5
    Samuel Kinney, 119, 402–403n4
    siren activated during the assassination,
      118–119
    unidentified figure encountered by Officer
      Joe Marshall Smith, 59–60, 142–143,
      357, 391n16
    Zapruder frame 313 and, 354
    See also Hill, Clint
Selby, Chip, 302, 304
Shaw, Clay, 112, 135
Shaw, J. Gary, 142, 143
Shaw, Robert, 83–84, 85

shots
    James Altgens's account of, 45–48
    Howard Brennan's account of, 398–399n5
    Clint Hill's account of, 424–425n29
    S. M. Holland's account of, 68, 70–71,
      242–243, 393n9
    Emmett Hudson's account of, 42–45
    LIFE magazine investigation and, 27, 28
    minimal mechanical firing time for
      Oswald's rifle, 352, 441–442n1
    the Newmans' account of, 32–38
    Officer B. J. Martin's account of, 57–58
    Officer Bobby Hargis's account of, 55–56
    Officer Douglas Jackson's account of, 51
    Officer James Chaney's account of,
      52–53
    Officer Joe Marshall Smith's account of,
      58–59
    portrayal of the assassination as two
      volleys of shots, 351–353
    Marilyn Sitzman's account of, 38, 40
    Texas School Book Depository as a source
      of, 4, 6 (*see also* Texas School Book
      Depository)
    Josiah Thompson's 1967 investigation into
      the number fired in the assassination,
      98–102
    Warren Commission on the number of, 6
    See also acoustic evidence; final shot;
      Kennedy head shot(s)
Should We Now Believe the Warren Report?
    (White), 402n2
Sibert, James, 255–256
Sibert-O'Neill report, 258
"Signal Processing Results for Both DPD
    Audio Files" (Mullen), 347, 377–386
Silber, John, 11
Simmons, James, 71, 72, 75, 76, 394n13
Simonstown (South Africa), 282, 283
simulcast, 338, 343, 344, 345, 441n19
simultaneous crosstalk, 295
    See also crosstalk
single-bullet theory, 83–85, 86
siren sounds, 118–119, 348
Sirica, John, 152
Sitzman, Marilyn, 29, 38–41, 118, 351
Six Seconds in Dallas (Thompson)
    appendix of measurements on the
      movements of Kennedy's head, 221
    James Barger's assessment of, 325

condensation in the *Saturday Evening Post*,
107–108, 109, 111
critical response to, 110, 112
FBI investigation of Josiah Thompson and,
400n2
Robert Groden and, 136
on Kennedy's forward head movement,
173
key pieces of evidence considered by
Thompson in the writing of, 94–103
national book tour for, 110–111
response of other assassination buffs to,
111
Josiah Thompson's reconstruction of the
Kennedy assassination, 103
Josiah Thompson's threshold question in,
93
writing and production of, 92–93, 105–107
Zapruder film frames controversy and the
Time Inc. lawsuit, 106–107, 109–110,
112–113
60-degree rule, 158–159
skull-shooting experiments, 126, 175,
261–262, 425n44
Skyhorse, Paul, 140
Smith, Gaddis, 387n2
Smith, Joe Marshall, 29, 49, 58–60, 142–143,
357
Smith, L. C., 395n14
smoke
S. M. Holland's account of, 69, 71, 72,
74–75
HSCA report on, 396n15
Snyder, Arthur, 197, 199, 202, 405n23,
433–434n37
Snyder, Margaret, 405n23
Society of American Acoustics (SAA), 145,
152, 323, 430n22
Soliah, Kathleen Ann, 190
Sorrels, Forrest, 20, 21, 43
Sound Surveillance System, 282
South Africa–Israeli nuclear test operation,
281–284, 428–429n13, 429n14
Specter, Arlen, 230, 253, 286
Specter, Shanin, 286, 432n27
spectrograms, 313–314, 318, 321–322, 326,
438
Spencer, Sandra Kay, 422–423n7
Sprague, Richard, 434n3
Stanton, Frank, 116, 121

startle responses. *See* jiggle theory
Stern, Samuel, 55, 68
Stetler, Morgan, 165
Stetler, Russ, 165, 185, 188
stockade (picket) fence
1978 HSCA hearings and, 164–165
acoustic reconstruction at Dealey Plaza
and, 153–154 (*see also* acoustic
evidence)
assassination account of Bill Newman
and, 36–37
assassination account of Lee Bowers Jr.
and, 62–67
assassination account of Officer Joe
Marshall Smith and, 58
assassination account of S. M. Holland
and, 70–82
final reconstruction of events in the
Kennedy assassination and, 355–356
key witnesses to the assassination and, 29
Josiah Thompson's August 1966 visit to
Dealey Plaza and, 13–14
See also grassy knoll
Stokes, Louis, 287–288
Stolley, Dick, 20, 21
Stone, Oliver, 189
Strauss, Lewis, 403n13
Stringer, John, 421–422n6
Sturdivan, Larry, 126, 175–176, 410–411n22
Summer, Anthony, 60
Susann, Jacqueline, 16
Suydam, Hank, 85, 86, 87
Swank, Arch, 20
Swank, Patsy
interviewed by Bob Porter, 388n3
LIFE's purchase of the Zapruder film and,
20–21
queries about the searching of car trunks
following the assassination and, 82
Josiah Thompson's description of, 20
Josiah Thompson's inquiries at Parkland
Hospital and, 21, 24, 26
Josiah Thompson's interviews of key
witnesses to the assassination and, 27,
28–29, 61
Swarthmore College, 134
Symbionese Liberation Army, 190

Taro, Gerda, 412n22
Texas Observer, 58

Texas School Book Depository
  accounts of witnesses on hearing shots, 399n5
  acoustic reconstruction at Dealey Plaza and, 152–154 (*see also* acoustic evidence)
  assassination account of Emmett Hudson and, 43
  assassination account of Howard Brennan and, 399n6
  assassination account of James Altgens and, 48
  assassination account of James Simmons and, 395n13
  assassination account of Officer Bobby Hargis and, 56
  assassination account of Officer Joe Marshall Smith and, 59
  final reconstruction of events in the Kennedy assassination and, 356–357
  Josiah Thompson's 1967 investigation into the number of shots fired and, 98–102
  Josiah Thompson's 1996 examination of Dealey Plaza and, 14
  Josiah Thompson's 2020 visit to Dallas and, 359, 360
  Zapruder film and, 6
30.06 rifle, 123–125, 126
.30 bullets, 24 26
.38 bullets, 24–26
  See also CE 399
.38-caliber pistol, 153
Thomas, Donald
  allegation of errors in the Ramsey Panel Report, 301–302, 303–305, 307, 433–434n37
  background of, 302–303
  James Barger's analysis of time synchronicity in crosstalk and, 338, 339
  on the continuity of the Dictabelt recording, 341
  conversation with Robert Blakey about a fifth shot, 408n17
  "I'll check it" crosstalk evidence and, 305–307, 311, 313, 326, 332
  reanalysis of the knoll shot echo location data, 161
  responses of the Ramsey Panel to the "I'll check it" crosstalk evidence, 307, 319–322

Zapruder frame 313 determined to be the next-to-last shot, 410n16
Thompson, Everson, 133
Thompson, Josiah
  2013 appearance on CNN, 275–276
  acoustic analysis of the DPD recordings and, 143–144
  antiwar movement and, 9–10, 105, 108–109
  biographical overview, 7–9
  biography of Kierkegaard, 133, 134, 139–140
  career as a private investigator, 140–141, 164, 165, 185–189
  children of, 12
  contact with James Barger regarding the crosstalk evidence, 323–326
  correspondence with Luis Alvarez concerning the jiggle theory, 119–121
  critique of the Ramsey Panel arguments supporting the "Hold everything" crosstalk, 339–343
  early independent investigations into the Kennedy assassination, 3, 9–15
  evidence for the purposeful omission of the "I'll check it" crosstalk by the Ramsey Panel, 312–318
  examination and critique of documents from the Ad Hoc Committee on Ballistic Acoustics, 284–289
  examination of Dealey Plaza in 1966, 3, 12–15
  examination of the DPD recordings for the "I'll check it" crosstalk, 308–313
  examination of the Ramsey Panel Report (*see* Ramsey Panel Report)
  FBI investigations of, 387n1, 400n2, 401
  first viewing of the Groden version of the Zapruder film, 135–136
  first viewing of the Zapruder film, 19
  Guggenheim Fellowship, 133
  Haverford College and, 9, 12, 104, 105, 133, 134–135, 140, 141
  investigation into Connally's wounds, 11, 12–13, 14–15
  John Kousi and, 387–388n1
  LIFE magazine investigation and (see LIFE magazine investigation)
  Sylvia Meagher and, 135
  personal life on the day of Kennedy's assassination, 3–6

ABOUT THE AUTHOR

Josiah Thompson received his PhD from Yale University in 1964. For the next twelve years, he taught philosophy at Yale and Haverford College. In 1976, he resigned his full professorship at Haverford and took up work as a private investigator in San Francisco. He worked as an operative for Hal Lipset and was trained by the extraordinary David Fechheimer. In 1979, he opened his own agency specializing in criminal defense. In a thirty-five-year career, he investigated numerous high-profile murder cases, including the Oklahoma City bombing as defense investigator for Timothy McVeigh.

His publications include two books on the Danish existentialist thinker Søren Kierkegaard and a memoir about his jump from professor to detective, *Gumshoe* (1988). His classic book on the Kennedy assassination, *Six Seconds in Dallas* (1967), has become a reference work on the case.

He and his wife, Nancy, live in northern California.